Faith and Reason Made Simple

(Training For the 21st Century Christian Believer)

RICK McGOUGH

DEDICATION

This book is dedicated to Christians everywhere who have found their faith under attack by those who attempt to use intellectual arguments to claim that the Christian faith and worldview is based on blind faith, rather than confirming evidence. My prayer is that pastors in local churches, as well as parents and grandparents in Christian homes will be better equipped to share not only what we believe, but also why we believe these things to be true. My prayer is also that believers of all ages will be better equipped to stand against the Goliath of our time that would intimidate and attempt to silence the voice of Christians. May this be a season of great victories in Jesus' Name!.

TABLE OF CONTENTS

Acknowledgments   *i*
Foreword by Josh McDowell   *iii*
Introduction - How to Use This Book   *vii*

I. Why Are These Issues Important?

1.	Be Ready to Give a Defense	1
2.	America in the Twenty-First Century	9
3.	The Devastating Consequences of Unbelief	19
4.	Are Faith and Science Opposed to Each Other?	29
5.	Regaining a Generation Already Gone	53
6.	David vs. Goliath: Propaganda and Intimidation	65

II. Understanding Your Worldview and Your Mission

1.	Total Truth and the Evangelical Movement	73
2.	The Importance of What We Believe	83
3.	The Meaning of Apologetics	89
4.	Foundational Issues of the Christian Faith	99

III. How to Share and Defend Your Christian Faith

	How to Use This Training Material	103
1.	Starting at the Beginning *(Creation Affirmed by Scripture)*	105
2.	Design Within The Universe Affirms Creation	113
3.	Design Within the Animal Kingdom Affirms Creation	131
4.	Design Within the Human Body Affirms Creation	147
5.	Design Within the Microscopic World Affirms Creation	153
6.	Design Within the Human Cell & DNA Affirms Creation	157
7.	Six Scientific Flaws in the Theory of Evolution	167
8.	Understanding Human History	187
9.	The Bible – God's Word *(Part 1)*	203
10.	The Bible – God's Word *(Part 2)*	235
11.	Jesus Christ – Son of God, Savior of the World	251
12.	Sharing the Gospel of Christ	299

13. Dealing with Questions and Criticisms of Skeptics   313
14. Dealing with Homosexuality and Other Social Issues   345
15. Christianity and Other World Religions   359
16. Christianity and Islam   375

IV. Bringing Apologetics into the Twenty-first-century Church

1. Reason, Love, and Holy Spirit Power   387
2. Equipping the Church and Family   395
3. A Challenge to Churches *(21st Century Apologetics)*   409
4. Appendix   415

ACKNOWLEDGMENTS

Thanks to my wonderful wife Val who has truly been a helpmate to me throughout our nearly 40 years of marriage and ministry together. I could not have given myself to the Lord's work in pastoring and now in Apologetics ministry if you had not been selfless and supportive, as you have been throughout our lifetime together. I love you so much!

Thanks to the wonderful people at New Life Fellowship and the leadership there for your loving support of our new ministry as we have stepped away from pastoring and into the ministry the Lord has now called us to!

Thanks to Josh McDowell for your encouragement and support in the past 3 years. Your belief in me and in what God has called me to accomplish has brought courage and strength to me! Thanks for your willingness to write the foreword to this book as well! I am so grateful for your friendship!

Thanks to Phil Stacey who has become a dear friend in the last 5 years and has on many occasions spoke words of encouragement and strength to me! Love you brother!

Thanks to Eric Hovind and to all the fine folks at Creation Today for your partnership and encouragement in so many ways as I have sought to make a difference in the body of Christ in the area of Apologetics! Eric, you have encouraged and helped me more than you will ever know!

Thanks to Willie Herath for your friendship and for making this book possible with all of your advice, wisdom and tutoring!

Thanks to Tom Williams for your great work in editing this work and for your patience with me as a novice!

Thanks to Shawn & Amber Karns for your amazing support and help in the Truth Conferences we put together around the nation!

Thanks to Sandy Muse and Sandi Conley for all you do! You guys are great!

Thanks to the directors and support team of Local Church Apologetics for all of your support, love and prayers! We couldn't do what God has called us to do without you folks!

Thanks to the churches, individuals and businesses that have come aside us and supported us in this work! Love you all!

Thanks to District and National leaders within the Assemblies of God who have been supportive of all we are trying to accomplish!

Thanks to my 3 sons, my daughter-in-laws, and my grandkids for bringing joy to my life in so many ways! I pray that you all grow in your faith and accomplish much in this life for Jesus and His Kingdom! Love you lots!

Thanks to my wonderful Mom & Dad who raised me to know and serve Jesus Christ! I am forever grateful for your love, example and training!

FOREWORD BY JOSH MCDOWELL

For 50 years I have sought to help Christian believers understand what we believe and why it is true. My own journey to faith was littered with doubts and questions about the reality of the Christian faith. Seeking to disprove the biblical narrative of God and His Son Jesus Christ, I found overwhelming evidence convincing me that the Bible and its message of salvation through Jesus Christ are historically accurate and true for all mankind. My personal journey to faith led me to a lifelong calling of helping others realize the transforming truth about the Christian faith.

Today, in America and in many parts of the world skepticism, agnosticism and unbelief have become a formidable opposition to the Christian faith. This is a stumbling block to many in regard to their own willingness to believe and trust Jesus Christ as Savior and Lord. Numerous research projects have shown that a great percentage of children who grew up in evangelical churches and families walked away from their faith by the time they reached their 20s. In many cases, it is intellectual doubts that are at the core of their turning away. Throughout our nation churches contain solid Christian families who now have a family member who no longer believes or who now claims to be an atheist or agnostic.

In the face of these challenges and realities, many local churches and much of the body of Christ have done little to purposely equip believers to know why we believe the foundational principles of the Christian faith to be true. Apologetics, the study of the evidences that allow us to give a defense about the hope that is within us, is often overlooked in the midst of ministry priorities. Many are intimidated by the word "apologetics," many are overwhelmed by the challenges that a skeptical culture presents, and many fail to see the value of prioritizing this area of Christian ministry.

"There is hope in the midst of this great battle! Many Christian leaders have seen the battle and are now looking for answers to help believers of all ages better understand how to defend their faith. Believers of all ages are beginning to take seriously the need to be equipped and articulate why they believe Christianity to be true.

It's not surprising that our Lord would call some of His servants into this battle for such a time as this. Rick McGough is one who is among those who have felt this specific calling upon his life.

After pastoring a local church for 34 years, Rick felt a growing burden concerning believers' need to know why they believe what they believe. This brought him to a time where he sensed God calling him to step down from pastoral ministry and devote the rest of his life to a ministry in apologetics. He came to believe that the Lord was calling him not only to equip individual believers to be able to defend their faith, but also to assist local churches and pastors in developing plans and resources to equip their congregations to better defend their faith. In January of 2016, he did just that and established a ministry called "Local Church Apologetics". I have served as a keynote speaker for several Truth Conferences which Rick has coordinated as part of the ministry he is now pursuing. I have observed the passion that God has put in Rick's heart to see believers equipped in how to defend their Christian faith.

This book is a result of that calling. Here, Rick uses his ability gained through over 30 years of pastoral ministry to simplify complex issues of apologetics and to present them in ways that the average church attendee can easily understand and communicate with others.

Faith and Reason Made Simple takes the reader through evidences which confirm that God created us in His image, the Bible is God's Word to us, and Jesus Christ is God's Son who was a historical person that died for our sins and bodily rose from the dead. Other critical issues are covered such as how to answer many of the questions/criticisms of skeptics, how do Christianity and Islam differ, and how should Christians respond to homosexuality today, etc..

This book is unique in its approach to the issues of apologetics, summarizing key points and even offering short points for the reader to memorize. It really is a training manual which can help believers develop an apologia for their faith.

Parents and grandparents can become better prepared to help their children and grandchildren face the challenges our culture presents. Church leaders will find a resource they can incorporate into their ministry to equip their people in how to defend the Christian faith.

Rick enters the apologetics world from a unique perspective, having been involved in pastoral ministry for over 30 years. His pastor's heart and his ability to simplify complex issues are evident throughout this book. I pray the Lord uses it greatly to make a difference in a multitude of believers in the coming years. I believe your faith will be strengthened and your life enriched as you read *Faith and Reason Made Simple*. May God bless you as you read, become better equipped, and stand up to the attacks upon the Christian faith so prevalent in our culture today.

Josh McDowell -Josh McDowell Ministry

INTRODUCTION

How to Use This Book

Faith and Reason Made Simple is designed to serve as a training manual and an apologetics handbook for Christian believers, from teenagers through senior adults. The first two sections of the book reveal the cultural challenges to the Christian faith in America today, and explain why every believer in Jesus Christ needs to be equipped to defend and share his or her faith within this increasingly secularized culture.

The actual training material begins in section 3. If you feel that you would benefit by going straight to that section to delve immediately into the meat of the book, you should feel free do so.

If you decide to do this you can come back and read the first 2 sections at your convenience. I certainly believe that you will benefit from the first 2 sections but I was concerned that those looking specifically for evidence to help them defend their faith might become concerned, reading through the first two sections and feeling as though the book was not dealing with the issues directly that they were looking for.

In section 3, where the actual training material is found, a summary is also included at the end of key chapters to help the reader retain the evidences presented within the chapter. You are encouraged to memorize the key points covered in these chapters for use in discussions you have with others.

To this end, memorization cards are included with the key chapters to assist you in memorizing the key points. Actual cards that can be printed, cut out and carried with you can be accessed at localchurchapologetics.org without cost. You are encouraged to use the cards and memorize key points within the materials here.

God bless you as you proceed!

Introduction

In January of 1982, my wife Val and I, along with our seven-month-old son, moved to Moline, Illinois, to become the pastors of a small church. The church had suffered a split and was struggling to survive. The church leadership had been looking for an older, experienced pastor who could settle things down and get them moving in the right direction. Through God's grace and His leading, they changed their minds and took a chance on a twenty-three-year-old who had been a youth pastor for two

Rick & Val McGough (Early 1980s)

years but had never pastored a church. The Lord blessed us at New Life Fellowship, and we continued to pastor the church until January 10, 2016, exactly thirty-four years from the day that we officially began our ministry there.

I had felt that my calling was to pastor a church for the rest of my life. What a surprise it was when in my mid-fifties, God began to stir my heart to step down from pastoring and spend the rest of my life equipping believers and local churches to defend the Christian faith from the intellectual attacks so prevalent within American culture today.

For well over twenty years I had been increasingly burdened by the things I saw happening within our culture. I was especially concerned about the teaching of evolution in our schools and the denial of God as our Creator. It was clear to me that teaching people that there is no Creator and that they are simply the results of evolutionary processes would inevitably erase from their minds the need for a Savior and the prospect of life after death.

It seemed to me that the cultural attacks on creation, the existence of God, the validity of the Bible, and the person of Jesus Christ were not being addressed adequately within local churches or within the body of Christ as a whole. There were exceptions of course, but by and large, it appeared that we were attempting to reach and strengthen our people by the same methods we used decades earlier when the Judeo-Christian worldview permeated

every aspect of life in America and the thinking of most its people.

The burden I felt to address this growing need increased to the point that in 2014 my wife, Val, and I made a decision to step away from pastoring the congregation we loved in order to pursue the calling God was laying upon our hearts. We established a ministry called Local Church Apologetics, which includes this book, Faith and Reason Made Simple, videos that present the teachings within this book, traveling and speaking across the nation, training people in how to better defend their faith, and a soon-to-be-developed website at localchurchapologetics.com, which will provide local churches with helpful resources and instructions to assist them in bringing apologetics into their ministries to children, teens, and adults. We are also working with Josh McDowell and other apologetics speakers to bring Truth Conferences to various states and regions across the nation.

In writing this material, I have attempted to present the complex subjects of apologetics in simple, easy to understand terms that the average, churchgoing believer can understand. I trust that this book will be a blessing to you. I hope that you will use the materials found within it to strengthen your own faith, help others understand the evidence that confirms the Christian faith, and to reach out to a lost and hurting world. God bless you!

Rick McGough

Faith and Reason Made Simple

(SECTION 1)

Why Are These Issues Important?

SECTION 1: CHAPTER 1

"Be Ready to Give a Defense"

If you wonder why a book on faith and reason is important or why you should take the time to better defend your Christian faith, consider the following: Christianity in America is declining at a rapid pace. A few decades ago, over 90 percent of Americans believed in God. Today that percentage is only 70 percent.[1] And only 48 percent of those who claim to believe are actually members of a church.[2] And it gets worse; less than 20 percent of those who claim church membership attend services at least once every four to six weeks.[3] And as every churchgoer knows, very few of those who do attend church are actively involved in its mission. Mainline churches which have buckled to secular values on morality and origins are losing members at a precipitous rate. Clearly, even evangelical churches are being affected, as many of their members claim Christianity but live largely by the values of the secular majority.

In their book Already Gone, Ken Ham, Britt Beemer, and Todd Hillard reveal that approximately two out of three teenagers sitting in our churches will leave the church by the time they are in their

---

[1] "America's Changing Religious Landscape" (Pewforum.org, May 12, 2015) http://www.pewforum.org/2015/05/12/americas-changing-religious-landscape/. Accessed May 20, 2017.

[2] John Shook, "Church-Goers Now a Minority in America" (Huffpost Website, May 24, 2012)http://www.huffingtonpost.com/john-shook-phd/churchgoers-now-a-minority _b_1537108.html. Accessed May 20, 2017.

[3] Rick L. Stonestreet, "Church Attendance is on the Decline" (Daily Republic website, September 27, 2015) http://www.dailyrepublic.com/news/locallifestylecolumns/church-attendance-is-on -the-decline/ Accessed May 20, 2017.

twenties. If their faith is not thoroughly destroyed by the morality and secular lives of their high school peers, the process will be completed by their college professors. All this is occurring because the increasingly secular values of American culture have made inroads into our churches, and the churches have largely failed to ground their members in the basics of the faith that would keep their beliefs intact and robust.

The purpose of this book is to equip concerned Christians to ground their fellow believers in the faith and to communicate to non-believers the basics of what Christians believe in a way that will enable them to see the validity and rationality of the faith.

Though much of the material in this book in later chapters comes from the realm of scientific data, certainly our understanding of the issues related to belief has its foundational source in scripture. The Bible is God's Word and is both our starting place for understanding life and our source of direction when it comes to how a Christian should respond to cultural challenges to faith.

THE MEANING OF APOLOGETICS

What we are doing in this book is often called apologetics. Apologetics may seem a strange word to use for explaining the rationality of faith, because at a glance it appears to indicate that we are in some sense apologizing for what we believe. That is not the case at all. As we will see, the term 'apologetics' does not speak of making an apology but rather giving a defense for something that we believe, that brings us hope. In the following scripture, the apostle Peter explicitly enjoins Christians to engage in apologetics:

> **But even if you should suffer for the sake of righteousness, you are blessed, and do not fear their intimidation, and do not be troubled, (15) but sanctify Christ as Lord in your hearts, always being ready to make a defense to everyone who asks you to give an account for the hope that is in you, yet with gentleness and reverence; (16) and keep a good conscience so that in the thing in which you are slandered, those who revile your good behavior in Christ will be put to shame.**
> **(1 Peter 3:14-16, NASB)**

This passage gives a number of directives to believers concerning their relationship to an unbelieving culture. First, in the face of persecution for the Christian faith, believers are instructed not to fear or to be troubled by their intimidation. This obviously involves a great amount of trust in God and a great amount of leaning upon His strength. Second, believers are instructed to sanctify, or to set apart, Jesus as Lord in their heart, and to be ready to make a defense to everyone who asks about the hope that they cherish in their hearts. Third, believers are told to always speak to unbelievers about their Christian faith in a spirit or attitude of gentleness and reverence. Finally, believers are instructed to make sure that their behavior represents Christ well and never contradicts the faith they are communicating to others.

In this chapter we will focus on the second directive this scripture gives us: "always being ready to make a defense to everyone who asks you to give an account for the hope that is in you." The phrase "to make a defense" is translated from the Greek word apologia, which is found in the original Greek version of 1 Peter 3:15. This is our source for the term "apologetics." Apologetics refers to Christian believers giving a defense for the hope they have in Christ to those who question them about their faith.

This defense will vary depending upon the challenges we face. In twenty-first century America, some of the main challenges to the Christian faith include the issue of origins, the questioning of the authority of the Bible, and the questioning of the deity and/or historicity of Jesus Christ.

THE VALUE OF APOLOGETICS

If we follow the directives of 1 Peter 3:15, we will recognize the need to prepare ourselves and to be ready with responses in the key areas noted above—origins, biblical authority, and the deity of Christ.

The good thing about challenges to faith is that they motivate believers to consider why they believe what they believe. In the end, this causes the believer's faith to become stronger and more reasonably explained. An unbelieving culture loves to accuse believers of having blind faith—faith based on nothing more than unthinking adherence to an outdated book or on what we've been told by parents or the church. Though it is true that some believers have never taken the time to understand the reasons behind the Christian faith and have simply followed the faith of others, we are not called to a blind faith, but rather to a faith that is reasonable and consistent with reality. The reasonable explanations for the Christian faith are available for all to find and understand. So, "being ready" (apologetics) not only prepares believers to share their faith in a reasonable way with others, but also strengthens believers' understanding of why they believe what they believe, and thus protects them from attacks that attempt to undermine their faith.

This book will explain the complexities related to key issues such as creation, the inspiration of Scripture and the deity of Jesus Christ in simple ways that will help believers of all ages understand, remember, and communicate them effectively to others.

THE NECESSITY OF APOLOGETICS

Some contend that defending the foundational truths of Christianity is not really necessary. They say we just need to preach the message of the cross and live for Jesus, and God will take care of everything else. This view overlooks the fact that if foundational truths such as "God created all things, including mankind", "The Bible is the Inspired Word of God", and "Jesus Christ is God the Son, who became the Incarnate Savior of the World" are not true, then none of the rest of the gospel message makes sense. Also, the moral directives of the Bible lose their strength if these foundational truths are ignored or forsaken.

The book of Psalms warns us of the devastation that will occur if the foundational truths of the Christian faith are no longer understood, proclaimed, and lived by: **"If the foundations are destroyed, What can the righteous do?" (Psalms 11:3, NASB).**

America and the Western nations today show vividly that when a people allow the foundations of the Christian faith to be destroyed, the moral fiber of that people crumbles, and when moral fiber crumbles, more than just faith will suffer.

Learning to defend the hope of the Christian faith that is within you is key to reestablishing the foundations for your own life and for the lives of many others that you will influence in your

4

lifetime, including children, grandchildren, neighbors, co-workers, friends, etc.

I am convinced that if we do not turn the corner in these critical issues, the cause of Christ will be greatly damaged. If you think that this statement does not communicate much faith, my response is that by failing to prepare Christians to give a defense for the hope within each believer, the church has been on a path of disobedience. If we will obey God's directive to "be ready to give a defense to everyone who asks us to give an account for the hope that is in us," then I believe with all my heart that the foundations can be strengthened and the cause of Christ can move forward with great strength and life.

THE LOVE DISPLAYED IN APOLOGETICS

Every believer is called to be a witness for Jesus Christ. In Acts 1:8 He said that His followers would be His witnesses. In 2 Corinthians 5:17-20 we are told that as believers in Christ we are ambassadors of His, representing Him to this world we live in. We are told that He makes His appeal to lost people through us.

These passages make it clear that "being ready to give a defense for the hope that is in you" is a very loving thing to do. If Christians claim that they do not need to expend the effort required to be ready to make a defense because they intend to avoid any challenges from unbelievers, they are taking a stance that is rooted in selfishness. In essence, those who take this approach are saying, "As long as I am a believer and have eternal life, that is all I am concerned about." God, however, is concerned for all people, wanting all to be saved. (1 Timothy 2:3-4). He has clearly expressed in His Word that all believers are called to reach out to those who do not know Christ as their Savior. One of the ways we do this is by preparing ourselves with knowledge that can help those who may be truly confused by the lies of an unbelieving culture.

> Love for people who do not know Jesus Christ as their Savior, love for young believers who are being challenged by an unbelieving culture, and love for our

> children and grandchildren should all be motivating factors in moving us to be ready to defend the hope that is found in Jesus Christ.

ATTITUDE: THE LUBRICATING OIL OF APOLOGETICS

In the last phrase of 1 Peter 3:15, God's Word instructs us to give a defense for the hope that is within us with the proper heart attitude. We are to give a defense "with gentleness and reverence." Even if believers become highly efficient in debate, they will not be effective if they speak to people with arrogance, cockiness or mocking tones. Believers are called to have a gentle demeanor toward those they are trying to reach with the truth. They are also called to maintain a reverent attitude toward God and His revealed purposes as they speak. Verse 16 adds that a believer's behavior is also a critical factor that facilitates the acceptance of his apologetic message: **"and keep a good conscience so that in the thing in which you are slandered, those who revile your good behavior in Christ will be put to shame." (1 Peter 3:16, NASB).** For his message to be taken seriously, he must "walk the walk" so that his everyday life reflects the faith that he is defending.

The directive given to believers in 1 Peter 3:15 is the foundational thought behind this entire book. Christians throughout the centuries since Christ have lived out their lives in many different cultures, facing many different challenges, deadly persecution, oppression, political tyranny, ridicule, and repression. It is critical for believers living in twenty-first century America to identify the challenges facing the church today and to respond accordingly. We cannot ignore the fact that the Christian faith is being attacked in the intellectual realm and that foundational truths of the Christian faith are being skewed and maligned in the realms of education, entertainment, and public policy.

Today, Christian believers have more information available to counter these attacks than at any point in history. Books, DVDs, Teaching CDs, Podcasts, online resources, and ministries devoted to training believers in apologetics are available to any who desire to learn and grow in their Christian faith. Many of these resources are available either without charge or at minimal cost. Utilizing resources such as these will enable us to "be ready." If enough of us take the time to prepare ourselves, we could see an army of believers raised up in this hour to face the challenges within our increasingly unbelieving culture.

My challenge to you is to ask yourself if you have responded to the scriptural directive given in 1 Peter 3:15: **"Be ready to make a defense for the hope that is in you!"**

Reminder – The actual training material begins in section 3. If you feel that you would benefit by going straight to that section to delve immediately into the meat of the book, you should feel free do so. You can come back and read the first 2 sections at your convenience.

BE READY TO GIVE A DEFENSE

"America in the Twenty-first Century"

Those among us who are fifty or over can remember America as a nation that displayed many of the characteristics of a Christian nation. The moral directives that most Americans lived by were guided by the words of the Bible. There were evidences, even decades ago, that the effects of the Christian faith upon American culture was diminishing. But most Christians could hold to their beliefs without a great deal of direct challenge.

Today, that tolerant atmosphere most certainly has changed. Christians now find their faith and beliefs challenged on many fronts. Public education may be the greatest culprit. Young Christians are often challenged by teachers and professors who insist that the Christian faith is not based on reality and facts and make it their mission to mock, attack, and destroy the faith of students that they teach. Entertainment sources, including movies, music, TV sitcoms, talk shows, and comedians also dishonor Christian values and regularly attack the Christian faith or specific aspects of it. The moral collapse of society has led to a demand for sexual freedom to the point that perversions have been normalized and endorsed by government and institutions, putting the secular values of the culture at odds with the values expressed by scripture and the Christian faith. Even law has begun to repress freedom of conscience, forcing Christians in certain businesses either to provide their services for homosexual weddings or close down. The influential voices that are often heard today do not merely express disbelief in the Christian faith, they denounce it as unreasonable, destructive, ludicrous, blind, unfounded, misguided, dangerous, counterproductive, repressive, intolerant, and bigoted. Christians today often endure ridicule for their faith at schools, in the workplace, and even among their unchurched friends.

These realities are among the reasons why it is so important for the church to reevaluate what ministry in the local church includes and what believers need to prepare them to stay in the faith and to proclaim their faith to others.

Consider the following quotes by some of today's popular speakers and educators: (Internet - Atheist Quotes - Images)

"Faith is the great cop-out, the great excuse to evade the need to think and evaluate evidence." (Richard Dawkins)

"The problem with faith is that it is a conversation stopper. Faith is a declaration of immunity to the powers of conversation. It is a reason, why you don't have to give reasons, for what you believe." (Sam Harris)

"Science knows it doesn't know everything: otherwise it'd stop. But just because science doesn't know everything doesn't mean that you can fill in the gaps with whatever fairy tale that most appeals to you." (Dara O'Briain on Science & Religion)

"Stupidity: If you can't understand science, choose religion." (George Carlin)

"Teaching creationism in science class as an alternative to evolution is inappropriate." (Bill Nye)

"We are a nation that is unenlightened because of religion. I do believe that. I think religion stops people from thinking. I think it justified crazies." (Bill Maher)

"If you could reason with religious people, there would be no religious people." (House)

"I submit that there is no question on which science was

once the authority, but now after years of progress, that authority has been ceded to the church. There are a functionally infinite number of questions where it has run the other way." (Sam Harris)

"Atheism is the absence of religion. We don't really need atheism. We just need to get rid of religion." (Penn Jillette)

Another indication of the ferocity of the present-day attacks upon the Christian faith is the many books written against God, the Bible, and the Person of Jesus Christ. Note these examples –

"How Jesus Became God" (Bart Ehrman)
"Forged: Why the Bible's Authors are Not Who We Think They Are" (Bart Ehrman)
"God's Problem: How the Bible Fails to Answer Our Most Important Question—Why We Suffer" (Bart Ehrman)
"The End of Faith: Religion, Terror, and the Future of Reason" (Sam Harris)
"The God Delusion" (Richard Dawkins)
"God is not Great" (Christopher Hitchens)
"The Da Vinci Code" (Dan Brown)

These titles give us just a few examples of the climate that exists in our world today—a climate of mockery and challenge to the Christian faith.

THE DECLINE OF CHRISTIANITY IN AMERICA

Fifty to seventy-five years ago, most citizens of the United States

had a Judeo-Christian background, even those who were not living a Christian life. Most people had been raised with a familiarity of the values and truths found in the Bible. In that era, ministering to people in our culture would be similar to the way Peter ministered to the Jewish people in

Jerusalem and surrounding towns in the years following Christ's death and resurrection. Most people at that time were very familiar with Old Testament law and foundational truths about creation, the fall of man, the Ten Commandments, the need for forgiveness, etc.

In cultural situations such as these where the foundational truths of God's love and forgiveness are already generally known and respected, the gospel message can be proclaimed by simply going straight to message of Jesus Christ and his atoning death and resurrection.

In contrast, when we look at America today we find a large number of people who have no Judeo-Christian background. They have within them no foundation of knowledge to build on. Many have no concept of what Christianity is about and no understanding of basic principles within Scripture that helps us to see our need for Christ and His forgiveness. While the message of the cross is certainly what they need to hear and understand, it may not be the best starting point for them. Think about it: If a person does not believe that he is created by God but is just a random collection of atoms and molecules that have developed over time by unguided processes, why would he think he needs forgiveness or salvation? If he does not believe there is a God, how could he be open to learning about God's love?

Given this radical loss of Christian knowledge in American culture, the church needs to reconsider its approach to evangelism. We must begin by giving answers to the questions that people are asking: "Is there a God?" "How did we get here?" "Is the Bible just a book of myths and fairytales?" "Did Jesus really live on the earth?" With these questions being asked by so many today, how can we not adjust the way in which we attempt to reach them? I heard a statement about the ministry of Jesus, I believe by Ravi Zacharias, which stuck with

Source: Pixabay, CC0 Public Domain

me. "He always got to the nerve of their question, and then touched their heart." That is good advice for us to follow in reaching our increasingly secularized world.

THE STRATEGIES OF THE APOSTLE PAUL

In the book of Acts, we learn a lot about how the church was established and how the gospel was preached in various places at that time. In Acts 2, Peter stands on the day of Pentecost and boldly  proclaims to the people in Jerusalem that the Jesus they had recently crucified is indeed the Christ, and that He is the One who has come to save them. He tells them they must repent and be baptized (which is a public testimony of one's true faith in the person of Jesus) so that they can be forgiven of their sins. Thus the church starts in Jerusalem among people who, for the most part, already had a good working knowledge of the Old Testament and its message.

As we read through the Book of Acts, we see the work of the church expanding and more and more people groups being reached. In Acts 8, the church is scattered by persecution, and the dispersing Christians take the gospel with them. In Acts 9, Saul of Tarsus, who becomes the Apostle Paul, is converted to the Christian faith. He will become the apostle to the Gentiles. In Acts 10, Peter is sovereignly called by God to preach the gospel to certain God-fearing Gentiles, thus setting the precedent for the taking of the gospel to all Gentile people groups.

When we reach Acts 14, we find Paul in Lystra, speaking to a people who do not have a background knowledge of the Old Testament. They are worshippers of idols. It is very important that we notice how he approached these pagans. In verses 8-14, we read that he encounters a man who had been lame from birth and heals him in the Name of Jesus. They are awed by the astounding miracle and attempt to worship Paul and his companion, Barnabas, calling them Zeus and Hermes. In verses 15-17, we see Paul's response and proclamation to them, which he bases on where they are in their knowledge of God at the time:

Men, why are you doing these things? We are also men of the same nature as you, and preach the gospel to you that you should turn from these vain things to a living God, who made the heaven and the earth and the sea and all that is in them. (16) In the generations gone by He permitted all the nations to go their own ways; (17) and yet He did not leave Himself without witness, in that He did good and gave you rains from heaven and fruitful seasons, satisfying your hearts with food and gladness.

(Acts 14:15-17, NASB)

Paul realizes that these people do not know who God is, so he begins by speaking to them about turning to the living God who made the heaven and the earth and the sea and all that is in them. Identifying the God they do not know becomes his starting point. Then in verse 16, he speaks of God allowing the nations to go their own way. This brings attention to the fall of mankind who had strayed from God and points toward humanity's need of redemption. He goes on to say that bringing the rains from heaven and bringing forth fruitful seasons that satisfy their hearts with food and gladness acts as a witness to His love and concern, even for people who have strayed far from Him. Paul's ultimate goal is always to share Jesus Christ with people, but sometimes the starting point needs to be adjusted to provide his hearers with background material that will enable them to comprehend the essence of his message.

At the beginning of Acts 17, we see Paul ministering to Jews and God-fearing Greeks in the synagogue in Thessalonica.

Now when they had traveled through Amphipolis and Apollonia, they came to Thessalonica, where there was a synagogue of the Jews. (2) And according to Paul's custom, he went to them, and for three Sabbaths reasoned with them from the Scriptures, (3) explaining and giving evidence that the Christ had to suffer and rise again from the dead, and saying, "This Jesus whom I am proclaiming to you is the Christ." (4) And some of them were persuaded and joined Paul and Silas, along with a large number of the God-fearing Greeks and a number of the leading women.

(Acts 17:1-4, NASB)

Here Paul's approach is quite different. He has no need to identify God or the fall of man to these believers, so he goes straight to the heart of the matter, proclaiming Jesus Christ to them using evidence from the Old Testament that the Christ had to suffer and rise from the dead. He ministered to them according to where they were in their current knowledge. Notice two key words in this passage: reason and evidence. "[He] reasoned with them from the Scriptures, explaining and giving evidence that the Christ had to suffer and rise again from the dead" (italics added). Our ministry and proclamation of the gospel to skeptical or religiously untaught people should include reason and evidence. As we will note later, reasoning alone will not convert people to Christ, but it is an important element of ministry that must not be left out.

PAUL AND THE PAGAN ATHENIANS

Later in Acts 17, Paul is in Athens, again among a people who do not know God and do not have a background of Old Testament truth to build upon. They have an interest in spiritual things but are very misguided in their beliefs. We are told that Paul is troubled by the widespread idolatry of the city. Acts 17:16 says that "his spirit was being provoked within him as he was observing the city full of idols." Verses 17-21 tell us that Paul reasoned regularly with Jews and God-fearing Gentiles in the Athens synagogue and with whomever he might encounter in the marketplace. His message aroused the curiosity of some of the Epicurean and Stoic philosophers. They invited him to explain his new religion to a forum in the Areopagus, a gathering place for discussion of novel philosophic or religious ideas.

> *So Paul stood in the midst of the Areopagus and said, "Men of Athens, I observe that you are very religious in all respects. (23) For while I was passing through and examining the objects of your worship, I also found an altar with this inscription, 'TO AN UNKNOWN GOD.' Therefore what you worship in ignorance, this I proclaim to you. (24) The God who made the world and all things in it, since He is Lord of heaven and earth, does not dwell in temples made with hands; (25) nor is He served by human hands, as though He needed*

anything, since He Himself gives to all people life and breath and all things; (26) and He made from one man every nation of mankind to live on all the face of the earth, having determined their appointed times and the boundaries of their habitation, (27) that they would seek God, if perhaps they might grope for Him and find Him, though He is not far from each one of us; (28) for in Him we live and move and exist, as even some of your own poets have said, 'For we also are His children.' (29) Being then the children of God, we ought not to think that the Divine Nature is like gold or silver or stone, an image formed by the art and thought of man. (30) Therefore having overlooked the times of ignorance, God is now declaring to men that all people everywhere should repent, (31) because He has fixed a day in which He will judge the world in righteousness through a Man whom He has appointed, having furnished proof to all men by raising Him from the dead.

(Acts 17:22-31 NASB)

As we noted above, Paul has already observed that the Athenians are pervasive idol worshippers. So he knows he cannot simply begin his message of salvation with a direct proclamation of Christ. Notice the brilliance of his strategy as he reasons with the Epicurean and Stoic philosophers. He begins at a starting point which is appropriate for them. He speaks about the God who made the world and all things in it, the God who is Lord of heaven and earth, the God who gives life and breath to all people and all things, the God who made from one man all  the nations of the world, the God who determined where different nations and people groups will abide, and the God who is not far from us. He speaks of the Creator and describes Him as One who is involved in the affairs of men and who is concerned about us all. He then proclaims a message of repentance and coming judgment. Finally, he speaks to them of Jesus Christ as the One who was raised from the dead and who will judge the world in righteousness.

Paul started at a place where the Athenians had questions and ended up proclaiming Christ. He revealed to them the God they did not know as the Creator, sustainer, and redeemer of their lives. This is our model for introducing Christ to the culture we live in today.

THE CRITICAL ROLE OF ATTITUDE

Notice Paul's attitude toward the Athenians as he ministers to them. We noted above that he was provoked in his spirit by the idolatry in Athens. Yet he approaches them with respect and love, saying, "Men of Athens, I observe that you are very religious in all respects." He could have begun his discourse with something like, "Men of Athens, I see that you are a bunch of heathen idolaters!" His gentle and kind attitude prevents them from automatically rejecting his message. He continues to demonstrate respect when he refers to their idols as "objects of your worship." He will later point out that they are worshipping in ignorance and that they need to repent, but by oiling the way with respect, he softens them up to receive central point of his message. Remember that Peter commanded us to explain our faith with "gentleness" and with "reverence" (1 Peter 3:15). Attitude makes a big difference when talking to people about God and their need for Him.

It is my conviction that to be effective in today's world skepticism and agnosticism, the church of Jesus Christ must adjust its approach to evangelism. We live in an age when all believers must be able to defend their faith and share it with others. We cannot go on ignoring the questions and attacks that are being cast at the feet of Christians. Gaining a thorough

apol - o - get - ics

understanding of foundational issues such as creation, the dependability of the Bible, and the historicity of Jesus Christ will both deepen the faith of seekers and equip them to be instruments in God's hands to reach people He desperately loves.

"The Devastating Consequences of Unbelief"

The passage of Scripture found in Romans 1:18-32 gives us a critical key to the topic of apologetics because it addresses three issues that are as relevant today as they were in the first century when Paul addressed them. Those issues are (1) the fact of creation; (2) the secular response to creation; and (3) the degeneration of culture that results when creation is denied. The passage also enables us to understand why many of the social issues of our day have become so prominent and divisive. Please read the passage carefully before we delve into it.

For the wrath of God is revealed from heaven against all ungodliness and unrighteousness of men who suppress the truth in unrighteousness, (19) because that which is known about God is evident within them; for God made it evident to them. (20) For since the creation of the world His invisible attributes, His eternal power and divine nature, have been clearly seen, being understood through what has been made, so that they are without excuse. (21) For even though they knew God, they did not honor Him as God or give thanks, but they became futile in their speculations, and their foolish heart was darkened. (22) Professing to be wise, they became fools, (23) and exchanged the glory of the incorruptible God for an image in the form of corruptible man and of birds and four-footed animals and crawling creatures. (24) Therefore God gave them over in the lusts of their hearts to impurity, so that their bodies would be dishonored among them. (25) For they exchanged the truth of God for a lie, and worshiped and served the creature rather than the Creator, who is blessed forever. Amen. (26) For this reason God gave them over to degrading passions; for their women exchanged the natural function for that which is unnatural, (27) and in the same way also the men abandoned the natural function of the woman and burned in their desire toward one another, men with men committing indecent acts and receiving in their own persons the due penalty of their error. (28) And just as they did not see fit to acknowledge God any longer, God gave them over to a depraved mind, to do those things which are not proper, (29) being filled with all unrighteousness, wickedness, greed, evil; full of envy, murder, strife, deceit, malice; they are gossips, (30) slanderers, haters of God, insolent, arrogant, boastful, inventors of evil, disobedient to parents, (31) without understanding, untrustworthy, unloving, unmerciful; (32) and although they know the ordinance of God, that those who practice such things are worthy of death, they not only do the same, but also give hearty approval to those who practice them.

(Romans 1:18-32 NASB)

It is easy to see the close parallel between the culture Paul is addressing and our American culture today. Obviously, the degenerating morality of our society is nothing new in history. What may surprise us more is what Paul reveals as a primary cause of this degeneration—a society's failure to accept the truth that God is the Creator of the universe. As this passage reveals, there is a critical connection between the acceptance of the Gospel and the truth of creation. Notice how Paul addresses this connection by contrasting the righteousness of God with His wrath.

In verse 17, which immediately precedes our topic passage, we are told that in the gospel "the righteousness of God is revealed from faith to faith." Then in verse 18 we are told that "the wrath of God is revealed from heaven against all ungodliness and unrighteousness of men who suppress the truth in unrighteousness." So God reveals His righteousness to men as men respond with faith to His revelation found in the gospel. Conversely, He reveals His

wrath to men as they respond with a lack of faith, suppressing the truth He reveals. The truth they are suppressing is the truth that God is the Creator of mankind and everything in the universe that surrounds him.

Verses 19 and 20 make this fact perfectly clear; it's a matter of simple logic: When people deny creation, they have no basis for receiving the Gospel of Christ by faith. This passage reminds us that to be successful in ministering to our American culture today, we must first address the fact that so many of them have suppressed the truth of creation.

THE WILLFUL DENIAL OF GOD AS CREATOR

We find the heart of this passage is verses 19-22 where Paul proclaims that God is the creator of all that exists and that He has revealed Himself in that which He has created. Then Paul boldly

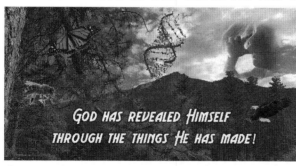

GOD HAS REVEALED HIMSELF
THROUGH THE THINGS HE HAS MADE!

proclaims that no person has an excuse for not believing in God, because He has made Himself known to everyone through the things He has created. Finally, he boldly proclaims that those who deny God as creator do so not because of a lack of evidence, but rather because they choose to suppress or push away the truth that is so obvious to all—the truth that God created the heaven and the earth and all that is within them.

Here we have an explanation as to why there is so much propaganda in our culture today which claims that science has proven that God did not create and that we are all here without

21

purpose, design, accountability, or destiny. Scientific evidence has not disproved God! Paul makes it clear that men suppress the truth not for lack of evidence, but because of their unrighteousness. Although they intuitively know God, they willfully suppress that knowledge and do not honor Him as God or give thanks. They have become futile in their speculations. Their foolish hearts have been darkened. Professing to be wise, they have become fools. Any open, honest heart can see ample evidence confirming that an intelligent, wise, powerful, and caring designer has brought all things into being. He has revealed so much of Himself through the things He has made.

Why Intelligent Design Is Wrong for Our Schools

NOT IN OUR CLASSROOMS

Edited by Eugenie C. Scott and Glenn Branch

Foreword by Rev. Barry W. Lynn

If this knowledge of God is so clear and easy to see, why isn't it proclaimed freely in every public school? The answer is found right here in this passage: The truth is suppressed in an attempt to deny God so that people can be their own god and live their lives by their own rules and values. What our public schools teach today is not taught because it is good science; it is taught because it is critical to the beliefs found in secular humanism. The foundational premises of secular humanism are dependent upon getting rid of God in the past, present, and future.

Verses 19 and 20 reveal three important points that we must understand if we are to develop a biblical worldview that can be defended and proclaimed in this skeptical culture:

---

(1) That which is known about God is evident to all people because God made it evident to them!

(2) God has revealed Himself to us through the creation of the world! He has revealed –

        * His Invisible Attributes!

        * His Eternal Power!

        * His Divine Nature!

These things are clearly seen, being understood through what has been made!

(3) No one has an excuse for not knowing God!

When you speak with an unbeliever about God, remember that buried somewhere within him is the revelation that God is real. God's invisible attributes—His eternal power and His divine nature—are clearly evident for him to see. He may deny it. He may have closed his heart to the point that it has become darkened. Still, the truth is that God has revealed Himself to this person through the things He has made. You can speak with confidence and boldness, though you should still speak with gentleness and reverence. You can know without a doubt that you are not starting from scratch with this person. God has already faithfully revealed Himself to him.

THE RESULTS OF DENYING GOD AS CREATOR

In verses 22-32, we read a detailed account of what God says will happen within any culture, nation, or people group which choose to deny Him as creator. If they suppress the truth in unrighteousness and refuse to honor God or give Him thanks, inevitable results will follow, and Paul lists those results in stunning detail in this passage. And it all begins with the denial of God as creator!

As we look at these verses, we can hardly help but think about where America is today as a people. I think you will see a clear parallel.

The downward spiral into depravity begins in verse 22 where we read that "professing to be wise, they became fools." This is easy to see today when brilliant men and women come up with very foolish ideas in an attempt to escape the obvious conclusion that God has created all things. Ideas like "the multiple universe theory" or "directed panspermia" are examples of foolish ideas that come about when people claim to be wise enough to remove God from the equation of life. It is often the most intelligent among us that lead the way down the path of foolishness as they proudly declare ideas and speculations that eliminate God from the picture.

Verse 23 speaks of the next step in this downward spiral—idolatry. It says they "exchanged the glory of the incorruptible God for an image in the form of corruptible man and of birds and four-footed animals and crawling creatures." Here Paul recognizes the fact that some cultures worship idols of stone and wood, while others worship people and living creatures. In America we have seen an increase in the worship of celebrities. Masses of people often wait in lines for hours, pay large sums of money, or even compromise their values just to get close to the movie stars, singers, athletes, or politicians they worship.

In verses 24-27 we see the next step in this downward spiral, which is sexual misconduct, especially homosexuality.

Here we learn what happens to people who "exchanged the glory of the incorruptible God for an image in the form of corruptible man and of birds and four-footed animals and crawling creatures" (v. 23). Verse 24 tells us that God "gave them over in the lusts of their hearts to impurity, so that their bodies would be dishonored among them." Then verse 25 restates the cause of all of this: "For they exchanged the truth of God for a lie, and worshiped and served the creature rather than the Creator."

Then verses 26 and 27 give specific information about the type of sexual sin any culture, nation, or people group who deny God as Creator will fall prey to. In verse 26 Paul gives a description of homosexuality among women: "For this reason God gave them over to degrading passions; for their women exchanged the natural function for that which is unnatural." The Bible here refers to homosexuality as unnatural and as a degrading passion. When people begin to worship and honor the creature rather than the Creator, God allows "degrading passions" to find a place within that culture.

In verse 27 Paul gives a description of homosexuality among men: "And in the same way also the men abandoned the natural function of the woman and burned in their desire toward one another, men with men committing indecent acts and receiving in their own persons the due penalty of their error." Clearly we can see here that the underlying reason that God gave these people over to sexual depravity was their refusal to honor God as Creator or to worship Him.

I think it is important to clarify that this is not saying that people who struggles with sexual sin—homosexuality in particular—are experiencing that struggle because they themselves have directly denied God as Creator. It is the culture as a whole that has been given over to these kinds of struggles because society in general has denied God as Creator.

It is also important to state here that the response of Christians to the issue of homosexuality should be the same response as to other sins. We must not compromise the Word of God and attempt to explain away homosexuality as something other than sin. But it is important that we reach out with love to those who have chosen this lifestyle or who struggle with this sin. We should never be guilty of name calling or hateful attitudes toward those who are caught in sin. It is very possible, and actually very natural, to stand firmly on the biblical teachings that homosexuality is a sin and at the same time be kind, loving, and caring toward those who are involved in this sin.

The church is often accused of treating homosexuality differently than all other types of sexual sin. Though this may be true in some instances, I am convinced that in the vast majority of situations it is the world, not the church, which attempts to make the distinction between homosexuality and other sexual sin. For example, rarely do you secularists saying to the church that it must declare adultery to be a valid lifestyle. Even those who commit adultery usually acknowledge that it is wrong. Yet, we often hear people in secular society urging the church to acknowledge homosexuality as a valid, normal, and non-sinful lifestyle. It is world, not the church, that attempts to treat one sin as different than all others. The response of the church toward those caught in any type of sin must be to continue to present the truth in love. As Jesus said, it is the truth that sets us free (John 8:32).

When we look at American history over the past 75 to 100 years, we see the pattern described in Romans 1 lived out in the modern world. In 1925, the so-called "Scopes Monkey Trial" took place in Dayton, Tennessee. Though the verdict upheld the law of that day, which disallowed the teaching of evolution in public schools, the trial became a rallying point for the proponents of evolutionary teaching. As naturalism became the pervasive scientific theory, evolution began to creep into public schools, and by the 1960s it was taught widely. It is probably not coincidental that by 1962 and 1963, prayer and Bible reading were removed from public schools, and moral indicators showed a major downturn in American moral behavior.

David Barton and his organization, Wallbuiders, did extensive research on the effects of the changes within our public schools in the early 1960s, and the results were staggering. Teenage pregnancy rose over 500 percent after 1962. The number of unwed mothers has increased dramatically since 1962. Crime rates have skyrocketed. After remaining relatively level since their inception, SAT scores dropped for eighteen years in a row after 1962. This downward trend in SAT scores reversed in the early 1980s with the rise of the Christian School and Home School movements. Many other moral indicators revealed the negative effects of what was now occurring in our public schools.

There can be little doubt that removing the teaching of creation, prayer, and Bible reading from public schools are all related to the drastic slide in our culture. All stem from the same root problem—a turning from God.

The issue of homosexuality did not become prominent immediately but the downward spiral of morality in America would eventually lead to exactly the kind of moral and sexual depravity that Romans 1 describes. Today we live in a nation where the homosexual marriage is legal in all fifty states. Entertainment, education, businesses, and public policy all promote homosexuality as normal, upright, and healthy. Romans 1 indicated that this would be the result in any nation where God is no longer honored as the Creator.

When verse 27 says that those who engage in homosexuality are "receiving in their own persons the due penalty of their error," it may be speaking of the sexually transmitted diseases that are so prevalent within the homosexual community, including the HIV/Aids virus. You will note that I used the term "may" because we cannot be sure that this is the meaning of the verse. But it well could be.

THE FINAL STEP IN THE DOWNWARD SPIRAL – A DEPRAVED MIND

As we continue through Romans 1, we come to verses 28 through 32, which describe the continuing downward moral spiral of any people who cease to honor God as Creator. The end result is "a depraved mind" which leads to "doing those things which are not proper."

The list of "things which are not proper" that Paul gives us here is staggering, but it hardly seems foreign to us. Actions and attitudes like these seem pervasive in people's lives in America today:

- **Filled with all unrighteousness**
- **Filled with wickedness**
- **Filled with greed**
- **Filled with evil**
- **Full of envy**
- **Full of murder**
- **Full of strife**
- **Full of deceit**
- **Full of malice**
- **Gossips**
- **Slanderers**
- **Haters of God**
- **Insolent people**
- **Arrogant people**
- **Boastful people**
- **Inventors of Evil**
- **Disobedient to Parents**
- **Without understanding**
- **Untrustworthy**
- **Unloving**
- **Unmerciful**

The Romans 1 passage closes by saying that though people know the ordinances of God and that those who practice improper and depraved things are worthy of death, they not only practice them as well, but also give hearty approval to others who practice them. To put it in other terms, they not only commit the evil acts themselves, they also approve of others who commit them. They create a culture where it is politically correct to both do and approve of sinful things.

It is both sad and alarming to realize how much America today resembles Paul's description of depravity in Romans 1. And we should feel shame when we realize that our decisions to reject God have brought our nation to this low point. When we deny God, we teach our children that man is his own god. Then we wonder why our streets are filled with murder, theft, drugs, alcohol, immorality, and riots. We wonder why families fall apart so often and people are so stressed and depressed. No political figure or party can turn these things around, but we know the root cause: If man has become his own god, then man will do only what feels good to him at the moment, disregarding long-term or eternal consequences. Only true repentance and turning back to God can change the course America is on today.

For the believer seeking to understand how to use apologetics to better defend and share his faith, it is important to understand the truth of Romans 1. It will confirm the critical importance of what people believe about creation and other foundational issues of the Christian faith.

SECTION 1: CHAPTER 4

"Are Faith and Science Opposed to Each Other?"

Before the eighteenth century, science and the Christian faith walked hand in hand. Faith was pervasive in the Western world, and the origin, composition, and order of the material universe were assumed to have their source in the same God who gave his Son for mankind's redemption. But with the inception of Enlightenment Philosophy in the 1700s, the seeds of conflict were planted. The Enlightenment elevated human reason as man's guiding light and began to discredit Christianity as blind faith unsupported by reasonable evidence.

Since the Enlightenment, science has made great strides, enabling the Industrial Revolution, finding cures to many diseases, unleashing atomic power, and exploring space. The discoveries of scientists have given humans longer life, greater comfort, mobility, communication, and entertainment. These successes have elevated science to a high pedestal in the human mind and emboldened unbelieving scientists and humanists to intensify the conflict with religion with increasingly antagonistic statements about the Christian faith and those who hold to it. Consider the following examples:

Thomas Huxley (1825-1895), who was known as "Darwin's Bulldog" and coined the term "agnostic," once said, "Extinguished theologians lie about the cradle of every science as the strangled snakes beside that of Hercules; and history records that whenever science and orthodoxy have been fairly opposed, the latter has been forced to retire from the lists, bleeding and crushed if not annihilated; scotched, if not slain." [1]

Chemist, philosopher, and photographic pioneer **John William Draper (1811-1882)** proclaimed that "The history of

Science is not a mere record of isolated discoveries; it is a narrative of the conflict of two contending powers, the expansive force of the human intellect on one side, and the compression arising from traditionary faith and human interests on the other." [2]

More recently **Alan Sokal (b. 1955),** a professor of mathematics at University College London and professor of physics at New York University stated, "'Faith' is not in fact a rejection of reason, but simply a lazy acceptance of bad reasons. 'Faith' is the pseudo-justification that some people trot out when they want to make claims without the necessary evidence." [3]

James D. Watson (b. 1928), who along with Francis Crick

won a Nobel Prize for their discovery of the double helix structure found in the DNA molecule, said, "Today, the theory of evolution is an accepted fact for everyone but a fundamentalist minority, whose objections are based not on reasoning but on doctrinaire adherence to religious principles." [4]

---

[1] Quoted from Goodreads.com,
http://www.goodreads.com/quotes/tag/science-vs-religion.
[2] ibid.
[3] ibid.
[4] ibid.

Robert G. Ingersoll (1833-1899), noted orator and political leader expressed his opinion concerning the relationship between faith (or religion) and science in even harsher words,: "There is no harmony between religion and science. When science was a child, religion sought to strangle it in the cradle. Now that science has attained its youth, and superstition is in its  dotage, the trembling, palsied wreck says to the athlete: "Let us be friends." It reminds me of the bargain the cock wished to make with the horse: "Let us agree not to step on each other's feet." [5] He has also said, "The telescope destroyed the firmament, did away with the heaven of the New Testament, rendered the ascension of our Lord and the assumption of his Mother infinitely absurd, crumbled to chaos the gates and palaces of the New Jerusalem, and in their places gave to man a wilderness of worlds." [6]

Luther Burbank (1849-1926), an inventor, botanist, and horticulturalist, found fame when he single-handedly saved US potato crops from a deadly blight by cultivating russet potatoes. He was a fan of Robert G. Ingersoll and an atheist. He once stated, "The integrity of one's own mind is of infinitely more value than adherence to any creed or system. We must choose between a dead faith belonging to the past and a living,  growing, ever-advancing science belonging to the future." He also spoke of children as the greatest sufferers of outgrown theologies. [7]

This examination of quotes showing the attempt to distance faith and religion from science would not be complete without some quotes from the virulent atheist **Richard**

---

[5] ibid.
[6] ibid.
[7] ibid.

Dawkins (b. 1941), author of The God Delusion and the University of Oxford's Professor for Public Understanding of Science from 1995 until 2008. Dawkins has said, "To an honest judge, the alleged marriage between religion and science is a shallow, empty, spin-doctored sham." [8] "Religious fanatics want people to switch off their own minds, ignore the evidence, and blindly follow a holy book based upon private 'revelation'." [9] In another place he is quoted as saying, "Religion is capable of driving people to such dangerous folly that faith seems to me to qualify as a kind of mental illness." [10] "Faith is the great cop-out, the great excuse to evade the need to think and evaluate evidence. Faith is belief in spite of, even perhaps because of, the lack of evidence." [11]

As you can see, there are and have been many who attempt convince people that faith (or religion) and science have no connection to one another. They would have us believe that faith is the product of blind faith held doggedly without evidence, while science is the result of growing amounts of evidence. They tell us that to be a person of reason and science, you must abandon your adherence to faith and religion. This is the type of bias that is used to ban the teaching of Creation in public schools while forcing the teaching of Darwinian Evolution but preventing the introduction of any critical thinking that would expose its weaknesses. Their basic stance is, "It's a done deal; we have proved it conclusively, but the supporting evidence is too difficult for you to understand, so just take our word for it."

Evolutionists will tell you that school textbooks do provide hard evidence for evolution. But examination will show that these evidences support only what we call "microevolution" which, as we will see later in this chapter, does not even begin to support the

---

[8] Quoted from the Brainy Quote.com,
  http://www.brainyquote.com/quotes/authors/r/richard_dawkins_3.html.
[9] ibid.
[10] ibid.
[11] ibid.

extravagant claims of evolutionists.

Are faith and science truly at odds with each other? A study of the development of science shows that this is definitely not the case. In fact, it was the belief that the universe is governed by laws and orderly, observable forces and movements that led early scientists to begin their studies. Science is built upon the presupposition that the universe is ordered and consistently  functions by pre-established laws. If the pioneers of modern science had believed that the universe was the result of unguided processes which followed a random explosion, they would not have believed that their observations could be trusted. Without consistent order, what you observe today might be totally different than what was observed yesterday or will be observed tomorrow. **It was their belief in a wise, powerful creator that led them to trust that processes and movements observed by scientific examination would be consistent and reliable. Their faith led them to their science.**

It is significant to the success of scientific advances that **most of the pioneers of modern science were Christians or believers in God.** The following list contains several of the most prominent scientists who ever lived, including a few who are still living. All share two things in common: their pivotal place in the history of science and their belief in God.

Nicholas Copernicus (1473-1543)

 Copernicus was the Polish mathematician and astronomer who put forward the first mathematically based system demonstrating that the planets orbited the sun. The publication of this model in his book, On the Revolutions of the Celestial Spheres, just before his death in 1543 is considered a major event in the history of science, triggering the Copernican Revolution and making an

important contribution to the Scientific Revolution.

Francis Bacon (1561–1626)

 Bacon is one of the fathers of empiricism. He is credited with establishing the inductive method of experimental science, which is what is called the scientific method today. His works argued for the possibility of scientific knowledge based only upon inductive and careful observation of events in nature. Most importantly, he argued that this knowledge could be achieved by use of a skeptical and methodical approach whereby scientists aim to avoid misleading themselves. He believed that greater knowledge in men brought glory to God. He wrote, "Knowledge is the rich storehouse for the glory of the Creator and the relief of man's estate." He also wrote. "A little philosophy inclineth man's mind to atheism, but depth in philosophy bringeth men's minds about to religion."

Johannes Kepler (1571-1630)

 Kepler was a brilliant mathematician and astronomer. He did early work on light and established the laws of planetary motion about the sun. He also came close to reaching the Newtonian concept of universal gravity well before Newton was born. His introduction of the idea of force in astronomy changed that science radically, moving it in a modern direction. Kepler also incorporated religious arguments and reasoning into his work, motivated by the religious conviction and belief that God had created the world according to an intelligible plan that is accessible through the natural light of reason. [12]

---

[12] Barker and Goldstein, "Theological Foundations of Kepler's Astronomy" The University of Chicago Press, 2001, 112–13.

Galileo Galilei (1564-1642)

Galileo was an Italian astronomer, physicist, engineer, philosopher, and mathematician who played a major role in the scientific revolution during the Renaissance. Galileo has been called the "father of observational astronomy," the "father of modern physics," and the "father of science." Galileo expressly said that the Bible cannot err, and he saw his system as an alternate interpretation of the biblical texts.

Blaise Pascal (1623–1662)

Blaise Pascal is well known for Pascal's law in the realm of physics and Pascal's theorem in math. Pascal influenced mathematics throughout his lifetime and is considered one of the first two inventors of the mechanical calculator. In the realm of physical sciences, Pascal's work in the fields of hydrodynamics and hydrostatics centered on the principles of hydraulic fluids. His inventions include the hydraulic press (using hydraulic pressure to multiply

force) and the syringe. In addition to being a mathematician, physicist, inventor, and writer, he was also a Christian philosopher.

John Ray (1627–1705)

John Ray (Wray) was an English botanist who published important works on botany, zoology, and natural theology. His classification of plants in his Historia Plantarum was an important step towards modern taxonomy. He was the first to give a biological definition of the term "species." In the 1690s, he published three volumes

on religion, the most important being The Wisdom of God Manifested in the Works of the Creation.

Sir Isaac Newton (1642-1727)

Isaac Newton is widely recognized as one of the most influential scientists of all time and as a key figure in the scientific revolution. His book Mathematical Principles of Natural Philosophy, first published in 1687, laid the foundations for classical mechanics. Newton made seminal contributions to optics, and he shares credit with Gottfried Leibniz for the development of calculus. Newton's Principia formulated the laws of motion and universal gravitation, which dominated scientists' view of the physical universe for the next three centuries. In optics, mechanics, and mathematics, Newton was a figure of undisputed genius and innovation. In all his science (including chemistry) he saw mathematics and numbers as central. What is less well known is that he was devoutly religious and saw numbers as involved in understanding God's plan for history as revealed in the Bible. In his system of physics, God was essential to the nature and absoluteness of space. In Principia he stated, "The most beautiful system of the sun, planets, and comets, could only proceed from the counsel and dominion of an intelligent and powerful Being." He was a devout but unorthodox Christian.

Gregor Mendel (1822-1884)

Mendel was the first to lay the mathematical foundations of genetics, in what came to be called "Mendelianism." He began his research in 1856 (three years before Darwin published his Origin of Species) in the garden of the Monastery in which he was a monk and gained posthumous fame as the founder of the modern science of genetics. His life as a priest certainly illustrates that he was both a man of science and a man of faith.

Louis Pasteur (1822-1895)

Louis Pasteur was a French chemist and microbiologist renowned for his discoveries of the principles of vaccination, microbial fermentation, and pasteurization. He is remembered for his remarkable breakthroughs in the causes and preventions of diseases, and his discoveries have saved countless lives ever since. He reduced mortality from  puerperal fever and created the first vaccines for rabies and anthrax. His work also was significant in disproving the notion of "spontaneous generation" and in establishing the scientific "Law of Biogenesis" which states that life can only come from life. Pasteur was a devout Christian, and did not see any conflict between science and Christianity, remarking that "A bit of science distances one from God, but much science nears one to Him." He also stated, "The more I study nature, the more I stand amazed at the work of the Creator."

Max Planck (1858-1947)

Planck made many contributions to physics, but he is best known for quantum theory, which revolutionized our understanding of the atomic and sub-atomic worlds. He was a deeply religious man, although his view of God was more that of a deist. He said: "Both Religion and science require a belief in God. For believers, God is in the  beginning, and for physicists He is at the end of all considerations... To the former He is the foundation, to the latter, the crown of the edifice of every generalized world view."

George Washington Carver (1864–1943)

George Washington Carver was an American scientist, botanist, educator, and inventor. Carver's reputation is based on his research into and promotion of alternative crops to cotton, such as peanuts, soybeans, and sweet potatoes, which also aided nutrition for farm families. Carver believed he could have faith both in God and science, and he integrated the two studies into his life. He testified on many occasions that his faith in Jesus was the only mechanism by which he could effectively pursue and perform the art of science.

John Lennox (b. 1945)

John Lennox is a mathematician, philosopher of science and pastoral adviser. His works include the mathematical thesis The Theory of Infinite Soluble Groups (co-written with Derek J. S. Robinson) and the religion-oriented God's Undertaker: Has Science Buried God? He has also debated religion with Richard Dawkins. He is a Fellow in Mathematics and Philosophy of Science at Green Templeton College, Oxford University.

Jennifer Wiseman

Dr. Jennifer Wiseman is a senior astrophysicist at the NASA Goddard Space Flight Center, where she serves as the Senior Project Scientist for the Hubble Space Telescope. In addition, she is a co-discoverer of 114P/Wiseman-Skiff (a periodic comet in our solar system). In religion, she is a Fellow of the American Scientific Affiliation, and on June 16, 2010 she became the new director for the American Association for the Advancement of Science's Dialogue on Science, Ethics, and Religion.

Stephen C. Meyer (b. 1958)

Dr. Stephen Meyer, formerly a geophysicist with the Atlantic Richfield Company, is presently the Director of the Center for Science and Culture at the Discovery Institute and Vice President and Senior Fellow at the Discovery Institute. Meyer's books include, Signature in the Cell and Darwin's Doubt.

John C. Sanford (b. 1950)

Dr. John Sanford earned a PhD in 1980 in plant breeding/plant genetics. Between 1980 and 1986 Sanford was an assistant professor of Horticultural Sciences at Cornell University, and from 1986 to 1998 he was an associate professor of Horticultural Science. He has published over seventy scientific articles in peer reviewed journals. Sanford is a prolific inventor with more than thirty-two issued patents. At Cornell, Sanford and colleagues developed the "Biolistic Particle Delivery System" or so-called "gene gun." He is the co-inventor of the Pathogen-derived Resistance (PDR) process and the  co-inventor of the genetic vaccination process. He was given the "Distinguished Inventor Award" by the Central New York Patent Law Association in 1990 and 1995. Formerly an atheist, from the mid-1980s, Sanford has significant research into Theistic Evolution, Old Earth Creationism and Young Earth Creationism. [13]

---

[13] The biographies of the scientists who profess Christianity in this section are adapted from two sources: (1) "List of Christians in science and technology," Wikipedia, https://en.wikipedia.org/wiki/List_of_Christians_in_science_and_technology#cite_note-99.

For lists of Scientists past and present who believe in God you can go to the Wikipedia page entitled "List of Christians in Science and Technology" or to the website entitled "Evidence for God".

How can we explain the fact that the names of great scientists appear on both sides of the conflict between faith and science? Each side deals with the same facts and evidence, but each reaches opposite conclusions. The answer is that both sides begin with their own presuppositions that force them to reach inevitable conclusions. The unbelieving scientists begin with the presupposition that God does not exist. That foundational belief forces them to interpret all evidence in a way that supports evolution. Their thinking, though seldom expressed in this way, goes something like this: "There is no God, therefore evolution must be true. The evidence may not demand an evolutionary interpretation, but we have no alternative but to interpret it that way because we are convinced at the outset that there is no God."

If you do not believe that any real scientist would allow an underlying, presupposed belief to affect his scientific objectivity, consider the following quotes: In a letter to Nature in 1999, a Kansas State University immunologist wrote, *"Even if all the data point to an intelligent designer, such an hypothesis is excluded from science because it is not naturalistic."* [14]

In the same vein, eminent geneticist Richard Lewontin wrote:

We take the side of science in spite of the patent absurdity of some of its constructs... in spite of the tolerance of the scientific community for unsubstantiated just-so stories, because we have a prior commitment, a commitment to materialism. It is not that the methods and institutions of science somehow compel us to accept a material explanation of the phenomenal world, but, on the contrary, that we are forced by our a priori adherence to material causes to create an apparatus of investigation and a set of

---

Accessed May 24, 2017. (2) "Famous Scientists Who Believed in God," God and Science.org, http://www.godandscience.org/apologetics/sciencefaith.html.

[14] Todd, S.C., correspondence to *Nature* 401(6752):423, 30 September. 1999.

concepts that produce material explanations, no matter how counterintuitive, no matter how mystifying to the uninitiated. Moreover, that materialism is an absolute, for we cannot allow a Divine Foot in the door. [15]

These frank admissions make it clear that the presupposition of atheism among scientists closes the door to an objective interpretation of evidence. Those who claim that faith and science cannot mix base that claim on their own religious beliefs (atheism or agnosticism), which erect a personal bias that closes off openness to opposing evidence. But to an open mind, the opposing evidence is plain to see. As we have shown above, the history of modern science—the foundations of which were developed largely by believing scientists—show clearly that **not only are faith and science compatible, but faith is actually a motivation and aide to the pursuit of true science**.

TERMS AND DEFINITIONS

To better understand the true relationship between religious faith and science, it is important that we define some key terms related to the issue.

Science

A simple definition of the word science is "knowledge." More specifically, "knowledge about or study of the natural world based on facts learned through experiments and observation." Another definition states it this way: "a branch of knowledge or study dealing with a body of facts or truths systematically arranged and showing the operation of general laws: knowledge, as of facts or principles; knowledge gained by systematic study." [16]

In summary, science involves knowledge derived from experimentation and observation. To qualify as scientific knowledge, a phenomenon or event must be observable, demonstrable, and

---

[15] Richard Lewontin, "Billions and billions of demons," The New York Review of Books (January 9, 1997), 28.
[16] https://www.dictionary.com/browse/science

repeatable. Understanding this will help us to see that when it comes to looking back into the past for answers about origins, even the most adamant, anti-religious materialist must incorporate an element of faith in his conclusions. No human was there to observe the event, and it is obviously not demonstrable or repeatable. Believing in the Big Bang, for example, requires an element of faith, because it can neither be demonstrated nor repeated.

Scientist

A scientist is a person who studies science and is involved in scientific discovery. Scientists are obviously blessings to society as they use their God-given abilities and acquired knowledge to develop products and medicines that benefit our lives.

You may have heard the claim that all true scientists believe that evolution explains man's origin and development. This is simply not true. Disagreement over issues does not disqualify one to bear the label of scientist. Nor is the claim true that scientists approach scientific research without any bias. Scientists are people; and like other people, they hold different worldviews, religious views, and political views. They are just as vulnerable as the rest of us to cultural influences and outside pressures. The idea that "Whatever position the majority of scientists hold at this moment must be fact" is no truer than the idea that "Whatever the majority of politicians hold at this moment must be good."

An example of the influences that often affect scientists is found in Ben Stein's movie Expelled. In this documentary, Stine reveals the occupational pressures placed on teachers in American schools and universities. If they fail to hold to the party line about Darwinian evolution, they face discipline or dismissal. This pressure causes many teachers to continue proclaiming evolution as a proven scientific theory even though they know that there are serious problems with the theory and that it does not match the scientific data.

Operational & Historical Science

Science in general is divided into two broad fields: operational and historical. Operational science deals with experimentation and observable processes that are repeatable. In operational science, dependable conclusions can be derived from repeated experimentation. Operational science is responsible for the development of the modern lifestyles and conveniences that we enjoy each day. To this branch of science we owe such things as microwave ovens, airplanes, cell phones, x-ray machines, televisions, and computers. Many Christian scientists have played critical roles in the development of modern operational science and its resulting technology.

Historical science deals with seeking answers about events that have occurred in the past. These events, for the most part, are neither observable, demonstrable, nor repeatable. Conclusions in areas of historical science usually involve speculation and always involve a measure of faith. This is true because we are observing evidences available in the present that indicate a past event and seeking to understand what these evidences tell us about that event. For example, the presence of ash provides evidence that a fire occurred. But the ash doesn't tell us how, why, when, or by what the fire was started. Answers to those questions require further evidence or speculation.

Many evolutionists today claim that the conclusions of historical science regarding past events are just as reliable as the observable, demonstrable, and repeatable evidences found in operational science. The reality is, however, that many of these conclusions are merely interpretations of evidence that cannot be proved or repeated. Many of them do not line up well with observable evidences such as the fossil record, the second law of thermodynamics, or genetic entropy. But since no observable, repeatable, or demonstrable evidence for evolution is available, evolutionary scientists often use creative means to push their theory.

One of their methods is the use of considerable artistic freedom to create the appearance that current evidences confirm their speculative opinions. For example, drawings are often used to support the theory that the fossil record reveals a slow, consistent evolution of humans from ape-like creatures of the past. Occasionally, a newly discovered fossilized tooth or a half-dozen bone fragments will be hyped as another missing link confirming that evolution has occurred. Published along with a photo of the fossil will be an artistic rendering of the creature from which the fossil is derived. The drawing will always be quite complete, creating exactly the impression the evolutionists want to communicate—that this creature actually existed somewhere in the ancestral line of humans.

The problem is, the drawing has no basis other than the imagination of an artist. A tooth or a few random bone fragments cannot indicate how tall a creature was, the shape of its skull or body, whether it walked upright, or whether it had hair. A classic example of this is found in the discovery of what was once called "Nebraska Man." Nebraska Man was proclaimed in the 1920s as a missing link in the evolution from ape-like creatures to man. The

"Nebraska Man"

supposed creature was based on a tooth that rancher and geologist Harold Cook found in Nebraska in 1917. Artistic renderings were produced to show what the creature looked like (see the drawing reproduced on this page). In the early 1920s, an article was published in the magazine Science announcing the discovery of a man-like ape in North America, and many were excited about how the new find confirmed evolution. But a few years later, further examination of the tooth revealed that it was actually from an extinct species of pig. Look at the picture again and think about the magnitude of the audacity and deception involved here. This highly detailed picture of a complete creature was extrapolated from one weathered tooth of an extinct pig to convince the world that a man-like ape had been found.

Many of us have seen computer animations that illustrate how the Big Bang initiated the development of the universe billions of years ago. When viewing such animations, we should always remember that what we are seeing are current creations developed by skilled technicians, not a filmed record of the past. Research can certainly help us speculate about past events, but we must always keep in mind that human interpretations of events that occurred in the past always involve an element of faith.

Faith

The Bible gives us the definition of faith in Hebrews 11:1 (KJV): "Now faith is the substance of things hoped for, the evidence of things not seen." Note the second part of this definition: Faith is evidence of things not seen. When we deal with things of the past, such as the origin of the universe and the origin of life, we are dealing with things we cannot see. Because of this, we examine the evidence that is available to us and come to conclusions. Conclusions about things we cannot witness directly always involve faith. This is true whether one is a creationist or an evolutionist. I examine the evidence that is found all around me in the known world and come to the faith conclusion that the Bible's proclamation that God created the heavens and earth and all that is within them is true. Someone else looks at the same evidence and comes to the faith conclusion that Darwin's proclamations that life has evolved by natural, unguided processes over billions of years is true. We both must invoke faith, because neither of us can travel back in time and witness God creating all things or witness life evolving from non-life and evolving into different life forms. We must apply faith to our interpretation of the evidence given to us in order to reach our separate conclusions.

The claim we often hear from evolutionists that faith and science are diametrically opposed is simply not true. As we have shown above, historical science always involves faith, whether one's conclusion is creation or evolution. Such conclusions inevitably involve faith, but they should never involve blind faith. God never requires anyone to hold their beliefs on the basis of blind faith. He has provided overwhelming evidences within the things He has made that enable us to develop faith about past events that is solid and dependable, confirming what He has told us in the Bible.

Easton's Bible Dictionary defines "faith" in this way, "Faith is in general the persuasion of the mind that a certain statement is true. Its primary idea is trust. A thing is true, and therefore worthy of trust. It admits of many degrees up to full assurance of faith, in accordance with the evidence on which it rests." So faith rests upon and is strengthened by evidence that confirms its claims.

Those who claim that Christians resist science are not telling the truth. We simply disagree with the speculative interpretations of current evidences that automatically eliminate God and supernatural causes from consideration.

Religion and Worldview

A Google search for "the meaning of religion" yields this threefold definition:

1. "the belief in and worship of a superhuman controlling power, especially a personal God or gods."
2. "a particular system of faith and worship."
3. "a pursuit or interest to which someone ascribes supreme importance." [17]

Another definition of religion is found at the website, All About Religion.

"Religion is a fundamental set of beliefs and practices generally agreed upon by a group of people. These sets of beliefs concern the cause, nature, and purpose of the universe, and involve devotional and ritual observances. They also often contain a moral code governing the conduct of human affairs." [18]

As you can see, religion is not always defined as being specifically related to belief in God and the supernatural. As the second, third, and fourth definitions above indicate, religion includes systems of faith that groups share, any shared pursuit that groups find important, and most tellingly, sets of shared beliefs about the nature and purpose of the universe. These definitions show that the

---

[17] https://www.google.com/webhp?sourceid=chrome-instant&ion=1&espv=2&ie=UTF-8#q=the+meaning+of+religion.

[18] "The Meaning of Religion," All About Religion.com, http://www.allaboutreligion.org/meaning-of-religion-faq.htm.

evolutionary view of origins is in itself a form of religion. To disbelieve in God is as much a religious point of view as it is to believe in God.

Most secular humanists agree that they adhere to a religious worldview. According to the Humanist Manifestos I & II: Humanism is "a philosophical, religious, and moral point of view." [19] In fact, in the fall of 2014, a federal district court in Oregon declared secular humanism to be a religion, paving the way for the non-theistic community to obtain the same legal rights as groups such as Christianity. [20]

Not all humanists, however, want to be identified as religious, because they understand that religion is (supposedly) not allowed in American public education. To identify secular humanism as a religion would eliminate the humanists' main vehicle for the propagation of their faith. [21] The reality is, it is a faith by their own admission. The Humanist Manifestos declare: "These affirmations [in the Manifestos] are not a final credo or dogma but an expression of a living and growing faith." [22]

It is important to understand the full meaning and application of the word religion so we will not be misled by attempts to exclude scientific conclusions that support creation or intelligent design because they affirm God and the supernatural. As these definitions of religion demonstrate, the word includes both belief and disbelief in God. By falsely classifying belief as religious and disbelief as scientific, humanists have succeeded in limiting all explanations and discussions within classrooms to those that support their worldview.

This brings us to the question, what is a worldview? The American Scientific Affiliation describes it in this way: "A worldview is a theory of the world, used for living in the world. A worldview is a

---

[19] Paul Kurtz, in the preface to Humanist Manifestos I & II (Buffalo, NY: Prometheus Books, 1973), p. 3.

[20] Jack Jenkins, "Atheists Score Major Win In Federal Court," Think Progress.org, November 3, 2014.
http://thinkprogress.org/justice/2014/11/03/3587801/district-court-declares-secular-humanism-a-religion/.

[21] "What is Secular Humanism?" Christian Answers.net,
http://www.christiananswers.net/q-sum/sum-r002.html.

[22] Kurtz, Humanist Manifestos I & II, p. 24. Italics added.

mental model of reality — a framework of ideas and attitudes about the world, ourselves, and life, a comprehensive system of beliefs — with answers for a wide range of questions." [23]   One's worldview encompasses his beliefs about the most significant concepts of life, such as God, the cosmos, knowledge, values, humanity, and history.

Everyone has a worldview, though not everyone is aware of it. Our worldview can be determined by many things, including our family life, environment, and peers. But normally, it will be especially impacted by our education—what principles, realities, and values are taught to us as truth.

A good illustration of how our worldview impacts the way we view things in life is the wearing of colored glasses. If we are wearing glasses with green-tinted lenses, then everything we look at will appear to have a green tint. If we are wearing glasses with red-tinted lenses, then everything we view will appear to have a red tint. This principle applies to our scientific and religious views. Our worldview provides the "tint" of our mental lenses, and our beliefs are determined by the worldview through which we see reality. We will look more closely at worldviews and their importance in a later chapter.

Those holding a materialist or atheistic worldview often discount the conclusions of Christian scientists, claiming that their religious worldview is bound to skew their objectivity when examining evidence. Is it possible that this is true—that a person's Christian worldview will always invalidate the objectivity of his conclusions? Before we address that question, we must ask another: Is there ever anyone—Christian or otherwise—who can evaluate scientific evidence without his conclusions being impacted by his religious beliefs? As we have noted above, secular humanists, agnostics, and atheists also have religious beliefs that affect their worldview and their interpretation of scientific evidences. It is grossly unfair for these secularists to claim that Christians cannot do science honestly because of their prior religious bias when they themselves are guilty of the same thing. Religious biases, whether pro-God or anti-God, will inevitably affect how scientists interpret

---

[23] "What is a Worldview?" American Scientific Affiliation, http://asa3.org/ASA/education/views/index.html.

available evidences to reach their conclusions in the realm of historical science.

Microevolution and Macroevolution

We need to understand the difference between microevolution and macroevolution because it is the basis of much of propaganda used to promote the theory of evolution in public school textbooks. These terms and issues surrounding them will be explored in greater detail later in the chapter, "Scientific Flaws of the Theory of Evolution." For now, we will simply define these two terms and briefly explain how they are often used and misused.

"Microevolution" refers to changes that occur within a particular kind of living thing. For example, variations within the beaks of finches that Darwin observed on the Galapagos Islands were examples of microevolution. Despite the changes in their beak sizes and shapes, the finches did not change into another kind of creature. They continued to be finches.

"Macroevolution" refers to changes occurring by mutations and natural selection that result in one kind of living creature becoming a different kind of living creature over extended periods of time. Supposed examples of macroevolution would be dinosaurs turning into birds or land mammals turning into whales.

Microevolution has been observed multitudes of times in scientific research. It is consistent with scientific data. Species do have the capacity to adapt to their changing environments with modifications to their size, shape, and color. We can even cause microevolution to occur, as in the selective breeding of animals such as cattle, horses, and dogs to modify the size and strength of animals within a species. No scientist, Christian or otherwise, denies the occurrence of microevolution. Macroevolution, on the other hand, has never been observed in scientific research and is not consistent with scientific data. The reason this is significant is that a common practice in many science textbooks is to cite examples of microevolution as proof of macroevolution. It is a dishonest bait-and-switch tactic that bases the totally unsupported theory of macroevolution upon obvious and universally accepted examples of microevolution.

Naturalism

Naturalism is the "idea or belief that only natural (as opposed to supernatural or spiritual) laws and forces operate in the world." Naturalism is a pillar of many of the evolutionary ideas that dominate science textbooks and classrooms in America today. Many who hold to a naturalistic worldview do not deny people's right and privilege to hold to faith in God or a supernatural world. They simply argue that any explanations of reality that include the supernatural or spiritual realms have no place in the science classroom. They claim that science must limit itself to explanations within the natural realm. It is this predisposed bias that causes many to refuse even to consider any explanation of the universe that allows the possibility of a supernatural designer.

I like to illustrate the effect of naturalism on modern science by imagining a grade school math class with a very peculiar set of rules. The teacher says to the students, "Today we are going to examine the question, what is 2 + 2? The only rule for our examination is that the answer '4' is not allowed into the discussion." The teacher may go on to urge the students to explore this math problem with open minds. She may congratulate various students for their ability to come up with intellectual-sounding arguments supporting their answers. But the reality is that the class will not be able to solve the math problem properly because the right answer has been eliminated before they even begin their exploration.

Naturalism has the same effect on historical science. It eliminates from the set of possible answers the very answer that all the scientific data points to—that of an intelligent, powerful designer.

Alternative speculations are deemed more intellectually appealing than the obvious answer.

Scientists who do not limit themselves to naturalism posit that the precise fine-tuning which enables the universe to support life gives evidence of a designer, because in mathematical terms, the vast complexity of this fine-tuning is beyond the possibility of random chance. Scientists who limit themselves to naturalism dismiss this assertion, claiming that to introduce the possibility of a supernatural realm is not scientific. Then those same scientists turn around and introduce the "multiple universe theory" which claim that the universe is fine-tuned because there have been millions of imperfect universes—for which there is absolutely no evidence—and that this one just happens to be perfect for the support of life by sheer accident. That, they say, is scientific!

Another example of how naturalism influences the conclusions of scientists is related to the amazing complexity of the DNA molecule. Dr. Francis Crick, who along with Dr. James Watson won a Nobel Prize for the discovery of the double helix structure of the DNA molecule, wrote in his book, Life Itself: Its Origin and Nature, that life at the cellular level is too complex to have possibly evolved from nonlife here on earth, even in 4.6 billion years. He then reveals his own hypothesis to explain life on earth. He calls it "Directed Panspermia." It postulates that highly evolved creatures from some other planet placed the spores (or seeds) of life on an unmanned spaceship and sent them across the universe to the earth. All life on earth was seeded by those spores. Dogged adherence to naturalism forces scientists to consider a supernatural creator to be a far-fetched fantasy while the possibility that advanced beings from another planet sent the seeds of life to earth is considered a realistic scientific possibility. Dedication to the naturalistic worldview can lead one to deny the obvious in favor of highly convoluted explanations more fit for science fiction than for science.

Christians must understand that true science is not the foe of Christianity. But limiting views such as those inherent within naturalism are used to make it seem that creation is a fantasy of the ignorant and unworthy of scientific consideration.

Natural Revelation and Worship

In the previous chapter, we discussed the critical passage of scripture found in Romans 1:18-32. Within this passage, we are told that God has revealed Himself to us through the things that He has made (v. 20). The verse goes on to state that because of this clear revelation of God's existence, we have no excuse for disbelief.

Some within the church have minimized the importance of creation, saying that it is not critical to the gospel. Unless man was created perfect and fell from perfection into the deadly state of sin, then Christ's atoning sacrifice would be meaningless. Not only is creation critical to the gospel message of Christ on the cross, it is also critical because it enables us to know and understand the nature of God and develop a deep relationship with Him. He has revealed Himself to us through the created things He has placed around us—an aspect of revelation which is often called "Natural Revelation" or "General Revelation."

In addition to Natural Revelation, God has given us "Special Revelation" in the forms of the Bible and of Jesus Christ, His Son. Special Revelation is critical to our understanding of God and his plans and purposes. Special Revelation does not negate the importance of Natural Revelation, but our understandings of God gleaned through Natural Revelation can never override what God reveals to us in Special Revelation.

Some people also experience "Supernatural Revelation," which occurs when God reveals Himself through dreams, visions, or prophesies. Just as with Natural Revelation, Supernatural Revelation can never override God's Special Revelation given to us through the Bible and the person of Jesus Christ.

Most of our worship of God tends to center on His Special Revelation—the Bible and the person of Jesus Christ. This is commendable and appropriate. But if you want to enhance your worship, you can do no better than to heighten your sensitivity to Natural Revelation. Through Natural Revelation, God has revealed to us His invisible attributes, His eternal power, and His divine nature. This includes phenomena such as the finely tuned universe, the earth which is so perfectly prepared to be inhabited, the amazing instincts and abilities of living creatures, the complex and exquisitely designed structures we call our bodies, the vast amount of usable information found in DNA, or the activities within the human cell, which has all the complex interrelated workings of a miniature city. The more we learn about these wonderfully designed things, the more our worshipping hearts will naturally blend with our voices in exultation when we sing "How Great is Our God!"

"Regaining a Generation Already Gone"

In their book Already Gone, Ken Ham, Britt Beemer, and Todd Hillard reveal that approximately two out of three teenagers sitting in our churches will leave the church by the time they are in their twenties. Many of them are "already gone," meaning they have already left in their heart and remain physically only out of courtesy or obligation to family or friends. Some will return to the church later in life after they settle down and have children of their own. However, the statistics show that many will not.

The book reveals that much of the reason so many young people are leaving the church is that they are not receiving answers to questions about why we believe in the Christian faith. Today they live in a culture that often attacks Christians as holding a blind faith contrary to reality, facts, and reason. With little or no understanding of the basis of our faith, they are left to assume that the world's accusations may be true. They are often easily swayed by teachers, peers, or other influences, which induces them to leave their Christian faith behind and follow the philosophies held by those around them.

Despite the fact that we live in a time when Christian television, radio, music, movies, games, websites, etc. are far more accessible than ever before, the younger generation is largely ignoring these attempts to retain their attention and turning away from the church in unprecedented numbers. Consider the following statistics:

> ## Twenty-somethings struggle to stay active in Christian faith
>
> **20% who are churched as a teen remain spiritually active at age 29**
> **61% who are churched as a teen become disengaged during their twenties**
> **19% are never churched as a teen, and still remain unconnected** [1]

The problem is not that the church has failed to bring children and teens into the church. In fact, through much effort, the church has been quite effective in this area. In 2000, the Barna Group did extensive surveys of more than 22,000 people and found that nearly 50 percent of American teens were regularly attending church. About three out of five attended a church youth group meeting sometime within a three-month period, and one-third participated in Christian clubs of some type at school. [2] The problem has been the number of teens who leave the church once they leave high school.

To probe deeper into the problem, Ken Ham of Answers in Genesis turned to Britt Beemer of America's Research Group, a leading marketing research and business analyst firm. Beemer specializes in studying human behavior. These two men embarked on a study of their own to find out why so many were leaving the church. In the course of their research, they interviewed 1,000 individuals from coast to coast balanced according to population and gender with just over half aged twenty-five to twenty-nine and just under half aged twenty to twenty-four. [3]

---

[1] Source: The Barna Group, LTD 2006
[2] Barna Research Online, "Teenagers Embrace Religion but Are Not Excited About Christianity," January 10, 2000, www.Barna.org.
[3] https://answersingenesis.org/christianity/church/already-gone/

> ### <u>Of the thousand 20 to 29-year-old evangelicals who no longer attend church:</u>
>
> **95% attended church regularly during their elementary and middle school years**
> **55% attended church regularly during high school**
> **Only 11% were still going to church during their early college years** [4]

We can see that the departure from church was not limited to those college age or older. A large number stopped attending church somewhere among their middle school or high school years. There are a number of reasons why people raised in the church might decide to leave, including job conflicts, peer pressure, involvement in lifestyles not approved by the church, or busy schedules. But the research uncovered an issue much nearer to the root of the problem. **If we do not know why we believe what we believe, and if we begin to doubt that what we believe is true, then all other reasons for departing from the church become more enticing.** In order to evaluate what part belief played in the decision of young people to leave the church, the researchers asked the sample group this question:

> ### <u>"Do you believe all the accounts/stories in the Bible are true and accurate?"</u>
>
> *** 38 percent of people who left the church answered yes**
> *** 44 percent said no**
> *** 18 percent didn't know** [5]

This statistic tells us that 62 percent of those surveyed said they either did not believe that the accounts and stories in the Bible are true and accurate or they didn't know if they were. With no more

---

[4] ibid.
[5] https://answersingenesis.org/is-the-bible-true/not-what-youd-expect/

confidence in biblical truth than that, it's little wonder that young people leave the church. How difficult is it to live for something that has a cost in terms of time, lifestyle, prestige, and peer acceptance if you are not convinced that it's true?

There are a number of issues that the church needs to address today, such as homes that reflect true Christian values, love shown consistently to all who come through the church doors, and living courageously in the face of increasing hostility to Christianity. But nothing outstrips the need to teach our young people why we believe what we believe! It is not enough merely to teach them what the church believes; we must also ground them solidly in why we believe it. We must prepare them to "always be ready to give a defense to everyone who asks you a reason for the hope that is in you" (1 Peter 3:15).

The research revealed that young people are typically not developing their doubts after they get to college; they begin doubting during their middle school and high school years.

> **When did young people begin to doubt the accuracy of biblical accounts:**
>
> - **39.8 percent first had doubts in middle school**
> - **43.7 percent first had doubts in high school**
> - **10.6 percent had their first doubts in college** [6]

This statistic shows that the church must recognize the need to begin at an earlier age to teach young people the "why" answers regarding the Christian faith.

When asked if they planned to return to church when they have children of their own, a little over one-third thought it likely; one-third thought it unlikely; and just under one-third didn't know. It is very telling to note the following answers showing how much the beliefs of those surveyed impacted their decision as to whether they planned to return to the church.

---

[6] https://answersingenesis.org/christianity/church/already-gone/

Comparison of Beliefs of Young People Who Plan to Return to the Church With Those Who Do Not Plan to Return	Planning on Returning	Never Coming Back
Do you believe all the books of the Bible are inspired by God?	76.4% said Yes	41.9% said Yes
Do you believe in creation as stated in the Bible?	92.1% said Yes	47.8% said Yes
Do you believe in the creation of Adam and Eve in the Garden of Eden?	91.3% said Yes	50.6% said Yes
Do you believe all the accounts/stories in the Bible are true/accurate?	58.5% said Yes	16.8% said Yes

As you can see, what people believe makes a big difference in their behavior, especially when it comes to church attendance and living out the Christian faith. For years we have been negligent within the local church, failing to teach more than Bible stories to our children—as well as to people of all ages, for that matter. We have, in most cases, not taught the evidences that confirm truth of our beliefs. We must make adjustments if we are going to be effective in the culture we now live in! It will involve diligence and work, but the good news is that wonderful resources showing why the Christian faith is trustworthy have been produced by dedicated and knowledgeable experts. This material is abundant, affordable, and easy to find.

THE ISSUE OF RELEVANCE

When we consider where one goes to learn about geology, anthropology, astronomy, biology, anatomy and history, we of course think of school. Ideally, we trust that at school we will be taught factual, truthful information about reality. At school we expect to learn true and verifiable facts about the world we live in. In contrast, at church we are usually taught

stories containing supernatural events that are merely asserted to be true, with no observable supporting evidence. Do you see the problem here? It is easy for kids to grow up thinking that school is relevant to the real world they live in, while church is not. In reality, the church has the capacity to teach geology, anthropology, astronomy, biology, anatomy and history in a more relevant way than our secular schools. This is because the Bible contains relevant information that coherently explains phenomena that puzzles secular educators.

For example, geology shows many sedimentary rock layers all over the world which are filled with billions of fossils. Contemporary  scientists are baffled by the existence of these fossils because all of them seem to have been formed in the same geologic era. Scientists are convinced that it takes millions of years for these strata to form, and they are puzzled by the uniformity of these fossils. The best and most coherent explanation for the fossils is the biblical account of the worldwide flood in Genesis. The layers of sedimentary rock were formed by the pressures and movement of enormous volumes of water. In answer to the belief that such layers take millions of years to form, sedimentary rock layers formed near Mt. St. Helens in a matter of days after its massive 1980 eruption.

Connecting the biblical account of the global flood in Noah's time with the geology that we see around us today can help students see that the Bible is relevant to the real world. This is just one example of many showing how the church today must learn to teach the Bible as it relates to reality and life.

When the church allows the public sector—which has bought totally into a non-biblical worldview—to be the sole source of information about important areas of learning, we are setting ourselves up to become irrelevant. If people believe that all the answers concerning the world they live in are found outside the church, the church loses its relevance and becomes easy for people to walk away from it.

When the Already Gone researchers asked the entire 1,000 young adults whether they believe that the Church is relevant, only 47 percent said "yes." A full 53 percent said either "no" or "I don't know." [7] When over half of our young people see the church as irrelevant, it becomes clear that we have a huge education task ahead of us.

How sad it is to see huge, beautiful church buildings across Europe which have become museums or practically vacant as the culture has become increasingly secular. American churches today struggle to stay relevant to avoid the same end as many of those in Europe. Unfortunately, churches often attempt to stay relevant by focusing on style, adding all the bells and whistles necessary to make church "cool" for the people they are trying to attract. There may be value in staying relevant stylistically and using the latest technologies for the kingdom of God, but ultimately it is the message we preach that must have relevance.

If we intend to restore the relevance of the church, we must address a number of questions: Are we seen just as another voice adding our opinion to the noise of the culture, or do we speak with the authority of "Thus sayeth the Lord"? Have we taken the time to know ourselves and to help others see that there is abundant evidence that confirms God as Creator of all things? Have we demonstrated with solid evidence that the Bible is His authoritative, dependable Word? Have we shown that God's sending His divine Son, Jesus the Christ, into the world to save us from our sin is verified by solid historical and rational evidence? Have we demonstrated the superiority of what the Christian faith teaches over what we are encountering in our decadent culture? Or have we allowed the notion to prevail that science is about facts and the Bible is about

---

[7] https://answersingenesis.org/christianity/church/the-real-deal/

myths and stories? Have we allowed professors and pundits to attack the dependability of the Bible without teaching why we can depend upon its historical accuracy and divine authority?

The evidence is all on the side of the church, but most churches have not focused on learning and communicating that evidence. It is time to step up to the plate and address the issue for the sake of future generations, for the sake of evangelism, and for the sake of the advancement of the kingdom of God.

MAKING ADJUSTMENTS

In a previous chapter, we spoke of how the Apostle Paul adjusted his presentation of the gospel to fit the culture he was addressing. Unlike Peter, who in Acts 2 was ministering to a predominantly Jewish crowd, Paul spoke in Acts 14 and 17 to Gentiles who did not have the Jewish foundation of belief in the Old Testament teachings. He began by speaking of the God of creation and from there made his way to telling them about the crucified and resurrected Christ. It is undeniable that the people we reach out to today with the gospel message do not have the same foundation of belief that people had fifty to seventy-five years ago.

In the fourth chapter of Already Gone, Ken Ham makes a statement that I believe every church leader and proclaimer of the gospel should understand:

> When Billy Graham retired, I saw that as symbolic. It was the end of the era of the "Jews" and the beginning of the era of the "Greeks." We will not have another Billy Graham type of response in today's present culture. His message can't be heard the same way in this culture. If they won't believe what the Bible teaches about earthly things, how will they believe about the heavenly things? [8]

---

[8] https://answersingenesis.org/christianity/church/the-short-road-to-irrelevance/

HOW YOUNG PEOPLE SEE TODAY'S CHURCH

In his 2007 book unChristian, David Kinnaman, president of the Barna Institute, points to other studies which show the negative perceptions of Christianity that many American young people have today. These perceptions are false, for the most part, and I believe they reflect the fact that our young people lack grounding in the foundational truths of Christianity.

As you can see on the chart, "Perceptions of Christianity," the vast majority of sixteen to twenty-nine-year-olds outside the church see Christianity as anti-homosexual, judgmental, hypocritical, old-fashioned, too involved in politics, out of touch with reality, and insensitive toward others. [9] Obviously, this image problem is not helpful in drawing these people into the church.

PERCEPTIONS OF CHRISTIANITY (Ages 16–29)

Perception	By Outsiders	By Churchgoers
anti-homosexual	91%	80%
judgmental	87%	52%
hypocritical	85%	47%
old-fashioned	78%	36%
too involved in politics	75%	50%
out of touch with reality	72%	32%
insensitive toward others	70%	28%

How do these perceptions relate to a lack of grounding in foundational truth? Look at the chart, "'Favorable' Image of Christianity." [10]

[9] David Kinnaman, unChristian, (Grand Rapids: Baker Books, 2007), 28.
[10] ibid.

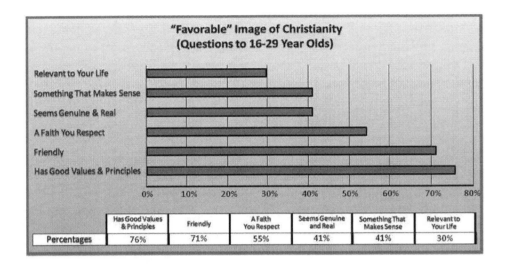

	Has Good Values & Principles	Friendly	A Faith You Respect	Seems Genuine and Real	Something That Makes Sense	Relevant to Your Life
Percentages	76%	71%	55%	41%	41%	30%

I believe this information is very revealing. Though the majority of non-churchgoers age sixteen to twenty-nine see the church as friendly and having good values and principles, only a small minority (30 percent) view Christianity as relevant to their life. Only 41 percent felt that Christianity made sense or seemed to be genuine and real. This tells us that the real disconnect is not due to the atmosphere or the values of the church. **The real disconnect is with the genuineness, the reality, the sensibility, and the relevance of Christianity**. I believe this relates to the fact that most have never heard the evidence that links the message of the Bible to historical fact and verifiable reality. We have been generally oblivious to the fact that the world is promoting a narrative that the Christian faith is based on myths and fairytales. Because the church has not countered this narrative with the truth, it has increasingly disconnected our young people from the Christian faith.

If a person does not have a worldview established upon the basic factual truths of the Bible, then the church's declarations on current social issues will seem to be doctrinaire and unfounded. An article by Focus on the Family states that **"A recent nationwide survey completed by the Barna Research Group determined that**

only 4 percent of Americans had a 'biblical' worldview." [11] No wonder so many young people have a misperception of Christianity! They are viewing the world through different glasses. To correct this problem, we must effectively communicate both the whats and whys of the foundational truths of Christianity. People are searching for something more than just what feels good. They are searching for something that is true and trustworthy!

The church and its leaders must respond to the challenges presented by a mocking, skeptical culture and do the things needed to regain a generation that is stumbling around in an environment of relativism devoid of absolute truth. We must obey the strong admonition found in 1 Peter 3:15:

> *Sanctify Christ as Lord in your hearts, always being ready to make a defense to everyone who asks you to give an account for the hope that is in you, yet with gentleness and reverence.*

This admonition was not limited to the first-century church. It is for the church today, and not just for specially trained teachers and leaders, but for every Christian who occupies a pew. Have we made ourselves ready? Have we prepared? Have we responded to the battle?

I do believe there are signs that the church and its leaders are beginning to wake up to this need, and a strong response is beginning to rise. Because Jesus Christ is Lord of His church, I have great faith that He will raise up the church to face this challenge, just as He has raised up His church to face every challenge it has faced throughout the centuries.

---

[11]

http://www.focusonthefamily.com/faith/christian-worldview/whats-a-christian-world view/whats-a-worldview-anyway

SECTION 1: CHAPTER 6

"David vs. Goliath: Propaganda and Intimidation"

The challenge facing Christians who desire to defend their faith is not a lack of evidence for it. We have plenty. Nor is it that we face contrary evidence against our faith. The challenge is the massive amount of propaganda and intimidation hurled at us by unbelievers. This is especially true when dealing with the issue of creation vs. evolution.

Intimidation and propaganda in promoting evolution appears in many venues in today's culture. Public television documentaries use propaganda when they make bold statements based on nothing more than unprovable assumptions about events purported to have occurred billions of years ago. Similar unsupported assumptions appear in books, in the news, in movies such as Inherit the Wind, a blatantly anti-Christian film dealing with the Scopes Trial, and on talk shows. But perhaps nowhere is this propaganda more aggressive and insidious than in our public schools and universities.

INTIMIDATION AND PROPAGANDA IN SCHOOLS

University professors often use their power and authority within the classroom to bully Christian students. Some take great joy in attempting to destroy the faith of Christian students. Their weapon of destruction is not evidence, for credible evidence against the Christian position does not exist. Rather, they play on the ignorance of their students and present naturalistic positions as confirmed fact. They give the impression of authority by using phrases such as "scientist now know" or "science has shown" to give the impression that evolutionary assumptions have been proven to be true, when in that evolutionary assumptions have been proven to be true, when in fact, they have not. They get by with such propaganda in a classroom filled with green, impressionable students, but when challenged to defend their position against prepared Christians who know better, it's a different story.

We recently found this to be true in the Quad Cities area of Illinois and Iowa where I live. We tried for weeks to find a professor within any of the local colleges to debate a Christian speaker who had experience in debates on college campuses. We eventually had to give up on the idea of a debate because we could not find a single willing evolutionist debater. Evolutionists often say they avoid such debates because they don't want to give creationists a platform that suggests their position might have credibility. In other words, they imply that creationist's views are too incredible even to be considered worthy of debate. I believe the real reason evolutionists avoid debate with Christians is clear: The scientific evidence for creation is too strong to be successfully refuted, which would cause evolutionists to lose face in a public arena.

Not all the intimidation in schools is against students. Teachers and professors who would attempt to treat the subjects of creation and evolution fairly are often threatened by the possibility of dismissal.

School textbooks provide blatant examples of the most common form of propaganda—promoting Darwinian evolution by presenting assumptions as though they were proven facts. We noted in a previous chapter that evolutionists use examples of microevolution (adaptations within a species) to prove that macroevolution (one kind of creature evolving into a completely different kind) has occurred, even though they know that macroevolution has never been replicated, proven, or observed in any scientific research.

In his DVD Evolution vs. God, Ray Comfort challenges various science students and university science professors to give one example of macroevolution that can be accepted on any basis other than blind faith. Not one is ever given, though some responders attempt to use documented instances of microevolution as examples of macroevolution. The video makes it abundantly clear that no

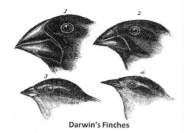

Darwin's Finches

examples of macroevolution have ever been found.

Textbooks often use the examples of color changes in peppered moths or beak adaptations in finches as proof of evolution. Both examples demonstrate only microevolution (which no one denies), and neither has anything to do with macroevolution. The modified finches were still finches and the differently pigmented moths were still moths. Yet these bait-and-switch examples are dishonestly used in textbooks as propaganda to influence students toward belief in evolution.

Here is a more specific example of how textbooks use misguided information and propaganda to influence students. In a Miller and Levine high school biology textbook, there is a discussion about sedimentary rock layers found around the world. The book references

Public Domain via. Wikimedia Commons

Charles Lyell and his views about uniformitarianism—the idea that the Earth was originally shaped by the same processes still in operation today. The discussion centers on Lyell's theories on how geological rock strata came to be distributed around the earth. The text dismisses the idea that these rock layers could be the result of a global catastrophe in the distant past, such as a worldwide flood, by citing Lyell's adherence to an accepted scientific method:

> Lyell also argued that scientists must always explain past events in terms of events and processes they could observe themselves. That, Lyell insisted, was the only way the scientific method could work. [1]

Here the textbook is saying, in essence, "You can't accept a global flood in the past as a scientific explanation for anything, because we cannot see it happening today."

About seventy pages later, the text deals with another subject:

---

[1] Charles Lyell, *"Biology"* - *Miller & Levine*, Prentice Hall, 1998, (page 272)

the scientific law of biogenesis, which states that life can only come from life. This law was established as the result of extensive scientific research and experiments by Louis Pasteur that disproved the idea of "spontaneous generation" (life coming forth from non-life). Yet as the discussion of biogenesis closes, the textbook asserts that life did indeed evolve from non-life here on earth about 3 billion years ago. How could that be if there is a proven scientific law which shows that life can only come from life? Are you ready for the explanation? Here it is, directly from the textbook:

> Hey, what's going on? you might exclaim. If we just said that life did arise from nonlife billions of years ago, why couldn't it happen again? The answer is simple: Today's Earth is a very different planet from the one that existed billions of years ago. [2]

Boom! There it is! Just take our word for it. The earth was different back in the primeval past, which is why life could emerge from non-life then but not now. Does that sound scientific? Of course not! It is the use of confident jargon to make a blatant assumption look like a fact that can be accepted. No proof or evidence is given because no proof or evidence is possible, even by the very scientific methods that the textbook authors endorse. On page 272, students are told that the only way the scientific method can work is for past events to be explained in terms of events observed by scientists to be happening today. Remember that the textbook used this method to eliminate the flood as an explanation of currently seen geologic features. Then on page 346, students are told that life evolved from non-life, contrary to currently held scientific law, because "the earth was a much different place back then." They cite the use of an accepted scientific method to discredit the biblical flood, then turn around and discard that method in order to affirm their theory of life spontaneously arising from dead matter. The double-standard is blatantly obvious. As you can see, this is not science; it is pure propaganda.

---

[2] *"Biology" - Miller & Levine*, Prentice Hall, 1998, (page 346)

INTIMIDATION BY MOCKERY

One of the most insidious methods of intimidation is the mockery and belittling inflicted by leading atheists on those who hold to creation and other Christian views. Perhaps the most notorious of these mockers is Richard Dawkins, the author of The God Delusion. I cited several of his anti-Christian quotes in chapter 4, but I here I will add two more that show how he often goes beyond mere opposition to the faith and indulges in outright mockery of it.

Rather than say he's an atheist, a friend of mine says, 'I'm a tooth fairy agnostic,' meaning he can't disprove God but thinks God is about as likely as the tooth fairy.

We cannot, of course, disprove God, just as we can't disprove Thor, fairies, leprechauns and the Flying Spaghetti Monster. [3]

Dawkins, of course, is not the only offender. The illustration on this page shows only one of the many other examples of scientists and entertainers who denigrate the Christian faith.

Statements like these, coming from well-known writers or celebrities, can be quite intimidating to those who want to be regarded well by their peers and associates. I

The simple fables of the religious of the world have come to seem like tales told to children.

- Francis Crick

am convinced that this intimidation is one of the reasons liberal theologians and pastors often abandon biblical truth and drift into secular beliefs. It is largely their fear of being labeled stupid, out of touch with reality, or backward in their thinking. The Bible tells us that in the last days there will be mockers who will come again those who proclaim Biblical truth. 2 Peter 3:3-6 says:

---

[3] http://www.brainyquote.com/quotes/authors/r/richard_dawkins_2.html

Know this first of all, that in the last days mockers will come with their mocking, following after their own lusts, (4) and saying, "Where is the promise of His coming? For ever since the fathers fell asleep, all continues just as it was from the beginning of creation." (5) For when they maintain this, it escapes their notice that by the word of God the heavens existed long ago and the earth was formed out of water and by water, (6) through which the world at that time was destroyed, being flooded with water.

Exactly this kind of mockery is occurring today in America and other parts of the world. Mockers mock Christianity and indulge their own lusts. They deny both the judgments of God in the past and the prophesied second coming of Christ in the future. In their mocking, there is an intimidating spirit that often causes fear in the hearts of believers.

FACING THE GOLIATH OF OUR DAY

The demonic forces that are behind the influences within this mocking culture use fear tactics to silence the church. It is much like the intimidating mocking spewed forth by the giant Goliath as he stood before the armies of Israel and dared them to send out a warrior to fight him. Standing well over nine-feet tall, Goliath was certainly intimidating. Fear gripped the hearts of Israel's warriors, and they shrank from the giant's challenge. It took a young man who saw the whole situation from a much different angle to respond to Goliath's intimidating words. The teenager David realized that the battle was not really Goliath against a soldier of Israel. The battle was Goliath against the living God whom Israel served. Courage filled David's heart, leaving no room for fear. He put his life on the line and faced the giant's challenge, trusting that the Lord his God would fight for him, with him, and through him. In 1 Samuel 17:45-46, we read of David's words to Goliath just before he slew him:

Then David said to the Philistine, "You come to me with a sword, a spear, and a javelin, but I come to you in the name of the LORD of hosts, the God of the armies of

Israel, whom you have taunted. (46) "This day the LORD will deliver you up into my hands, and I will strike you down and remove your head from you. And I will give the dead bodies of the army of the Philistines this day to the birds of the sky and the wild beasts of the earth, that all the earth may know that there is a God in Israel."

Clearly David's trust was not in his own ability but in the Name of LORD of hosts. He realized that it was God that Goliath was taunting, and it was God who would bring Goliath down. He also realized that this victory would cause all the earth to "know that there is a God in Israel."

We have a Goliath in our day that calls out to the church with intimidating threats and mockery. He boasts that anyone who steps out into the public arena and attempts to proclaim biblical truth will be brought down in ridicule and shame. For this reason, a great majority within the church have not come out to face the challenge. As a result, many souls are wounded and killed by the lies that this Goliath continues to spew.

Praise God that there are also many whom the Lord is raising up in this hour to stand in faith and come out against the lying, mocking Goliath of our day. God's Spirit was upon David, and God's Spirit is upon those today who humbly trust the Lord and move out in faith to speak the truth in love.

What about you, my friend? What about you, pastor? What about you, mom and dad? What about you, Christian teacher? What about you, believer in Christ? Will you stay in the shadows while many souls are being destroyed by lies? Will you allow yourself to be blinded to the real battle that is now raging around us? Will you choose not to be ready to give an answer to everyone who asks about the hope within you? Or will you study to show yourself approved unto to God? Will you choose to take the time to look at the wonderful evidences that confirm the foundational issues of the Christian faith? Will you step up and step out in faith, trusting the Lord to be with you in every conversation and in every situation, speaking through you to be a part of the victory over the Goliath of our culture and our day? The New Testament tells us that "greater is He who is in you than he who is in the world" (1 John 4:4) David understood this truth before it was written for us to see. We must understand this truth and stand upon it today!

A call is going out to the church today. God's spirit is speaking to pastors, church leaders, Christian parents, and believers of all ages. The call will not be the same for each person, but we all are being called to stand up and proclaim God's truth in this day. This call has led me down a path I did not expect to be on. After thirty-four years as the senior pastor of the local congregation that I love, I have stepped out of my comfortable world to follow a vision the Lord has placed in my heart. I believe He has called me to spend the rest of my life responding to the challenge of our time, which is the current attack upon God's truth. I don't really know what that will ultimately look like, but I know that when that stirring in my heart came to me, it continued to grow until I knew that I needed to devote full time effort to address this need.

What is God saying to you? Will you do your part and follow His leading today?

Faith and Reason Made Simple

(SECTION 2)

Understanding Your Worldview and Your Mission

"Total Truth and The Evangelical Movement"

I do not recall how I ended up with a copy of Nancy Pearcey's book Total Truth, but I do recall an inner drawing to read it. This was strange to me, since I have always been more prone to learning through DVDs and videos, rather than reading lengthy, detailed books. Total Truth is a lengthy, detailed book and deals with sobering issues, but I felt in my spirit that it contained something the Lord wanted me to know. I read the entire book within a week or so. The historical perspective I gained from that reading has confirmed to me the need for evidence, teaching, doctrine, and apologetics in the church today.

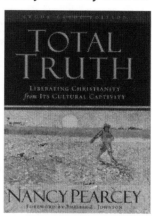

Before I divulge my main take-away from the book let me give you an idea of what the book is about. Here is a description of it from the Amazon website.

> Does God belong in the public arena of politics, business, law, and education? Or is religion a private matter only-personally comforting but publicly irrelevant?
>
> In today's cultural etiquette, it is not considered polite to mix public and private, or sacred and secular.

This division is the single most potent force keeping Christianity contained in the private sphere-stripping it of its power to challenge and redeem the whole of culture.

In *Total Truth*, Nancy Pearcey offers a razor-sharp analysis of the public/private split, explaining how it hamstrings our efforts at both personal and cultural renewal. Ultimately it reflects a division in the concept of truth itself, which functions as a gatekeeper, ruling Christian principles out of bounds in the public arena.

Pearcey teaches readers how to liberate Christianity from its cultural captivity. She walks readers through practical, hands-on steps for crafting a full-orbed Christian worldview.

Finally, she makes a passionate case that *Christianity is not just religious truth but truth about total reality. It is total truth* (italics added). [1]

I love that last line! It summarizes so succinctly what people need to understand today. Christianity is not just religious truth, but truth about total reality. It is total truth!

THE PROBLEM OF THE EVANGELICAL PENDULUM

Pearcey does a superb job of walking the reader through a period of church history that is not often talked about. We hear a lot about ancient church history and the era of the reformation, but not so much about the past 250 years or so.

It is hard to imagine what the church would be like today without the broad influence of the Evangelical movement. Pearcey reveals some of the salient factors involved in the rise of this movement. Before it began, much of the church world had become spiritually dead, or dormant at best. Young people typically went through catechism or confirmation classes to learn the doctrines of the church but often were not impacted by what they were taught. Churches were full of people who did not have a relationship with

---

[1] http://www.amazon.com/Total-Truth-Study-Guide-Edition/dp/1433502208

Jesus Christ. They had neither been born again nor changed by their Christian faith. They had some head knowledge of the faith, but it was not life-changing.

From this environment, the Evangelical movement arose. Evangelical pastors and leaders began to proclaim that people needed to come to know Christ, be born again, and experience God. They proclaimed that the Christian faith was not just a religious ritual or a set of doctrinal facts. They helped people to see that true Christianity involved a relationship with Jesus Christ. They instituted altar calls, drawing people to public acceptance of Christ as Savior and Lord. Sounds good doesn't it? Praise God for the emergence of the Evangelical movement!

There was, however, a problem that came along with the new movement that is still affecting the church today. As humans typically do, church leaders swung the pendulum so far that a new imbalance developed. Emphasis on the teaching of doctrine was associated with the dead churches of the past, so doctrine was largely dropped from the curricula of church classes. This meant that Christian young people were no longer grounded in Bible doctrines and evidences that confirm the foundational teachings of Christianity. Note the following quote from the book summary:

> The bad news of evangelicalism ironically lies in many of the factors that made the movement so successful. The focus on an intense emotional conversion experience was highly effective in bringing people to faith. Yet the emphasis on religion as an emotional experience, in turn, led to a neglect of theology and doctrine and the whole cognitive element of belief. The use of the vernacular and simple folk music reached many ordinary, uneducated people, but revivalists tended to go even further, taking great pride in their ignorance while making fun of the "highly

educated, but spiritually dead" clergy "back east. [2]

In most Evangelical churches today, youth ministries focus almost totally on worship, music, games, friendly atmosphere, inspirational preaching, and the use of technology to reach and disciple young people. "Come and experience God" or a similar call is commonly heard. Much of this very good, but it has gone out of balance. The same is often true in the ministries designed for adults and children. It's almost entirely about experience. The teachings of the Christian faith and the evidences that confirm them are seldom emphasized. People don't have time to study, and doctrine is considered boring—or worse yet, divisive. So we continue to draw people into an experience with God and wonder why so many abandon their faith when confronted by the world or life's temptations. A faith that is not grounded in knowledge of truth is a faith that does not stand strong when challenged. We must know what we believe and why we believe it.

Please understand that I am not denying the need for altar calls or for appeals to experience God or come into a relationship with Jesus. I have been committed to these things my entire adult life. What I am saying is that we have swung the pendulum too far. This is the central idea that so impressed me in Total Truth. We should embrace the relationship and feeling aspect of Christianity, but we must also embrace the learning aspect as well. Learning truth, doctrine, and evidences that confirm our faith is critical. If we do not make the adjustments and bring this balance into the ministry of the church, I believe we will continue to see large numbers of people walking away from the faith.

Another aspect of the swinging pendulum has been the abandonment of the creeds of the early church and the often-voluntary removal of Christian thinking from the public discussion of truth and reality. Note the following:

It may seem as though the evangelical revivalists were

---

[2] Total Truth by Nancy Pearcey, 2004 by Nancy R. Pearcey. Summarized by permission of the publisher, Crossway Books, a division of Good News Publishers, Wheaton, Illinois. 472 pages. ISBN: 1-58134-458-9. (page 6)

simply carrying on the tradition passed on by the Reformation. However, while the Reformers insisted that the Bible was plain to anyone and that Scripture was the final authority, they did not dismiss history or corporate statements of faith. They maintained an allegiance to the ecumenical creeds and councils of the Church's first five centuries when the fundamental doctrines of the Trinity and the deity of Christ were deliberated and defined.

Evangelicalism did not overcome the age-old "two-story division" of knowledge. In fact, it intensified the split by contributing to the idea that religion is a private and emotional experience, effectively moving it from the public realm to a completely private one. Evangelical churches and seminaries voluntarily withdrew from intellectual confrontation with the secular world. [3]

TURNING THE EVANGELICAL SHIP AROUND

Years of neglect in teaching evidences and the confrontation with untruth in the secular world have taken a toll on today's church. Fortunately, the church has what it needs to turn things around: the truth of God's Word, the power of the Holy Spirit, and the love of Jesus Christ. It's not too late for us to impact people for Christ in this culture. We must study to show ourselves approved unto God, workmen who do not need to be ashamed and servants who rightly divide the Word of truth.

In the foreword to Nancy Pearcey's follow-up book, Finding Truth, J. Richard Pearcey writes about the evidences that God gave to believers throughout the Bible. The shepherds were able to come and see the baby in the manger, which confirmed the words of the angel spoken to them. The crowd in Mark 2 was able to see the

---

[3] ibid.

authority of Jesus as He told the lame man to get up, take up his pallet, and walk, which confirmed His authority to forgive the lame man's sins.

J. Richard Pearcey goes on to say this concerning the ministry of Jesus:

His ministry was a public work of question and answer and give and take. He set forth propositions that can be considered and discussed, and He invited people to observe public miracles that confirmed His claims in the here and now.

It is true that not every person in Jesus' own day would have observed every miracle He performed, heard every sermon He delivered, or encountered the physically raised Jesus of Nazareth. Nevertheless, whether in His day or ours, the total body of His actions and communications evinces an attitude of openness to examination so that inquisitive people are welcome to explore and investigate.

It is against this historical backdrop that Paul argued that the events grounding the Christian worldview were not "done in a corner" (Acts 26:25-26). Shepherds, kings, doctors and tax collectors could all check out the facts that are central to the Christian message. What is being communicated is an accurate description of reality, not a belief system about it.

This reality orientation is the positive intellectual climate in which the core propositions and events of the gospel live and breathe. It is a mentality in which people are liberated by verifiable truth to challenge tradition, question power, and fight for life and healing against death and decay.

Despite this auspicious heritage, many of our contemporaries find solace in what Francis Schaeffer describes as an "escape from reason." They accept polite society's dumbed-down redefinition of faith as something totally privatized – that is, a commitment so private and so personal that evaluation and evidence are irrelevant.

This is a far cry from the holistic respect for information that characterizes a biblical worldview. Scripture nowhere encourages the notion the "faith" equals commitment quarantined from evidence or isolated from the mind....

To accurately reflect the biblical emphasis, we must acknowledge that a falsified "faith" is quite properly a discarded faith. It is a futile faith and therefore not worth keeping. But this sharp challenge cuts in a positive way as well.

For we must also say that a confirmed faith, or better, a well-grounded trust, is well worth embracing by the whole person. In fact, the "trust," rather than the now-privatized words "faith" or "belief," better captures the understanding of commitment set forth in the Bible. The New Testament Greek word often translated as "believe" is more accurately rendered as "trust" (from the word pistis, "trust" or "believe," rooted in the peitho, "I persuade"). the biblical attitude is one of persuasion, a will to verity and know what is true and to respond accordingly. [4]

Here we are reminded that the claims of Jesus were confirmed with evidence that His believers could build their faith upon. He never asked them to exercise blind faith, nor does he ask it of us. Our faith in Him is solidly confirmed by many solid evidences. Those evidences come in many forms—the revelations found in created things, the verified historical accounts of the Bible, the historical confirmations of the resurrection of Jesus Christ, the verifiable indestructibility and growth of the Christian faith despite great opposition over the centuries, the changed lives of millions of people who have come into a relationship with Jesus Christ, and the

---

[4] Nancy Pearcey, *Finding Truth*, David C. Cook Publishing, 2015, (Forward by J. Richard Pearcey)

testimonies of modern-day miracles and healings.

I love the last part of J. Richard Pearcey's quote where he states that "a confirmed faith, or better, a well-grounded trust, is well worth embracing by the whole person." I am convinced that our faith in Christ is greatly strengthened when the challenges of our culture lead us to seek out the confirming evidences for faith. The good thing about the church's current situation is that it may give rise to a host of believers who will no longer hide from the intimidating culture, but will by necessity seek out the evidences that confirm their faith, and then rise up in boldness to witness for Jesus Christ.

HOW EVIDENCE CHANGES LIVES

Think of the difference that evidence made in the lives of the twelve disciples of Jesus. These men had forsaken Jesus when He was

captured and falsely accused. They made no attempt to save Him from the brutal scourging or the crucifixion. They hid themselves from the world after Jesus was crucified. By all appearances, they had succumbed to fear and were responding as cowards. Yet something happened to these men that changed them dramatically. Over the next forty days, the resurrected Jesus appeared to them several times. He showed them His nail-scarred hands. He explained to them the Old Testament scriptures that spoke of Him and the suffering He would endure. He gave them instructions concerning how they were to be His witnesses throughout the known world. Then He ascended into heaven in plain view before them. As you can see, Jesus gave His disciples an enormous amount of evidence on which to base their faith.

The results were astounding. These men who had run away and hid in fear suddenly began to turn the world upside down. They preached boldly, challenging those who stood against the faith. They performed miracles in the Name of Jesus. They faced up to threats by governmental and religious authorities What made the difference? Evidence! Solid evidence strengthened their faith to the point that they were willing to die for it. In fact, this willingness to die for their faith gives us powerful evidence that the Resurrection of Christ actually occurred. Many men and women have died for good causes, and many have died for causes they mistakenly thought were true. But no one will willingly die for a cause he knows to be false. These men would never have changed from abject cowards to courageous heroes had they not been absolutely certain that the Resurrection occurred. They would never have put their lives on the line to perpetrate a lie.

These twelve men experienced one other significant event that affected their witness and behavior. They were all filled with the Holy Spirit (see Acts chapter 2). The combination of a faith and trust built upon verifiable evidence and the empowering of the Holy Spirit changed these men from cowards to courageous, powerful witnesses.

We have entered a difficult time in church history, wherein believers are being intimidated by mockers, scoffers, intellectual agnostics, and an army of unbelievers who ridicule the faith of Christian believers. It may seem that the church has become too weak to face these challenges because believers are not sure about what they believe. But isn't it possible that the opposition we face will give rise to a revived church filled with believers as bold and powerful as those first disciples? Could it be that as these cultural pressures force believers to search out the evidence that so powerfully confirms their faith, they will rise up and reach out to the unbelieving culture and challenge the demonic forces behind it?

Extreme persecution of Christian believers in China during the second half of the 20th century has given rise to an army of bold and courageous believers who are now taking the gospel of Jesus Christ to the most difficult parts of the world. I pray that in the same way, the extreme intellectual attacks upon Christian believers in America and Europe will give rise to an army of bold and courageous believers who will proclaim the confirming evidences of the Christian faith to a lost and dying world. I believe this is possible, and I believe that by God's grace and by the power of His Holy Spirit, it will occur!

SECTION 2: CHAPTER 2

"The Importance of What We Believe"

In today's postmodern, post-truth society, many think that it doesn't matter what you believe as long as you are sincere about it. The word "tolerance" has been redefined to indicate that we must accept any belief that others may adopt as being just as valid as what we believe ourselves. To say that what they believe is incorrect is supposedly intolerant. At the core of this mode of thinking is idea that there is no absolute truth, which means no belief is actually true; whatever you choose to believe is nothing more than your opinion.

What we believe is critical to who we are in many ways. Even atheists acknowledge the importance of what we believe. In an internet article on the nature of belief, Austin Cline writes, "Beliefs are important because behavior is important and your behavior depends upon your beliefs. Everything you do can be traced back to beliefs you hold about the world." He goes on to say, "All this means that beliefs are not an entirely private matter. Even beliefs you try to keep to yourself may influence your actions enough to become a matter of legitimate concern of others." [1] The point that Cline hints at here is that religious beliefs can bring people into negative behavior that affects others. Religious belief, therefore, may be fair game for suppression. Though I certainly do not agree with Cline's conclusions, I do agree that what we believe affects our behavior and affects who we are as a person.

What we believe is important. The Gospel of John indicates this in a unique way. The purpose of this gospel is to present who Jesus Christ is and our need to believe in who He is. Toward the end

---

[1] http://atheism.about.com/od/definitionofatheism/a/BeliefImportant.htm

of the book, the purpose is stated in this way: "Therefore many other signs Jesus also performed in the presence of the disciples, which are not written in this book; but these have been written so that you may believe that Jesus is the Christ, the Son of God; and that believing you may have life in His name" (John 20:30-31). What we believe about Jesus is expressed as that which determines whether we find the life God has provided for us.

We can see John's emphasis on what we believe about who Jesus is by the fact that he makes this point ninety-eight times in his gospel, using various forms of the word "believe." He uses "believe" fifty-five times; "believes" fourteen times; "believed" twenty-four times, and "believing" five times. In each of these cases the various forms of the word "believe" is used in direct reference to whether or not a person or group of people believed in who Jesus is. In case you think this emphasis on belief is found everywhere in scripture, note the use of these terms in the three synoptic gospels:

> • **The Gospel of Matthew uses a form of "belief" 11 times with only one referring to believing in Jesus**
> • **The Gospel of Mark uses a form of "belief" 15 times with only two referring to believing in Jesus**
> • **The Gospel of Luke uses a form of "belief" 10 times with none of them referring to believing in Jesus**

As you can see, the Gospel of John is unique in its strong emphasis on the importance of believing who Christ is. My point is that this belief is so important that there is a book of the Bible dedicated specifically to it. What we believe is critically important. What we believe ultimately determines our behavior. It also determines our eternal destiny beyond the grave.

Another example of the Gospel of John's emphasis on believing is that the phrase "truly, truly" is found twenty-five times in the NASB translation of the New Testament. Every one of them is in the Gospel of John, and each time the phrase is spoken by Jesus. When Jesus said "truly, truly I say unto you" He was emphasizing that the things He proclaimed to His followers were absolutely true and trustworthy. The NIV translates the phrase as "Very truly I tell you." The NKJV translates it as "Most assuredly I say to you."

From the Gospel of John we learn two things about belief and truth. First, John emphasizes that what we believe about who Jesus is, is very important. Second, he emphasizes that what Jesus said to us is true and should be believed.

Both of these points leads us to the need for effective apologetics. We need to believe the right thing—the truth—and we need to know why we believe it. That is what apologetics does; it helps us to know what we believe and why we believe it. This includes not only what we believe about Jesus, but also what we believe about creation, the Bible, truth, and morality.

DEVELOPING A BIBLICAL WORLDVIEW

What we believe about foundational issues will determine our worldview. A worldview is a comprehensive conception of the universe and of humanity's relation to it based on one's personal  philosophy of human life and meaning. Worldviews vary from person to person because their personal philosophies filter their perceptions. Some have illustrated a worldview by comparing it to a pair of eyeglasses, as we did in an earlier chapter. If your glasses have green lenses they will cause everything to look different than if you wear a pair that have blue or red lenses. Your worldview affects your belief about every issue of life.

To illustrate, compare a person whose worldview includes God as creator with a person whose worldview accepts evolution as the instrument of origins. The beliefs of these two people about the value of human life, marriage, moral standards, and truth will differ greatly because of their differing worldviews. One sees human beings as uniquely created in the image of God and therefore of immense value. The other sees human beings as having no greater value than any other living things, for everything is what it is due to random, accidental processes. One will believe that abortion is wrong because it involves the taking of a unique, highly valued human life with a potential for eternal joy. The other will usually endorse abortion because he or she believes human life has no unique value. Therefore, they feel free to destroy the baby if it interferes with someone's lifestyle or inconveniences them in any way.

A worldview needs to answer the four basic questions that apply to every person. Ravi Zacharias says it this way: "Everyone—pantheist, atheist, skeptic, polytheist—has to answer these questions: 'Where did I come from? What is life's meaning? How do I define right from wrong and what happens to me when I die?' Those are the fulcrum points of our existence." [2] He has also said "I am totally convinced the Christian faith is the most coherent worldview around." [3]

Apologetics involves learning how our Christian faith answers these four questions and how it fits with the reality around us. God never calls us to have blind faith. He calls us to develop a strong faith that can be confirmed by evidence, that does not conflict with reality, and that provides reasonable answers to the four questions related to the meaning of life. Many Christians do not have a Biblical worldview because they have believed only isolated aspects of the Biblical message. Many believe Jesus was a good person but not the Son of God. Some believe in the historically verified narratives but not the miracles. Some believe God created the world initially and then brought man into existence by a process of theistic evolution. When we accept all of the Bible as God's inerrant, authoritative Word, then we will be able to develop a biblical worldview and everything we believe will fit together as God intended. Life will make sense.

A good illustration of how our worldview determines our beliefs, values, and behavior can be seen in the structure of an iceberg. As you can see in the picture on this page, only the top portion of an iceberg is visible above the water. By far the greater mass of it is submerged beneath the surface. This larger, invisible part determines the nature of the smaller visible part above the surface. In that sense, the iceberg is like a person. At the base of who we are is our worldview, which is our perception of the nature of

---

[2] http://www.brainyquote.com/quotes/authors/r/ravi_zacharias.html
[3] ibid.

reality. From our worldview emerges our beliefs, which are formed from our conclusions about what is real. From our beliefs come our values, which are our conclusions about what is right and good. Our values form the basis for our behavior patterns which are what those around can see as visible evidences of our invisible values, beliefs, and worldview. It is the things under the surface, our worldview, our beliefs, and our values, that determine how we behave and interact with the world around us. When "Christians" don't act

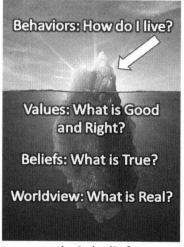

like Christians on an ongoing basis, it is because their belief system underneath their actions isn't really Christian.

The apologetics organization Answers in Genesis has devised a teaching system to help people see how the truth of the Bible,

history, and reality all fit together. It is titled The Seven C's of History. The seven Cs are alliterative section titles for seven stages in world history: Creation, Corruption, Catastrophe, Confusion, Christ, Cross, and Consummation. In Chapter 7 of Section 3 we review these seven points and show how they reveal the historical accuracy of the biblical message.

Believers need to see the logic involved in a Biblical worldview—how utterly rational and cohesive it is, not only to strengthen the foundations of their own faith, but also to enable them to help non believers to know the truth and understand why it is true.

SECTION 2: CHAPTER 3

"The Meaning of Apologetics"

The word "apologetics" seems to have two strikes against it at the very outset. First, when coupled with the term "Christian" as in "Christian apologetics," it seems to the uninitiated to mean that we are, in some sense, apologizing for our culturally out-of-step religious beliefs. Second, Christians who do understand the term often think it involves a complicated, intellectual system of thought meant to be explored only by the more studious Christians among us.

Both of these impressions are misguided. In using apologetics, we are not offering excuses or asking pardon or offering a copout for our Christian beliefs. Nor is apologetics an activity reserved just for specialized Christians; it is one that every Christian is called to exercise.

The term "apologetics" is translated from the Greek word apologia, and it simply means "reasoned arguments or writings in justification of something, typically a theory or religious doctrine." Apologetics is the branch of Christian studies that deals with the defense or the establishment of the Christian faith.

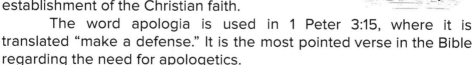

The word apologia is used in 1 Peter 3:15, where it is translated "make a defense." It is the most pointed verse in the Bible regarding the need for apologetics.

Sanctify Christ as Lord in your hearts, always being ready to make a defense to everyone who asks you to give an account for the hope that is in you, yet with gentleness and reverence. (1 Peter 3:15)

This verse says so much that is critical for every believer to understand as we live out our faith in a culture that openly attacks Christianity. Note that it gives us three important directives:

> (1) Sanctify Christ as Lord in your hearts
> (2) Always be ready to make a defense to everyone who asks you to give an account for the hope that is in you
> (3) Make your defense with gentleness and reverence

First, we are first reminded of the focus and the foundation of our faith, Jesus Christ, who is the Lord of our lives. It is on this firmly set foundation that our hope is founded and from which a defense of that hope can be made.

Second, we are always to be ready. This indicates preparation ahead of time. We must study and learn so that we understand why we believe what we believe. Then whenever anyone asks us about the hope that is within us, we can "make a defense" or give answers as to why we believe what we believe. We can demonstrate that our belief in Christianity does not rest on blind faith, but is rational, reasonable, and supported by numerous evidences.

Third, we are instructed to always have the right heart attitude when speaking with others about our faith in Christ. That attitude is to involve gentleness toward those to whom we are speaking and reverence toward God. It is easy to see how these characteristics

gentleness
power under control

lead toward a heart attitude of love, which is central to the Christian faith. We are never called to bully people into belief. We are always called to communicate powerful truths with a gentle spirit.

DEALING WITH WHY, NOT JUST WHAT

Proclaiming the gospel involves teaching and explaining what we believe. This can be done without ever referring to why we believe it. In many situations, the proclamation of the gospel alone reaches the hearts of people and leads them to salvation. Paul said of the gospel, "...it is the power of God for salvation, to everyone who believes" (Romans 1:16).

Decades ago, the simple, straightforward proclamation of the gospel message was pretty much all that the church had to focus on in order to reach people for Christ. Unfortunately, the culture has changed, and in many cases people are now filled with questions and skepticism that hinder them from hearing and responding to the gospel. For this reason, it has become increasingly important that we share not only what we believe, but also why we believe it.

Source: Pixabay, CC0 Public Domain

As I have noted before, God does not require blind faith. Jesus performed many miracles to confirm that the claims He made about His deity were true. In John 10:25-38, He challenged people to believe because of the works and miracles He performed, which He

said testified of Him. Christians today can offer a similar challenge. We can point to many evidences which confirm our beliefs that God created us, the Bible is God's Word, and that Jesus Christ is God's Son and a historical person who died on a cross and rose from the dead. There is ample evidence of these facts from science, archaeology, historical records, and fulfilled prophecies. Apologetics involves Christians learning these evidences and sharing them with others. This is how we obey the command rendered in 1 Peter 3:15.

WHAT DOES AN APOLOGIST LOOK LIKE?

Many believers have a stereotypical view of what a Christian apologist is like. They think he is highly intellectual, unusually knowledgeable, well-educated, and a bit of a geek. He loves delving into deep, complicated topics, and apologetics just happens to be his particular hobby. When we hear him speak about apologetic issues, we find it fascinating and enlightening. We are glad he is doing apologetics, but we feel that the special knowledge required to do it puts it far over the head of the average Christian. It's great for him, but it's not for me.

The reality is, however, that apologetics is for every believer in every Christian church. We are not all called to do the original research, give seminars, produce videos, or write books on the subject. But we are all called to learn and share information that defends the hope that is within us. This information widely available. Thinkers and researchers such as C.S. Lewis, Josh McDowell, Ravi Zacharias, Ken Ham, and Lee Strobel have written excellent apologetic material that is easily digestible for the average person. The second half of this book is dedicated to teaching believers simple outlines and bullet points that can be easily communicated and easily remembered, so that the average churchgoing believer can begin to use apologetics in his everyday encounters with skeptics and searchers.

Let me use an illustration from the realm of sports. In the game of golf, there are professionals who play extremely well and make a lot of money doing so. Despite their incredible abilities, it is not these pros who make the game one of the most popular sports in the world. What makes golf so popular is the fact that millions of average people play the game. The average golfer makes the same golf shots as the professionals, just not as well. One thing that keeps average golfers coming back is the fact that at any given moment, he is capable of hitting a shot that will rival that of any professional. The average golfer may only hit one or two such shots per summer, while the professional may hit forty per round. But both are playing the same game, and both are capable of enjoying the moments of victory the game provides. We can enjoy watching the professionals on TV, but to truly reap the benefits of the game, there is nothing like getting out and playing it yourself.

In apologetics, there are "professionals" who make their living leading the church in defending the faith. They are greatly needed, and we should be grateful for them. Still, just as golf is not intended for just the professionals, neither is apologetics. All believers are called to experience the joy of defending the hope that is within them, explaining why they believe what they believe. You don't have be one of the world's leading apologists to share truth with your neighbor, your co-worker, your child, or your grandchild. Learn what you can and share it with others. Learn a little more and share a little more. That's the way it works.

I am privileged to have a cousin who is perfect example of an average believer who loves and uses apologetics very effectively. My cousin, Scott Dyal lives out in the country near a small town in Missouri. Scott is truly a "country boy". He delivers mail to make a living. Scott is just an average guy who loves Jesus, loves the truth of God's Word, and loves people. Because of this he has studied apologetics and uses it regularly to speak with atheists on line, talk to people in his community about Jesus and to teach young people in the church he attends. Scott has led dozens of people to Jesus and influenced hundreds for Christ! Just an average country boy, churchgoer, but greatly used by God because he is ready to make a defense to those ask about the hope within him!

Many believers avoid apologetics because they are terrified that they will be asked a question for which they don't know the answer. The solution to this dilemma is amazingly simple: Just say, "I don't know the answer to that question." No one knows the answer to every question, so it is certainly okay to acknowledge that you are not omniscient. That is much better than giving an inadequate or obfuscating answer to cover the fact that you don't know. Be humble! That is a great Christlike attribute. But don't leave the questioned issue hanging. Say, "That's a great question. I will be glad to look into it and get back to you with an answer."

Failure to involve oneself in apologetics can indicate an attitude of selfishness. Too many believers don't question their own faith and therefore feel no need to bother with apologetics. This reveals a focus on self and an unconcern for the salvation of others—in other words, a lack of love.

To make this point vivid, let's put a modern-day twist on the famous story Christ told about the good Samaritan.

A young man was beaten up spiritually by atheistic and skeptical intellectuals and left on the street as spiritually dead. A church deacon walked by and said to himself, "I don't have time to get involved in this type of thing. Too many questions would have to be answered, and learning the answers is not my ministry."

Then a church worship pastor walked by and said, "I'm too busy preparing the church's music to deal with young people like this guy. Besides, I'm afraid to try. What if I said the wrong thing? It could aggravate his spiritual wounds and make matters worse. Anyway, he probably brought all this on himself. If he had been more into praise and worship music, he would have been a lot more spiritual and this wouldn't have happened to him."

Finally, a young believer who had a heart for others came by. He had prepared his heart for such a time as this, so he went to the young man and began to share with him the evidences that confirm the validity of the Christian faith. It took time and effort, but in the end the beaten-up young man recovered from his spiritual wounds and was brought back to a vibrant faith in Christ. Immediately, he began to prepare himself to help others being attacked by the lies of the culture.

It is not enough for us to be secure in our own faith. We are called to love one another. That love must not be limited to saying, "I love you." It is to be backed up by action. That action may involve practical acts, such as providing needed food or shelter. It may also involve providing spiritual and intellectual help to others. (Nothing specific intended against deacons or praise & worship pastors – just an illustration to make a point to us all.)

APOLOGETICS IN CHRISTIAN HISTORY

Though the need for Christian apologetics has increased because of the rise of secularism of our culture, it is not a new thing. As we have already noted, the word itself comes from a biblical verse written 2,000 years ago, showing that apologetics has existed throughout church history. Church fathers such as Augustine and Irenaeus engaged in apologetics. In the Reformation period of the 1500s,

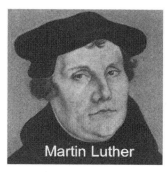

Martin Luther

apologetics became a vital part of the reformers' stand for truth. Their defense of the Christian faith was not primarily against atheists and agnostics, but rather against church leaders who had corrupted much of the truth found in the Bible. In that era, apologetics would have taken on a different slant from the apologetics of today because the attacks were not the same. But the principle of defending the faith was the same. Thank God for those who stood strong to defend the Christian faith in that critical time! Some of them gave their lives in that defense.

In the early years of American history, we read of the First Great Awakening, a widespread spiritual revival that swept across the American colonies and impacted thousands upon thousands of lives. This awakening influenced the emerging nation spiritually, morally, socially, and politically. One of its leaders was Jonathan Edwards, who pastored a church in Northampton, Massachusetts. Because of his role in the First Great Awakening, Edwards is considered one of the early leaders of the evangelical movement.

Jonathan Edwards combined his commitment to theology with a tremendous interest in science. He saw the natural world as evidence of God's masterful design, and throughout his life, he often went into the woods as a favorite place to pray and worship. He was fascinated by the discoveries of Sir Isaac Newton and other scientists of his time. It was clear to him that the laws of nature were derived from God and demonstrated His wisdom and care.

One of the things that Jonathan Edwards is remembered for is his preaching that not only appealed to the intellect of the hearers, but also impacted their emotions and brought forth an

Jonathan Edwards

experiential evidence of saving grace. Edwards' most famous sermon was entitled "Sinners in the Hands of An Angry God." Many were drawn to Christ by this powerful message.

Even though Edwards preached with passion and emotion, stirring the hearts of people, he recognized the need for apologetics in his time. He saw that the Christian faith must be more than an emotional faith. It must be both something that you can feel and something that you can believe by the reasoning powers of the mind.

Note the following statements from Jonathan Edwards' biography regarding the importance of apologetics.

> He viewed himself as having a high calling from God, nothing less than to present the definitive defense of the Christian religion in relation to all knowledge and all possible objections. [1]

> Like many men of his time Edwards was determined to know everything and how it all fit together in God's universe. [2]

Edwards' eagerness to complete his "Harmony of the Old and New Testaments" reveals the urgency he felt in demonstrating how the Bible was a unique God-given book. He had spent a lifetime collecting arguments on that topic and seems to have spent increasing time in his later years answering specific critical challenges to biblical history. At the same time, characteristically, he did not see the question of biblical authority as settled simply by arguments. Ultimately, the truth of Scripture, like God's redemptive work itself, would be recognized only through the illumination of the Holy Spirit. [3]

It is easy to see that Jonathan Edwards valued apologetics and saw the defending of the Christian faith as important in his day. The following quotes by Edwards himself show that he believed in apologetics because he was convinced that the Christian faith is

---

[1] George M. Marsden, *Jonathan Edwards A Life*, Yale University Press (2003) p. 110
[2] ibid. (p.62)
[3] ibid. (p. 481)

based solidly on reason. He realized that authentic Christianity involves a healthy balance between head knowledge and heart experience.

> All truth is given by revelation, either general or special, and it must be received by reason. Reason is the God-given means for discovering the truth that God discloses, whether in his world or his Word. While God wants to reach the heart with truth, he does not bypass the mind. [4]

> As on the one hand, there must be light in the understanding, as well as an affected fervent heart [in true religion], where there is heat without light, there can be nothing divine or heavenly in that heart; so on the other hand, where there is a kind of light without heat, a head stored with notions and speculations, with a cold and unaffected heart, there can be nothing divine in that light, that knowledge is no true spiritual knowledge of divine things. [5]

According to his biography, Jonathan Edwards strongly opposed the misuse of the word "reason" in his day:

> He acknowledged the proper use of "reason" as being the same as "argument or evidence." He acknowledged that it would be right to say that we should not believe anything without reason or contrary to reason … or against evidence. On the other hand, he strongly opposed the misuse of the word "reason" which illegitimately enthroned "reasonable opinions" that humans arrived at on their own as necessarily higher than what they could learn from special revelation. [6]

---

[4]https://beaconapologetics.wordpress.com/2013/01/23/my-favorite-christian-apologetics-quotations-pt-3/

[5] Jonathan Edwards, *Religious Affections*, Originally published in 1746, p. 120.

[6] George M. Marsden, *Jonathan Edwards A Life*, Yale University Press, (2003) p. 476

This great man realized that apologetics is necessary to stand against the arguments that sought to destroy the Christian faith. His example, along with that of the early church fathers and other reformers, show clearly that apologetics has been important for the body of Christ throughout church history. It is of the utmost importance today in light of the attacks which continue to come against the Christian faith.

Apologetics is not a scary word when you understand what it means. All Christians can learn the basic information that will enable us to defend the hope that is within us.

"Foundational Issues of the Christian Faith"

The second half of this book is dedicated to helping Christian believers understand the foundations of the faith and the issues prevalent in today's culture that erect obstacles to belief in Christianity.

In this short chapter, I will give the reader a brief introduction to each of these areas and why they have been chosen as objects of our focus. These foundations include creation, the Bible, Jesus Christ, key passages upon which our faith rests, the uniqueness of Christianity, responding to social issues, and answering key questions that skeptics tend to ask.

CREATION AND OUR CREATOR

I am convinced that the issue of Creation vs. Evolution is one that every believer needs to understand thoroughly, both for the support of his own faith and to equip him to defend the truth. The current of his own faith and to equip him to defend the truth. The current opposition to the Christian faith depends heavily on evolutionary teaching and thinking. I think few realize that the external evidence that confirms the Bible's account of creation is abundant and marvelous, and Christians are obligated by their love for the lost to know and understand this evidence thoroughly enough to present it to others.

This issue is critically important, because without an understanding of creation, none of the other issues make sense or really matter. If we are not created by God, then life has no true meaning, and there is no life after death or accountability for our current life. If we are the products of random, evolutionary processes with no designer, then everything about the Christian faith becomes meaningless—as does all of life itself. Creation is the key issue that separates atheists from Christians at the outset and places one on a path either to a biblical or a secular worldview.

We will delve deeply into the issue of creation and show the scientific flaws in the theory of evolution and the vast scientific support for creation.

THE BIBLE: INSPIRED, INERRANT, AND INFALLIBLE

The second item of major importance is the Bible, God's Word.

Everything we know about the Christian faith is based upon the teachings of the Bible. In particular, our understanding of salvation and Jesus Christ the Savior comes from the Bible.

Today the Bible is under severe attack from atheist authors, speakers, and university professors, even in some so-called Christian universities. They claim the events and claims of the Bible are largely mythical, historically inaccurate, corrupted in transmission, and contradictory. This issue is of crucial importance because these attacks undermine the faith of many Christians, particularly young people whose faith is vulnerable for lack of solid, foundational teaching in the local church.

In a later chapter where we explore this subject thoroughly, we will look at the internal and external evidences that confirm to us that the Bible is the Word of God. We will demonstrate that it is God-inspired, historically accurate, accurately transmitted, believable in its accounts of miracles and prophecy, and non-contradictory. In short, we can trust the Bible to be God's way of transmitting His will to humanity.

JESUS CHRIST: HIS DEITY AND HISTORICITY

The third area of evidence we will explore supports our belief in the person of Jesus Christ. Both Christ's historicity and deity are under severe attack today by modern critics, atheistic writers, and university professors. Even those who admit his existence deny His deity, His atoning sacrifice, and His resurrection. In the next section we will address these questions: Did Jesus really live here on earth? Who was He? Is Jesus God? Is Jesus the Savior of the world and the only way of salvation? We will use both Biblical and external  evidence to show that the answers to these questions affirm all the claims of Christianity concerning Jesus Christ.

KEY PASSAGES OF SCRIPTURE

One way to secure a better grasp of foundational truths of the Christian faith is to understand the unique purposes of particular books and passages in the Bible. Within the second chapter dealing with the reliability of the Bible, we will explore several of these books and passages and learn their unique purposes and how they relates to the whole of scripture.

THE UNIQUENESS OF CHRISTIANITY

With the proliferation of religions in America today, many see

Christianity as just one among many. The redefinition of tolerance, which says that all belief systems should be accepted as equally valid, means that Christianity is largely seen as just one way among many to reach God.

To counter this false view, we will explore the distinctive features of Christianity and show how radically it differs from all other religions and how its uniqueness reveals it as the only true and authentic religion on earth. In particular, we will show the radical differences between Christianity and Islam, demonstrating conclusively that any attempt to reconcile or combine the two religions is futile.

RESPONDING TO SOCIAL ISSUES

Several unbiblical social practices are ripping apart the moral fabric of America today. These include abortion, euthanasia, same-sex relationships, gender identity fluidity, and radical feminism. Responses to these issues range from total acceptance to mean-spirited hostility. Most Christian believers understand that our responses need to be both true to biblical teachings about sin and loving toward those caught in sin.

We will assist believers in understanding and remembering key Bible passages about same-sex issues. A little bit of prayerful study can go a long way in preparing us to have a right response to all these issues.

ANSWERING COMMON QUESTIONS OF
SKEPTICS AND SEEKERS

Believers are often confronted with tough questions, such as the perennial, "If God is a loving God, how can He send people to hell?" We will look at this question and some of the other most common ones that skeptics and seekers ask about God, the Bible, Jesus Christ, life, and the afterlife.

This concludes our summary overview of the type of information you will learn in the next section of this book, which is the heart of the entire volume.

Faith and Reason Made Simple

(SECTION 3)

How to Share and Defend Your Christian Faith

INTRODUCTION TO SECTION 3

How to Use This Training Manual

The title of this book indicates the main purpose of the book, to present the issues of faith and reason to the average believer in a local church in a simple way, making them easy to understand and retain. Here in the third section of the book, we will get into the actual training materials that can be used to defend and share the Christian faith. The first chapter reminds us of what the Bible says about creation and then the remaining chapters give confirming evidence for the Christian faith. Before we begin, I will give you a brief explanation as to how you can best benefit from this material.

For Personal Reading & Training
For simply personal use of this book, your primary need is to understand the connection between the memorization cards and the information in the chapters of this section. Numerous key chapters are aligned with a set of memorization cards. (The memorization cards shown at the end of chapter 2 are for the material covered in chapters 2-6.) For the best results, read the chapter(s) to gain understanding of the simple points on the cards, and then use the cards to memorize those points. You can create a packet of cards and carry them with you for memorization practice at times when you find a few moments to spare, like you would if you were memorizing scripture verses. The cards are shown at the end of key chapters but can be downloaded and printed by going to localchurchapologetics.org. There is no cost to download the memorization cards and no restrictions for printing them.

Much of the material in this book is also available in video form online at localchurchapologetics.org, or on a companion DVD which is available for purchase at the same website.

Keep in mind as you begin this process that the information within these chapters and on these cards only scratches the surface of the mountains of material available concerning these subjects. I have purposely limited the information here to enable the reader to learn about evidence that will help them without getting bogged down in extensive, intricate details. If you wish to continue your study beyond what this book offers, I have included information in the appendix at the end of the book about many of these additional resources to help you find what you need.

For Church, Small Group, or Classroom Use

If you are using this book in a group setting, you can either teach from it directly, using it as a text, or you can use the video materials mentioned above. There are also Powerpoint slides available that you may find helpful. The teaching sessions should be followed by classroom discussion, role-playing, or other teaching techniques that fit the teacher's strengths. One unique possibility to consider is to take the class on outings into "real life" where students can encounter and discuss these issues with live unbelievers. The use of the memorization cards will remain the same. Students will learn the material from the presentations and then use the cards to commit it to memory.

The fact that we are using the word "training" indicates that the intent of this book is that the reader should do more than just read through it. At a minimum, the memorization cards should be used to commit key points to memory for future use. I also encourage you to open conversations with others using the information you are learning. What you don't use, you tend to lose. As you learn this material and begin to converse with others about it, I encourage you to seek out some mature believers you can turn to if you get stumped or confused on any point.

God bless you as you dive into this training section!

"Starting At The Beginning: Creation"

We will begin our study of how to defend the faith with the most foundational issue of all: creation. The first words of the Bible give us a solid proclamation of that foundation: "In the beginning God created the heavens and the earth" (Genesis 1:1). If this statement were not true, then we would have no need for apologetics because Christianity would not exist. It is easy to see why this truth is attacked by so many today in the secular world.

Before we look at the evidence that confirms the Bible's bold statements that God created all things, we will lay some preliminary groundwork by looking at a few key scriptural passages that teach us this important truth. Biblical statements are not evidences or proofs of creation, but they are testimony from the only witness who was there and saw it happen. That testimony alone may be enough for believing Christians, but it is not enough for skeptics and seekers who need evidence that what the biblical testimony is true.

The scientific evidence we will look at serves to confirm the teachings of Scripture (not to establish them) and shows that our faith in what Scripture teaches is both rational and defensible. This procedure will help us see that the fact that we look first to the Bible for truth about reality does not invalidate the supporting proofs of our belief that we find in science. Atheists do the same thing. They start with a metaphysical premise that says God does not exist, and from that foundation they seek evidential proof in science. As we noted in an earlier chapter, everyone who looks at scientific evidence as it relates to historical science and theories of origins interprets that evidence through their preconceived biases. Both rely on their faith in their foundational belief about origins, and both attempt to confirm that faith through scientific evidence. The question is, does verifiable scientific evidence confirm what the Bible says about origins or what Darwin has said about origins.

So, let us begin by looking at a few key passages of Scripture that attest to the fact that God is the Creator of all that exists. Then in the following chapters we will confirm the biblical witness with external evidence that validates everything the Bible tells us about creation.

KEY SCRIPTURES PROCLAIMING CREATION
(Note – Bold print indicates the portion of Scripture that appears on the memorization cards)

God created the heavens & the earth.

> Genesis 1:1: **In the beginning God created the heavens and the earth.**

God created mankind in His image & likeness.

> Genesis 1:26-27: Then God said, "Let Us make man in Our image, according to Our likeness; and let them rule over the fish of the sea and over the birds of the sky and over the cattle and over all the earth, and over every creeping thing that creeps on the earth." (27) **God created man in His own image, in the image of God He created him; male and female He created them.**

God formed each of us in our mother's womb.

> Psalms 139:13-14: **For You formed my inward parts; You wove me in my mother's womb. (14) I will give thanks to You, for I am fearfully and wonderfully made;** Wonderful are Your works, And my soul knows it very well.

Creation includes both the visible natural world and the invisible spiritual world.

> Colossians 1:16: For by Him all things were created, both in the heavens and on earth, visible and invisible, whether thrones or dominions or rulers or authorities—**all things have been created through Him and for Him.**

As these passages show, the Bible boldly proclaims that God created the heavens and the earth and all that are within them. The New Testament includes two additional details that are important for us to understand.

JESUS CHRIST IS THE AGENT OF CREATION

We are told that God the Son (the second person of the Godhead) whom we know as Jesus Christ is the agent of creation. The Scripture below expresses this fact quite clearly. It is supported by three other passages: John 1:1-3, John 1:10, and Hebrews 1:1-3.

All things were created through and for Jesus Christ.

> Colossians 1:16-17: For by Him all things were created, both in the heavens and on earth, visible and invisible, whether thrones or dominions or rulers or authorities—**all things have been created through Him & for Him. (17) He is before all things, and in Him all things hold together.**

CREATION REVEALS THE GLORY AND CHARACTER OF GOD

God has revealed Himself to us through the things that He has made. Psalms speaks of revealing His Glory, and Romans speaks of revealing his character.

Romans 1:18-32: For the wrath of God is revealed from heaven against all ungodliness and unrighteousness of men who suppress the truth in unrighteousness, (19) because that which is known about God is evident within them; for God made it evident to them. (20) **For since the creation of the world His invisible attributes, His eternal power and divine nature, have been clearly seen, being understood through what has been made, so that they are without excuse.** (21) For even though they knew God, they did not honor Him as God or give thanks, but they became futile in their speculations, and their foolish heart was darkened. (22) Professing to be wise, they became fools,

In verse 20 above, Paul tells us that (1) God's invisible attributes, (2) His eternal power, and (3) His divine nature are clearly seen through the things that He has made. Because of this, no one has an excuse for not knowing God. It is important to see what is written before and after this verse in Romans 1:18-32 so that we can understand why creation is not widely accepted, though to unbiased minds open to clear scientific evidence, it is obvious. The Bible says that men will suppress this truth in unrighteousness (v.18). In other words, they will suppress the obvious truth about creation because they want to go on living in an unrighteous way. They must convince themselves there is no God who created them. Verses 21-32 show what happens when any group of people deny God as their creator. This passage describes what we see happening in America today with deadly accuracy. (Note – Romans 1:18-32 is covered in more detail in Section 1, Chapter 3.

The Old Testament also reveals that the heavens show us the glory of God.

Psalms 19:1: **The heavens are telling of the glory of God; And their expanse is declaring the work of His hands.**

The truth about creation is critical to defending and sharing the Christian faith. If we were not created, we certainly would not need a savior or the forgiveness of sin. The entire gospel of Jesus Christ would become meaningless if we were not created. The Bible clearly says we are created by God, and as we will see, scientific data confirms this truth over and over again.

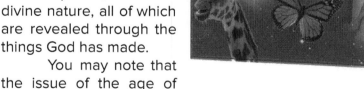

Worship, for the believer is enhanced by our understanding of God as Creator. Our worship of Him grows as we grow in our knowledge of His invisible attributes, His eternal power, and His divine nature, all of which are revealed through the things God has made.

You may note that the issue of the age of the earth is not directly addressed in this book. It is the one issue about creation that Christians disagree on the most. "Young earth" and "old earth" views often define various groups, ministries and teachers. I personally believe that the Bible describes 6 literal 24 hour days in Genesis, chapter 1, so I would be among those who believe in a young earth. I do however also believe that there are many wonderful Christians who believe and teach that the earth is billions of years old. There are many Christians who believe the earth is approximately 6 thousand years old & many who believe the earth is billions of years old. Others believe that the age of the earth is not a critical issue.

I have chosen to not make this issue a major focus of this book because often times believers tend to turn off others because they are either "young earth" or "old earth". My passion is to see believers obey the Bible's command to always be ready "to make a defense to everyone who asks you to give an account for the hope that is in you". I would hate to see someone choose not to learn the basic evidences that will help them defend their Christian faith concerning creation, the Bible, the Person of Jesus Christ, etc., because they felt the author of a book designed to help them, was "young earth" or "old earth".

As we look at our evidences confirming creation we will focus on design and information that is seen throughout God's wonderful creation which confirm that God created the heavens and the earth.

I do believe that our interpretation of the book of Genesis is important and that many doctrinal issues are affected by our interpretation of Genesis 1, but in this book I have felt it necessary to avoid focusing on the issue. Many books, teachings, etc. are available on the subject of the age of the earth for those seeking a deeper understanding of this issue.

Genesis 1:1

"In the beginning, God created the heavens and the earth!"

Genesis 1:27

"God created man in His own image, in the image of God He created him; male & female He created them."

Psalm 139:13-14a

"For You formed my inward parts; You wove me in my mother's womb. (14) I will give thanks to You, for I am fearfully and wonderfully made ..."

Colossians 1:16-17

"...all things have been created through Him & for Him. (17) He is before all things, & in Him all things hold together."

Romans 1:20

"For since the creation of the world His invisible attributes, His eternal power & divine nature, have been clearly seen, being understood through what has been made, so that they are without excuse."

Psalm 19:1

"The heavens are telling of the glory of God; And their expanse is declaring the work of His hands."

Memorization Cards Available for Free Download at localchurchapologetics.org

"Design Within the Universe Affirms Creation"

What would we look for to find scientific evidence that confirms the Bible's proclamation that God created the heavens and the earth?

Answering this question relates to our discussion of the difference between "Operational Science" and "Historical Science" in chapter 4 of the first section of this book. Operational science deals with those things that can be tested and observed repeatedly in the present. Historical science seeks answers to events that happened in the past and cannot be observed happening today. The study of origins falls into the category of historical science because we cannot reproduce the events of the past to prove scientifically just how everything began. This applies whether one claims that origins occurred by evolution or creation. We can, however, search out the observable universe and find evidence that confirms or discredits either scientific theories or the biblical account of how all things have come into being. The truth is, there is an enormous amount of scientific evidence that confirms the biblical account of creation.

Now, back to our question: What would we look for to find evidence of a creator when studying various aspects of the observable universe? Two things: design and information. Design always points to a designer, and things that are not designed, like the chaotic debris left after an explosion, show evidence of random, unguided processes. Information is always the result of a source of intelligence. So if we can find design features and usable information in the observable universe and in living things, we will have evidence that confirms what the Bible says: God created the heavens and the earth.

With this in mind, we will begin our search by looking first into the vastness of the universe, and end it by peering into the microscopic world of the human cell. **("From Biggest to Smallest")** As we explore these areas and every stage between, we will find astounding evidence of design and information everywhere we look.

> **These 5 chapters are formatted in a way to help you remember their content and memorize their major points. We start with the largest realms of creation and move progressively to smaller realms to find evidences that point to a creator. The eight different areas of evidence presented here are as follows: (1) The Universe (2) Our Solar System (3) The Earth (4) Living Creatures on the Earth (5) The Human Body (6) The Microscopic World (7) The Human Cell (8) DNA.**

As you can see, we will be looking from realms that are incomprehensibly enormous to realms that are extremely small. The first three levels of evidence which come from the universe, the solar system and the earth will be examined in this chapter.

LEVEL 1 – (THE BIGGEST) THE UNIVERSE IS FINELY TUNED

Modern Science has now been able to identify numerous laws of physics and the physical constants within the universe that are set very precisely and are very stable (constant), allowing galaxies, stars, planets, and intelligent life to exist. This precision is referred to as "The Finely Tuned Universe." The more that scientists have learned about the laws governing the physical universe, the more they realize that these laws are all set with such 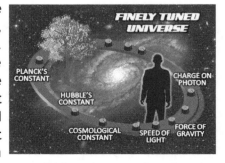 precision that even a slight variation would be devastating for the order, function, and even the very existence of the universe. Here are just a few of the constants within the universe that are in place:

> **The force of gravity (the gravitational constant)**
> **The speed of light**
> **The expansion rate of the universe**
> **The cosmological constant**
> **The ratio of protons to electrons**

It is readily accepted that there are at least thirty or more of these constants that are precisely set to allow the universe to function, and some observers now point to many more than thirty. For a couple of lists of these constants you can go to the following web pages:

http://www.godandscience.org/apologetics/designun.html
http://en.wikipedia.org/wiki/Physical_constant

As one example of this fine tuning, we can look at the force of gravity. If the force of gravity, which is constant, was slightly stronger or slightly weaker, it would not be possible for planets to form or for life forms to exist. Gravity is set at the perfect strength to maintain cohesive structure and life. The force of gravity

$$F_g = G\frac{m_1 m_2}{r^2}$$

is expressed through the equation displayed on this page. Its value can be expressed as (6.67408(31)×10−11 m3•kg−1•s−2). You and I may

not comprehend the details of such mathematical calculations, but the point to remember is that this is just one of the constants that are set precisely, enabling forms to cohere and life to exist.

To think that this precision is the result of a huge explosion and unguided processes over billions of years goes against common sense. All observable examples of things that function with precision indicate the presence of an intelligent designer. The universe being finely tuned is evidence of an amazingly wise and powerful Creator.

Another example of precisely set things that allow life to exist in the universe is found in the atomic and nuclear world. The quantity of "Proton Mass" is expressed as *mp* and is another of the physical constants in the laws of physics. The value of "Proton Mass" is (1.672 621 777(74) × 10−27 kg). Most of us will not understand what this really means but we can see how precise this is. These examples merely begin to show the precision that can be found in the constants that govern the formation and function of the universe.

Consider the table below that shows how much variation is possible within just five of the constants that have been found to be critical for the universe to function. When we begin to multiply these maximum possible variations, we quickly come up with numbers that reveal it is virtually impossible for these things to be set this way by accidental chance.

FINE TUNING OF THE PHYSICAL CONSTANTS OF THE UNIVERSE	
PARAMETER	MAX. DEVIATION
Ratio of Electrons: Protons	$1:10^{37}$
Ratio of Electromagnetic Force: Gravity	$1:10^{40}$
Expansion Rate of Universe	$1:10^{55}$
Mass Density of Universe	$1:10^{59}$
Cosmological Constant	$1:10^{120}$
These numbers represent the maximum deviation from the accepted values, that would either prevent the universe from existing now, not having matter, or be unsuitable for any form of life.	

To understand more about this truth, you may want to watch the following YouTube video clips: (The first one, which includes helpful illustrations, is probably the best.)

http://www.youtube.com/watch?v=1iwzzR0lUKw
http://www.youtube.com/watch?v=plpCfXKKYLE
http://www.youtube.com/watch?v=3nl1rAEKMUA

All scientists who study the universe see this fine tuning. As we will see in a moment, some try to explain it away, but many, even many who are not Christians, acknowledge that this fine tuning is great evidence of a Creator, or a Designer, who has put the universe together with amazing precision. Consider the following quotes by various scientists:

Fred Hoyle (British astrophysicist): "A common sense interpretation of the facts suggests that a super intellect has monkeyed with physics, as well as with chemistry and biology, and that there are no blind forces worth speaking about in nature. The numbers one calculates from the facts seem to me so overwhelming as to put this conclusion almost beyond question." [1]

Paul Davies (British astrophysicist): "There is for me powerful evidence that there is something going on behind it all.... It seems as though somebody has fine-tuned nature's numbers to make the Universe.... The impression of design is overwhelming." [2]

John O'Keefe (astronomer at NASA): "We are, by astronomical standards, a pampered, cosseted, cherished group of creatures.... If the Universe had not been made with the most exacting precision we could never have come into existence. It is my view that these circumstances indicate the universe was created for man to live in." [3]

George Greenstein (astronomer): "As we survey all the evidence, the thought insistently arises that some supernatural agency—or, rather, Agency—must be

[1] Hoyle, F. 1982. *The Universe: Past and Present Reflections*. Annual Review of Astronomy and Astrophysics: 20:16.

[2] Davies, P. 1988. *The Cosmic Blueprint: New Discoveries in Nature's Creative Ability To Order the Universe*. New York: Simon and Schuster, p.203.

[3] Heeren, F. 1995. *Show Me God*. Wheeling, IL, Searchlight Publications, p. 200.

involved. Is it possible that suddenly, without intending to, we have stumbled upon scientific proof of the existence of a Supreme Being? Was it God who stepped in and so providentially crafted the cosmos for our benefit?" [4]

Vera Kistiakowsky (MIT physicist): "The exquisite order displayed by our scientific understanding of the physical world calls for the divine." [5]

Frank Tipler (Professor of Mathematical Physics): "When I began my career as a cosmologist some twenty years ago, I was a convinced atheist. I never in my wildest dreams imagined that one day I would be writing a book purporting to show that the central claims of Judeo-Christian theology are in fact true, that these claims are straightforward deductions of the laws of physics as we now understand them. I have been forced into these conclusions by the inexorable logic of my own special branch of physics." [6]

Frank Tipler, a highly respected physicist who converted to Christianity has authored a book entitled The Physics of Christianity in which he demonstrates that the essential beliefs of Christianity are wholly consistent with the laws of physics.

You may ask, if this fine tuning of the universe is so obvious and widely accepted, how do scientists explain it apart from a Creator? The answer reveals how desperate many people become in their attempt to deny the God of all creation. Many non believing scientists attempt to explain the fine tuning of the universe by suggesting that there may have been multiple millions, billions or even trillions of universes, and this one just happens to be just right. They suggest that our universe is a

---

[4] Greenstein, G. 1988. *The Symbiotic Universe*. New York: William Morrow, p.27.
[5] Margenau, H and R.A. Varghese, ed. 1992. *Cosmos, Bios, and Theos*. La Salle, IL, Open Court, p. 52.
[6] Tipler, F.J. 1994. *The Physics of Immortality*. New York, Doubleday, Preface.

part of something called the "multiverse," which is made up of millions of universes. Please note that these proposed additional universes cannot be observed and are purely speculative. The following statement from Wikipedia regarding the multiverse is very telling. "Multiple universes have been hypothesized in cosmology, physics, astronomy, religion, philosophy, transpersonal psychology and fiction, particularly in science fiction and fantasy."

Everything in the observable world around us consistently tells us that things which are precisely put together have a designer or creator. To deny this truth and to suggest that millions of universes can explain this finely tuned universe that we live in is obviously dishonest intellectually.

Another interesting note regarding the fine tuning of the universe is what some scientists have called "the anthropic principle" which states that the universe is especially suited for the wellbeing of mankind. In other words, the more we learn about the observable universe, the more we see amazing details that appear to be designed specifically for mankind's benefit. This, of course, is exactly what we would expect to find if God created all things and then created man and placed him in the world to rule over it.

So the first level of evidence of a creator is found in the biggest thing we know of, the universe that we live in. It does not look at all like it has come about as the result of a massive explosion billions of years ago. It is precisely governed by finely tuned laws of physics. It looks very ordered. It looks designed! It confirms what the first verse of the Bible says, "In the beginning God created the heavens and the earth."

Before we move from our examination of the universe let me mention briefly one other thing that I find fascinating. You may have heard of the terms "dark matter" and "dark energy". These are terms that scientists have made up to describe mysterious forces within the universe that help form stars and hold galaxies together (dark matter) and assist the universe in its continual expansion (dark energy). Recent calculations suggest that the universe is made up of 96% dark matter and dark energy. We can't see, hear or detect dark matter or dark energy. These terms are made up because there is not enough visible matter within galaxies to hold them together or to allow stars to form and there is not enough detectable energy to cause the universe to continue to expand at the rate it is expanding. Neil deGrasse Tyson has stated in YouTube videos that we the terms "dark matter" and "dark energy" make it sound like we know something, but we don't. He says we could call these "Fred" and "Wilma".

The Bible actually explains the mysteries that modern science attempts to explain by the invention of "dark matter" and "dark energy". Colossians 1:17 says that in Jesus "all things hold together." Hebrews 1:3 says that Jesus "upholds (holds together) all things by the word of His power." So, from a biblical perspective we would expect that galaxies would be held together and stars would form. In 10 or more Old Testament passages including Isaiah 40:22 we are told that God "stretches out the heavens like a curtain (or tent)" so we would expect to see the universe expanding. Isn't that amazing! The very things that modern science are baffled by within the study of the universe are spoken of, and explained in the Bible!

LEVEL 2 - OUR SOLAR SYSTEM IS WELL ORDERED
In our search for scientific evidence that confirms the biblical account of creation, we will now move from the vastness of the universe to something closer to home. We find our own solar system to be another example of tremendous order and design.

Our solar system is so well ordered that we can know the exact placement of the planets within the solar system 100 years ahead of time. The orbit of the planets is like clockwork.

Each of the planets within the solar system is made up of different types of materials, some gaseous and some terrestrial. Each is unique and has its own rotation rate and direction. In many cases, we can even identify the purpose within the solar system that various planets fulfill. For instance, the large gaseous planets of Jupiter and Saturn protect the Earth from potentially dangerous objects by their strong gravitational pull upon objects entering our solar system.

The fact that some of the planets and moons in our solar system rotate in opposite directions than most others reveals that the solar system is not the result of an explosion of spinning matter. If it were, all the planets and moons would rotate in the same direction. The fact that they are made of various materials also is problematic for the idea of random development after an explosion.

An example of design can be seen in the precision of size and distance involved in our Moon and our Sun that allows for total solar eclipses. The Moon's size ratio compared to the Sun's size is precisely comparable to the distance ratio of the Moon's distance from the Earth compared to the Sun's distance from the Earth. It is this precision that causes the Moon to be just the right size from our vantage point to allow it to cover the entire Sun, allowing scientist to analyze the light coming from around the rim of the Moon.

The sun's ability to produce usable energy and light as well as the earth's ability to utilize that energy and light while warding off the harmful aspects of the sun's rays all show amazing design.

Recent scientific discoveries have shown that each planet in our solar system shows specific characteristics of design and defies the theorized views of evolutionary development. To learn more about this you can go to the following YouTube video: http://www.youtube.com/watch?v=Gr8Az3QQZdl

Additional information about our solar system's design and function is available in an article entitled "Revelations in the Solar System" which can be found at http://creation.com/revelations-in-the-solar-system

So at level 2, our solar system we again see design features that point to the handy work of a creator.

LEVEL 3 - THE EARTH IS DESIGNED WITH PRECISION

As we move closer still and observe our home, the Earth, we find great design features that allow the Earth to sustain living creatures.

In Isaiah 45:18 the Bible tells us, "For thus says the LORD, who created the heavens (He is the God who formed the earth and made it, He established it and did not create it a waste place, but formed it to be inhabited), 'I am the LORD, and there is none else.'"

Since God says that He specifically formed the Earth to be inhabited, we would expect to find evidence within scientific study that confirms this truth and shows that the Earth is a unique and special place, allowing life to exist.

Many have speculated for decades that there may be life forms living on another planet somewhere in the universe. But the reality is, nothing has yet been found to show life existing anywhere else in the universe.

There are more than seventy-five different specific parameters found on the Earth that enable life to exist. The more that scientists learn about what is involved in the Earth's ability to sustain life forms, the more obvious it becomes that the earth was designed and made by God for the purpose of being inhabited by living things.

Here is a partial list of factors that enable the Earth to be habitable:

1. Located in the right part of the galaxy
2. Orbiting the right type of atar
3. The right distance from the Sun
4. The right magnetic field
5. The right oxygen to nitrogen ratio in the atmosphere
6. The right amount of liquid water
7. The right axis tilt of 23½ degrees
8. The right rotation rate (speed)
9. The right amount of water vapor in the atmosphere
10. The proper ozone quantity in the atmosphere
11. The right thickness of the Earth's crust
12. The right amount of carbon dioxide in the atmosphere
13. Right gravitational interaction with the Moon
14. Right distance from Jupiter, (strong gravity that provides protection to the Earth from asteroid and comet collisions)
15. Right tectonic activity

Some scientists have attempted to calculate the probability that these parameters, along with the many others that enable the

Earth to sustain life, could have come about on earth by random chance. One calculation has estimated that there would be one chance in ten to the 99th power. Obviously, it did not happen by chance. The Earth was clearly designed by God as a place to be inhabited, just as Isaiah 45:18 says. [7]

A great tool to understand more about the Earth's unique design is the DVD entitled The Privileged Planet, which can be found at localchurchapologetics.org, Christian Book Distributors, Amazon, or at this website: http://www.privilegedplanet.com

As we look at the Earth, we can also see some amazing features that affect our daily lives in a very tangible way. Consider the water cycle which is so essential for life. Water evaporates from the seas and oceans and ascends into the atmosphere to form clouds. These clouds are moved over the Earth by upper wind currents. Water vapor condenses, releasing rain or other forms of precipitation from the clouds across the land to irrigate the soil. Water then runs back into streams and rivers to be carried back into the seas and oceans. The cycle continues and makes life possible.

I once did some calculations to determine how much water is released from a thunderstorm. I based my calculations upon a storm that would release an average of 2 inches of rain across an area that is 500 miles wide by 500 miles long. That's a pretty big storm, but not at all unusual when you figure that some storms produce rain all the way across America, which is about 3,000 miles wide. The amount of water released from my theoretical storm (2 inches by 500 miles by 500 miles) would fill a lake 20 feet deep, 10 miles wide,

"Lake Rainstorm"

_____

[7] http://www.godandscience.org/apologetics/probabilitieslife.html
http://www.reasons.org/articles/fine-tuning-for-life-on-earth-june-2004

and 200 miles long. To help you visualize this, consider that it is about 175 miles across Illinois, from Chicago to the Mississippi River in Moline, IL. This lake would be bigger than any lake in the state of Illinois (not counting the adjacent Lake Michigan).

The trees and other plants are also significant participants in this hydrological cycle. Trees draw moisture through their roots from the ground and draw the moisture to very top of tree through amazing design features that allow them to overcome gravity in this task. The underside of a tree leaf has pores that can open and close as needed to release all the excess moisture back into the atmosphere, assisting in the earth's water cycle. The hotter the day, the more the tree pulls up moisture, and releases the excess after it has been nourished by the moisture. This process is called "transpiration". When we sweat it is called "perspiration" and when a tree or plant sweats it is called "transpiration". You might be thinking that the amount of moisture a tree or plant "transpires" is probably minimal. Think again! For example, a maple tree can transpire 50-60 gallons of water per hour on a  hot summer day! Wow! This is another example of God's wonderful design on this planet that we benefit from every day!

Another wonderful aspect of God's design of the Earth is the amazing balance which causes our atmosphere to stay filled with life-giving oxygen. Billions of people and billions of animals are continually breathing in the oxygen from the atmosphere and breathing out carbon dioxide into the atmosphere. How does the air keep from getting depleted of oxygen and filled with lethal amounts of carbon dioxide? The answer is found in the trees and plant life that permeate the earth. Plants breathe in carbon dioxide and release oxygen into the air continually. This symbiotic exchange keeps the atmosphere balanced with the right amount of oxygen and carbon dioxide needed for both life groups. If we could identify only one or two nice "coincidences" like this that enable the Earth to sustain life, we might be tempted to chalk it up to mere chance. The truth is, however, that wonderful "coincidences" like this exist all around us, confirming that we have an awesome Creator.

Our earth truly displays additional evidence of a Creator!

THE GLOBAL FLOOD AND NOAH'S ARK

This subject is not related directly to creation, but because the biblical flood affected the Earth in ways that are apparent today, I have chosen to address it here.

The Bible gives a full account of the flood in Genesis chapters 6–9, and there are references to it in 1 Peter 3:18-20 and 2 Peter 3:3-7. The Genesis account tells us that God destroyed the Earth and all the living creatures that lived upon it except for Noah, his family, and the animals that were taken into the ark.

Many have denied the reality of the Bible's account or claimed that the flood was limited to a local area. The issues surrounding the flood are very important to a biblical worldview, because the flood explains many phenomena that we observe in the Earth today.

All around the world we find sedimentary rock layers, and within those layers we find millions of fossils. The evolutionary explanation says that these rock layers were formed slowly and gradually over millions of years, and that the fossils found within them are, therefore, millions of years old. An alternate interpretation of the same evidence is that the rock layers and the fossils within them are there as a result of the global flood recorded in Genesis. We absolutely know that sedimentary rock layers can be formed very quickly because they were observed to be formed in a matter of hours and days after the eruption of Mt. St. Helens in 1980. Based on the results of that relatively small catastrophic event, it is easy to see how a global catastrophic event such as the flood of Genesis that involved "the fountains of the deep" bursting forth, as well as rain coming from above, would have produced much more sedimentary rock layers. These rock layers would inevitably be full of fossils, since multitudes of living creatures would have been buried quickly during and immediately after the flood.

Fossils are formed when the body of a creature is trapped inside a layer of sediment. After the sediment hardens into stone, the creature's body decays, leaving an empty space shaped to the contours of the creature's body. When that space fills again with sediment, the previously hardened layer acts as a mold. As the new sediment hardens, the mold forms it into a stone replica of the creature.

Considering what it takes for a fossil to be formed before it decays to nothing, the explanation of a global flood fits the evidence found today much better than the theory of creatures dying and being buried gradually over millions of years. If a creature is not buried alive or very quickly after its death it has no chance of becoming a fossil.

Another evidence of a global flood is that many sedimentary rock layers are curved or bent, showing that the material making up  these layers had to have been laid down quickly, while it was soft and pliable. Had earthquakes or tectonic movement caused the distortion, the layers would not have been formed into smooth curves. The layer lines would have been broken and fragmented because the sediment would already have been formed into rock as the movements of millions of years reshaped them into contorted forms.

Bent Rock Layers

Many mock the biblical account of the flood, claiming it would have been impossible for two of every kind of animal to have fit within the ark. It is important to note that the Bible does not say that the ark held two of every "species," but rather two of every "kind." The ark would not have housed two poodles, two German shepherds, two beagles, etc. There would simply have been two of the dog kind. All the necessary genetic information needed to account for all the species of dogs existing today within the dog kind would have been latent within the two dog kind that were in the ark.

The larger animals probably would not have been represented on the ark by adults, but by much smaller infant or young creatures. Research results shown in John Woodmorappe's book Noah's Ark: A Feasibility Study reveals that there would have been only about 16,000 animals on the ark, and that the median size of all those animals would have been that of a small rat. Woodmorappe's research also included consideration of how much space would have been needed for food and drinkable water. His research also showed that there would have been plenty of room for all that was needed to allow all the inhabitants of the ark to survive.

The ark is described in the Bible as having been 300 cubits long, 50 cubits wide, and 30 cubits high. Using the smallest description of a cubit measurement, the ark would have been a minimum 437.5 feet long, 72.9 feet wide, and 43.75 feet tall. If we use a larger description of a cubit measurement, it may have been as much as 515 feet long, 85.8 feet wide, and 51.5 feet tall. The Bible says it had three levels, or floors, so the available square footage would have been somewhere between 95,681 and 132,561. That is approximately three acres of floor space!

It is important for believers to realize that the Bible's account of the global flood in Noah's day is both factual and consistent with the confirming evidence we see today. For more information, see the articles found at:

http://creation.com/how-did-all-the-animals-fit-on-noahs-ark

or

http://njbiblescience.org/presentations/Noahs%20Ark%20-%20A%2
0Feasibility%20Study.pdf

EVIDENCES OF A CREATOR - GOD

FINELY TUNED UNIVERSE !

Scientists now know that the universe is held together by precisely set laws of physics (constants) such as "the law of gravity" & "the speed of light". If these constants were set just slightly different, galaxies, stars and planets would not exist! This precision shows great design and confirms the involvement of a designer!

(1)

EVIDENCES OF A CREATOR - GOD

OUR SOLAR SYSTEM !

Our Solar System is so well ordered that we can know exactly where each planet will be within its orbiting cycle around the sun a century from now. Also, each planet is unique in design, rotation, etc. The order of our Solar System points to a designer!

(2)

EVIDENCES OF A CREATOR - GOD

THE EARTH !

There are approximately 75 different characteristics that a planet needs, to be able to sustain life. Examples of these are "being the right distance from the sun", "the right rotation rate", "the right atmosphere", "the right amount of liquid water", "a moon to control the tilt of the earth and the ocean tide", etc. The earth is perfectly designed with all of these characteristics to allow for life to inhabit the earth!

(3)

EVIDENCES OF A CREATOR - GOD

THE EARTH !

Isaiah 45:18 (NASB) For thus says the LORD, who created the heavens (He is the God who formed the earth and made it, He established it and did not create it a waste place, but formed it to be inhabited), "I am the LORD, & there is none else.
2 Practical Examples of God's great design on the Earth!
(1) The Water Cycle
(2) The Balance of Oxygen & Carbon Dioxide in the Atmosphere

(4)

EVIDENCES OF A CREATOR - GOD

LIVING CREATURES !

Living creatures, including insects, marine creatures, birds, mammals, etc. all exhibit amazing instincts and abilities that defy evolution. In many cases their existence is dependant upon their special abilities. Consider the Australian Brush Turkey, Honey Bees, Giraffes, Woodpeckers, Monarch Butterflies, and Beavers as examples. (5)

EVIDENCES OF A CREATOR - GOD

THE HUMAN BODY (1)

Psalm 139:13-14 tells us that we were formed by God in our mother's womb and we are "fearfully & wonderfully made". Every aspect of the development of a baby in the womb is amazing. Consider the fact that in 9 months 1 cells multiplies into about 100 trillion cells. In addition to multiplying, the cells diversify into blood cells, bone cells, skin cells, etc. The entire process is amazing!

(6)

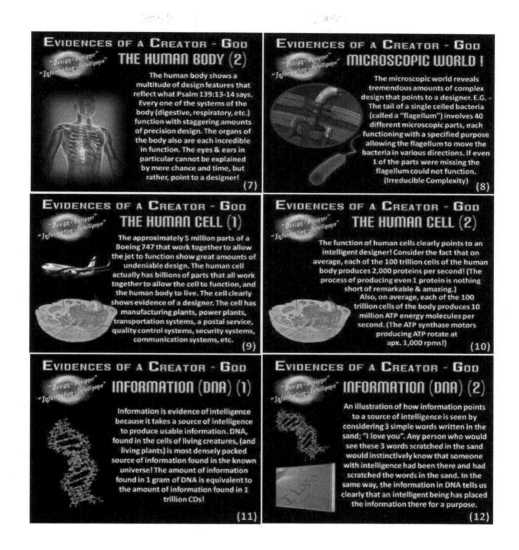

(Above) Evidence for a Creator from the largest realm (the vastness of the universe) down to nearly the smallest realm known (the microscopic world and DNA in the nucleus of living cells) *** **("From Biggest to Smallest")** *** (These cards coincide with the material found in Sec. 3, Chapters 2-6)

Memorization Cards Available for Free Download at localchurchapologetics.org

"Design Within the Animal Kingdom Affirms Creation"

LEVEL 4 - LIVING CREATURES ON THE EARTH

The DVD series entitled Incredible Creatures That Defy Evolution is a wonderful source of information, showing us that God's amazing design features can be seen throughout the animal kingdom. From the largest mammals to the smallest insects, we find design features within living organisms that could not have evolved by mutations or natural selection over millions of years. Countless numbers of animals and insects have instincts and abilities that cause us to marvel at the wisdom of God. We will briefly touch on a few of these.

Those who cling to Darwinian evolution will claim that all the marvelous design features we will speak of here could have come about by evolutionary means. But as we review these design features, I ask you to consider whether an honest investigation confirms the idea of gradual unguided processes or creation by an intelligent designer. If we continue to see design features that are produced by usable information, we may not have proved that these creatures were created, but we have certainly confirmed through research that the view of an intelligent designer fits the evidence better than the idea of random, unguided processes.

The **Australian Brush Turkey** (also called "the incubator bird") builds its nest on the ground. The nest, or mound, is quite large,

measuring ten to twelve feet wide and three to six feet high. After the female deposits her egg under the mound, it is the job of the male brush turkey to keep the temperature and humidity at precise levels for the seven weeks of incubation until the chick is hatched and makes its way out of the mound. The male brush turkey will keep the temperature within the mound within a degree or two of 91 degrees Fahrenheit for seven weeks or more by placing and moving sticks, sand, and leaves to cover various locations on the mound as needed to reduce or increase the temperature. He has an amazing ability to maintain steady temperature and humidity levels within the nest that cannot be explained by slow evolutionary processes. If the brush turkey had not been given this ability by God from the beginning, brush turkeys would have become extinct long before this ability could be developed.

Honey Bees also have a marvelous ability that shows the glory of God. When a scout bee finds a food source, she will return to the hive to communicate its location to the other bees in the hive. As many other bees gather around her in the hive, she will give out small samples of the food, and then she will do a dance in the midst of the other bees to communicate to them the direction of the food source, how far away it is, and how much food is available. The dance of the honey bee

incorporates the bee's internal clock and knowledge of the location of the sun as a part of its explanation to the other bees. We can easily see that this behavior appears to be designed and does not look like something that developed randomly over millions of years. The bee's communication system also involves a method of sending messages through the hive by passing along special chemicals, ultimately communicating information about the condition of the hive to the queen bee. She uses this information to determine what type and how many eggs to lay in order to keep the hive balanced and healthy. A queen honey bee will often lay 175,000 to 200,000 eggs in a year.

A colony of honey bees can consist of 20,000 to 60,000 bees. Don't be fooled by the appearance of chaos when you see bees swarming in a hive. The truth is, honey bees are amazing architects and engineers. For 2,000 years, mathematicians and architects have studied and marveled at the bee's engineering skills. The bee's honeycomb consists of many perfectly shaped six-sided hexagons. This geometric shape provides the strongest  structure possible for use as a nursery for their young and the production of honey. The shape also provides maximum space to be constructed with the minimum amount of material. Humans have, in many cases, incorporated the engineering design of honeycombs into their designs and plans. Not only do the bees build perfect hexagon structures, they also build each hexagon at an incline, angled at 9 to 14 degrees toward the center of the honeycomb for maximum efficiency.

To produce one pound of honey, it takes 556 honey bees flying a total of 55,000 miles, gathering nectar from 2 million flowers. One of the skills that enables honey bees to do this work so efficiently is their incredible, unimaginative ability as mathematicians. In a research study done by scientists at Royal Holloway University in London, honey bees were found to have the ability to compute the most efficient path to travel to each flower in a field of millions of flowers. They found that it took supercomputers days to figure out what the bees figure easily each day, without error. Their brains are the size of a grain of grass seed, yet their abilities are beyond understanding. Evolved by random mutations, or designed by an awesome God? The answer is obvious!

To learn more about the dance of the honey bee or to simply see the bees performing their dance, view the YouTube video at this location: http://www.youtube.com/watch?v=bFDGPgXtK-U .

In the case of the **Giraffe**, it is not an instinct or ability that is so amazing, but rather a special body design that points to the engineering expertise of our God. A bull giraffe typically grows to a height of eighteen feet. As you might imagine, this may cause some real challenges for proper blood flow to and from the giraffe's head. The truth is that the giraffe is designed with a number of features that are not found in other creatures, enabling the giraffe to live and function without problem despite his height. The giraffe has special valves in the blood vessels of his neck that open and close when he raises and lowers his head, regulating the amount of blood allowed to run up and down his neck. This is essential, since the long neck of giraffe must compensate for the gravitational force created when he lowers his head.

The giraffe also has a very large heart to produce high blood pressure levels, allowing blood to be pushed adequately up to his head when he is standing. A giraffe's heart weighs up to twenty-six pounds. In addition to these special features, the giraffe also has a unique sponge in his head that retains a portion of blood when he raises his head up quickly after having gotten a drink of water. Though the blood now rushes out of his head downward, enough blood is stored in the sponge and released into the brain to prevent the giraffe from passing out while his body adjusts and begins to push blood up his long neck.

There are a few other special features of the giraffe's circulatory system that also help to overcome the special challenges posed by his height. All these features show great design by a wonderful Creator. These features could not be the result of evolution, because all of them are necessary to the giraffe's survival at the outset. Giraffes could not wait for them to develop slowly over millions of years.

To learn more about these special features within the giraffe, you may want to view the following YouTube videos:

http://www.youtube.com/watch?v=PEnv8eq_v-8

http://www.youtube.com/watch?v=pcWYdxNks3s&index=1&list=PLN
MUF52D1L9CVSIIaSXxII8KdBMLd_p9y
http://www.youtube.com/watch?v=BMz9o9LP9WI

Woodpeckers also have special design features that allow them to live and perform their unique function. First, the woodpecker has special shock absorbers in his neck to prevent him from harming his brain and head as he spends his day banging his beak into trees. Second, his tongue design is also unique. It coils up in the back of his mouth and can then be extended up to ten inches beyond his beak so that he can reach into a tree to collect a bug for food. His tongue is barbed at the end, allowing him to stab bugs that he finds inside of trees. His tongue also produces a sticky glue-like substance to assist him in drawing bugs out of trees. While this feature is obviously beneficial for that function, it would be  very detrimental once the bug was in the woodpecker's mouth if it were not for a solvent that is excreted into the mouth to dissolve the glue-like substance. This allows the woodpecker to swallow the bug.

The woodpecker also has specially designed feet and tail feathers that enable him to cling vertically to the side of a tree as he drills a hole with his specially designed beak, which is much stronger than the beak of other birds. His skull is thicker per body weight than any other creature.

Finally, the woodpecker has an incredible ability to open and close his eyes every time he strikes the tree. He opens his eyes to see where he is going to strike and closes them immediately as he strikes. This opening and closing sequence occurs numerous times per second.. Research has found that the force produced through the strike of the woodpecker's beak is so strong that it would cause his eyeballs to pop out of his head if he were not able to close his eyelids multiple times per second at the exact moments he strikes the tree.

These special features are clear indicators that the woodpecker is created by God and is not the product of evolutionary processes over long periods of time. To learn more about the woodpecker, you may want to view the following YouTube video:

http://www.youtube.com/watch?v=vKR9vS4df-l&list=PLNMU
F52D1L9CVSIlaSXxII8KdBMLd_p9y&index=2

Monarch Butterflies are truly remarkable. They live through the winter months in some isolated forest areas of Central Mexico. In the spring, they are stirred to begin a journey to the north. This generation of monarchs lays their eggs on milkweed plants in northern Mexico and the southern portion of the U.S. and then die. As the eggs hatch into caterpillars, the milkweed becomes their food source. The caterpillars then go into the chrysalis stage inside of their cocoon and are transformed into butterflies. This process is a marvel of God's creative genius.

The new generation of butterflies will travel north as summer approaches and will live six to eight weeks. This generation will find milkweed plants now growing further north, where they will lay their  eggs and then die. The same process will take place for three to four generations, with a generation of monarchs now living in the northern parts of the U.S. and the southern parts of Canada. Here's where it gets truly amazing. The generation of monarchs born in late summer in the northern U.S. and southern Canada will not live a mere six to eight weeks like the previous generations, but will live approximately eight months. They will migrate back to very same trees in Mexico where their great, great grandparents spent the winter in the previous year. The marvelous patterns that define the life cycle and the migration abilities of the monarch butterfly defy evolutionary explanations and point again to an intelligent, wise Creator. For more information on monarch butterflies you may want to view these YouTube videos:

http://www.youtube.com/watch?v=7AUeM8Mbalk
http://www.youtube.com/watch?v=AZk6nZGH9Xo
http://www.youtube.com/watch?v=LawHWsIqa5s

Beavers show the creative work of God in their special abilities to build very effective water dams without the aid of high-tech tools or human ingenuity. In some cases, crews of men have worked through the day to remove a beaver dam only to find it back in place by the next morning. The Beavers know-how when it comes to building water dams is truly incredible. In addition to building water dams beavers build their lodges in similar fashion. They are sealed from the cold, yet with designed ventilation in the roof. They are only accessible from underwater with multiple entrances and exits in case the need for a quick exit comes about.

As we would expect, the beaver has more than just great engineering abilities. He has some very special equipment perfectly suited for his habitat. Beavers have special valves in their nose and ears which automatically close when they are under water to prevent water from coming in. They also have special fur mouth flaps in their mouths between their front scissor teeth and their back molars so they can chew sticks underwater without swallowing water. Since they live under water so much of the time they also have special eye lids that are transparent, allowing them to see well underwater and have their eyes protected.

Beavers are great examples of God's design!

Chickens: God's Amazing Birds!

When we think about creatures with amazing, unique abilities, chickens are not likely the first that come to mind. A few years ago, I

was thinking about how God has revealed Himself through the things that He has made, and for some reason my thoughts went to chickens. I started thinking about how critical chickens are to our food supply—in terms of both meat and eggs. We should all praise God for the lowly chicken. Let's look at how critical chickens are to our everyday lives and how uniquely equipped they are to play their role in sustaining life here on Earth.

Consider these facts about birds in general and their egg-laying abilities:

- Bald eagles typically will lay one to three eggs per year — up to forty in a lifetime.
- Cardinals lay two to five eggs in a clutch, usually two times per year.
- Penguins egg-laying capacity varies among species, but they generally lay a maximum of fifteen eggs in a lifetime.
- Blue jays lay three to six eggs each year in a clutch.
- Ringneck doves lay two eggs per clutch and up to sixteen to eighteen eggs per year.
- Turkeys (Another great food source) lay a maximum of 100 eggs per year.
- Chickens are egg-laying machines. A hen hits puberty only eighteen to twenty-four weeks after hatching out of an egg herself. It only takes about twenty-six hours for a hen to make an egg, and she can start producing another one forty to sixty minutes after laying. What's more, hens lay a lot of eggs—up to 300 per year.

Now consider these facts about our consumption of chickens and chicken eggs, and you can see the importance of this bird's highly prolific, unique egg production.

- Americans eat 8 billion chickens per year. That's almost twenty-six per person each year, or one per person every other week.
- In 2014, Americans consumed an average of 256 chicken eggs per person. That's over 81 billion eggs in just one year!
- Ask.com reports that Americans consume an average of 25 billion chicken wings each year, including 1.25 billion during Super Bowl weekend alone!

Note these stats from the USDA for the year 2008:

<u>USDA Slaughter Stats 2008</u>

Cattle: 35,507,500
Pigs: 116,558,900
Turkeys: 271,245,000

Chickens: 9,075,261,000
(Over 90% of the Total)

http://www.animalliberationfront.com/Practical/FactoryFarm/USDAnumbers.htm

The stats above show egg consumption just for the United States. It has been estimated that over 53 million tons of chicken eggs are consumed per year worldwide. If there were no chickens, think of how it would affect our world! Of course, chicken eggs are not just eaten by themselves; they are also ingredients in many of our other foods. I think it is safe to say that if chickens were suddenly removed from the world, the impact on our lives would be catastrophic.

It should not be surprising, since God is a masterful designer, to discover that chicken eggs are very, very nutritious. In an online article, Dr. Fred Kummerow discusses how mother's milk is nature's most perfect food, and then he puts the egg in second place "because its amino acid content mimics the levels in mother's milk. Moreover, the egg is also inexpensive and readily available. If you doubled the portion to two whole eggs, these would contain even more essential amino acids than one quart of human milk."

Later in the article Dr. Kummerow adds, "Although maligned in nutritional recommendations, eggs are the most nutritious and the least expensive protein source in the grocery store. At only 68 calories, one egg provides about 11 percent of your daily protein requirement. Eggs contain a variety of important nutrients including every vitamin, mineral and natural antioxidant that your body needs." [1] He, Dr. Kummerow also dispels the myth that eggs are a source of high cholesterol.

So here we have a bird that is highly prolific in producing eggs, and those eggs are arguably the most nutritious form of food available to us. I do not believe this is a coincidence. We should praise God for creating the under-appreciated chicken. He designed them with unique abilities knowing that they would be a much needed food source for us.

The **Bombardier Beetle** is another truly amazing creature that shows great design features. This little insect has a built-in defense system that involves a number of specially designed functions and parts. The bombardier beetle has the ability to fire a hot, noxious chemical spray mixture into the face of a would-be predator. The spray is produced from a reaction between two chemical compounds, hydroquinone and hydrogen peroxide, which are

stored in two reservoirs inside the beetle's abdomen. The beetle also stores an inhibitor which prevents the two explosive compounds from exploding inside the beetle. When released through the gland outlets in the rear of the beetle, the compounds create a series of about 70 mini-explosions at a rate of about 500 per second. Though the process takes only a fraction of a second, the resulting chemical reaction is powerful enough to drive away would-be predators and in some cases can be fatal to them. In some species of bombardier beetles, the gland openings that shoot out the explosive compounds can swivel up to 270 degrees, helping the beetle to fire the explosive compounds more accurately into the face of the predator.

Evolutionists acknowledge that the evolutionary process of

---

[1]http://www.westonaprice.org/health-topics/abcs-of-nutrition/protein-building-block s-of-the-body/

this defense system is unknown, but they claim that the system could have theoretically evolved from defenses found in other beetles in incremental steps by natural selection. Creationists claim that the bombardier beetle is an example of "irreducible complexity" which means that if you reduced the complexity of the system by subtracting any part of it, the whole system would fail to work and be useless. Irreducible complexity therefore says that the whole system must be fully designed and put in place at the same time. It makes no sense to think the separate parts of the system could develop over time independently, for each part would be meaningless and useless during development. Yet each part would have to develop in such a way that it would fit perfectly and be completely functional when integrated with the other parts into the completed system.

Added to this problem is the dilemma of time. If the bombardier beetle must have its complex spraying mechanism intact in order to survive, it could not have survived during the millions of years it would have taken the system to evolve.

Consider **Australian Aquatic Frogs** (also referred to as "gastric-brooding frogs"). After the eggs of these frogs are laid and fertilized, the female swallows them. Once the young are in her stomach, the mother stops eating for the next eight weeks. After eight weeks, fully developed little frogs come out of the mother's mouth. This is possible because she releases fine threads of special chemicals which prevent the mother's stomach from making digestive acids. Her stomach becomes a comfortable, protective nursery for her developing young. (Note: It is believed that these frogs became extinct in the 1980s, though the reason is not known.)

The **Camel** is perfectly designed for living in desert areas, and for that reason camels are highly helpful to humans who live in arid climates. Camels can drink up to forty-four gallons of water in a day, up to twenty-seven gallons of water at once in a ten-minute period. They store the water in the hump on their back, which enables them to live for weeks without

drinking more. The hump (or humps) also contains stored fat reserves that allows camels to go for long periods of time without eating. During these long periods, their humps will shrink away until the animals eat again and build them back up.

Camels have several lesser-known features which make them perfect for travel in the desert. The camel's nose creates condensation as it breathes and helps him to bring in needed moisture continually. The camel has three sets of eyelids to protect its eyes from the sand. The third set is transparent. These eyelids cover the camel's eyes during a sandstorm, enabling him to see without incurring eye damage.

The camel's feet are of special design as well—broad and flat like snowshoes to keep him from sinking in the desert sands. His knees are covered with a protective layer of tough skin, allowing him to kneel in the hot sand. The camel has specially designed red blood cells that allow him to utilize water internally much more efficiently than humans. These cells enable a camel to lose up to 40 percent of its body weight through water loss and still be healthy. That loss can be as much 500 pounds.

Everything about the camel's design allows him to help humans travel in the dessert. Many lives have been saved by the camel's unique abilities. When looking at the camel, we again must ask ourselves if these features look designed and if the camel is not still another example of evidence for a Creator.

The **North American Bison** is an example a "ruminant"—a grazing animal that chews the cud and has a uniquely designed four-stomach digestive system. It is hard to imagine how we would survive without grazing animals such as cows, bison, sheep, and goats. These animals spend their lives eating grasses, plants, and leaves, becoming wonderful sources of food for humans. The ingenious four-part stomach system of ruminants is specially designed to digest grass and plants. The first two stomachs utilize billions of friendly bacteria or probiotics which break down the food to begin the digestive process. Then specially designed muscles push the food back into the animal's mouth to be re-chewed. When the food is again swallowed, it goes into the third stomach, where water and minerals are absorbed into the bloodstream. Finally, the food enters the fourth stomach, which is much like the human stomach.

Evolutionists claim that the complex four-stomach system of ruminants evolved from simpler digestive systems in the past. The fossil record does not bear this out. Studies on ancient bison have shown that they contained identical proteins and amino acids as found in current bison. Without a fully formed and functioning system, the bison and other ruminants such as cows would have not survived. Considering the billions of probiotics, the hydrochloric acids, the muscles, and the interactions of these elements with other organs,  the idea of random mutations developing this complex digestive system is a stretch of faith at best. The digestive system of ruminants appears to be another example of a wonderfully designed system for life.

Below is a table listing some of the special abilities and traits of the creatures we have looked at as examples. I encourage you to evaluate this table with an honest heart. Answer this question regarding the features listed for each creature: Do these features appear to be designed, or do they display what we would expect to see in creatures that are the product of random, unguided processes over millions of years? Both believers and unbelievers have access to the same evidence. Believers say the evidence supports creation while unbelievers say it supports evolution. The question you must answer is, which seems the more rational conclusion? Which best fits what the evidence shows us?

Creature	Special Features & Abilities	Design?	Random Chance?
Brush Turkey	Male keeps nest (mound) at precise temperature & humidity for 7 weeks by moving sand, leaves, sticks, etc.		
Honey Bee	Communicates precise information with a dance. Builds perfectly engineered hives. Calculates best flying routes. Etc.		
Giraffe	Has special valves in its neck and a special sponge in its head, allowing proper blood flow. (Plus has huge heart)		
Woodpecker	Has special shock absorbers built into its neck and a uniquely designed tongues, perfect for retrieving bugs from trees.		
Monarch Butterfly	Migrates from Mexico to Canada over 3-4 generations. Fall generation back to the same trees in Mexico & lives for 8 months.		
Beaver	Special design features for living under water. Engineering wonder building effective dams on flowing waterways.		
Chicken	Reproductive wonder (hens lay up to 300 eggs per year) Chickens & Chicken Eggs are critical food sources for humans.		
Bombardier Beetle	Protects itself from predators by shooting explosive gases out its behind. Gases produced in inner chambers along with inhibitor.		
Gastric-Brooding Frog	Female swallows eggs & hatches them in stomach which becomes a nursery. Digestive fluids cease until babies born by mouth.		
Camel	Has many unique features perfectly suited for life and travel in the desert. (Water storage, feet, knees, eyelids, nostrils, etc.)		
Ruminants (Cow)	The 4 stomach digestive system of "Ruminants" is a marvel of digestive efficiency. Perfectly suited for grazing.		
All The Above	Consider the above examples together as a whole!		

Romans 1 says that God has revealed Himself through the things that He has made. So it should not be surprising that the evidence points overwhelmingly to a designer with unlimited intelligence, imagination and creativity.

There are so many different creatures that display traits pointing to an intelligent, wise creator. Space will not allow us to treat such phenomena as the salmon's ability to return to its birthplace to lay its eggs, the dolphin's sonar system, the hummingbird's ability to fly or the robin bird's ability to detect worms in the soil. From the insect world to the creatures of the air and sea, to the land-dwelling animals, we find amazing instincts, abilities, and design features that point to God's wisdom. Evolutionists claim that evolution can produce these features if given enough time, but such claims involve choosing not to see the obvious. When something looks designed, sounds designed, and acts designed, it is safe to say that it is designed. Faith in our Creator is reasonable and consistent with all we observe in living creatures. Faith in evolution involves choosing to look blindly past all the design features we see around us.

Living creatures provide additional evidence of a great Creator!

SECTION 3: CHAPTER 4

"Design Within the Human Body Affirms Creation"

LEVEL 5 - THE HUMAN BODY

All living creatures show evidence of design, but there is none that is designed so exquisitely as the human body. Every system, organ, and part of the human body is remarkable in itself. When looked at as a whole, it is an unsurpassed masterpiece.

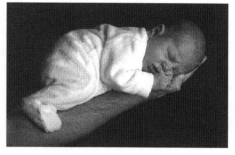

Consider the development of a human being prior to birth. One cell multiplies to trillions of cells within nine months. This kind of multiplication is remarkable in itself, but even more remarkable is the fact that these cells diversify into about 200 different types of cells as they multiply, becoming bone cells, blood cells, skin cells, etc. Somehow all these various types of cells develop in their proper place and begin to function uniquely, as needed for the benefit of the entire body that is being formed. Considering that all the bones, organs, and systems develop from a single cell reminds us of what Psalm 139:13-14 tells us:

> *"For You formed my inward parts; You wove me in my mother's womb. (14) I will give thanks to You, for I am fearfully and wonderfully made; Wonderful are Your works, And my soul knows it very well."*

Our skeletal system has over 200 uniquely designed bones providing protection, strength, and mobility to our body. Working with the muscles, tendons and ligaments, our bones are able to perform many different tasks. Some of our muscles are voluntary and some are involuntary, functioning automatically without our 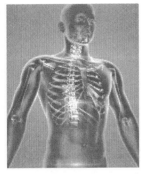 conscious control. Our heart muscles, for example, function continually throughout our lifetime. If this were not the case we would obviously be in big trouble.

Our circulatory system involves enough blood vessels that if we could connect them all end to end they would stretch around the world two and one-half times. Our heart will pump enough blood in an average lifetime to fill a train of tanker cars twenty-five miles long. The valves in our heart are paper thin, yet strong enough to open and close successfully about 100,000 times per day for seventy years or more.

Our respiratory system is designed to continually bring in needed oxygen from the Earth's atmosphere and filter the incoming air to protect us from harmful influences. One of the miraculous things about the respiratory system takes place within the walls of our lungs. With every breath we take, an amazing process must take place or we would die.

Tiny sacs called "alveoli" in the walls of our lungs work with the tiny capillaries surrounding them to exchange inhaled oxygen molecules, which the body needs, with carbon dioxide molecules, which are waste materials that need to be exhaled. Red blood cells in the tiny capillaries surrounding the alveoli release the carbon dioxide molecules through the membrane shared by the capillaries and the alveolus. At the same time oxygen

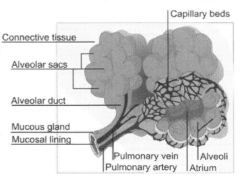

molecules pass through the membrane and attach to hemoglobin proteins within the red blood cells as they pass by. It is like little rafts picking up needed cargo as they pass by on their journey to the heart and from there to other parts of the body. The average human lung has about 300-500 million alveoli with a combined inner surface area that is about the same size as half of a full-size tennis court. That's forty times the surface area of a person's skin. Amazing! This process occurs with every breath that we take throughout our lifetime without us even thinking about it.

This is one of many processes within the human body that brings glory to God our Creator. How could this system have possibly evolved? One breath without this transformation and exchange process would kill the creature before evolution could occur.

There are even special enzymes in the lungs that are like tiny vacuum cleaners taking care of any debris that may make it through the other safety nets the body has set up to keep dust particles out. Proverbs 20:12 says, "The hearing ear and the seeing eye, The LORD has made both of them." Among the many wonders of the human body are those found in the design and function of the human ear and the human eye.

Think about these facts related to the human ear and our ability to hear. When someone speaks, the movement of their vocal cords causes fluctuations in the air pressure. Air molecules then create a sequence of movement events like billiard balls hitting one

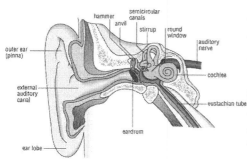

another, each causing the next to move. The air pressure fluctuations and movement of air molecules reaches the human ear, which is so sensitive that it can detect an air pressure change caused by a change in altitude of 1/30,000th of an inch. That is much less than the thickness of a sheet of paper. So if you stand on the floor and then step up onto a single sheet of paper, your ear can detect the difference in altitude.

Sound wave vibrations are transmitted by air to the outer ear, where they hit the eardrum, which transfers them to the middle ear.

The vibrations are moved from the middle ear to the inner ear by three tiny bones that function together in the middle ear. These bones magnify and transmit the sound signals into the inner ear, where they enter a structure called the cochlea, which is filled with fluid. Inside the cochlea is another structure called the organ of Corti. Inside the organ of Corti are tiny cilia (hair-like structures) which move according to the pressures in the fluid, creating electronic signals that are transmitted to the brain for cognitive translation and understanding of exactly what the sound is. Throughout this intricate process, we are not only able to discern that we have heard a sound; we can also tell who the speaker is (if we are familiar with his or her voice), and what words they are saying. It starts with nothing more than air molecules moving across the room.

The middle ear bones are there because of an impedance difference between air (in the outer ear) and liquid (in the inner ear). If you have ever tried to speak to someone under water, you know that sound does not travel well from air into water or through water. The middle ear takes care of this problem.

Even the earwax in the outer ear serves an important purpose. It functions as a type of electrostatic filter that cleans the incoming air of debris, thus protecting the ear and the body from damage by incoming dust or other tiny debris. We might ask how the buildup of the debris in the earwax will be removed. The answer involves a pretty neat fact! The skin on all other parts of the body grows from bottom to top and then falls off in the form of dead skin cells. In the ear, however, the skin grows from inside (at the eardrum) to the outside. As it grows, it continually moves the earwax in the outer ear from the inside to the outside for removal. You can picture this growth and movement pattern by thinking of one of those moving sidewalks in an airport.

The inner ear also gives us our sense of balance. The system that controls this is called the vestibular system. Inside the cochlea there are three semicircular canals which contain a fluid substance. Inside the fluid there are little stones (to detect motion through gravity pulling them downward) and cilia hair which detect motion as well. Through this ingenious system, our brain is able to continually detect our posture and movements, allowing us to stay balanced.

The human eye is just as complicated, efficient, and amazing as the human ear. The various parts of the eye work together much like the parts of a camera, only much more effectively. Rather than attempt to give you details about how the eye works, I will give you some quotes from a 2010 online article in the New York Times about the efficiency of the human eye.

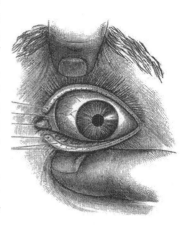

In an article entitled "Seeing the Natural World with a Physicist's Lens," Natalie Angier speaks of the level of efficiency of the human eye.

"The basic building blocks of human eyesight turn out to be practically perfect. Scientists have learned that the fundamental units of vision, the photoreceptor cells that carpet the retinal tissue of the eye and respond to light, are not just good or great or fabulous at their job. They are not merely exceptionally impressive by the standards of biology, with whatever slop and wiggle room the animate category implies. Photoreceptors operate at the outermost boundary allowed by the laws of physics, which means they are as good as they can be, period." [1]

She goes on to talk about a principle researchers are finding regularly in living things, which they have called "optimization." This principle speaks of how living things are often found to be designed in an optimized way, allowing them function extremely efficiently. Related to this, Angier says,

"Photoreceptors exemplify the principle of

---

[1] http://www.nytimes.com/2010/11/02/science/02angier.html

optimization, an idea, gaining ever wider traction among researchers.... In each instance, biophysicists have calculated, the system couldn't get faster, more sensitive or more efficient without first relocating to an alternate universe with alternate physical constants." [2]

Wow! The human eye could not be more efficient, according to scientific research. This article does give evolution the credit for this perfection, but that is certainly because in the secular humanistic worldview, evolution is assumed as fact and evidence to the contrary cannot seem to break through that stubborn philosophical wall. It amazes me that people could honestly think that this kind of perfect design is the result of random evolutionary processes. (Note that the researchers refer to the design of living things.) All of the precise design we see in the human body is blueprinted in the vast amount of usable information contained in DNA. The body is manufactured according to the pattern found in this directive information. As a building is built according to the information on a blueprint, so the human body is built according to the information in the DNA code.

Evolution is supposed to be driven by mutations in DNA, but mutations almost never cause positive changes or add more information. Furthermore, evolution cannot account for the origin of DNA. Also, it defies common logic to assume that perfect design can be created over and over again by random processes that have their origin in a chaotic explosion.

The human body is a masterpiece that points to a masterful designer!

The function of the human brain, the processes within human skin, the healing processes of the body, our capability of speech, the processes within the digestive system and the nervous system, as well as the function of the organs of the body are all remarkably complex and precise. Every part of the human body is testament to the wisdom of God our Creator!

---

[2] ibid.

"Design Within the Microscopic World Affirms Creation"

Level 6 - The Microscopic World

As we have already seen, the stars, planets, and forces of the universe display precision, order, and design. The pervasiveness of design and order continued as we explored our solar system, our planet, its living creatures, and our human bodies. This prevalence of order and design is not diminished when we look into the smallest of worlds that can only be viewed with the use of high-powered microscopes.

Dr. Michael J. Behe, professor of biochemistry at Lehigh University in Pennsylvania, has researched much of the complexity that can found in the microscopic world. In his book Darwin's Black Box, Dr. Behe introduces the term "irreducible complexity," We defined this term previously when describing the defense mechanism of the bombardier beetle. Irreducible complexity applies to any complex machine which cannot function if any of its parts are removed.

Irreducible complexity can be found throughout the microscopic world. One example is the bacterial flagellum. Single-celled bacteria, though extremely small, have the ability to move about freely because of their flagellum, which is a tail-like structure attached to their rear end. The flagellum functions like an outboard motor, propelling the bacteria in various directions. The remarkable thing is that the bacterial flagellum consists of forty different usable parts, all of which are needed for the flagellum to function. These forty necessary parts raise two questions for evolutionists to answer: First, how did the flagellum exist while its motor mechanism was evolving? Second, how did all of these forty separate parts evolve independently of the others into a mechanism

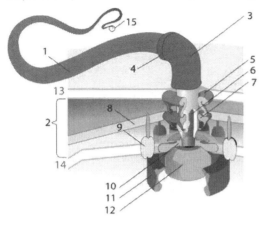

where all of them fit together perfectly to perform their necessary function? What good is a halfway developed part? It has no use until fully developed, and during the developmental stage, there would have to be some kind of pre-set design for evolution to achieve, or the whole evolutionary process would be meaningless. In other words, evolution would have to "know" in advance that it was evolving an item that was useless during the evolution process and would have meaning only when completed. This defies all reason and all logic, for evolution is a blind and random process. Any time you find separate parts fitting together to perform a needed function, there is no way to get around the need for a designer. The design of the flagellum is another example of scientific evidence that confirms God as the Creator of all things.

Dr. Richard Dawkins, an evolutionist and atheist who is very outspoken against creationism and belief in God, has said this about the issue of design:

> "For many years, for many centuries indeed ... you only had to look at living creatures, the sort of magnificent diversity we see in this museum, and everything looks designed. So it was clearly preposterous to suggest that it was due to any kind of freak accident. Darwin came along and showed that it's not actually a freak accident, but nor is it designed. There's a third way

which in the case of biology is evolution by natural selection, which produces a close imitation of something that is designed. It's not designed, we know that now. We understand how it happened, but it looks very designed." [1]

Dawkins acknowledges that living things look as if they were designed. He chooses to take an unsupported leap of faith and believe that living things are not as they appear to be, but rather they are the result of a process that we cannot see happening because it supposedly took place in the prehistoric past. The sensible conclusion is that things that look designed and function like they are designed, are indeed designed!

To learn more about the microscopic world and irreducibly complex systems within that world, you may want to watch the YouTube video at this link:

http://www.youtube.com/watch?v=NaVoGfSSSV8

---

[1] Richard Dawkins, spoken during a debate between Richard Dawkins and John Lennox on October 3, 2007 at the University of Alabama, Birmingham.

"Design Within the Human Cell and DNA Affirms Creation"

Level 7 - The Human Cell

Within the microscopic world, we find the foundational form of life: the cell. Living cells are found in all living things. Plants, insects, animals, and humans are all made of living cells. Even bacteria are a form of a living cell.

In Charles Darwin's time, very little was known about cells. It was assumed that the cell, which constituted life at its most basic form, was a very simple organism. This assumption was partly what brought Darwin to his conclusion that life could evolve from simple to complex forms through mutations and natural selection. Today we know that cells are extremely complex and are ordered by highly sophisticated coded information systems.

After James Watson and Francis Crick discovered the molecular structure of DNA in the 1950s, they came to understand just how complex life is at its most basic form. In fact, Francis Crick wrote in his book Life Itself: Its Origin and Nature of his conclusions that life is too complicated at the cell level to have evolved from non-living substances here on Earth, even if billions of years were a part of the equation. Unfortunately, since Dr. Crick did not believe in God, he came up with another theory of how life may have come to be here on Earth. He proposed a theory called "directed panspermia," which in essence says that highly evolved creatures on another planet somewhere in the universe took the spores of life and sent them on an unmanned spacecraft across the universe to the Earth, thus seeding life upon this planet.

The point here is that even those who believe in evolution recognize that life is extremely complex at its most basic level, and it is highly unlikely that it could have come about from nothing by random processes. It is noteworthy that many who claim that proposing God as the creator of life is unscientific, are willing to accept the idea of life on earth coming from unknown aliens as a valid scientific hypothesis.

Living cells are remarkably complex in their construct and in their various functions.

The human cell in particular is truly fascinating, and its complex design and function gives confirming evidence of a wise Creator.

As we noted above, the human body consists of 60 to 100 trillion cells. Each of these cells is built from the DNA encoded blueprint information existing within the first cell formed after initial fertilization and conception.

How utterly wrong Darwin was about the simplicity of the cell! Each human cell consists of billions of working parts and is like a microscopic city with bustling activity occurring continually. The cell contains manufacturing plants, energy plants, communication systems, a postal system, a transportation department, defense systems, security systems, waste management systems, etc. All of this goes on within each of our 100 trillion cells. You might say that you are a walking universe.

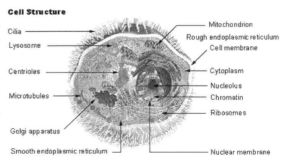

The complexity of each living cell within our body points to a very intelligent designer. The following quote from the Discovery Institute website confirms this:

"Our cells contain incredible complexity, like miniature factories using machine technology but dwarfing the complexity and efficiency of anything produced by humans. Cells use miniature circuits, motors, feedback loops, encoded language, and even error-checking machinery to decode and repair our DNA. Darwinian evolution struggles to build this type of integrated complexity. As biochemist Franklin Harold admits: "there are presently no detailed Darwinian accounts of the evolution of any biochemical or cellular system, only a variety of wishful speculations." [1]

Consider this aspect of life within the cell. On average, each of our 100 trillion cells produces 2,000 proteins per second. That's 200,000 trillion proteins per second. As highly efficient as that is, it is magnified when we consider the process involved in protein synthesis—the production of a single protein.

It begins in the nucleus of the cell where our DNA coded information is found. A section of DNA, called a gene, is unfolded and is copied by an organelle called an RNA polymerase. A start signal and a stop signal assists in this process. The copy of the section of DNA is called an RNA messenger molecule. This newly formed RNA messenger molecule is transported out of the cell nucleus through one of the pores of the nucleus membrane (wall) which are like the gatekeepers of the cell nucleus, determining what is allowed in and out of the cell nucleus.

Once the RNA messenger molecule is outside of the nucleus, it is attached to an organelle called a "ribosome." (Note that a ribosome is made out of eighty-two proteins, which is intriguing since a protein cannot be formed without a ribosome. Think about that!) The ribosome is equipped to accomplish a very important part of protein synthesis. It is here that the language of DNA-coded information is translated into the language of amino acids. In other words, from the coded information within the RNA messenger molecule, a string of amino acids—usually hundreds of amino acids

---

[1] http://www.discovery.org/id/faqs/

long—is formed. (The amount of amino acids and which ones are placed in the string depends upon what protein is being produced.)

Once the string of amino acids is formed, it is moved along by a chaperone molecule into a barrel-shaped organelle in which the string of amino acids will be folded into a protein. The newly formed protein is released into the endoplasmic reticulum and then moved into the Golgi apparatus, which is like the post office of the cell. Here the protein will be placed in a package with other like proteins and labeled for delivery. The package of newly formed proteins is called a vesicle. The vesicle is now ready for delivery to the proper address for its assigned purpose.

Ribosome

Delivery of the vesicle full of proteins is accomplished by motor proteins called "kinesin" which have two arms, two legs, and a body. The kinesin picks up the vesicle and carries it on the highways of the cell called "microtubules" and delivers the protein to its prescribed location for its prescribed purpose.

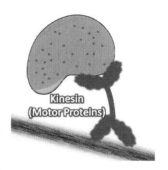

Kinesin
(Motor Proteins)

This is a simplified explanation of the production of one new protein. It is mind boggling to think that this process occurs about 2,000,000,000,000,000,000 times per second in your body. Trillions of kinesin are walking around in you right now carrying newly produced proteins to their prescribed locations. It all happens without you thinking about it, and it is scientific information that clearly indicates that we are created by God.

This is probably the most efficient production and delivery process in the known world. To think that this astounding system could occur by random, accidental chance takes an incredible amount of blind faith. Our hearts should leap with joy and with praise to our Creator as we behold this remarkable process that is occurring within our bodies each second!

The process of energy production within the cell is just about as amazing as protein production. It takes place within other organelles of the cells called "mitochondria." These are the power plants of the cell. There are a great number of mitochondria within each of our cells. Within the membrane folds of mitochondria are tiny rotary motors called "ATP synthase motors." These motors turn at approximately 1,000 rpms and turn ADP molecules, which are like depleted batteries, into ATP molecules, which are like recharged batteries. Three ATP molecules are produced with each rotation of the ATP synthase motor. These ATP molecules are the

Mitochondria

energy source for all the activities taking place within the body. For instance, every step that a kinesin takes uses up one ATP molecule. It is estimated that it would take 125,000 steps for a Kinesin to move one millimeter, so this may give you an idea of how many ATP molecules must be produced for the body to function. It is estimated that each of our cells produce an average of 10 million ATP molecules per second. That is a total of 100 trillion times 10 million per second. We truly are fearfully and wonderfully made.

ATP Synthase Motor
Image – Alex X.-enWiki

Other processes within the human cells are also truly remarkable. For example, the process of white blood cells fighting infections that enter our body is amazing. To see this process explained, you can view a YouTube video with Dr. Georgia Purdom at this link:

http://www.youtube.com/watch?v=nn8GfMGXoso

In my opinion, the human cell is the most convincing evidence within science that confirms that God created us. I like to think of the human cells as "100 Trillion Reasons to Believe in God." I believe every Christian should learn at least the basics about the human cell and the functioning parts of it. It is a great way to strengthen your faith and to enhance your worship of the loving God who created you with such care and thoughtfulness.

To learn more about the human cell and other living cells, I recommend the YouTube videos at the following links:

http://www.youtube.com/watch?v=W5AVOnuP76U
http://www.youtube.com/watch?v=rUV4CSsOHzl
http://www.youtube.com/watch?v=i8c5JcnFaJ0
http://www.youtube.com/watch?v=B_zD3NxSsD8

Level 8 - The Wonders of DNA

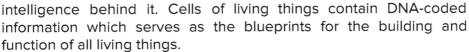

We have been looking at design features of everything from the vast and enormous universe to the microscopic world of the living cell. No matter where we look, we can easily observe design that points to a designer.

In addition to all of these design features all living things contain vast amounts of information that guide the processes involved in their various functions. The existence of information always indicates a source of intelligence behind it. Cells of living things contain DNA-coded information which serves as the blueprints for the building and function of all living things.

The amounts of information found in the tightly wound strands of DNA within our 46 chromosomes is staggering. Bill Gates has been quoted as saying that "DNA is like a computer program but far, far more advanced than any software we've ever created" [2] According to calculations by Leonard Adleman of Los Angeles South California University, just one gram of DNA can contain the amount of data equivalent to the capacity of trillion CDs. [3] Others have estimated that there is enough information in just one pinhead volume of DNA to fill a stack of books from the earth to the moon 500 times.

---

[2] Website "goodreads" – Quotes from the book *The Road Ahead* by Bill Gates.
[3] Article entitled "Scientists Tap DNA to Try and Build 'Perfect Computer'" The Christian Science Monitor (Jan. 13, 2000).

Some evolutionists have pointed to so-called "junk DNA" as evidence that DNA could not have been created by a wise and powerful God. They have said that junk DNA shows that the genetic code is really not that efficient. These arguments have been proven wrong by more recent scientific studies which revealed more and more uses of the so-called junk DNA. The more that scientists learn about the functions of DNA, the more it becomes apparent that it is anything but junk.

Evolutionists have also pointed to the similarities between human DNA and the DNA of chimps as evidence of common ancestry. They have claimed that human DNA and chimp DNA show commonalities of 98 percent. This is highly misleading, because when these comparisons were made, the researchers chose only sections of the genome that they knew to be similar. Dr. Jeffrey P. Tomkins addresses this issue in the following statement:

"For the past several decades, the standard mantra has been that humans are 98 percent genetically identical to chimpanzees. However, this claim is based on cherry-picked data and does not take into account the vastly different regions of the two respective genomes.

Major research published over the past decade comparing human and chimpanzee DNA was recently reviewed and critiqued. In every single publication, researchers only reported on the highly similar DNA sequence data and discarded the rest—apparently because it was too dissimilar. In fact, when the DNA similarities from these studies were recalculated using the omitted data, markedly lower levels—between 81 and 86 percent similarity—were found. Even the well-known chimpanzee genome paper published by evolutionists in 2005 provides a genomic similarity of only about 80 percent when the discarded nonsimilar data are included and only 70 percent when the estimated size of the chimpanzee genome is incorporated." [4]

In the same article, Dr. Tomkins goes on to say, "In reality, many chromosomal regions are vastly different between chimps and humans, and several areas of the genome that are present in chimps are completely absent in humans—and vice versa." [5]

In another article, he explains more about the differences current research is finding between human DNA and chimpanzee DNA. He says,

> "Increasingly, orphan genes defy evolution and support the Genesis account of creation. These genes are unique sets of coding sequences specific to particular creatures. This is a big problem for evolutionary ideas to explain. In a recent research report, scientists describe a new set of 1,307 orphan genes that are completely different between humans and chimpanzees.
>
> Orphan genes, as the name implies, are found in no other type of creature and therefore have no evolutionary history. This finding is another key prediction of the creation model. Not only should creatures have similar code for similar functions, but they should also have unique code that makes them distinct from other creatures. In support of this creation prediction, scientists discovered that orphan genes are incredibly important for specific biological processes and traits that correspond with specialized adaptations." [6]

Understanding that all life is governed by vast amounts of coded information gives us additional evidence that all life has been brought about by an intelligent being. We know this intelligent being

[4] https://www.icr.org/article/7892.
[5] ibid.
[6] http://www.icr.org/article/9145/282/

as God, the Creator of all things.

If you and I were to walk along an ocean beach and saw the words "I love you" scratched into the sand, we would know that someone with intelligence had written that information. Even though  we had not been there to observe a person writing the words, we would be sure that some person had written them. No one could convince us that those words were the result of random waves crashing in upon the shore. The amount of information in those three simple words would be enough to convince us that someone with intelligence had purposely written this message. The amount of coded, usable information in DNA that is contained within every one of our cells should tell us just as clearly that our God, who is intelligent and wise, has given us life and has said to us, "I love you."

Consider another example. We know that the information contained in the instruction manual for repairing a particular type of car was written by intelligent experts who knew everything about the design and function of that car. To think for a moment that these detailed instructions came together through random, undirected processes without a source of intelligence is ludicrous. DNA contains an even more detailed set of blueprints and instructions that guides the building and repairing of all living cells. To think that DNA came into existence through random, 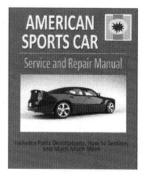 undirected processes without a source of intelligence is at least as ludicrous as thinking a car repair manual had no originator. The existence of DNA is maybe the greatest evidence in the universe of an intelligent, purposeful, and personal Creator.

Summary - Design and Information
We cannot prove that God created everything because it happened in the past and there were no human witnesses. Neither can evolutionists prove that life came about through evolutionary

processes because no one was there to see it happen. What we can do is look at the evidence acquired through scientific observation to determine much about events and their causes in the past. What we find at every level of observation is highly efficient design and astounding amounts of information which confirm the biblical account of a wise, powerful Creator, God.

The chart below gives you a summary of the information presented in these chapters on design. By using this summary and the memorization cards associated with these chapters, you can learn basic information about the scientific evidence that confirms the biblical account of creation. You can then memorize the basic points and utilize this information to strengthen your own faith and that of others, whether they are schoolmates, co-workers, strangers, friends, neighbors, family members, children or grandchildren.

Scientific Evidence Confirming Creation	
Design Features & Usable Information Seen (From Biggest to Smallest)	
B i g g e s t - s m a l l e s t	THE UNIVERSE - FINELY TUNED BY THE LAWS OF PHYSICS (CONSTANTS)
	OUR SOLAR SYSTEM - PRECISELY ORDERED YET DIVERSIFIED
	OUR HOME (EARTH) - MEETS OVER 75 PRECISE PARAMETERS NEEDED TO BE INHABITED
	LIVING CREATURES - EACH SHOW UNIQUE, AMAZING DESIGN FEATURES & ABILITIES
	HUMAN BODY - ENGINEERING MARVEL (SYSTEMS, ORGANS, ETC.)(UNDENIABLY DESIGNED)
	MICROSCOPIC WORLD - INTRIQUITE DESIGN (IRREDUCIBLE COMPLEXITY)
	HUMAN CELLS - TRILLIONS, EACH LIKE A MINIATURE CITY (AMAZINGLY EFFICIENT)
	DNA - VAST AMOUNTS OF USABLE INFORMATION (BLUEPRINTS FOR ALL LIVING THINGS)

To help you remember these points you should remember "from biggest to smallest".

"Six Scientific Flaws in the Theory of Evolution"

Six Scientific Flaws in the Theory of Evolution

The theory of evolution is presented by many as established scientific fact. In reality the claims of Darwinian evolution should be referred to as a hypothesis instead of a theory because there is not enough evidence supporting it to truly label it as a theory. In this chapter we will look at six of the scientific flaws within the proposed ideas of Darwinian evolution. Out of courtesy and to avoid confusion we will refer to it as the theory of evolution as we proceed.

Flaw No. 1:
The Theory of Evolution Violates the
Second Law of Thermodynamics

The theory of evolution holds to the idea that everything we see in the known universe today is the result of a "big bang," a massive explosion that supposedly took place about 13.8 billion years ago. This explanation is inadequate, for it does not answer the question of ultimate origins. Where did the matter and energy come from that caused the big bang? The bigger problem, however, has to do with the events between the proposed big bang and now. How does the big bang account for life and the universe to exist in the forms we observe today? The theory of evolution asserts that matter and energy have developed the great order and complicated systems seen throughout the known universe without any guiding force. This contradicts a scientifically observed principle observed to be so consistent that a scientific law has been established to express it.

The second law of thermodynamics, also referred to as "entropy," states that the amount of usable energy in any closed system always decreases over time. In other words, things wear out; things run down; things move from order to chaos, and nothing develops greater amounts of ordered processes on its own. Observation and common sense also tell us that explosions do not bring  about tremendously sophisticated systems and processes like we see throughout the known universe. No one would ever believe that a jumbo jet airliner was brought about through an explosion in a steel factory. Yet, the human cell, for instance, is much more complicated than a jumbo jet airliner.

To put the contradiction in simple terms, the second law of thermodynamics says the universe is running down and playing out. Evolution says it is winding up and improving. Despite this contradiction, nonbelievers persist in pushing evolution because they need it so desperately as a foundation to their alternative to religion—secular humanism.

Observable examples of entropy include the wearing out or burning down of stars and the deterioration of the human genome.

The second law of thermodynamics, on the other hand, fits perfectly with the Bible's account of the results of sin that not only affected man, but all of creation (Romans 8:19-23).

Flaw No. 2:
The Theory of Evolution Violates the Law of Biogenesis
The law of biogenesis is a proven scientific law which states that life can only come forth from life. In contrast to the law of biogenesis is the idea of "spontaneous generation," which speculates that life can come from non-life. Scientific research by Louis Pasteur and others have proven that spontaneous generation is a false concept. Life has never been observed to have come forth from

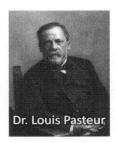

Dr. Louis Pasteur

non-life in any scientific research. Even secular textbooks admit that this is true. Biogenesis obviously contradicts the premise of the theory of evolution, which states that life arose on Earth billions of years ago from non-living material.

Experiments by American chemist Stanley Miller in the 1950s are often referenced to propose that life could have come forth from non-life under certain conditions. Actually, Miller was not successful in bringing forth any living material. He did produce some amino acids under manipulated laboratory conditions, but those acids were both right-handed and left-handed. Only left-handed amino acids can contribute to the bringing about of life. Right-handed amino acids are actually detrimental to life. Brilliant scientists have attempted for decades to produce living materials from non-living materials under carefully controlled conditions without success. Yet we are told that it happened by random, unguided, chance events in the distant past.

The technical term for spontaneous generation is "abiogenesis." According to RationalWiki, "Abiogenesis is the process by which life arises naturally from non-living matter. Scientists speculate that life may have arisen as a result of random chemical processes happening to produce self-replicating molecules." [1] It is worth noting that the RationalWiki site consistently mocks creationists and the Christian faith. It is not surprising, therefore, that the rest of their page on abiogenesis presents a defense for it. Note, however, that this defense is far from scientific, even in its first sentence. It says that "scientists speculate that life may have arisen as a result of random chemical processes happening to produce self-replicating molecules."

Interestingly, the article later makes this statement to separate the problem of biogenesis from the theory of evolution: "Often brought up in the origins debate is how evolution does not explain the origin of life. Let's get something abundantly clear: abiogenesis and evolution are two completely different things. *The theory of evolution says absolutely nothing about the origin of life.* It merely describes the processes which take place once life has

---

[1] http://rationalwiki.org/wiki/Abiogenesis.

started up" (italics added). [2]

It is good to see an admission here that the theory of evolution does not explain the origin of life. But the fact is, evolution is indeed presented that way in classrooms today. Included in textbooks presenting the theory of evolution is the theory of "chemical evolution" which is defined in this way: *"The formation of complex organic molecules from simpler inorganic molecules through chemical reactions* in the oceans during the early history of the Earth; *the first step in the development of life on this planet"* (italics added). [3] "Organic" indicates "living," while "inorganic" indicates "non-living." As they say, you can't have your cake and eat it too. In this case you can't explain the origin of living things by chemical evolution and then avoid the problem of abiogenesis by claiming that the theory of evolution says absolutely nothing about the origin of life.

Even Dr. Francis Crick who with Dr. James Watson won a Nobel Prize in the 1950s for his discovery of DNA, has stated that life in its most basic form of the cell is way too complicated to have evolved on the Earth from non-life. Though he attributed life on earth to the equally irrational theory of "directed panspermia" (which we explained in a previous chapter), he was honest enough to recognize the obvious fact that life could not have developed on Earth from inorganic matter.

---

[2] ibid.
[3] http://www.dictionary.com/browse/chemical-evolution

Flaw No. 3:
The Theory of Evolution Purposefully Confuses
Micro-Evolution with Macro-Evolution

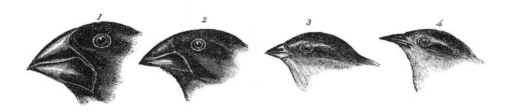

The first example usually cited as evidence for the theory of evolution is Charles Darwin's discovery of finches on the Galapagos Islands whose beaks were observed to have changed under various conditions. These changes ensured their survival by enabling them to obtain food better. This observation was then extrapolated to claim that small changes like those observed in the finches' beaks could accumulate over long periods of time and result in the emergence of a totally new animal. Over 150 years of scientific research since Darwin has consistently shown that living creatures can adapt the shape, size, and color of features within a kind, but there has never been any observation of one kind of creature changing into a different kind. The beaks of the finches that Darwin observed reverted to their original form when weather conditions altered and increased their food supply. Adaptation within a kind is a highly beneficial design feature and is made possible by the genetic information present within each kind of living being. One kind changing into another kind would involve the addition of new genetic information. It is not scientific to suggest that this has taken place in the past, since it has never been observed in scientific research. It is based on pure speculation and assumption.

In his DVD Evolution vs. God, Ray Comfort asks university science students and four university professors to give one scientifically verified example of "one kind changing into a different kind." One professor spoke of a type of stickleback fish which developed certain adaptive characteristics, but remained the same kind of fish. This professor, along with others, spoke of bacteria which adapted to conditions, but were still bacteria. Not one person was able to give a single example in the observed history of science of one kind of living creature changing into another kind of creature.

The Stickleback Fish is a perfect example of how evolutionists use examples of microevolution (adaptation within a kind) in their attempt to prove that macroevolution has occurred. An Internet page dedicated to this subject can be found at http://learn.genetics.utah.edu/content/selection/stickleback/

On this page, the survival and multiplication in freshwater lakes of freshwater sticklebacks is cited as modern day proof of the theory of evolution. Freshwater sticklebacks have less protective armor 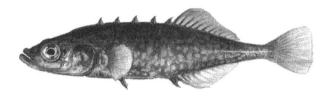 plates covering their bodies but grow faster and move quicker, compared to their ocean-dwelling cousins, which have more protective armor plates covering their bodies. After discussion about the details of the observed survival tendencies in the sticklebacks, the page presents a section entitled "Studying Sticklebacks to Understand Evolution.". A highlighted box is found in this section that expresses the following:

MISCONCEPTION
Evolution may have happened in the past, but it is no longer happening today.

REALITY
Scientists observe evolution in progress today.

Here you can see a classic example of purposely using a case of microevolution (adaptation within a kind) to claim that we are observing macroevolution (one kind of creature turning into a totally different kind of creature). I would encourage you to look at this article online. It shows clearly the weakness of the examples used to support the theory of evolution.

High school and college biology textbooks regularly use examples of microevolution to convince students that macroevolution has occurred. The peppered moth is another frequently used example. Light colored peppered moths have been shown to survive better on trees with lighter colored bark, and dark colored peppered moths have been shown to survive better when soot from factories darkened the trees. When the trees no longer are covered by soot and become lighter again, the darker moths don't fare as well. It is easy to see that this example has nothing to do with macroevolution, yet it is still cited as support for it in textbooks today.

The fact that textbooks, teachers, and professors must consistently point to examples of adaptation within a kind to attempt to prove macroevolution is good evidence that they have no examples of macroevolution. If they had such examples, they would use them. They don't have them because they don't exist.

Flaw No. 4:
The Theory of Evolution Contradicts What is Found in the Fossil Record

The fossil record is critical to understanding the Earth's history, particularly to learn what creatures have lived upon the Earth in the past.

When Darwin proposed the theory of evolution, he knew that fossils had not been found to confirm the evolutionary process of one kind of creature changing into another kind. He attributed this lack of evidence to the fact that fossil exploration was a new branch of science. He thought that continued research in the coming years would confirm his theory by the discovery of many "transitional forms" showing creatures in the process of evolving from one kind to another. He acknowledged that if these transitional forms were not found, his theory would be invalid. In his book On the Origin of Species, Darwin writes the following in chapter 9, which is entitled "On the Imperfection of the Geological Record."

> "The several difficulties here discussed, namely our not finding in the successive formations infinitely numerous transitional links between the many species which now exist or have existed; the sudden manner in which whole groups of species appear in our European formations; the almost entire absence, as at present known, of fossiliferous formations beneath the Silurian strata, are all undoubtedly of the gravest nature." [4]

Over 150 years of fossil discoveries since that time have proven that the fossil record is void of transitional forms. If Darwin's theory were true, transitional fossils should be present by the millions. There are a few disputed samples of supposed transitional forms, such as the "archaeopteryx," which was supposedly a link between reptiles and birds, and "Lucy," which was supposedly a link between apes and humans. "Archaeopteryx" is now known to have been a bird and "Lucy" an ape. These are not transitional forms. In some instances, supposed transitional forms have actually been found to be frauds such as "Piltdown Man", probably the most famous fossil fraud ever, and the famous Triceratops dinosaur fossil at the National Museum of Natural History, Smithsonian Institution. The Triceratops fossil was eventually revealed to be composed of

---

[4] Charles Darwin, "*On Origin of Species By Means of Natural Selection*", D. Appleton and Company, 1859, p.271

the bones of 14 different animals.

The late Dr. Colin Patterson, was the senior paleontologist (fossil expert) at the prestigious British Museum of Natural History. After Dr. Patterson had written a book entitled Evolution, creationist Luther Sunderland wrote to him inquiring why he had not shown one single photograph of a transitional fossil in his book. Patterson wrote back with the following amazing confession which was reproduced in its entirety in Sunderland's book Darwin's Enigma:

> "I fully agree with your comments on the lack of direct illustration of evolutionary transitions in my book. If I knew of any, fossil or living, I would certainly have included them. You suggest that an artist should be used to visualize such transformations, but where would he get the information from? I could not, honestly, provide it, and if I were to leave it to artistic license, would that not mislead the reader?" [5]

In 1979 Dr. David Raup, a Paleontologist with the University of Chicago wrote this very telling statement about the lack of transitional fossils in the fossil record.

> "Well, we are now about 120 years after Darwin and the knowledge of the fossil record has been greatly expanded ... The record of evolution is still surprisingly jerky and, ironically, we have even fewer examples of evolutionary transition than we had in Darwin's time. ... some of the classic cases of Darwinian change in the fossil record ... have had to be discarded or modified as a result of more detailed information." [6]

The fossil record actually shows a sudden development of life forms on the Earth, some of which are now extinct, many of which are found in the same form today. Some evolutionists try to explain

---

[5] http://creation.com/that-quote-about-the-missing-transitional-fossils
[6] D. Raup, "Conflicts Between Darwin and Paleontology," Field Museum of Natural History Bulletin 50(1), 1979, p.25.

the lack of transitional fossils by pointing to the fact that fossils are difficult to form. Living creatures must be buried very quickly at the time of death so that they do not deteriorate before becoming a fossil. This explanation points to another problem for the theory of evolution. The fact that there are fossils in rock layers reveals that these rock layers were

Image by Dr. Steve Austin

formed very quickly, not gradually over millions of years. Fossils of marine creatures are found near the tops of mountains in some cases, showing evidence for the global flood recorded in Genesis 6–8. Examination of the areas around Mt. St. Helen after its catastrophic eruption show with certainty that rock layers can be formed in days, even in hours.

The fossil record and the rock layers that fossils are found in solidly contradict the theory of evolution and confirm the accounts of the Bible.

Flaw No. 5:
The Theory of Evolution Contradicts the Fact That Mutations Do Not Generate Increased Amounts of Genetic Information

The theory of evolution states that living creatures have evolved from one stage to another through the process of beneficial mutations, which are chosen by natural selection, enabling the fittest creatures to survive and reproduce. In short the process is described in this way: Mutations

MUTATIONS

occur through errors in the copying of DNA (genetic) information during the reproduction of living things. When these mutations bring about an advantage in life, the living thing acquiring the advantage survives better than similar living things without the mutational advantage. This explains that common evolutionary phrase we've all heard, "the survival of the fittest." Those creatures made fittest by mutations mate with each other ("natural selection") and pass along to their offspring the newly gained mutational advantage. This process is then multiplied in tiny increments over millions and billions of years, allowing for the formation of more sophisticated forms of life as time moves on.

It might be a nice story, but it has some major problems from a scientific point of view. Actual research has shown that mutations are almost always detrimental, not beneficial. In an article on mutations, Barney Maddox, M.D. states,

> "The underlying genetic mechanism of evolution is random mutation, and specifically mutation that is beneficial to life. Biology textbooks in theory present positive and negative mutations to students as though these were commonplace and roughly equal in number. However, these books fail to inform students that unequivocally positive mutations are unknown to genetics, since they have never been observed (or are so rare as to be irrelevant)." [7]

Dr. Maddox goes on to speak about the examples of mutations that evolutionists sometimes point to as being beneficial. Writing about bacteria that through a mutation become resistant to antibiotics, he says,

> "In bacteria, several mutations in cell wall proteins may deform the proteins enough so that antibiotics cannot bind to the mutant bacteria. This creates bacterial resistance to that antibiotic. Does this support

---

[7] http://www.icr.org/article/mutations-raw-material-for-evolution/

evolutionary genetic theory? No, since the mutant bacteria do not survive as well in the wild as the native (non-mutant) bacteria. That is, the resistant (mutant) bacteria will only do well in an artificial situation, where it is placed in a culture medium with the antibiotic. Only then can it overgrow at the expense of the native bacteria. In the wild, the native bacteria are always more vigorous than the mutant bacteria." [8]

Evolutionists often point to one mutation in humans that they say is beneficial. This example, strangely, is sickle cell anemia, which they claim makes those afflicted with it more resistant to malaria. Concerning this claim, Dr. Maddox points out the obvious. I won't give the quote because it is quite technical but simply stated he refers to the fact that sickle cell anemia is a deadly disease. Though it may prevent malaria in specific environments it causes great devastation for those affected by it. It certainly does not show itself to be beneficial.

I'm amazed that evolutionists would point to such a terrible disease as an example of a beneficial mutation. To say that sickle cell anemia is beneficial because it resists malaria is like saying death is beneficial because it prevents further diseases. I personally have seen the devastation caused by sickle cell anemia. During my years of pastoring, a family from Africa began to attend our church. They had a teenage son who had sickle cell anemia. He was a wonderful young man, and he and I developed a good friendship. He lived in a wheelchair and often spent days at a time in the hospital before he died at a very young age. It was heart-wrenching to see the pain and difficulty that sickle cell anemia brought to this young man.

To use such a terrible disease as an example of a beneficial mutation shows how desperately lacking evolutionists are in true evidence to support their claims.

Another piece of scientific evidence that is contrary to evolution's ideas about beneficial mutations is the fact that the

---

[8] ibid.

human genome is deteriorating from generation to generation. This is not surprising from a biblical worldview, because the Bible speaks of the deterioration that is a result of man's sin. But this fact creates another problem for evolutionists. It reveals the opposite of what would be expected if evolution were occurring as a result of the accumulation of beneficial genetic mutations.

Dr. John C. Sanford, well-known scientist, Courtesy Associate Professor at Cornell University, plant geneticist, and inventor of the "gene gun," is an expert in the human genome. He has said,

> "This generally accepted fact of modern science strongly implies, therefore, that we have devolved, not evolved, from an originally superior state, as a species or collective gene pool, compared to our current rapidly degenerating condition. We are all heading downhill, genetically, very rapidly in fact." [9]

Even the small percentages of those mutations that show any type of benefit do not involve additional genetic (DNA) information. The mutation is caused by missing genetic information. For simple living creatures to evolve into more and more complex creatures would require a continual increase of genetic information not previously present in that kind of living thing.

Flaw No. 6:
The Theory of Evolution Contradicts the Order, Beauty, Design and Information that is Observed Throughout the Known Universe
Evolutionists offer various explanations for the order, beauty, design, and information observed throughout the universe, but the fact remains that everything we observe appears to be designed. Even the outspoken atheist, Richard Dawkins, has said, "Biology is the

[9]http://www.educatetruth.com/featured/dr-john-sanford-lectures-on-inevitable-genomic-deterioration/

study of complicated things that have the appearance of having been designed with a purpose." [10]

It is inconsistent to assume that things which display superb design features are not designed. We can choose to assume that this is the case, but it is not an assumption based on actual evidence. When we see design features in machines, languages, buildings, electronics, etc., we do not question the presence of a designer. We see the same type of design features in living things and the vastness of the universe, so it is very strange to deny that they too are the products a designer. It should be clear to an unbiased, rational observer that random, unguided processes could not account for anything in our highly ordered universe.

Information always points to a source of intelligence. The fact that we can clearly see vast amounts of information involved in the foundational structures of living creatures absolutely necessitates the presence of an intelligent designer. To deny this is to deny both common sense and the scientific method.

Design features, ordered processes, beauty, and great amounts of information can be found in the microscopic world, in plant life, in living creatures of all types and sizes, in the function of the Earth, in the ordered solar system, and even in the vastness of the universe around us. Nowhere is there even a slight indication of random, unguided processes.

Not All Scientists Believe in Evolution

The notion that all scientists believe in the theory of evolution is simply not true. Many scientists openly deny the validity of the theory. There are many more who privately do not believe in evolution but do not openly express their denial because of the pressures placed upon them by peers and institutions they work for. Ben Stein, in his 2008 movie Expelled, No Intelligence Allowed, gives an account of the occupational pressures placed on teachers and professors, pressing them to toe the line when it comes to the teaching of evolution. The same type of pressure is faced by scientists who rely upon institutions of higher learning for their

---

[10] http://www.brainyquote.com/quotes/authors/r/richard_dawkins.html

source of work and income. There are also a large number of scientists who do not totally reject the theory of evolution but are skeptical of its claims.

The claim that virtually all scientist believe in evolution is one of the intimidation tactics used to defend Darwinism, since true evidence to support the theory is lacking. Richard Dawkins is one of the intimidators. He asserts in one of his books that, "no qualified scientist doubts that evolution is a fact." [11] Dawkin's claim reveals how apart from reality ardent supporters of the theory of evolution can be. Compare his assertion that no qualified scientist doubts

evolution with the information found on the website, A Scientific Dissent from Darwinism.

The Discovery Institute established this website, which is dedicated to displaying a list of scientists who are skeptical of the claims of the theory of evolution. (See http://www.dissentfromdarwin.org/) All the scientists listed on the website have attested to the following statement, which is displayed on the website:

> ### A Scientific Dissent from Darwinism
> *"We are skeptical of claims for the ability of random mutation and natural selection to account for the complexity of life. Careful examination of the evidence for Darwinian theory should be encouraged."* [12]

Here is a quote from the website defining its purpose:

> "The statement was drafted and circulated by Discovery Institute in 2001 in response to widespread claims that no credible scientists existed who doubted Neo-Darwinism. Discovery Institute subsequently took

---

[11] Richard Dawkins, *"A Devil's Chaplain"*, Boston: Houghton Mifflin, 2003, p. 220.
[12] http://www.dissentfromdarwin.org/faq/

out an ad in The New York Review of Books and elsewhere showcasing over 100 scientists who were willing to publicly express their scientific skepticism of Neo-Darwinism. Since 2001 the signatories of the statement have grown to over 800 scientists, both in the United States and around the world." [13]

The list can be downloaded in a PDF format. It appears that the updated list, as of July, 2017, now includes nearly 1,000 scientists. It includes scientists from the US National Academy of Sciences, Russian, Hungarian, and Czech National Academies, as well as from universities such as Yale, Princeton, Stanford, MIT, UC Berkeley, UCLA, and other prominent institutions.

In another statement concerning the purpose for creating the list, the website states:

> "During recent decades, new scientific evidence from many scientific disciplines such as cosmology, physics, biology, "artificial intelligence" research, and others have caused scientists to begin questioning Darwinism's central tenet of natural selection and studying the evidence supporting it in greater detail. Yet public TV programs, educational policy statements, and science textbooks have asserted that Darwin's theory of evolution fully explains the complexity of living things. The public has been assured that all known evidence supports Darwinism and that virtually every scientist in the world believes the theory to be true." [14]

Here is an example of why many scientists seriously doubt the claims of the theory of evolution. This quote is by Chris Williams, Ph.D., a biochemist at Ohio State University:

> "As a biochemist and software developer who works in

---

[13] http://www.dissentfromdarwin.org/about/
[14] ibid.

genetic and metabolic screening, I am continually amazed by the incredible complexity of life. For example, each of us has a vast "computer program" of six billion DNA bases in every cell that guided our development from a fertilized egg, specifies how to make more than 200 tissue types, and ties all this together in numerous highly functional organ systems. Few people outside of genetics or biochemistry realize that evolutionists still can provide no substantive details at all about the origin of life, and particularly the origin of genetic information in the first self-replicating organism. What genes did it require — or did it even have genes? How much DNA and RNA did it have — or did it even have nucleic acids? How did huge information-rich molecules arise before natural selection? Exactly how did the genetic code linking nucleic acids to amino acid sequence originate? Clearly the origin of life — the foundation of evolution — is still virtually all speculation, and little if no fact." [15]

It is easy to see that not all scientists believe in the theory of evolution. As was the case in the pioneering days of modern science, many scientists today are Christians, or at least theists. They approach science with the mindset that because the universe is created by an intelligent person, they can expect it to be intelligible and consistent. Creation and true science are actually very good companions. We must always be diligent to differentiate between science and the intimidating propaganda of secular humanism and atheism that attempts to masquerade as science.

Summary: Scientific Problems with the Theory of Evolution
Below is a summary of the information found in this chapter that coincides with the six memorization cards for the chapter. Use the summary and the memorization cards to retain the main points of the chapter for use in strengthening your faith and helping others to understand the fatal flaws in the theory of evolution.

---

[15] http://www.dissentfromdarwin.org/scientists/

Scientific Flaws in the Theory of Evolution
(These 6 Flaws do not Constitute a Complete List of Flaws That Can be Seen)

Scientific Contradictions	
	1. CONTRADICTS THE 2ND LAW OF THERMODYNAMICS (ENTROPY)(ORDER TO CHAOS)
	2. CONTRADICTS THE LAW OF BIO-GENESIS (SPONTANEOUS GENERATION IS NOT SCIENTIFIC)
	3. CONFUSES 'MICROEVOLUTION' (SEEN) WITH 'MACROEVOLUTION' (NEVER SEEN)
	4. CONTRADICTS THE FOSSIL RECORD - (TRANSITIONAL FORMS NOT FOUND)
	5. MUTATIONS DO NOT ADD GENETIC INFORMATION & ARE ALMOST ALWAYS HARMFUL
	6. CONTRADICTS BEAUTY, ORDER & DESIGN SEEN EVERYWHERE IN THE UNIVERSE
	NOTE TO REMEMBER - NOT ALL SCIENTISTS BELIEVE IN THE THEORY OF EVOLUTION

THE FLAWS OF THE THEORY OF Evolution

1 – The Theory of Evolution Violates the 2nd Law of Thermodynamics

The amount of usable energy in any closed system always decreases
(Things move from order to chaos, Not from chaos to order)
("Entropy")

 THE FLAWS OF THE THEORY OF Evolution

2 – The Theory of Evolution Violates the Law of Bio-Genesis

Life only comes from life!
The idea of "spontaneous generation" which is life coming from non-life has been tested and proven to be false!

 THE FLAWS OF THE THEORY OF Evolution

3 – The Theory of Evolution Purposely Confuses Micro-Evolution w/Macro Evolution (New Kind)

Micro-Evolution (adaptation within a kind) can be observed & verified scientifically.
Macro-Evolution (one kind evolving into a new kind) has <u>never</u> been observed in nature or by scientific discovery!

THE FLAWS OF THE THEORY OF Evolution

4 – The Theory of Evolution Contradicts The Fossil Record

If the theory of evolution were true the fossil record would be filled with "transitional" life forms. It is not!
Also, fossils found in rock layers give evidence that rock layers were formed quickly!

 THE FLAWS OF THE THEORY OF Evolution

5 – The Theory of Evolution Contradicts the fact that Mutations Do Not Bring Increased Genetic Information!

For more complex life forms to evolve from simpler life forms an increase of genetic information would be needed. Mutations are the result of missing genetic information!

 THE FLAWS OF THE THEORY OF Evolution

6 – The Theory of Evolution contradicts the Order, Design, Beauty & Information we observe in the Universe!

Everywhere from the vast universe, to the planet earth, to the living creatures we observe, to the microscopic world & the human cell we observe tremendous amounts of order, design, beauty & information!

(Above) Six scientific flaws of the theory of Evolution are summarized on these memorization cards to assist you in retaining the essential information from this chapter.

Memorization Cards Available for Free Download at localchurchapologetics.org

"Understanding Human History"

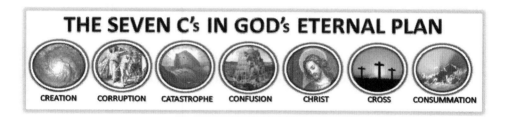

THE SEVEN C's IN GOD's ETERNAL PLAN

CREATION   CORRUPTION   CATASTROPHE   CONFUSION   CHRIST   CROSS   CONSUMMATION

Understanding Human History

Because the Bible is the inspired Word of God, it is useful in many more ways than just as a textbook to learn moral values and how to get to heaven. The Bible is also a book of history, giving us many answers to questions we often ask about why things are the way they are in today's world. God's plans and purposes revealed in the Bible are consistent with the reality we observe in the world. In this chapter we will present an overview of world history from a biblical perspective, using an easy-to-remember alliterative arrangement labeled "The Seven Cs of History." The seven Cs are Creation, Corruption, Catastrophe, Confusion, Christ, Cross, and Consummation." **(The contents and graphic ideas of this chapter are taken from materials developed by "Answers in Genesis". There are no memorization cards associated with this chapter.)**

The Bible – Inspired by God

- Explains Origins & History of the Universe
- Reveals Purpose
- Explains Suffering, Disease, Evil, Death
- Explains Geology & Paleontology
- Explains Anthropology
- Reveals God's Love & Plans
- Brings Hope For Salvation & Eternity
- **Answers Key Questions** about life, man, the earth, suffering, the future, etc.

---

1. Creation: The Beginning

The first of our seven Cs is Creation. The basic point of this section as it relates to our study of apologetics is the biblical assertion that God is the Creator of all that exists. He created everything in perfect form and set it into flawless operation. Below are several key Scriptures that reveal various aspects of this basic truth.

> *Genesis 1:1: In the beginning God created the heavens and the earth.*

> *Genesis 1:31: God saw all that He had made, and behold, it was very good. And there was evening and there was morning, the sixth day.*

> *John 1:1-3: In the beginning was the Word, and the Word was with God, and the Word was God. (2) He was in the beginning with God. (3) All things came*

into being through Him, and apart from Him nothing came into being that has come into being.

Colossians 1:15-17: For by Him all things were created, both in the heavens and on earth, visible and invisible, whether thrones or dominions or rulers or authorities--all things have been created through Him and for Him. (17) He is before all things, and in Him all things hold together.

Hebrews 1:1-2: God, after He spoke long ago to the fathers in the prophets in many portions and in many ways, (2) in these last days has spoken to us in His Son, whom He appointed heir of all things, through whom also He made the world.

Romans 1:20: For since the creation of the world His invisible attributes, His eternal power and divine nature, have been clearly seen, being understood through what has been made, so that they are without excuse.

In addition to the basic fact that God created all things, Scripture teaches us many other important truths about creation that explain things we observe today.

• The Habitable Earth: The world was created to be inhabited. (Isaiah 45:18).
• The Expanding Universe: God made the Earth as a sphere, and the heavens are expanding (Isaiah 40:22).

• Our Personal God: He revealed Himself to us (Romans 1). He formed us, knows us, and is involved in our lives (Psalm 139).
• Man is Unique: He is created in God's image and likeness and derives his

dominion, value, and purpose from God. He is endowed with creativity, emotion, intellect, imagination, love, conscience, and will (Genesis 1:26-28; 2:15-17).
• Sexuality and Marriage: Marriage is valid only between one man and one woman (Genesis 2:21-25).
• Origins of Kinds and Species: God created animals to reproduce consistently "after their kind" (Genesis 1:21-25).
• Apostasy: Romans 1:18-32 explains what will happen to any people who deny God as Creator, as we see happening today in America.
• Jesus Christ is the Agent of Creation: By Him all things are made (John 1:2-3).

2. Corruption: The Fall

The second of the seven Cs stands for Corruption. This speaks of man's fall away from God and into sin. God had warned Adam that disobedience (sin) would bring death. Yet Adam sinned, and spiritual death, which is separation of our spirit from God's Spirit, happened immediately. Physical death, which is separation of our spirit from our body, became inevitable. Because God had given man dominion over all the Earth, his sin impacted not only himself, but also the creation around him. Romans 8 speaks of the corruption that has come upon all of creation because of man's sin. When we see the second law of thermodynamics (entropy) in full operation today, we are seeing exactly what the Bible tells us we should expect to see. We are seeing the inevitable result of the fall of man.

The following Scriptures give us a quick overview of the fall and its still reverberating consequences.

Genesis 2:16-17: The LORD God commanded the man, saying, "From any tree of the garden you may eat freely; (17) but from the tree of the knowledge of good and evil you shall not eat, for in the day that you eat from it you will surely die."

Romans 5:12: Therefore, just as through one man sin entered into the world, and death through sin, and so death spread to all men, because all sinned.

Romans 8:19-23: For the anxious longing of the creation waits eagerly for the revealing of the sons of God. (20) For the creation was subjected to futility, not willingly, but because of Him who subjected it, in hope (21) that the creation itself also will be set free from its slavery to corruption into the freedom of the glory of the children of God. (22) For we know that the whole creation groans and suffers the pains of childbirth together until now. (23) And not only this, but also we ourselves, having the first fruits of the Spirit, even we ourselves groan within ourselves, waiting eagerly for our adoption as sons, the redemption of our body.

All around us in today's world, we see clear evidence of the truth of these Scriptures. Things go wrong all the time; pain, disease, grief, death, strife, and disasters, both natural and man-made, are daily parts of our environment. For confirmation of this truth, we need only observe the following facts:

• **The Second Law of Thermodynamics:** The entropy principle confirms that everything is running down, moving from order to chaos, and inevitably deteriorating. Even our genome (genetic information) is deteriorating with each generation.
• **The "Law of the Jungle":** Man without God becomes self-centered and motivated only by what brings him satisfaction, even at the expense of others. This creates dishonesty, strife, wars, estrangement, hate, crime, and rebellion.
• **Man's Personal Problems:** The daily lives of humans are filled with stress, despair, hopelessness, lack of purpose, and futility. These factors lead to anger, relationship breakdown, drug, alcohol, cigarette, and pornography addictions, infidelity, sexual promiscuity and the resulting diseases, and suicides.

• **The Suffering in the World:** Diseases, natural disasters, man-made disasters, pain, death, and grief are all attributable to the effects on the Earth caused by the fall of man.

• **Man's Sinful Flesh:** The above conditions that we face daily make it clear that something has gone wrong with the nature of mankind. Other worldviews promoted today, saying that man is basically good and improving, do not match the reality we observe. Only the fall and its resulting corruption of man's nature account for the clear reality observable around us, as the following Scriptures affirm:

> ***James 1:13-15:** Let no one say when he is tempted, "I am being tempted by God"; for God cannot be tempted by evil, and He Himself does not tempt anyone. (14) But each one is tempted when he is carried away and enticed by his own lust. (15) Then when lust has conceived, it gives birth to sin; and when sin is accomplished, it brings forth death.*

> ***1 Peter 2:11:** Beloved, I urge you as aliens and strangers to abstain from fleshly lusts which wage war against the soul.*

While man bears total responsibility for his fall, we must not discount the evil influence of our spiritual enemy, Satan, who tempted man and whose influence still operates in today's world. For further study on the topic of Satan and his evil, see the following Scriptures: Genesis 3:1-6; Isaiah 14:12-15; Ezekiel 28:11-19; Revelation 12:3-12; Ephesians 6:10-18.

3. Catastrophe: The Flood

The third C represents Catastrophe, which speaks of the flood that God brought upon the entire world as recorded in Genesis 6–9. Genesis 6:5 tells us that God sent the flood as judgment upon the sinfulness and wickedness of mankind:

> *Genesis 6:5 Then the LORD saw that the wickedness of man was great on the earth, and that every intent of the thoughts of his heart was only evil continually.*

Because man had been given dominion over all the world, much more than just human life was impacted by the flood judgment. Almost all living creatures, except those that could live under water, were impacted. The earth itself was also impacted. All around the world today geological structures bear the imprint of the flood.

Challenges to the validity of the biblical account of the flood reflect an inadequate understanding of it. The Bible makes it clear that the flood was not merely the result of forty days of rain upon the earth. It says that "all the fountains of the great deep burst open, and the floodgates of the sky were opened" (Genesis 7:11).

Contrary to the claims of skeptics, the ark was large enough to house all the animals the Bible says it carried. Noah did not have to take two of every species of animal, but rather two of every kind. For example, He would have taken two of the dog kind, not two of every species of dogs. The genetic information for all the different species of modern dogs would have been inherent in those original dogs. The ark was also very seaworthy in design. The ratio of its dimensions are used today by many shipbuilders.

Peter wrote that in the last days, mockers would scoff at the second coming of Christ, treating that future event as a fantasy in the same category as the flood, which they do not believe ever occurred.

2 Peter 3:3-6: Know this first of all, that in the last days mockers will come with their mocking, following after their own lusts, (4) and saying, "Where is the promise of His coming? For ever since the fathers fell asleep, all continues just as it was from the beginning of creation." (5) For when they maintain this, it escapes their notice that by the word of God the heavens existed long ago and the earth was formed out of water and by water, (6) through which the world at that time was destroyed, being flooded with water.

Peter's prophecy has come to pass. Many people today deny the occurrence of the flood despite the abundant evidence of it seen in sedimentary rock layers and fossils all around the world. The massive pressures caused by the eruption of the "fountains of the deep" explain many of the tilts, fissures, and convolutions of rock layers everywhere. Those pressures explain the Grand Canyon, the tectonic movement of the continents, the  existence of marine fossils on mountaintops, and even the formation of many valleys and mountains. The eruption of Mt. St. Helens in 1980 and the resulting "mini-grand canyon" formed within days confirms that the global flood described in the Bible could certainly have brought about the formation of the Grand Canyon and other sedimentary rock layers around the world.

Image by Dr. Steve Austin

The flood also explains a lot about the results of sin and the coming judgment that is nearing as the culture of the world moves further and further from God—just as they did in the days of Noah.

194

4. Confusion: The Tower of Babel

The fourth C stands for Confusion and refers to the historical account of the Tower of Babel in Genesis 11:1-9. Here we see mankind again in rebellion against God, proclaiming that they will "build a tower to reach into heaven." Why was this pursuit so displeasing to God? It was an act of rebellion against Him. The tower was to be a citadel of self-government independent of God, drawing all men together under human rule. God quelled the rebellion by dividing their single language into many, and the resulting mass confusion ended tower construction and forced men to separate from one another throughout the world. Much of what we understand of anthropology today can be related to the events found in Genesis chapter 11.

> *Genesis 11:7-9: "Come, let Us go down and there confuse their language, so that they will not understand one another's speech." (8) So the LORD scattered them abroad from there over the face of the whole earth; and they stopped building the city. (9) Therefore its name was called Babel, because there the LORD confused the language of the whole earth; and from there the LORD scattered them abroad over the face of the whole earth.*

It is interesting that the Hebrew word for "Babel" is the same as for "Babylon." There is no difference. It is translated Babel only here in Genesis 11 and once in Genesis 10, where Babel is said to have been the beginning of the kingdom of Nimrod, who is called "a mighty hunter before the Lord." Every other time this Hebrew word is used in Scripture it is translated "Babylon" or "Babylonians." In the book of Revelation, chapters 17-18, we see that the kingdoms of men who will rise up together to oppose the second coming of Christ, and who have filled the world with wickedness, are referred to again as "Babylon." It is not hard to see this same independent, rebellious attitude or spirit that was present at Babel at work again today.

The many people groups and languages throughout the world today are explained by the confusing of the languages in Genesis 11. Again, we can see that the biblical account and the characteristics of the real world around us today fit together perfectly.

There may also be an explanation of the separate continents and land masses present today in the Bible's reference to the Days of Peleg. Peleg means "division."

Genesis 10:25: Two sons were born to Eber; the name of the one was Peleg, for in his days the earth was divided; and his brother's name was Joktan.

There are varying view on this point. Some believe the separation spoken of here may just be a reference to the separation of language and people groups, while others believe it refers to the separation of land masses, which they think occurred about 100 years after the flood.

What occurred at Babel certainly explains the numerous people groups and languages in the world today. Note the following:

The reference book "Ethnologue" (20th Edition) lists over 6,900 living languages extant today. Of these, about half are spoken by less than 10,000 people, and about a quarter of them are spoken by less than 1,000 people. [1]

As a side note, it is interesting that the earliest known written alphabets are said to have originated about 4,000 to 5,000 years ago. That happens to be just about the time of the flood and the tower of Babel. Interesting! [2]

---

[1] http://www.education.rec.ri.cmu.edu/fire/naclo/pages/Ling/Fact/num-languages.html
[2] http://www.ancient.eu/alphabet/

5. Christ: The Messiah

The fifth of the seven Cs stands for Christ, who has impacted all of human history by His coming to the Earth to be the substitutionary sacrifice for man's sin. In the first few pages of the Bible we find the first prophecy of his coming:

> **Genesis 3: 14-15: The LORD God said to the serpent, "Because you have done this, Cursed are you more than all cattle, And more than every beast of the field; On your belly you will go, And dust you will eat All the days of your life; And I will put enmity Between you and the woman, And between your seed and her seed; He shall bruise you on the head, and you shall bruise him on the heel."**

The Old Testament pointed to Christ in many ways through types, shadows, and prophetic words. Isaiah prophesied Christ's coming in this well-known passage:

> **Isaiah 9:6-7: For a child will be born to us, a son will be given to us; And the government will rest on His shoulders; And His name will be called Wonderful Counselor, Mighty God, Eternal Father, Prince of Peace. There will be no end to the increase of His government or of peace, On the throne of David and over his kingdom, To establish it and to uphold it with justice and righteousness From then on and forevermore. The zeal of the LORD of hosts will accomplish this.**

In the New Testament the heavenly proclamation at the Birth of Jesus Christ confirms the significance of His coming.

> **Luke 2:10-14: But the angel said to them, "Do not be afraid; for behold, I bring you good news of great joy**

which will be for all the people; (11) for today in the city of David there has been born for you a Savior, who is Christ the Lord. (12) "This will be a sign for you: you will find a baby wrapped in cloths and lying in a manger." (13) And suddenly there appeared with the angel a multitude of the heavenly host praising God and saying, (14) "Glory to God in the highest, And on earth peace among men with whom He is pleased."

John 3:16 reveals the reason behind His coming. ***"God so loved the world that He gave His only begotten Son"***

John 1 speaks of who Jesus Christ is and says much about His attributes, including His preexistence, His deity, His role as Creator and as the giver of life and light. It also speaks of His incarnation, rejection, and limited reception.

John 20:31: But these have been written so that you may believe that Jesus is the Christ, the Son of God; and that believing you may have life in His name.

Jesus Christ is the central point of all history. Our measurement of time itself is based on the moment of His birth, with every event prior to it labeled BC (or BCE) and every event subsequent labeled AD (or CE).

6. Cross: The Sacrifice for Redemption

The sixth C stands for Cross and points to the sacrifice of Christ that brought redemption and reconciliation to a world separated from God by sin with no hope of salvation. No event in history has impacted the world like the birth of Christ, His death upon the cross for our sin, and His resurrection from the dead. Evidence of the impact is seen in the testimonies of millions of people around the world. History shows that entire nations have been impacted for good when the good news about Jesus Christ was proclaimed and accepted.

The Old Testament sacrifices were symbolic types, or acted-out analogies that pointed to an ultimate sacrifice for sin that was yet to come. Some celebrations and events also pointed to Christ's coming redemption, such as Passover (Exodus 12) and the serpent in the wilderness (Numbers 21). Isaiah spoke of the sacrifice for sin that Christ would make in this passage:

> ***Isaiah 53:3-6: He was despised and forsaken of men, A man of sorrows and acquainted with grief; And like one from whom men hide their face He was despised, and we did not esteem Him. Surely our griefs He Himself bore, And our sorrows He carried; Yet we ourselves esteemed Him stricken, Smitten of God, and afflicted. But He was pierced through for our transgressions, He was crushed for our iniquities; The chastening for our well-being fell upon Him, and by His scourging we are healed. All of us like sheep have gone astray, Each of us has turned to his own way; But the LORD has caused the iniquity of us all To fall on Him.***

John 1:29 proclaims, ***"Behold the Lamb of God who takes away the sin of the world."*** John 10:17-18 says that He laid down His life voluntarily and that He will rise again. In 1 Peter 3:18 we read that ***"Christ also died for sins once for all, the just for the unjust, so that He might bring us to God."***

The Gospels tell of His crucifixion and resurrection. History confirms both events. Hebrews 2:14 tells us that by His death, Jesus has destroyed him who had the power of death, that is the devil.

The book of Hebrews explains that Jesus would not sacrifice the blood of bulls or goats, as did the Old Testament priests, but He would sacrifice of His own blood on our behalf. It also says that He is our Great High Priest and that He always lives to intercede for us.

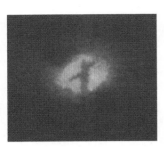

John 14:6 says that *Jesus is the way, the truth and the life, and that no one comes to the Father except through Him.*

History has revealed the impact that the sacrifice of Christ upon the cross has made in the lives of all who put their trust in Him.

There is even a reminder of the cross of Christ in the heavens. Note the picture of the Whirlpool Galaxy seen here that was taken from the Hubble spacecraft.

7. Consummation: The Restoration of All Things

The final of our seven Cs stands for Consummation. It addresses what the Bible says will happen in the future.
Because the future is yet to occur, we cannot yet see the shape it will give to human history, as we can with the other six Cs. Still, we can see the signs all around us that confirm what the Bible said we should look for during the times that will immediately precede the second coming of Christ and the consummation of God's plans.

Note the following passages that speak of that time of consummation that will occur when Jesus returns.

> *Acts 3:19-21: Therefore repent and return, so that your sins may be wiped away, in order that times of refreshing may come from the presence of the LORD; and that He may send Jesus, the Christ appointed for you, whom heaven must receive until the period of restoration of all things about which God spoke by the mouth of His holy prophets from ancient time.*

> *Revelation 21:1-5: Then I saw a new heaven and a new earth; for the first heaven and the first earth*

passed away, and there is no longer any sea. (2) And I saw the holy city, new Jerusalem, coming down out of heaven from God, made ready as a bride adorned for her husband. (3) And I heard a loud voice from the throne, saying, "Behold, the tabernacle of God is among men, and He will dwell among them, and they shall be His people, and God Himself will be among them, (4) and He will wipe away every tear from their eyes; and there will no longer be any death; there will no longer be any mourning, or crying, or pain; the first things have passed away." (5) And He who sits on the throne said, "Behold, I am making all things new." And He said, "Write, for these words are faithful and true."

Other passages that speak of these future consummation events include Acts 1:11; Matthew 24:29-31; Revelation 19-20; Revelation 21-22; 1 Thessalonians 4 & 5; 2 Thessalonians 2; 1 Corinthians 15; Matthew 24; The book of Daniel; The book of Revelation.

Summary: The Seven Cs of History

CREATION   CORRUPTION   CATASTROPHE   CONFUSION   CHRIST   CROSS   CONSUMMATION

In these seven Cs of history, we find how much the Bible corresponds to the history of the world and thus explains the reality we see around us today. The Bible's account of creation fits perfectly with the order, beauty, and design we see in all creation. It also affirms the special place that man has in God's creation.

The fall of man and its results are confirmed everywhere we look. Pain, suffering, disease, war, crime, hatred, etc. all are visible results of what the Bible describes as having happened at the time of Adam and Eve. Even the second law of thermodynamics affirms what the Bible says about the result of man's sin.

The global flood described in Genesis 6–9 explains the geology and paleontology findings that we observe today. What we see is exactly what we would expect as the results of a global flood.

The confusion of the languages described in Genesis 11 explains the anthropology of the world today, including the thousands of different languages and people groups known around the world.

The coming of Jesus Christ has so impacted nations, people groups, and individuals that even our calendars date back to the time of His birth. Nothing in history has impacted the world like the coming of Jesus Christ to bring salvation.

The sacrifice of Jesus Christ upon the cross explains the amazing change in the lives of all of those who trust Him as their Savior and follow Him and His Word.

The consummation of all things is yet to come, but the signs that it is drawing close are all around us.

These seven Cs that outline the biblical account explain very well the world we live in today.

"The Bible - God's Word (Part 1)"

The Bible - God's Word

God has revealed Himself to us in a number of ways. According to Romans 1:20, God has revealed Himself through the things that He has made. This is called "natural revelation" or "general revelation." Though we learn much about God through natural revelation, we are in need of much more specific revelation to know His ways, His commands, and His plans. To accomplish this, God has also given us "special revelation" through the  Bible and through Jesus Christ, who is the radiance of God the Father's glory and the exact representation of His nature (Hebrews 1:3). In this section we will examine information related to the Bible, God's special revelation to us.

Is there evidence to confirm that the Bible is the Word of God, or are we to accept that claim simply because the church makes it? The answer is, there is ample evidence to confirm to us that the Bible is the Word of God. That evidence does not eliminate the need to exercise faith, but it certainly does confirm that our faith is solidly supported by fact. We are not called to have a blind faith.

In the next two chapters we will look at twelve different areas of evidence that confirm the Bible as the Word of God. As you look at these twelve areas of evidence, you are encouraged to use the cards provided to memorize the basic points, thus strengthening your understanding and your faith.

Before we proceed, please note the image of an anchor shown here. This anchor appears on each of the accompanying memory cards to remind us that the Bible and the faith we develop through the Scriptures becomes an anchor for our lives, preventing us from drifting to and fro on the waves of false doctrines, false prophets, philosophies of men, politically correct statements, etc. The Bible enables us to know God's plan of salvation and His directives for every area of our lives.

1. Evidence from the Internal Unity of the Bible

The Bible claims to be inspired by God. Over 2600 times the phrase "God said" or its equivalent is used in the Bible. Also, 2 Timothy 3:16 says that "All Scripture is inspired by God." The authority of the Bible is first seen by its own claim to inspiration and divine origin.

Though the Bible was written by approximately forty men over a period of more than 1500 years, the message of every part of it is in beautiful unity and harmony with every other part. God's plans for mankind are revealed from Genesis all the way through to Revelation. One way to outline the Bible is as follows:

(1) God created mankind in His image and likeness to dwell with Him eternally (Genesis 1–2).
(2) Mankind sinned and was separated from God by his sin (Genesis 3).
(3) God reveals that He has redeemed mankind through His Son Jesus Christ (Genesis 3:15 - Revelation 20).
(4) God's original plan to have mankind dwell with Him eternally has been restored through Jesus Christ (Revelation 21-22).

Jesus Christ is the central character throughout the Bible. He is seen in the Old Testament through prophecies, types, and shadows. He is revealed clearly in the New Testament—who He is, what He has done to redeem us, and what He will do in the future to complete God's plan of salvation and redemption.

Examples of the Old Testament types and shadows that point to the person and purpose of Jesus Christ are the Passover (Exodus 12), the scarlet cord in the window of Rahab (Joshua 2 and 6), the manna eaten by Israel in the wilderness (Exodus 16), the sacrifice of Isaac (Genesis 22), the brazen serpent lifted in the wilderness (Numbers 21), and the scapegoat released on the day of atonement (Leviticus 16). Joshua was also a type of Jesus as he led the people into the promised land. Noah and the ark were a shadow of the salvation and safety that would be provided through Christ as God's judgment comes upon a rebellious world. Even the substance God instructed Noah to seal the ark with was a shadow of things to come. It was  called "pitch." The Hebrew word for pitch means "a covering" and is the same word elsewhere translated as "atonement." The tabernacle was a shadow of the work that Jesus Christ would accomplish. The book of Hebrews tells us that the Old Testament tabernacle and temple had to be built exactly according to God's instruction because it was a duplicate of the true tabernacle in heaven where Jesus would offer His blood for the sins of the world.

David's psalms spoke much of Jesus and what He would accomplish. The prophets prophesied many things about the coming Messiah that were fulfilled by Jesus hundreds of years later. Jesus said Himself that the Old Testament Scriptures speak of Him and reveal Him (John 5:39-47).

The message of the Bible could not be more unified if one man had labored long and hard over a story that he wanted to tell in great detail. The Old Testament and New Testament are unified. The Torah (the books of the law), the historical books, the poetic books, and the prophetic books of the Old Testament are all in unity. The four gospels of the New Testament are in unity. (It is a wonderful study to look at the uniqueness of the Gospel of John. Though it is in perfect harmony with the other three gospels, it is written with a distinct purpose, revealing who Jesus is). In the New Testament, the gospels, the book of Acts, the writings of Paul, the general epistles, and the book of Revelation are all in unity with one another. This unity reveals that though God used human agents to record the Scriptures, the source of the Bible is God, the Holy Spirit, who inspired each writer to record all that He wanted written.

The internal unity of the Bible speaks of its authenticity and of the fact that it is inspired by God.

2. The Bibliographical Evidence

Author	Written	Earliest Copies	Time Span	# of copies
Caesar	100-44 B.C.	A.D. 900	1,000 yrs.	10
Plato (Tetralogies)	427-347 B.C.	A.D. 900	1,200 yrs.	7
Thucydides	460-400 B.C.	A.D. 900	1,300 yrs.	8
Sophocles	496-406 B.C.	A.D. 1,000	1,400 yrs.	100
Catullus	54 B.C.	A.D. 1,550	1,600 yrs.	3
Euripides	480-406 B.C.	A.D. 1,100	1,500 yrs.	9
Aristotle	384-322 B.C.	A.D. 1,100	1,400 yrs.	5
THE SECOND RUNNER UP.....				
Homer (Iliad)	750-700 B.C.	200 B.C.	500 yrs.	643
AND THE WINNER IS......				
God (The N.T.)	A.D. 40-100	A.D. 125	25 yrs.	24,000+

Some critics argue that the Bible we have today is so far removed from the originally written manuscripts that it cannot be trusted. To answer these critics, it is important to look at the bibliographical evidence. The bibliographical evidence for any ancient writing involves how many ancient copies of manuscripts are available and how close to the time of the original writings they were copied. Bibliographical evidence shows us that the Bible as we have it today is much more reliable than any other ancient writing, including many that secular scholars readily accept as trustworthy. The table on this page lists popular ancient writings that are accepted as authentic. It lists the number of manuscript copies or partial copies still around today and gives the timespan from the original writings to the oldest manuscript copies known. You can easily see from this data that the Bible far surpases all other ancient writings when it comes to bibliographical evidence.

Some critics have suggested that the books of the New Testament were written well after the first century, but this argument is defeated by the fact that many of the early church fathers quote the New Testament Scriptures continually. In fact, the early church fathers quoted the New Testament so frequently that if we did not have any New Testament manuscripts, we could piece together practically the entire document by using the writings of the early church fathers. It would be impossible for them to quote Scriptures if those Scriptures had not yet been written. Other scholars today confirm that all of the New Testament books were written within the first century AD (or CE).

In 1947, the discovery of the Dead Sea Scrolls confirmed to us how accurately the Bible has been preserved throughout the centuries. Copies of the book of Isaiah found among the Dead Sea Scrolls, believed to be 1,000 years older than the previously oldest copies of Isaiah known, revealed almost no differences. One report says that only one word was found to be different, and that word had no effect on the original meaning. One word in a thousand years! This is a testament to the meticulous way that the scribes copied the Scriptures and preserved their integrity.

The bibliographical evidence affirms that the Bible we read today is accurate and trustworthy.

3. Archaeological and Historical Evidence

Another external confirming evidence that the Bible is the Word of God is found in archaeological evidence and additional historical documents. These sources confirm that the events, places, and people spoken of in the Bible are true history and not made up stories. The Middle East is a popular destination for archaeological expeditions, and the findings of those expeditions continually confirm the accuracy of the Bible. Noted archaeologist Nelson Glueck has said, "It may be stated categorically that no archaeological discovery has ever contradicted a biblical reference. Scores of archaeological findings have been made which confirm in clear outline or exact detail historical statements in the Bible. And, by the same token, proper evaluation of Biblical descriptions has often led to amazing discoveries." [1] That is quite amazing when you think of all of the archaeological finds over the years. If the Bible were simply a group of fictitious writings, as some critics claim, then the findings of archaeology would not have continued to confirm the historicity of the Bible's accounts.

Although it is not possible to verify every incident in the Bible, the archaeological discoveries since the mid-1800s have consistently demonstrated the reliability and plausibility of the Bible narrative. The following examples of this archaeological reliability are taken from christiananswers.net.

(1) The discovery of the Ebla archive in northern Syria in the 1970s has shown the biblical writings concerning the patriarchs to be viable. Documents written on clay tablets from around 2300 BC demonstrate that personal and place names in the patriarchal accounts are genuine. The name "Canaan" was in use in Ebla, a name critics once said was not used at that time and was used  incorrectly in the early chapters of the Bible. The word tehom ("the deep") in Genesis 1:2 was said to be a late word demonstrating the

---

[1] http://www.apologetics315.com/2009/07/sunday-quote-nelson-glueck-on.html

late writing of the creation story. Tehom was part of the vocabulary at Ebla, in use some 800 years before Moses. Ancient customs reflected in the stories of the patriarchs have also been found in clay tablets from Nuzi and Mari.

(2) The Hittites were once thought to be a biblical legend, until their capital and records were discovered at Bogazkoy, Turkey.

(3) Many thought the biblical references to Solomon's wealth were greatly exaggerated. Recovered records from the past show that wealth in antiquity was concentrated with the king, and Solomon's prosperity was entirely feasible.

(4) It was once claimed there was no Assyrian king named Sargon as recorded in Isaiah 20:1, because this name was not known in any other record. Then, Sargon's palace was discovered in Khorsabad, Iraq. The very event mentioned in Isaiah 20, his capture of Ashdod, was recorded on the palace walls. What is more, fragments of a stela memorializing the victory were found at Ashdod itself.

(5) Another king who was in doubt was Belshazzar, king of Babylon, named in Daniel 5. The last king of Babylon was Nabonidus, according to recorded history. Tablets were found showing that Belshazzar was Nabonidus' son who served as coregent in Babylon. Thus, Belshazzar could rightfully offer to make Daniel "third highest ruler in the kingdom" (Dan. 5:16) for reading the handwriting on the wall. Here we see the eye-witness nature of the biblical record, as is so often brought out by the discoveries of archaeology.

If there were only one archaeological discovery confirming biblical information, it might be explained away as coincidence, or an alternative interpretation might be given to disassociate it from the Bible. It is the weight of a myriad of discoveries that demonstrates the Bible to be the Word of God.

The Three Categories of Archaeological Discoveries
(1) Archaeological evidence demonstrates the historical and cultural accuracy of the Bible.
(2) The Bible's message of a loving Creator God who interacts in the affairs of mankind and has provided a

209

means of salvation stands in sharp contrast to the pagan fertility religions of the ancient world as revealed by archaeology.

(3) Archaeological findings demonstrate that the biblical prophets accurately predicted events hundreds of years before they occurred—something that lies beyond the capability of mere men. [2]

Along with archaeological evidence of biblical accounts, we have the confirming accounts of other historical documents to verify the Bible's accuracy. Many of these documents also fall into the category of archaeological finds because of the way they were discovered. Some archaeological finds reveal ruins of places or objects with specific names engraved on them. Some involve actual historical writings describing events and people that are spoken of in the Bible. Note the following examples taken from author Bryant Wood of Associates for Biblical Research:

The most documented biblical event is the world-wide flood described in Genesis 6–9. A number of Babylonian documents have been discovered which describe the same flood.

For example, the Sumerian King List (pictured here) lists kings who reigned for extremely long periods of time. Then a great flood came. Following the flood, Sumerian kings ruled for much shorter periods of time. This mirrors the pattern found in the Bible. Men had long lifespans before the flood and shorter lifespans afterward. The 11th tablet of the **Sumerian King List**

---

[2] https://christiananswers.net/q-aiia/aiia-arch1.html

Gilgamesh Epic speaks of an ark, animals taken on the ark, birds sent out during the course of the flood, the ark landing on a mountain, and a sacrifice offered after the ark landed.

Sumerian tablets record the confusion of language as we have in the biblical account of the Tower of Babel (Genesis 11:1-9).

More Examples of Extra-Biblical Confirmation of Biblical Events (from Bryant G. Wood, Ph.D)

(1) Campaign into Israel by Pharaoh Shishak (1 Kings 14:25-26), recorded on the walls of the Temple of Amun in Thebes, Egypt.

(2) Revolt of Moab against Israel (2 Kings 1:1; 3:4-27), recorded on the Mesha Inscription.

(3) Fall of Samaria (2 Kings 17:3-6, 24; 18:9-11) to Sargon II, king of Assyria, as recorded on his palace walls.

(4) Defeat of Ashdod by Sargon II (Isaiah 20:1), as recorded on his palace walls.

(5) Campaign of the Assyrian king Sennacherib against Judah (2 Kings 18:13-16), as recorded on the Taylor Prism.

(6) Siege of Lachish by Sennacherib (2 Kings 18:14, 17), as recorded on the Lachish reliefs.

(7) Assassination of Sennacherib by his own sons (2 Kings 19:37), as recorded in the annals of his son Esarhaddon.

(8) Fall of Nineveh as predicted by the prophets Nahum and Zephaniah (2:13-15), recorded on the Tablet of Nabopolasar.

(9) Fall of Jerusalem to Nebuchadnezzar, king of Babylon (2 Kings 24:10-14), as recorded in the Babylonian Chronicles.

(10) Captivity of Jehoiachin, king of Judah, in Babylon (2 Kings 24:15-16), as recorded on the Babylonian Ration Records.

(11) Fall of Babylon to the Medes and Persians (Daniel 5:30-31), as recorded on the Cyrus Cylinder.

(12) Freeing of captives in Babylon by Cyrus the Great (Ezra 1:1-4; 6:3-4), as recorded on the Cyrus Cylinder.

(13) The existence of Jesus Christ as recorded by Josephus, Suetonius, Thallus, Pliny the Younger, the Talmud, and Lucian.

(14) Forcing Jews to leave Rome during the reign of Claudius (A.D. 41-54) (Acts 18:2), as recorded by Suetonius.

In summary, archaeological evidence and other historical documents confirm the history recorded in the Bible. The

discoveries of archaeology can be helpful in removing doubts about the historical trustworthiness of the Bible. The miracles and the spiritual message must be accepted on faith, which is the basis of our relationship with God, but confirmation of the history, people, and geography of the Bible gives us solid

Site believed to be the Burial Site of Zechariah

reason for faith in all the Bible says.

For more information see - https://answersingenesis.org/archaeology/does-archaeology-support-the-bible/

4. Evidence from Medical Facts

Numerous medical facts found in the Bible have been confirmed by modern medicine. This is wonderful confirmation that the Bible is the Word of God, because the diagnoses and treatments of diseases it describes could not have been known by natural means at the times in which they were reported. The only possible source of this information had to be God Himself.

Consider the many passages in the first five books of the Bible that express the importance of avoiding germs (see Numbers 19:3-22, Leviticus 11:1-47; 15:1-33, Deuteronomy 23:12). Numbers 19:22 says, "Furthermore, anything that the unclean person touches shall be unclean; and the person who touches it shall be unclean until evening." All of these explicit directions about avoiding germs were written approximately 3500 years ago. Consider the following,

> "For centuries doctors denied the possibility that disease could be transmitted by invisible agents. However, in the late 19th century Louis Pasteur demonstrated in his Germ Theory of Disease that most infectious diseases were caused by microorganisms originating from outside the body. This new understanding of germs and their means of transmission led to improved sanitary standards that resulted in an enormous drop in the mortality rate. Yet these core principles of sanitation were being practiced by the Israelites thousands of years earlier." [3]

Another example of modern medical knowledge found in the Bible is seen in Leviticus 13:52: "So he shall burn the garment, whether the warp or the woof, in wool or in linen, or any article of leather in which the mark occurs, for it is a leprous malignancy; it shall be burned in the fire." This statement about leprosy seemed silly to many critics until modern medicine confirmed that leprosy is a bacteria that can survive on walls and garments. In fact, the online site entitled BibleEvidences.com sites the Medic-Planet.com encyclopedia and says that leprosy "can survive three weeks or longer outside the human body, such as in dust or on clothing." [4]

In Leviticus 12:3, God instructed His people to circumcise their baby boys on the eighth day of their life: "On the eighth day the flesh of his foreskin shall be circumcised." There certainly was no human knowledge available at that time that would have caused Moses to write "the eighth day" as a part of this instruction. Consider

---

[3] https://bibleevidences.com/medical-evidence/
[4] ibid.

the following: "Medical researchers recently discovered that the two main blood clotting factors, vitamin K and prothrombin, reach their highest level in life, about 110 percent of normal, on the eighth day after birth. These blood clotting agents facilitate rapid healing and greatly reduce the chance of infection. You can verify with any obstetrician that the eighth day of life is the ideal time for a circumcision, and that any circumcision done earlier requires an injection of Vitamin K supplement." [5] Wow! Only God could have known this fact 3500 years ago. These are the kinds of things that confirm to us that the Bible is the Word of God.

Another example is found in Leviticus 17:11, where we are told, "For the life of the flesh is in the blood, and I have given it to you on the altar to make atonement for your souls; for it is the blood by reason of the life that makes atonement." The Bible tells us here that life is found in the blood. We know this fact today, but 250 years ago medical physicians did not. In fact, as late as the nineteenth century physicians often bled patients in an attempt to cure them of sicknesses believed to be located in the blood. George Washington reportedly died because of this faulty medical practice.

Actually, he was bled 4 times by the 3 doctors that attempted to raise him from an illness that had overtaken him.[6] Again we see that the Bible had it right 3500 years ago even though modern medicine did not catch up until the last couple of hundred years.

These and other examples show that the medical facts in the Bible, written hundreds of years before they were understood by modern medicine, confirm that the Bible is the Word of God.

---

[5] ibid.
[6] Quoted from The Death of George Washington, http://www.mountvernon.org/digital-encyclopedia/article/the-death-of-george-was hington/

5. Evidence from Scientific Facts

The Bible records considerable scientific information that modern science has discovered only in recent decades and centuries. For

example, though skeptics love to mock Bible believers by calling them "flat earthers," it is actually the Bible that first told us the Earth is round: "It is He that sits upon the circle of the earth" (Isaiah 40:22). At a time when science believed that the Earth was flat, it was the Scriptures that inspired Christopher Columbus to sail around the world.

Around 1500 BC, a time when it was believed that the Earth was supported by a large animal or a giant, the Bible spoke of the Earth's free float in space: "He stretches out the north over empty space And hangs the earth on nothing" (Job 26:7). As we can see, the Bible gave us scientific facts long before modern science was able to confirm them. The first half of this verse has also been confirmed by recent scientific discoveries that have shown a huge hole in space in the direction of the northern hemisphere.

The second law of thermodynamics was regarded by Albert Einstein to be the premier law in science. The Bible accurately describes this law: "For the heavens will vanish away like smoke, the earth will grow old like a garment" (Isaiah 51:6). The biblical theology of the fall of man also confirms the second law of thermodynamics:

"For the anxious longing of the creation waits eagerly for the revealing of the sons of God. (20) For the creation was subjected to futility, not willingly, but because of Him who subjected it, in hope (21) that the creation itself also will be set free from its slavery to corruption into the freedom of the glory of the children of God. (22) For we know that the whole creation groans and suffers the pains of childbirth together until now." (Romans 8:19-22)

The circulation and conservation of the Earth's water is called the hydrologic cycle. Only recently has the hydrologic cycle been truly understood, but the Bible speaks of various aspects of it in a number of verses, including Job 36:27-28 (NIRV): "He makes mist rise from the water. Then it falls as rain into the streams. (28) The clouds pour down their moisture. Rain showers fall on people everywhere." Ecclesiastes 1:7 (NIRV) adds, "Every stream flows into the ocean. But the ocean never gets full. The streams return to the place they came from."

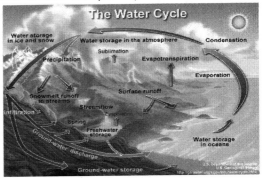

The complex nature of how water is supported in clouds despite being heavier than air is clearly implied as God asks in Job 37:16 (NKJV), "Do you know how the clouds are balanced, those wondrous works of Him who is perfect in knowledge?"

Job 38:31 speaks of star constellations, the Pleiades and Orion: "Can you bind the chains of the Pleiades, Or loose the cords of Orion?" The Bible reveals here that the stars of Pleiades are gravitationally bound while the stars of Orion are not, a fact which modern astronomy has confirmed. The only explanation for this scientific fact being in the Bible is that the Bible truly is from the God who created the universe we are now discovering.

In at least ten different Old Testament passages the Bible speaks of God "stretching out the heavens". Modern cosmology has confirmed that the universe is expanding, just as the Bible proclaimed.

Modern science has discovered springs on the ocean floors, but the Bible spoke of these springs 3500 years ago in Job 38:16 "Have you entered the springs of the sea? Or have you walked in search of the depths?"

For more information on scientific facts confirmed in the Bible, go to https://www.livingwaters.com/witnessingtool/scientificfactsintheBible .shtml   or   http://www.bibleevidences.com/scientif.htm

6. Evidence from Fulfilled Prophecies Concerning Ancient Cities

One category of biblical prophecy concerns predictions of the destruction of ancient cities. Many of these cities were centers of power in their day, but the Bible foretold their destruction with detail and precision.

Petra was the capital city of Edom, which was located southeast of Israel. It was situated in a mountainous area near Mt. Seir and was considered impenetrable because it was built in a large cavern accessible only through a narrow passageway between sheer rock walls. Invading forces had to approach the city by marching into this narrow space between the vertical stone cliffs, making them easy targets for the city's defenders. Yet Petra and Edom were conquered, and the Bible had much to say about its destruction. Note the following passages.

> *Ezekiel 25:12-13: "Thus says the Lord GOD, 'Because Edom has acted against the house of Judah by taking vengeance, and has incurred grievous guilt, and avenged themselves upon them,' (13) therefore thus says the Lord GOD, 'I will also stretch out My hand against Edom and cut off man and beast from it. And I will lay it waste; from Teman even to Dedan they will fall by the sword.'"*

> *Jeremiah 49:15-18: "'For behold, I have made you small among the nations, Despised among men. (16) As for the terror of you, The arrogance of your heart has deceived you, O you who live in the clefts of the rock, Who occupy the height of the hill. Though you make your nest as high as an eagle's, I will bring you down from there,' declares the LORD. (17) 'Edom will become an object of horror; everyone who passes by it will be horrified and will hiss at all its wounds. (18) Like the overthrow of Sodom and Gomorrah with its neighbors,' says the LORD, 'no one will live there, nor will a son of man reside in it."*

(Also see Ezekiel 35:1-8 and Isaiah 34:10-15.) Isaiah 34 says that this mighty fortress will become the home of wild animals, various crawling creatures, and birds of prey.

Just as the Bible predicted, Petra was conquered by Rome in AD 106 and became less and less used until it was almost uninhabitable from the seventh to the twelfth centuries. After a slight reviving in the twelfth century, it

was almost forgotten until rediscovered in the 1800s. At this point it was ancient ruins inhabited by hawks and wild animals, just as the Bible had predicted. People visit the area as a tourist site today, remembering what once was.

Here is a summary of the fulfilled prophecies concerning Edom and Petra:

(1) Edom was overthrown as a nation.

(2) The nation and city have become a desolation, as
Ezekiel 25:13; 35:4,7 and Isaiah 34:11-13 predicted.

(3) It has never been populated again, as Jeremiah 49:18 predicted.

(4) It has had a bloody history, as Ezekiel 25:13 and 35:6,8 predicted.

(5) Edom became populated with wild animals and birds (instead of people), as Isaiah 34:11-15 predicted.

The likelihood that these prophecies came true by some random chain of events is all but impossible.

Tyre, in modern Lebanon, was one of the wealthiest trading cities in history due to its advantageous geographical position and its good ports. This great Phoenician city was located on the eastern shore of the Mediterranean Sea, and it stood as one of the most ancient and prosperous cities in all the world. Part of the strength of Tyre from a military standpoint was that it was divided into two parts, the mainland part and the island part that was less than a mile off shore. This island fortress seemed indestructible in its day. The Bible has some very descriptive words to describe the coming destruction of Tyre.

> *"Now in the eleventh year, on the first of the month, the word of the LORD came to me saying, (2) "Son of man, because Tyre has said concerning Jerusalem, 'Aha, the gateway of the peoples is broken; it has opened to me. I shall be filled, now that she is laid waste,'" (3) therefore thus says the Lord GOD, "Behold, I am against you, O Tyre, and I will bring up many nations against you, as the sea brings up its waves. (4) They will destroy the walls of Tyre and break down her towers; and I will scrape her debris from her and make her a bare rock. (5) She will be a place for the spreading of nets in the midst of the sea, for I have spoken," declares the Lord GOD, "and she will become spoil for the nations. (6) Also her daughters who are on the mainland will be slain by the sword, and they will know that I am the LORD." (7) For thus says the Lord GOD, "Behold, I will bring upon Tyre from the north Nebuchadnezzar king of Babylon, king of kings, with horses, chariots, cavalry and a great army. (8) He will slay your daughters on the mainland with the sword; and he will make siege walls against you, cast up a ramp against you and raise up a large shield against you." (Ezekiel 26:1-8)*

Note some of the specifics about this prophecy against Tyre. It would be destroyed and laid waste. It would have many nations come up against it. Its buildings and towers would be thrown down, and it would have its debris scraped from it making it a bare rock. It would be invaded by Nebuchadnezzar and people on its mainland would be killed. It would become a place where fishermen would spread their nets. I italicized a couple of things here because of how specific and unique they are.

Not long after this prophecy was written in about 590 BC,

Nebuchadnezzar did come against Tyre, kill its inhabitants, and destroy its buildings and towers, leaving it in ruin. Following this, the city of Tyre was repeatedly attacked during the reign of the Medes and the Persians. Then in 332 BC, Alexander the Great besieged Tyre and crushed it. Soon after this defeat, Tyre continued to be attacked and conquered by Ptolemy of Egypt and by Atigonus of Syria. During Alexander's siege of Tyre, he did an amazing thing that fulfilled Bible prophecy precisely. He desired to conquer the island fortress of Tyre, and to reach it he scraped all the debris of the destroyed mainland city into the sea to create a causeway to the island

Modern arial photograph of Tyre showing the causeway (landbridge)built by Alexander now covered & expanded by silt & sand

fortress. He used tens of thousands of men to accomplish this and thus fulfilled the prophecy that Tyre would have its debris scraped from it, making it bare rock.

The ancient Phoenician city of Tyre was never rebuilt. The modern fishing city in Lebanon that now has built over the ancient ruins of Tyre ensures that the ancient Phoenician city will never be revived. The modern city of Tyre (about 120,000 in population) is a place where fishermen spread their nets to dry on the areas near the sea ports, again fulfilling Biblical prophecies in amazing detail.

Babylon was the ancient capital of the Babylonian Empire. It was a powerful city in its day that no one thought could be

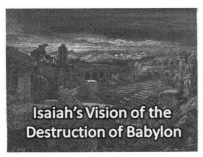

Isaiah's Vision of the Destruction of Babylon

conquered. It had been built to be impregnable. The walls of Babylon were so thick that chariot races could be run on top of them. One report says the wall around Babylon was 56 miles long, 300 feet high, and 25 feet thick, with another wall placed 75 feet behind the first wall and extending 35 feet below the ground. Others say that the walls were less than 300 feet high but that the area between the outer and inner walls was filled in, creating a massive fortress barrier.

The 250 towers along the wall are believed to have been 450 feet high, and a moat, both deep and wide, encircled the city. These defensive structures made Isaiah's prophecies of the coming destruction of Babylon seem impossible.

> *"Behold, I am going to stir up the Medes against them, Who will not value silver or take pleasure in gold. (18) And their bows will mow down the young men, They will not even have compassion on the fruit of the womb, Nor will their eye pity children. (19) And Babylon, the beauty of kingdoms, the glory of the Chaldeans' pride, Will be as when God overthrew Sodom and Gomorrah. (20) It will never be inhabited or lived in from generation to generation; Nor will the Arab pitch his tent there, Nor will shepherds make their flocks lie down there."*
> *(Isaiah 13:17-20)*

By 605 BC, when Nebuchadnezzar became king of Babylon, the Babylonian Empire had become the leading empire in the world.

Nebuchadnezzar focused on expanding his empire and on expanding Babylon to become the greatest city in the world. He built a beautiful palace, rebuilt and repaired the city walls, improved the streets, embellished the temples, and built the hanging gardens. When Nebuchadnezzar died in 562 BC, Babylon was truly one of the most magnificent cities in the world. Isaiah had prophesied that God would destroy Babylon, but now Babylon was greater than it had formerly been, making that prophecy seem highly improbable. However, Babylon's greatness would not last forever.

The Greek historian Herodotus, who wrote about Babylon years after its destruction, described how Cyrus captured the city.

Part of his army went north of Babylon and dug a trench from the Euphrates River to a nearby marsh. When the army connected the trench to the Euphrates River, much of the water in the river flowed toward the marsh, while only a little water continued to flow toward Babylon. While the Babylonians were confidently celebrating a feast, the strong river and moat protecting the city became very shallow, and the Medes and Persians were able to enter the city (Herodotus 1.191). They captured the city without a battle, and Darius the Mede was put in charge. Daniel, chapter 5 records the events of that night from the perspective of God's communication to Belshazzar the Babylonian king through the handwriting on the wall. The miraculous handwriting was interpreted by Daniel for the king just before the city was overtaken and Belshazzar was killed.

Though Saddam Hussein attempted to rebuild the ancient city of Babylon, it remains today as a place where visitors come to remember the past as they view its ruins. Josh McDowell, in his book Evidence That Demands a Verdict quotes Floyd Hamilton concerning the aspect of the prophecy that says "Nor will the Arab pitch his tent there, Nor will shepherds make their flocks lie down there." Hamilton says: "Travelers report that the city (Babylon) is absolutely uninhabited, even by Bedouins.  There are various superstitions current among the Arabs that prevent them from pitching their tents there, while the character of the soil prevents the growth of vegetation suitable for the pasturage of flocks."

The Bible's accuracy in these matters is great confirmation that it truly is the Word of God.

7. Evidence from Fulfilled Prophecies Concerning World Empires

The book of Daniel, written in the sixth century BC, contains a series of prophetic passages that give us a comprehensive history of world empires from Daniel's time to today. Daniel contains many prophecies, but in this section we will focus on the prophetic passages found in chapters 2, 7, and 8. These three chapters give prophetic pictures of what world empires would emerge and fall over the centuries. These prophecies also include indications of what we are to look for in the last days before Jesus Christ returns to the earth. If you have ever wondered why Bible teachers who focus on the end times are interested in developments toward a New World Order, you will understand more as you look at the prophecies of the book of Daniel.

In Daniel 2, the Babylonian king Nebuchadnezzar has a dream that deeply troubles him. He cannot understand the dream, nor can he remember the details of it. But he is determined to find out its meaning, and he makes the unreasonable demand of his counselors that they both describe the dream to him and interpret its meaning. God reveals the dream and its interpretation to Daniel, who recites both its content and meaning to the king.

In the dream, the king saw a statue with a head of gold, breasts and arms of silver, loins of brass (or bronze), legs of iron, and feet of iron mixed with clay. Then he saw a stone cut without hands from a mountain, and it struck the statue on its feet, crushing them and shattering the entire image. The stone then grew to become a great mountain that filled the whole earth.

The interpretation of the dream is given in Daniel 2:36-45.

"This was the dream; now we will tell its interpretation before the king. (37) You, O king, are the king of kings, to whom the God of heaven has given the kingdom, the power, the strength and the glory; (38) and wherever the sons of men dwell, or the beasts of the field, or the birds of the sky, He has given them into your hand and has caused you to rule over them all. You [Nebuchadnezzar of Babylon] are the head of gold. (39) After you there will arise another kingdom inferior to you, then another third kingdom of bronze, which will rule over all the earth. (40) Then there will be a fourth kingdom as strong as iron; inasmuch as iron crushes and shatters all

things, so, like iron that breaks in pieces, it will crush and break all these in pieces. (41) In that you saw the feet and toes, partly of potter's clay and partly of iron, it will be a divided kingdom; but it will have in it the toughness of iron, inasmuch as you saw the iron mixed with common clay. (42) As the toes of the feet were partly of iron and partly of pottery, so some of the kingdom will be strong and part of it will be brittle. (43) And in that you saw the iron mixed with common clay, they will combine with one another in the seed of men; but they will not adhere to one another, even as iron does not combine with pottery. (44) In the days of those kings the God of heaven will set up a kingdom which will never be destroyed, and that kingdom will not be left for another people; it will crush and put an end to all these kingdoms, but it will itself endure forever. (45) Inasmuch as you saw that a stone was cut out of the mountain without hands and that it crushed the iron, the bronze, the clay, the silver and the gold, the great God has made known to the king what will take place in the future; so the dream is true and its interpretation is trustworthy."

The prophecy of Daniel 2 tells of four world empires that would follow each other sequentially, starting with the Babylonian Empire. It finally reveals a world empire that is a continuation of the fourth empire (the legs of iron) but is a mixture of various peoples (the feet of iron mixed with clay). According to the prophecy, it is in the days of that final world empire that God will come and destroy the kingdoms of men and establish His eternal kingdom.

World history unfolded exactly as predicted in Daniel's prophecy. Visions given to Daniel in chapters 7 and 8 add more details to the prophetic revelation of chapter 2. In these two

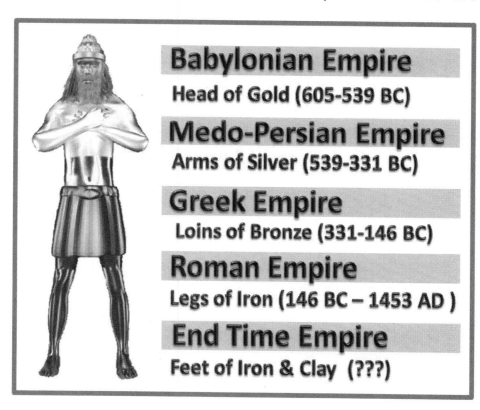

Babylonian Empire
Head of Gold (605-539 BC)

Medo-Persian Empire
Arms of Silver (539-331 BC)

Greek Empire
Loins of Bronze (331-146 BC)

Roman Empire
Legs of Iron (146 BC – 1453 AD)

End Time Empire
Feet of Iron & Clay (???)

chapters, animals are seen as representations of the same world empires that are represented by the parts of the statue in chapter 2. The second empire is that of the Medes and Persians. Cyrus, head of the Medo-Persian Empires, defeated Babylon during the reign of Belshazzar as described above in the section on the fall of Babylon. The Medo-Persian Empire was large and powerful, but it lacked the glory of Babylon, and is thus represented in the statue of Nebuchadnezzar's dream as being of silver rather than the more precious gold.

What happened next is described in another of Daniel's visions in which he saw a titanic battle between a two-horned ram and a shaggy goat with a single horn. After the battle, which the attacking goat wins, God tells Daniel the specific meaning of it:

> *"The ram which you saw with the two horns represents the kings of Media and Persia. (21) The shaggy goat represents the kingdom of Greece, and the large horn that is between his eyes is the first king. (22) The broken horn and the four horns that arose in its place represent four kingdoms which will arise from his nation, although not with his power." (Daniel 8:20-22)*

The Macedonian prodigy Alexander the Great conquered the Medo-Persians and established an empire under Greek rule. His empire was the loins of brass in the statue. Daniel was told that after aggressively conquering nations and peoples, the original leader of the Greek Empire would be cut off (or would die) and his empire would be then broken up into four parts.

As Daniel prophesied, Alexander died at the age of thirty-three, shortly after completing his conquests. His kingdom was then divided into four parts, each ruled by a leader of considerably less ability than Alexander.

Rome swept through the Mediterranean world and became the next dominant empire. It is represented in Nebuchadnezzar's dream as the legs of iron. The Roman Empire divided into Eastern and Western sections in about AD 1453.

Through Nebuchadnezzar's vision, the Bible gives us a prophetic view of world history. It played out exactly as prophesied including the details regarding Alexander the Great. The Babylonian empire was followed by a Medo-Persian Empire, followed by a Greek empire, followed by a Roman empire. The Roman empire is the last world empire yet seen. In the last days there will be an end-time empire with the strength of the Roman empire mixed with other peoples and nations, spoken of in Daniel 2, 7 & 8. The Bible predicted these major events perfectly, showing again that it is the Word of God!

8. Evidence from Fulfilled Messianic Prophecy

We will not spend a lot of space here on this subject because it is treated in more detail in a later chapter. Messianic prophecies of the Old Testament give many details of the birth, life, ministry, death, resurrection, and future reign of the coming Messiah (Christ). All of these prophecies are fulfilled in the person of Jesus Christ. Many New Testament passages tell us directly of the fulfillment of various Old Testament prophecies. Over 300 Messianic prophecies are included in the Old Testament, and all are fulfilled by Jesus Christ in the New Testament.

The only possible explanation for this fact is that these prophecies were given and recorded in the Bible by the inspiration of God, proving again that the Bible is a miraculously produced book.

The table below gives just a sampling of the biblical examples of fulfilled Messianic prophecies.

PROPHECIES OF JESUS IN THE OLD TESTAMENT

PROPHECIES	ACCOUNT	FULLFILLMENT
Isaiah 7: 14 & Micah 5	BORN OF A VIRGIN	Matthew 1:23/Luke 1:26-35
Isaiah 9:7 and Jeremiah 23:5	HOUSE OF DAVID	Mat. 1:1, 6/John 7:42
Micah 5:2.	BIRTHPLACE	Mat. 2:1-6/ Luke 2:4
Jeremiah 31:15	KILLING OF BABIES	Mat. 2:17-18
Hosea 11:1.	FLIGHT INTO EGYPT	Matthew 2:15
Isaiah 9:1, 2	MINISTRY IN GALILEE	Mat. 4:15-16
Psalm 110:4	PRIEST LIKE MELCHISEDEK	Heb. 5:6/6:20/7:17, 21
Psalm 69:9	PURIFICATION OF THE TEMPLE	John 2:17
Isaiah 62:11; Zech. 9:9	TRIUMPHAL JERUSALEM ENTRY	Mat 21:1-10
Psalm 41:9	BETRAYAL BY A FRIEND	Mat. 26:15/Mark 14:10, 21
Zech. 11:12, 13	30 PIECES OF SILVER	Mat. 26:15/Mark 14:10, 21
Isaiah 53:9-12	DEATH WITH CRIMINALS	Mat. 27:38/Luke 23:40-43
Psalm 22:16 & Zech. 12:10	PIERCED HANDS & FEET	John 20:27
Psalm 69:21	OFFERED GALL & VINEGAR	Mat 27:34, 48/Jo 19:29
Psalm 22:18	LOTS CAST FOR GARMENTS	Mk 15:24/Jo 19:24
Ex. 12:46 and Psalm 34:20	NO BONES BROKEN	John 19:36
Psalm 16:9 and Isaiah 53:9	BURIAL WITH THE RICH	Mat. 27:57-60
Psalm 16:10 and Hosea 6:2	RESURRECTION	Mat. 27:63; 28:6
Psalm 68:18 and Psalm 110:1	ASCENSION	Luke 24:51/Acts 1:9/Heb. 1:3

(Passages chosen from "Prophecies Fulfilled Concerning Jesus Christ", Dickson New Analytical Study Bible, World Publishing, 1973, p. 1476)

9. Fulfilled Prophecy Regarding the Dispersion and Regathering of the Jews

If a person had to rely on just one area of evidence to the Bible as God's Word, this might very well be the the one. One reason this piece of evidence is so profound is that it is happening right in front of us daily.

It is hard to imagine a nation of people being scattered and intermixed with other nations all around the world for many centuries and yet remaining true to their original national heritage. It is even harder to imagine these people actually returning to their homeland and becoming a nation again. Yet this is exactly what has happened to the Jewish people. Even more amazing are the biblical prophecies that predict these events and give details, such as the land blossoming and the cities being reinhabited. It would be impossible to write such predictions hundreds of years before they happen to a specific group of people and then to orchestrate their fulfillment—unless of course the writer is God, the sovereign ruler over the events of history. Here is a sampling of these prophecies.

Scriptures Predicting the scattering and regathering of the Jewish people

> *Deuteronomy 28:64: "Moreover, the LORD will scatter you among all peoples, from one end of the earth to the other end of the earth; and there you shall serve other gods, wood and stone, which you or your fathers have not known."*

> *Ezekiel 36:24: "For I will take you from the nations, gather you from all the lands and bring you into your own land."*

> *Ezekiel 36:28, 30, 33-38: "You will live in the land that I gave to your forefathers; so you will be My people, and I will be your God.... (30) I will multiply the fruit of the tree and the produce of the field, so that you will not receive again the disgrace of*

famine among the nations....*(33) On the day that I cleanse you from all your iniquities, I will cause the cities to be inhabited, and the waste places will be rebuilt. (34) The desolate land will be cultivated instead of being a desolation in the sight of everyone who passes by. (35) They will say, 'This desolate land has become like the garden of Eden; and the waste, desolate and ruined cities are fortified and inhabited.' (36) Then the nations that are left roundabout you will know that I, the LORD, have rebuilt the ruined places and planted that which was desolate; I, the LORD, have spoken and will do it. (37) ...This also I will let the house of Israel ask Me to do for them: I will increase their men like a flock. (38) Like the flock for sacrifices, like the flock at Jerusalem during her appointed feasts, so will the waste cities be filled with flocks of men. Then they will know that I am the LORD."*

Ezekiel 37:21-22, 28: *"Say to them, 'Thus says the Lord GOD, "Behold, I will take the sons of Israel from among the nations where they have gone, and I will gather them from every side and bring them into their own land; (22) and I will make them one nation in the land, on the mountains of Israel; and one king will be king for all of them; and they will no longer be two nations and no longer be divided into two kingdoms.... (28) And the nations will know that I am the LORD who sanctifies Israel, when My sanctuary is in their midst forever."*

Isaiah 11:12: *"And He will lift up a standard for the nations And assemble the banished ones of Israel, And will gather the dispersed of Judah From the four corners of the earth."*

Isaiah 43:5-7: "Do not fear, for I am with you; I will bring your offspring from the east, And gather you from the west. (6) I will say to the north, 'Give them up!' And to the south, 'Do not hold them back.' Bring My sons from afar And My daughters from the ends of the earth, (7) Everyone who is called by My name, And whom I have created for My glory, Whom I have formed, even whom I have made."

Jeremiah 29:14: "'I will be found by you,' declares the LORD, 'and I will restore your fortunes and will gather you from all the nations and from all the places where I have driven you,' declares the LORD,"and I will bring you back to the place from where I sent you into exile.'"

Jeremiah 32:37-38: "Behold, I will gather them out of all the lands to which I have driven them in My anger, in My wrath and in great indignation; and I will bring them back to this place and make them dwell in safety. (38) "They shall be My people, and I will be their God."

The return of the Jewish people into the land of Israel over the past 125 years is nothing short of astounding. The territory God originally promised to the Hebrews had been ruled and occupied by one nation after another, and finally by the Ottoman Empire beginning in 1517. The British

defeated the Ottoman Empire in 1917 during World War I—ending exactly 400 years of Ottoman rule—and Israel became a British protectorate.

In the late 1890s, Jewish people began to feel stirred in their hearts to return to Israel. A few did. This movement was aided on November 2, 1917 during WWI when the Balfour Declaration was signed. It was actually a letter from British Foreign Secretary Arthur James Balfour to Britain's most illustrious Jewish citizen, Baron Lionel Walter Rothschild, expressing the British government's support for a Jewish homeland in ancient Israel. It said in part, "His Majesty's Government view with favor the establishment in Palestine of a national home for the Jewish people, and will use their best endeavors to facilitate the achievement of this object, it being clearly understood that nothing shall be done which may prejudice the civil and religious rights of existing non-Jewish communities in Palestine, or the rights and political status enjoyed by Jews in any other country." These events paved the way for more Jews to return to Israel.

During WWII, millions of Jewish people were slaughtered in the holocaust. That horrible time produced one positive result, however, spurring another step toward making Israel a homeland for Jewish people. The newly formed United Nations partitioned the land, giving the Jewish people a place to call home. In 1948 Israel became a nation again for the first time in nearly 2,000 years. It was the first time in approximately 2500 years that the Jews were not in bondage to some other nation or nations.

Jewish people have continued to come back to Israel in large numbers since WWII. The Jewish population in Israel was less than 750,000 in 1948. Today it is well more than 6 million. Over a million returned from the former Soviet Union after the fall of the iron curtain in 1989. They continue to return today  from around the world, especially from European nations where anti-semitism abounds. It truly is a miracle happening before our eyes, during our lifetime, in direct fulfillment of Bible prophecy.

When the Jews began returning to Israel, the land was desolate, uncultivated, wild, and unfruitful. Mark Twain recounted his impression of Israel in his book The Innocents Abroad after his visit in 1867. He wrote that Israel is a...

> "...desolate country whose soil is rich enough, but is given over wholly to weeds—a silent mournful expanse....A desolation....We never saw a human being on the whole route....There was hardly a tree or a shrub anywhere. Even the olive and the cactus, those fast friends of the worthless soil, had almost deserted the country." [7]

Today Israel has become extremely fruitful in many ways. The land has truly blossomed, as the Bible said it would. Rains have returned to this area, supplemented by modern irrigation systems. Nearly a half a billion trees have been planted, fruits are exported, and cities have been rebuilt with vitality and commerce abounding. To show the extent of Israel's revitalization in the modern world, consider the following examples:

- Israel exports $2.5 billion worth of agricultural products and technology annually.
- Israel is a major player in the high-tech industry with 200 business start-ups annually and 2500 start-up companies presently in operation.
- Israel is the home of Teva Pharmaceutical Industries, the largest generic drug manufacturer in the world.
- Israel is one of the world's three major centers for polished diamonds.
- Israel is fast becoming a leader in venture-capital

---

[7] Quoted from Zionism and the State of Israel, https://zionismandisrael.wordpress.com/2008/08/28/mark-twain-in-the-holy-land/

outlays, new company launches, hedge fund industries, and information technology.

• Israel's solar companies work on projects around the world.

• Discoveries of natural gas fields have made Israel an exporter of natural gas.

• Israel has a technologically advanced market economy. As of 2013, Israel ranks nineteenth among 187 nations on the UN's Human Development Index, placing the nation ahead of France, Austria, and  Belgium. Israel ranked twenty-fifth in the world in GDP per capita in 2014 with a GDP per capita of 36,991.

All of this rebounding of the lushness and vitality of Israel was prophesied in the Old Testament. For lack of space, I will not list all these prophetic Scriptures, but for a sampling of them I urge you to see Ezekiel 36:8-12; Amos 9:11-15; and Isaiah 27:6.

We could spend additional time speaking of the amazing victories that Israel has won in numerous wars since May 14, 1948,  even though they were greatly outnumbered each time. We could also speak about the current oil field developments in Israel where many discoveries of huge petroleum supplies are based on Old Testament scriptures. We could also speak of the world focus on the city of Jerusalem, the most contended-for place on the face of the earth—again in fulfillment of biblical prophecy. Then of course there is the topic of the plans and preparations being made to rebuild the Jewish Temple in Jerusalem, also according to biblical prophecy. There is also the aligning of nations such as Turkey, Russia, and Iran toward the fulfillment of the war of Gog and Magog spoken of in Ezekiel 38 and 39. Though each of these topics are worthy of extensive attention, for the sake of space we will forego them and just mention a couple of additional points about modern Israel.

The Hebrew language has been restored in Israel as the national language in fulfillment of Zephaniah 3:9 (NKJV), which states: "For then I will restore to the peoples a pure language, That they all may call on the name of the LORD, To serve Him with one accord."

Finally, Israel was born as a nation in one day on May 14, 1948 in fulfillment of Isaiah 66:8 (NIV), which says, "Who has ever heard of such things? Who has ever seen things like this? Can a country be born in a day or a nation be brought forth in a moment? Yet no sooner is Zion in labor than she gives birth to her children."

Truly, all that is happening today in Jerusalem, Israel, and the Middle East shows unquestionably that the words written 2500–3500 years ago in the Bible had to have been inspired by God, since they are coming to pass with such accuracy!

"The Bible - God's Word (Part 2)"

The Bible - God's Word (Part 2)

Fulfilled Prophecy Related to the End Times

Another area of Bible prophecy that confirms the Bible as the Word of God is that of the End Times. End time prophecies occur in both the Old and New Testaments, describing what the world will be like and what events will take place in the days that precede the return of Jesus Christ.

We can break down End Time prophecy into four major categories: (1) Israel, Jerusalem and the Middle East, (2) Increased Lawlessness and Immorality, (3) Deception in the Earth (Including False Christs and False Prophets), and (4) New World Order. The first of these categories, Israel, Jerusalem, and the Middle East, was discussed in the previous chapter. So in this chapter, we will move directly to the next category, "Increased Lawlessness and Immorality."

Lawlessness and Immorality

Here are a few examples of prophetic Scriptures that describe the lawlessness and immorality we will find in the last days.

> *Matthew 24:7-10: "For nation will rise against nation, and kingdom against kingdom, and in various places there will be famines and*

earthquakes. (8) But all these things are merely the beginning of birth pangs. (9) Then they will deliver you to tribulation, and will kill you, and you will be hated by all nations because of My name. (10) At that time many will fall away and will betray one another and hate one another."

2 Timothy 3:1-4: "But realize this, that in the last days difficult times will come. (2) For men will be lovers of self, lovers of money, boastful, arrogant, revilers, disobedient to parents, ungrateful, unholy, (3) unloving, irreconcilable, malicious gossips, without self-control, brutal, haters of good, (4) treacherous, reckless, conceited, lovers of pleasure rather than lovers of God"

We are living in a time of increasingly extreme lawlessness and immorality. Terrorism takes lives daily. Crime is continually on the rise. Many government officials are now openly dishonest and corrupt. National, state, and local governments obey only the laws they like. Immorality in America is rampant as never before. Sexual immorality heads the list, with widespread pornography use and unrestrained sexual freedom, leading to high out-of-wedlock births, abortions, and a divorce rate hovering at 50 percent. Homosexuality, gay marriage, and gender fluidity have become socially accepted. It is clear that the Bible was extremely accurate with its prophecies of the increased lawlessness and immorality that would occur before Christ's second coming.

Deception in the Earth

Here are a few examples of prophetic scriptures picturing the deception that will infect the Earth in the last days.

In Matthew 24:5 and 11, Jesus told His disciples, "For many will come in My name, saying, 'I am the Christ,' and will mislead many. Many false prophets will arise and will mislead many."

2 Thessalonians 2:3: "Let no one in any way deceive you, for [the day of the Lord] will not come unless the apostasy comes first, and the man of lawlessness is revealed, the son of destruction."

1 Timothy 4:1: "But the Spirit explicitly says that in later times some will fall away from the faith, paying attention to deceitful spirits and doctrines of demons"

Daniel 11:32: "By smooth words he will turn to godlessness those who act wickedly toward the covenant, but the people who know their God will display strength and take action."

The "man of lawlessness," the ultimate tool of Satan who will appear in the last days, has not yet been revealed. Yet those who know and understand the Bible can already see massive deception taking place in America and the Western world as people turn away from churches in droves and begin to endorse the standards and immorality of  culture. Even many churches are endorsing sexual immorality, some going so far as to not only endorse homosexuality as a valid lifestyle, but also to ordain gays as pastors and bishops.

New World Order
Many prophetic Scriptures in both the Old and New Testaments prophesy the coming of a new world order—a one-world government headed by an extremely powerful, extremely evil, deceptive, and tyrannical leader. Here is a sampling of those Scriptures:

2 Thessalonians 2:8-9: "Then that lawless one will be revealed whom the Lord will slay with the breath of His mouth and bring to an end by the appearance of His coming; (9) that is, the one whose coming is in accord with the activity of Satan, with all power and signs and false wonders."

2 Thessalonians 2:4: [The man of lawlessness] who opposes and exalts himself above every so-called god or object of worship, so that he takes his seat in the temple of God, displaying himself as being God."

Revelation 13:16-18: "And he causes all, the small and the great, and the rich and the poor, and the free men and the slaves, to be given a mark on their right hand or on their forehead, (17) and he provides that no one will be able to buy or to sell, except the one who has the mark, either the name of the beast or the number of his name. (18) Here is wisdom. Let him who has understanding calculate the number of the beast, for the number is that of a man; and his number is six hundred and sixty-six."

Today we see several evidences of a movement toward a New World Order. In the fall of 2015, the United Nations implemented Agenda 2030, also referred to as a plan for "Sustainable Development." Though this plan was presented with wonderful goals, a closer look clearly reveals that it is a major, purposeful step toward the  breaking of national sovereignty and the establishing of a one-world system, or a New World Order.

The continual push toward globalism is an attempt to diminish national sovereignty in favor of a centralized system of control. The founding of the European Union was a step in that direction. The tendency of governments to relinquish increments of power to world courts also indicates a willingness to move toward a globalistic order of centralization.

The primary danger of this movement, as the Bible makes clear, is that the further government gets from the people, the more tyrannical it will become. So these globalistic clouds on the world horizon are harbingers of things to come that should make Christians extremely watchful and wary. The Bible tells us exactly what is behind these movements.

The words of Revelation 13:16-18 are familiar to most people because of their prophetic reference to the number 666 as the mark of the beast. My explanation of this passage is that in the last days, a world empire led by a world leader will have the ability to control a global electronic economic system. The system will involve scanning a device implanted in the hand or forehead of every individual engaged in buying or selling. Those who resist this leader and refuse to accept the implantation of the electronic number in their bodies will not be able to buy or sell.

The technology to implement this system is already with us, and it involves the number 666. In fact, this number is already

marked on the packages of products we buy daily through the use of the UPC (Universal Product Code). The first two lines of the code, the middle two lines, and last two lines are always identical to each other. They are longer than the other lines in the code, and based on the established code each of them represents the number 6. Put the three sets of lines together and you have 666 marked on every product we buy today. The same is true of products marked with an alternative form of the UPC.

What are the chances that the number that the Bible identifies as the mark of the beast in the last days is the very number chosen as the master number of the UPC marked on all the products we buy worldwide? The chances would probably be zero unless the God Who knows the end from the beginning is the author of the Bible.

Another note about End Time prophecy: Daniel 12:4 says something very pointed about the end times that doesn't fit our four main prophecy categories. In this passage God says to Daniel, "But as for you, Daniel, conceal these words and seal up the book until the end of time: many will go back and forth,

and knowledge will increase." Here we have a prophecy indicating two things that will be very significant in the developing world of the last days—the increase of travel and the increase of knowledge. Wow! Think about it! What two things have increased at astounding rates in the

past 100 years? Clearly, the answer is travel and knowledge. Again, this is exactly what the Bible said would happen.

11. Biblical Confirmation Through Changed Lives
Another wonderful confirmation that the Bible is the Word of God is the millions of changed lives its message has brought to people around the world throughout the centuries. The Bible is God's Word, and it is truth. Jesus said that when people follow Him and His words, they will know the truth and the truth will set them free! (John 8:32). If this were not true, Christianity would not have survived. Because it is true, Christianity still thrives today around the world.

One example of this fact can be seen in the nation of China. Christianity has grown in phenomenal ways as tens of millions have come to know Christ in China over the past 50 years or so. This despite the difficulties encountered by those who accept Christ and begin to follow Him. Many are persecuted and imprisoned for their faith. Some are tortured and even killed. Still, the number of Christians meeting in underground house churches continues to grow at an amazing rate. The change that Jesus brings into the lives of these Chinese believers is so powerful and so real that millions risk much to follow Christ and the teachings of the Bible.

The changed lives of those who come to know Christ bear witness to the fact that Jesus is the Savior of the world and the Bible is the Word of God.

12. The Indestructibility and Distribution of the Bible

Throughout the centuries since Jesus Christ established Christianity, the Bible, which is the book of Christianity, has been attacked in many ways by people and governments intent on destroying its teachings. Those attacks continue today, though they mostly come in more covert ways than in the past. Yet lies about the Bible and attempts to destroy its influence still abound. Through all these attacks, the Bible has stood through time and  remained by far the most widely distributed book throughout the world. It is translated into more languages than any other book.

In an article entitled "The Indestructibility of the Bible" on the website, Truth Magazine, Cecil Willis notes that every Roman ruler from the time of Christ until the reign of the emperor Constantine stood against the Christian church. He explains,

> "Many of their efforts were directed toward destroying the Bible. Of Diocletian (284-316), the ruler immediately preceding Constantine, Eusebius, the historian said, "royal edicts were published everywhere, commanding that the churches be leveled to the ground and the Scriptures destroyed by fire" (Church History, Book VIII, Ch. 1). Diocletian went on to say that if one had a copy of the Scriptures and did not  surrender it to be burned, if it were discovered, he would be killed. Furthermore, if any other should know of one who had a copy of the Scriptures, and did not

report it, he also would be killed. During this time many, many copies of the Bible were burned, copies laboriously written in longhand. Of this period, the historian Newman said, "Multitudes . . . hastened to deny the faith and to surrender their copies of the Scriptures; many more bore the most horrible tortures and refused with their latest breath to surrender the Scriptures or in any way to compromise themselves" (Newman, Church History, p. 169). After this edict had been in force for two years, Diocletian boasted, "I have completely exterminated the Christian writings from the face of the earth!" (Rimmer, Seven Wonders of the Wonderful Word, p. 15). But had he completely destroyed it? History tells us that the next ruler, Constantine, became a Christian. He requested that copies of the Scriptures be made for all the churches." [1]

This is just one example of many throughout the ages where rulers have attempted to eliminate the Bible, yet each attempt has failed and the Bible's influence on the lives of people has continued.

In his article, Willis refers to another example that occurred many years after the attacks of Diocletian.

"Voltaire, the noted French infidel, who died in 1778, made his attempt to destroy the Bible. He boldly made the prediction that within 100 years the Bible and Christianity would have been swept from existence into oblivion. But Voltaire's efforts and his bold prophecy failed as miserably as did those of his unbelieving predecessors. In fact, within 100 years, the very printing press upon which Voltaire had

---

[1] Quoted from article *The Indestructibility of the Bible*, http://www.truthmagazine.com/archives/volume19/TM019211.html

printed his infidel literature, was being used to print copies of the Bible. And afterward, the very house in which the boasting Voltaire had lived, was literally stacked with Bibles prepared by the Geneva Bible Society. Voltaire and all his cohorts had miserably failed." [2]

Guinness World Records says that the Bible is clearly the most widely read and sold book of all times. Note the following from their website: "Although it is impossible to obtain exact figures, there is little doubt that the Bible is the world's best-selling and most widely distributed book. A survey by the Bible Society concluded that around 2.5 billion copies were printed between 1815 and 1975, but more recent estimates put the number at more than 5 billion." They go on to say, "the whole Bible had been translated into 349 languages; 2123 languages

have at least one book of the Bible in that language." Wycliffe Bible Translators say that the number of languages that have complete Bibles is now up to 550. They exist to complete the work of translating the Bible into every known language so that all may hear the message of the Bible in their language.

Even though many today still attempt to discredit and destroy the Bible, especially in universities and schools across America, the Bible continues to be the best selling, most read book in the world generation after generation. The impact that the Bible has had upon the world is another evidence that it is the Word of God.

---

[2] ibid.

Conclusion

In addition to all of the things we have looked at here it should be noted that the Bible speaks with authority as the inspired Word of God! Over 2600 times the term "and God said" or its equivalent are found in the Bible. 2 Timothy 3:16 speaks to this: "All Scripture is inspired by God and profitable for teaching, for reproof, for correction, for training in righteousness."

Every Christian should realize that we do not accept the Bible as the Word of God just because the church or some person in authority tells us to. We accept the Bible as the Word of God because it is inspired by God, telling of historical events written during the lifetime of eye witnesses. Finally, there are many confirming evidences given to us that help us to see without question that the Bible is the Word of God.

Key Passages to Understand

Certainly all of the Bible is very important, but a few sections are especially important, enabling us to understanding critical aspects of a biblical worldview and God's plan of salvation. I will mention these passages briefly here and encourage you to study them on your own.

1. Genesis 1-11 – Foundations

Chapters 1–11 of the book of Genesis are especially important because they tell of our origin and several early events that shape the world as we know it. Chapters 1 and 2 tell of the creation of all things and give us our understanding of the value and purpose of mankind. We also gain our understanding of man's relationship to the world around him and our understanding of marriage and family.

Genesis 2 and 3 explain the fall of man into sin and show us the consequences of sin, which is clearly reflected in today's world. Genesis 4 and 5, as well as 10 and 11, give us a detailed genealogy from Adam to Abraham, including a timeline that can be measured. Genesis 6 through 9 give us a detailed account of the flood judgment that God brought upon the world, which explains much of the geology and paleontology we encounter today.

Finally, Genesis 11 gives us the account of the confusing of languages that occurred at the tower of Babel. This explains much of what we see in anthropology and in the nations, people groups, and languages of the world today.

2. The Gospel of John

The Gospel of John is written specifically to reveal who Jesus Christ is and to show us the importance of believing in Him as our Savior and Lord. The book opens with, "In the beginning was the Word, and the Word was with God, and the Word was God." The passage goes on to say that all things were created by Him (the Word) and that He is life and the light that has come into the world. We're told that He was rejected by many, but "as many as received Him, to them He gave the right to become children of God, even to those who believe in His name." In verse 14 "the Word" is clearly identified as Jesus Christ when it says that "the Word became flesh and dwelt among us, and we saw His glory, glory as of the only begotten from the Father, full of grace and truth."

In John 20:31 we are given the purpose of this book—"that you may believe that Jesus is the Christ, the Son of God; and that believing you may have life in His name." The entire book is dedicated to this purpose, bringing us to a point of believing in Jesus Christ so that we may have life in His name.

The Gospel of John differs from the other three gospels (the synoptic gospels) in a number of ways, all related to the distinct purpose of the book. Whereas the other three gospels give many details of the ministry of Jesus, the Gospel of John focuses on only a few events, but spends a great deal of time addressing the discussions about who Jesus is that occurred in conjunction with specific miracles He performed. This underscores John's purpose—to show who Jesus is.

Only eight of Jesus' miracles are recorded in the Gospel of John, and they are always called "signs" in this book. Each time a miracle is recorded, there is an ensuing discussion about who Jesus is or whether or not people believed in Him.

The emphasis of John's gospel on showing the deity of Christ is especially evident in the recording of twenty-three "I Am" statements throughout the book. These relate to God's words to

Moses in Exodus 3 when Moses was told to tell the people in Egypt that he was sent by the God called "I Am." The term "I Am" speaks of God's eternal existence and is related to the name "Jehovah." Often, in the Old Testament the name "Jehovah" was combined with descriptive terms such as "Jireh" which means "provider" or "Shalom" which means peace. In the same way, the Gospel of John adds descriptive terms to "I Am," such as "the resurrection and the life," "the door," "the good shepherd," "the light of the world," "the way, the truth and the life," etc. In other cases Jesus is simply referred to as "I Am," as in John 8:58.

The term "believe" or other forms of that word are used ninety-eight times in the Gospel of John. In each case the context relates specifically to believing or not believing in Jesus Christ. In contrast, in Matthew, Mark, and Luke, the word "believe" and its variants are only used a total of only thirty six times. Only three of those times are references specifically related to believing or not believing in Jesus Christ.

The Gospel of John is the book we normally tell new Christians to read first. This is because it is dedicated to revealing to us who Jesus Christ is and to showing us the vital importance of believing in Him.

3. The Book of Hebrews

The book of Hebrews is critical for our understanding of the sacrifice Jesus made on our behalf and His ongoing intercession for us as our great high priest. The book compares Jesus to angels, to Moses, and to the Old Testament priests, showing in each case His clear superiority.

The book of Hebrews is also significant in its comparison of the Old Covenant, revealed in the Old Testament, to the New Covenant, revealed in the New Testament. The New Covenant is seen to be superior to the Old in many ways.

The book was written to Hebrew converts who were facing trials and persecutions for their embrace of the New Covenant. It challenged them to stay true to their faith until the end. The book gives many warnings about the terrible consequences of turning back from faith.

4. The Books of Romans and Galatians

To gain a proper understanding of the plan of salvation as laid out in the New Testament, we need to study the books of Romans and Galatians. These two books give us detailed information as to why we need salvation, how salvation through faith in Christ fits with the justice and holiness of God, and how the Old Testament law was given—not to save us but to point us to salvation through faith in Christ.

5. The Books of Daniel and Revelation

The book of Daniel in the Old Testament and the book of Revelation in New Testament give us the majority of our information from Scripture about the future. This includes the second coming of Jesus Christ and the establishing of the kingdom of God. These two books are usually studied together, along with various related passages in other books of the Bible.

Study to Show Yourself Approved

When we study specific parts of the Bible to understand their unique purposes, we follow the admonition in 2 Timothy 2:15 (KJV) to "Study to shew thyself approved unto God, a workman that needeth not to be ashamed, rightly dividing the word of truth." I encourage you to enjoy the Bible and prayerfully seek to understand the truth that is in it. Remember that "All Scripture is inspired by God and profitable for teaching, for reproof, for correction, for training in righteousness" (2 Timothy 3:16).

Summary of Section 3 – Chapters 9 & 10

Below is a summary of the information presented in this chapter that corresponds to the memorization cards related to this chapter. You are encouraged to study the summary chart and the memorization cards so that you can retain and use this information in your witnessing and teaching.

Confirming Evidence - The Bible is God's Word
Both Internal & External Evidences Confirm the Bible to be God's Word

2 T I M O T H Y 3 : 1 6 - I N S P I R E D	
	INTERNAL UNITY - THE BIBLE CLAIMS TO BE GOD'S WORD & HAS A UNIFIED MESSAGE BEGINNING TO END
	BIBLIOGRAPHICAL EVIDENCE - CONFIRMS ORIGINAL CONTENT HAS BEEN PRESERVED
	ARCHAEOLOGICAL EVIDENCE CONFIRMS HISTORY, PLACES, PEOPLE & EVENTS OF THE BIBLE
	MEDICAL FACTS IN THE BIBLE - DISCOVERED IN THE PAST 250 YEARS BY MODERN MEDICINE
	SCIENTIFIC FACTS IN THE BIBLE - NOW CONFIRMED BY MODERN SCIENCE (E.G. - EARTH IS A SPHERE)
	FULFILLED PROPHECIES OF THE DESTRUCTION OF POWERFUL ANCIENT CITIES (WITH DETAIL)
	FULFILLED PROPHECIES OF WORLD EMPIRES - NOW FULFILLED IN HUMAN HISTORY
	FULFILLED MESSIANIC PROPHECIES (OVER 300) IN THE O.T. (FULFILLED BY JESUS CHRIST)
	FULFILLED PROPHECY - SCATTERING & REGATHERING OF THE JEWISH PEOPLE TO LAND OF ISRAEL
	FULFILLED PROPHECY - END TIME SIGNS & EVENTS LEADING TO 2ND COMING OF CHRIST
	CHANGED LIVES - MILLIONS AROUND THE WORLD CHANGED BY BELIEVING & FOLLOWING SCRIPTURES
	INDESTRUCTIBILITY OF THE BIBLE (THROUGH GREAT ATTACKS) & UNPARALLELED DISTRIBUTION

The Bible – God's Word!

The Bible was written by apx. 40 different authors over a period of more than 1500 years. Still, the unity of the message of the Bible is amazing. God's plan of creation & redemption from sin is consistently seen from Genesis - Revelation. Jesus Christ is the central character throughout. He is seen in the O.T. by prophecies, types & shadows. He is revealed clearly in the N.T. God's original plan in Genesis 1 & 2 is fulfilled in Revelation 21 & 22, redeemed man with God.

Internal Unity

(1)

The Bible – God's Word!

Though we do not have any of the original manuscripts of the Bible, we do have ancient copies of the original manuscripts that were written within 125 years of the originals. Great care was taken in the copying process to ensure accuracy. The number of manuscript copies of the Bible compared to other ancient writings such as Caesar's Gallic Wars & Homer's Iliad is vastly greater. Also, the copies of Bible manuscripts are much closer in time to the originals than that of the copies of other ancient writings. The Dead Sea Scrolls confirmed the accuracy of the manuscript copies.

Bibliographical Evidence

(2)

The Bible – God's Word!

Archaeological findings, as well as other historical documents continue to confirm the Bible's account of history. People, places and events are confirmed and continue to be confirmed as Archaeological exploration continues. Nelson Glueck, noted Archaeologist has said, "It may be stated categorically that no Archaeological study has ever contradicted a Biblical reference!"

Archaeology & History

(3)

The Bible – God's Word!

There are numerous medical facts found in the Bible that have now been confirmed by modern medicine. Three of them to consider are (1) The danger of germs in causing disease (found in many places in the O.T. law – Exodus through Deuteronomy)(Written apx. 3500 years ago) – (2) 8th Day chosen for circumcision (Lev. 12:3) & (3) Life is in the Blood (Lev. 17:11)

Medical Facts

(4)

The Bible – God's Word!

There are scientific facts in the Bible, now confirmed by modern science. For example Is. 40:22 reveals that the earth is round & that the heavens are being stretched out. Also, Job 38:31 speaks of star constellations, "the Pleiades" & "Orion". The Bible reveals that the stars of "Pleiades" are gravitationally bound while the stars of "Orion" are not.

Scientific Facts

(5)

The Bible – God's Word!

The Bible includes detailed prophecies concerning the destruction of ancient cities such as Petra, Tyre and Babylon. History books and encyclopedias reveal the accuracy of these Biblical prophecies which not only spoke of the destruction of these cities in general but in some cases gave details of how they would be destroyed.

Fulfilled Prophecy (a)

(6)

The Bible - God's Word!

The Bible includes prophecies of the World Empires from the time of Daniel (apx. 600 B.C.) through today. In Daniel 2, 7 & 8 the Bible prophesies that there would be (1) the Babylonian Empire, (2) the Medo-Persian Empire, (3) the Greek Empire, and (4) the Roman Empire. It also speaks of an End Time World Empire that is now referred to often as "The New World Order."

Fulfilled Prophecy (b) (7)

The Bible - God's Word!

The Bible includes over 300 Messianic prophecies in the O.T. that are fulfilled by Jesus Christ in the N.T. through His birth, life, ministry, death & resurrection. These fulfilled prophecies attest to the fact that the Bible is the Word of God & are another example of the unity of the message throughout the Bible. They also confirm that Jesus Christ is the Messiah!

Fulfilled Prophecy (c) (8)

The Bible - God's Word!

The Bible includes amazing prophecies concerning the scattering of the Jewish people into the nations of the world (e.g. – Deut. 28:64) and the regathering of the Jewish people from the nations of the world back to Israel in the last days. (e.g. – Ez. 36:23-24 & Ez. 37:21-22) It is also prophesied that the land will become fruitful again (Ez. 36:6-12) & Israel will become a nation (Is. 66:8)

Fulfilled Prophecy (d) (9)

The Bible - God's Word!

The Bible includes detailed prophecies concerning the end times (or last days) that are being fulfilled before our eyes. Of these (increase of immorality, wars & rumors of wars, movement toward a new world order, attention to Jerusalem, etc.) the most specific seems to be the use of the number 666 (Rev. 13:16-18) which is now used in the Universal Product Code on products.

Fulfilled Prophecy (e) (10)

The Bible - God's Word!

The changed lives of millions and millions of people who have accepted and followed the message of the Bible bears witness to the Bible being the Word of God. For centuries, including today, people all around the world give testimony of the dramatic change (for the good) that they have experienced when obeying the words of Scripture and putting their faith in Jesus Christ!

Changed Lives (11)

The Bible - God's Word!

The Bible has been attacked by kings, emperors and "intellectual" skeptics for centuries but has stood through every attack. All the while, the Bible has continued to be the undisputed leader when it comes to the number of copies produced and distributed, year after year after year!

Indestructibility & Distribution (12)

(Above) These 12 memorization cards deal with the evidences that confirm to us that the Bible is the Word of God. You are encouraged to use them to help you retain the critical information within these two chapters on the Bible.

Memorization Cards Available for Free Download at localchurchapologetics.org

"Jesus Christ - Son of God and Savior of the World"

Jesus Christ - Son of God and Savior of the World

In this chapter, we will focus on the person of Jesus Christ. He is both the author of and the central figure in the gospel message presented in the Bible.

While Christ is central to Christianity, we have deliberately preceded our discussion of Him in this chapter with a chapter containing evidences supporting the authenticity of the Bible. This is because the Bible is our primary source of information about Christ. Before we can trust what we learn of Him in the Bible, we must first have confidence in the reliability of the Bible.

Who Do You Say That Jesus Is?

This is the most important question each of us will answer in our lifetime. Our life now and for eternity depends upon our answer. In Matthew 16:13-18, Jesus had this discussion with His disciples:

> *Now when Jesus came into the district of Caesarea Philippi, He was asking His disciples, "Who do people say that the Son of Man is?" (14) And they said, "Some say John the Baptist; and others, Elijah; but still others, Jeremiah, or one of the prophets." (15) He said to them, "But who do you say that I am?" (16) Simon Peter answered, "You are the Christ, the Son of the living God." (17) And Jesus said to him, "Blessed are you, Simon Barjona, because*

flesh and blood did not reveal this to you, but My Father who is in heaven. (18) I also say to you that you are Peter, and upon this rock I will build My church; and the gates of Hades will not overpower it.

The importance of knowing who Jesus is can be seen in this passage. After the disciples expressed the variety of opinions held by others concerning His identity, Jesus asks them very pointedly, "But who do you say that I am?" Simon Peter answers the question thoughtfully, and correctly through the revelation given to him by God the Father. He replied, "You are the Christ, the Son of the living God." Jesus says that Peter is blessed because he has received this revelation.

Peter's answer reveals two critical points. The first is related to Peter's identity and nature. When Jesus first met Peter, He "looked at him and said, 'You are Simon the son of John; you shall be called Cephas' (which is translated Peter)" (John 1:42). Simon means "pebble," while Peter means "rock." Jesus was prophesying that Simon's inner nature would change, and he would become strong like a rock. When Peter receives and proclaims the revelation of who Jesus is, the inner transformation occurs and Jesus declares to him, "... you are Peter." The earlier prophecy is now fulfilled, and it is brought about by Peter coming to know who Jesus is and by his proclamation of that truth. We become capable of fulfilling God's destiny for our life by coming to know who Jesus is, and by proclaiming (confessing) who He is. Certainly, Peter had struggles in his character development after this moment, but it was at this moment that his inner identity changed.

The second critical thing that was revealed immediately was that Peter and his confession of who Jesus is would become the rock upon which Jesus will build His church. It is clear from the context of the passage that Peter's confession of Jesus Christ's identity is the key here. To this day, the understanding of who Jesus truly is, is so powerful that the church is established upon it and will never be defeated by Satan and all of hell's powers.

Who Jesus Is Makes Christianity Unique

Christianity is different from all other religions because it is based upon the person of Jesus Christ. All other belief systems may have key persons who are merely messengers, but Christianity is based on the understanding that Jesus Himself is the very source and means of salvation.

All other belief systems are based upon one or more of the following philosophical concepts:

> (1) **Epistemological** – The path to God
> or enlightenment is through knowledge.
> (2) **Pragmatic** – The path to God
> or enlightenment is through works.
> (3) **Existential** – The path to God or
> enlightenment is through an experience.
>
> Only Christianity is **"ontologically"** based. That means it is based upon a person. The path to God and enlightenment is through the person of Jesus Christ.

Seeing Who Jesus Is in the Scriptures

Jesus Christ is the central figure through all the Bible. He is seen throughout the Old Testament through types, shadows, and prophecies. He is seen clearly in the New Testament as God the Son, the Messiah (Christ), and as the Savior of the world. Here is list of only a few of the ways Christ is identified in Scripture.

The Scriptures Present Jesus Christ as:

(1) The Cornerstone that the Church is Built Upon - Psalm 118:22-23; Luke 20:17-18; Acts 4:10-12; 1 Peter 2:4-8

(2) God the Son (Having Deity) - John 1:1-3, 14; John 8:24, 58; John 19:35; John 20:31; Joel 2:32 with Romans 10:9; Philippians 2:5-8; Colossians 2:9; Titus 2:13; Hebrews 1:6-8

(3) Second Person of the Trinity - Matthew 28:18-20; Matthew 3:16-17; Hebrews 1:1-8

(4) God Incarnate - Isaiah 9:6-7; Matthew 1:23; John 1:1,14; Philippians 2:5-8; Colossians 2:9; Hebrews 2:14-18

(5) The Revelation of God the Father's Character - John 1:18; John 14:9; Hebrews 1:3

(6) Eternal - John 8:58; John 17:5; Hebrews 7:3

(7) Agent of Creation - John 1:1-3; Colossians 1:15-16; Hebrews 1:1-3

(8) Christ (Messiah) - Psalm 22; Isaiah 7:14; Isaiah 9:6-7; Isaiah 53; Matthew 16:13-17; Mark 14:61-62; John 20:31; Acts 2:36

(9) Holy and Sinless Lamb of God Who takes away the sins of the world - John 1:29,36; John 6:69; 1 Corinthians 5:7; 1 Peter 1:18-19; Revelation 5:6, 6:9 7:17, 19:9, 21:23

(10) Our Great High Priest - Romans 8:34; Hebrews 7:17-28; Hebrews 8; Hebrews 9:11-28;

(11) Redeemer of all Humanity and all of Creation - John 19:30; Romans 3:23-24; 1 Peter 1:18-19

(12) Risen from the Dead/Alive Forevermore - Acts 2;23-36; Ephesians 1:19-22; Revelation 1:17-18

(13) Victorious Over All Enemies (Spiritual and Physical) - 1 Corinthians 15:24-28; Ephesians 1:19-22; Colossians 2:13-15; Hebrews 2:14; Revelation 19:11-21

(14) The Only Way of Salvation – John 14:6; Acts 4:10-12; Romans 10:9-10; 1 Timothy 2:5-6

(15) The Author and Perfecter of Our Faith – Hebrews 2:10; Hebrews 12:2

The first nine of our memorization cards for this chapter deal with who the Bible says Jesus Christ is. The tenth deals with what the Bible says about our need to believe in Jesus Christ. Much of our attention in this chapter will be given to the truths presented on the last two cards, which deal with the fact that Jesus was an historical person who rose bodily from the dead. Before we look into these matters, we will look into the issue of who the Bible says Jesus Christ is.

The Cornerstone

In Acts 4:10-12, Peter proclaims that Jesus Christ has become the Chief Cornerstone and that there is salvation in no one else.

> *Let it be known to all of you and to all the people of Israel, that by the name of Jesus Christ the Nazarene, whom you crucified, whom God raised from the dead--by this name this man stands here before you in good health. (11) He is the STONE WHICH WAS REJECTED by you, THE BUILDERS, but WHICH HAS BECOME THE CHIEF CORNERSTONE. (12) And there is salvation in no one else; for there is no other name under heaven that has been given among men by which we must be saved.**

Peter's proclamation of Jesus as the Chief Cornerstone and the Stone which the builders rejected comes from Psalm 118:22-23.

> *The stone which the builders rejected Has become the chief corner stone. (23) This is the LORD'S doing; It is marvelous in our eyes.*

In this Psalm, David prophesied of the coming Messiah. He declared that the Messiah would be rejected by those who were leaders within the Jewish religion, but would be used by God to become the Cornerstone of the church that God would build for Himself. The prophecy makes it clear that this would be God's doing.

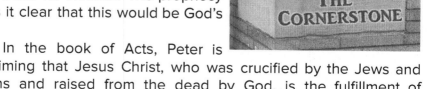

In the book of Acts, Peter is proclaiming that Jesus Christ, who was crucified by the Jews and Romans and raised from the dead by God, is the fulfillment of David's messianic prophecy in Psalm 118.

The title "Cornerstone" indicates that it is God's plan for the church to be built upon the Lord Jesus Christ.

Jesus refers to Himself in this way in Luke, chapter 20. He adds that every person who falls upon Him will be broken—that is, they will humble themselves, turn from their self-centered ways, and become completely dependent upon Him. He also indicates that every person who chooses to not fall upon Him will eventually be destroyed by the judgment that will come upon them for rejecting His salvation.

> *But Jesus looked at them and said, "What then is this that is written: 'THE STONE WHICH THE BUILDERS REJECTED, THIS HAS BECOME THE CHIEF CORNERstone'? (18) "Everyone who falls on that stone will be broken to pieces; but on whomever it falls, it will scatter him like dust." (Luke 20:17-18)*

In 1 Peter 2, the apostle Peter expounds upon this truth, showing in greater detail how it affects us as believers when we come to Jesus, who is the Cornerstone that we build our lives upon.

> *And coming to Him as to a living stone which has been rejected by men, but is choice and precious in the sight of God, (5) you also, as living stones, are being built up as a spiritual house for a holy priesthood, to offer up spiritual sacrifices acceptable to God through Jesus Christ. (6) For this is contained in Scripture: "BEHOLD I LAY IN ZION A CHOICE STONE, A PRECIOUS CORNERSTONE, AND HE WHO BELIEVES ON HIM WILL NOT BE DISAPPOINTED." (7) This precious value, then, is for you who believe; but for those who disbelieve, "THE STONE WHICH THE BUILDERS REJECTED, THIS BECAME THE VERY CORNERSTONE," (8) and, "A STONE OF STUMBLING AND A ROCK OF OFFENSE"; for they stumble because they are disobedient to the word, and to this doom they were also appointed. (1 Peter 2:4-8)*

When the Bible refers to Jesus as the Cornerstone or the Choice Stone that has been laid in Zion, it is proclaiming that God has established a plan of redemption and salvation for Jews and Gentiles that is based upon the person of Jesus Christ, the Son of God.

The Deity of Jesus Christ

The question of whether Jesus is God is central to distinguishing the Christian faith from many false religions and cults. Most, if not all, cults fall short of declaring Jesus Christ to be God. Most other world religions acknowledge Jesus in some way or another, but none of them believe Him to be God. Many modern skeptics and liberal scholars deny the deity of Jesus Christ, and many say that He never claimed to be God. They say that the status of deity was added to Jesus by the church centuries after Jesus lived.

The Bible actually declares clearly that Jesus Christ is God. Jesus Himself proclaimed His deity in a number of passages of Scripture. We will look at a number of examples of this here.

The Deity of Christ as Seen in the Gospel of John

John writes his gospel with the expressed purpose of revealing who Jesus is. John records only eight of Jesus' miracles, which he refers to as "signs." These signs indicate who Jesus is and instigate the discussions about His identity. This explains why, as we discussed in the previous chapter, that John uses the term "believe" and its variants a total of ninety-eight times—all in reference to belief in Jesus.

John explicitly states the purpose of his gospel in chapter 20.

> *Therefore many other signs Jesus also performed in the presence of the disciples, which are not written in this book; (31) but these have been written so that you may believe that Jesus is the Christ, the Son of God; and that believing you may have life in His name. (John 20:30-31)*

It couldn't get much clearer than that! John's purpose is also clearly affirmed in the very beginning of his gospel, where he opens with a clear proclamation of Christ's deity:

> *In the beginning was the Word, and the Word was with God, and the Word was God. (2) He was in the beginning with God. (3) All things came into being through Him, and apart from Him nothing came into being that has come into being. (John 1:1-3)*

"The Word" was with God and "the Word" was God. This is a clear and bold proclamation of the deity of Christ. In addition, these verses attest that Jesus is eternal and that He is the Creator of all things. We know that "the Word" refers to Jesus because of what verse 14 of the same chapter tells us.

> *And the Word became flesh, and dwelt among us, and we saw His glory, glory as of the only begotten from the Father, full of grace and truth. (John 1:14)*

The revelation of Christ as God in the Gospel of John is further buttressed by the "I Am" statements of Jesus that are strong and overt claims to His deity. The term "I Am" is applied to Jesus twenty-three times in the Gospel of John. These "I Am" statements are unique to the gospel of John and are not found in Matthew, Mark or Luke.

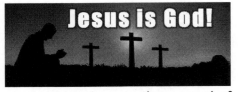

To understand the significance of this, we must go back to Exodus 3:13-15. In this passage, Moses has seen the burning bush, and God is calling him to go back to Egypt. Moses asks God, "Who shall I say has sent me?" God answers, "I AM WHO I AM"; and He said, "Thus you shall say to the sons of Israel, 'I AM has sent me to you'" (Exodus 3:14).

God identifies Himself as "I AM," which encompasses the idea of being self-existent and eternal. The Jews so reverenced this name of God that they would not even speak it, choosing rather to use only the consonants that essentially represented the words "I AM WHO I AM." These consonants are transliterated from the Hebrew language into English as YHWH, from which we get Yahweh or Jehovah.

With this understanding, we can see the significance of Jesus referring to Himself as "I Am" many times in the Gospel of John.

In the Old Testament, names were often added to "Jehovah" that were descriptive of God. Examples are "Jehovah Jireh" (Genesis 22:14) which means "God our provider" or "God will provide"; "Jehovah-Nissi" (Exodus 17:15) which means "God our banner" or "God our banner of victory"; and "Jehovah Shalom" (Judges 6:24) which means "God of peace".

In the same way, Jesus combined additional descriptions or names with "I Am" to refer to Himself throughout the Gospel of John. Many times these "I Am" statements were distinct expressions of His saving relationship to the world. Here are seven examples.

- "I Am the bread of life" (John 6:35, 41, 48, 51)
- "I Am the light of the world" (John 8:12)
- "I Am the door of the sheep" (John 10:7 & 9)
- "I Am the good shepherd" (John 10:11 & 14)
- "I Am the resurrection and the life" (John 11:25)
- "I Am the way, the truth & the life" (John 14:6)
- "I Am the true vine" (John 15:1 & 5)

These "I Am" statements both convey Jesus' claim to deity and convey who He is in relationship to our redemption and salvation.

Jesus also proclaimed Himself as "I Am" at times without adding other descriptive terms. Here are three examples that clearly show His claim to deity. He certainly knew and understood Exodus 3:13-15 when He purposely made these statements.

1. John 8:24: Jesus proclaims that we must believe that He is "I Am" in order to be saved, and to avoid dying in our sins.

> *And He was saying to them, "You are from below, I am from above; you are of this world, I am not of this world. (24) Therefore I said to you that you will die in your sins; for unless you believe that I am He, you will die in your sins." (John 8:23-24)*

Notice that the word "He" in verse 24 is in italics. This lets us know that the word was added to the text by the translators. This is a common practice. When translators added words like this, they were attempting to communicate in English what the Greek language was communicating in the text. In most cases, this is very helpful. In this case, however, I think it is helpful to read the text without the added word. Jesus said, "... unless you believe that I Am, you will die in your sins." The context of the passage does not necessitate the adding of the word "He." Even with "He" added, the passage is a powerful proclamation of Jesus' deity, authority, and power, but without it we have an even more powerful statement of His deity.

2. John 8:58: Here Jesus makes a statement that is a clear claim to His deity. It is also a clear reference to His eternal existence, which is a characteristic of God. I love this passage of Scripture. Jesus is having a heated discussion with a crowd of Jewish religious leaders about who He is and who they are. At one point, He says that Abraham rejoiced to see His day. They come back with an expected response:

> *So the Jews said to Him, "You are not yet fifty years old, and have You seen Abraham?" (58) Jesus said to them, "Truly, truly, I say to you, before Abraham was born, I am." (John 8:57-58)*

Jesus' response is highly significant. If He had said, "Before Abraham was, I was" or "Before Abraham was, I existed," we could say that the only thing He was communicating was that He is eternal or that He existed before, during, and after the time of Abraham. This in itself would be significant. But Jesus went beyond declaring that He is eternal. He chose this moment to clearly proclaim not only that He is eternal, but also that He is God. Jesus said to the crowd, "Before Abraham was, I AM!" By using the name "I AM," the same as "Jehovah," He was proclaiming His deity to them. Their angry response confirms that they understood exactly what He was saying; He was declaring Himself to be God! Verse 59 says that they picked up stones to stone Him.

3. John 18:4-6: Here Jesus proclaims Himself as "I AM," and a supernatural manifestation occurs to confirm Who He is.

> ***So Jesus, knowing all the things that were coming upon Him, went forth and said to them, "Whom do you seek?" (5) They answered Him, "Jesus the Nazarene." He said to them, "I am He." And Judas also, who was betraying Him, was standing with them. (6) So when He said to them, "I am He," they drew back and fell to the ground. (John 18:4-6)***

As the crowd led by Judas came to capture Jesus in the Garden of Gethsemane, Jesus asked them whom they had come to seek. He already knew the answer, so why would He ask this? It could very well be that He asked this question to precipitate the event that would follow, which would confirm who He truly is. The crowd replied that they were seeking Jesus the Nazarene. Again, our translations add the word "He" to Jesus' reply. In the original, He replied to them by saying simply, "I AM."

The moment He proclaimed that He is "I AM," the crowd "drew back and fell to the ground." Why did they fall? I think it is obvious. They were struck by a supernatural force that had nothing to do with the natural realm. The disciples did not suddenly intimidate them. No strong wind just happened to blow in at that moment. They were knocked down by the power of God! It was a supernatural witness to the truth of His claim to be God.

It is hard to comprehend why the crowd did not turn from their mission at that point. Especially after watching Jesus miraculously restore the ear that Peter had sliced off of one of the arrestors. You would think that many of them would have said, "I'm out of here!" Yet their ridiculous actions are indicative of the actions of many today who continue to attack Jesus' identity despite the overwhelming evidence that He is Creator, God, and Savior of the World.

In John 20:28 we have another case of Jesus being referred to as God in the Gospel of John. After Thomas, who had doubted the resurrection of Jesus, finally saw the resurrected Christ, he bowed before Him and proclaimed, "my Lord and my God." The Greek words used here for "Lord" and "God" are Kurios and Theos, showing absolutely that Jesus is being worshipped here as Jehovah God.

Jesus is revealed to be all the following in the Gospel of John: • Word made flesh • Creator • Light of men • Giver of life • Lamb of God • Giver of eternal life • Giver of living water • The Christ • Judge of all • Bread of life • Light of the World • Son of Man • Door of the sheep • The Good Shepherd • The Resurrection and the Life • The Way, The Truth, and The Life.

Throughout the Gospel of John, Jesus is seen to be God and to be the Christ. I encourage you to read the Gospel of John again with this understanding. Notice the proclamation of deity in the first verses, the discussions about who He is and whether or not people believed in Him, the many "I Am" statements, the many uses of the word "believe" and its variants, and the purpose statement at the end of the book. You will find the Gospel of John exciting and very informative in revealing Who Jesus is.

The Deity of Christ as Seen Beyond the Gospel of John

Though John is very specific about his intention to reveal the deity of Christ in his gospel, many other places in the Bible reveal it as well.

1. Gospel of Mark

Some critics have dismissed the emphasis on the deity of Christ found in the Gospel of John because it is the last of the four gospels to be written (probably around AD 90-95). They claim that the Gospel of Mark, which is believed to be written first, doesn't proclaim Jesus as God. By the time John wrote, they say, the message was adjusted to exalt Jesus to a status fitting for the founder of a religion. This is a faulty argument because Mark does indeed assert the deity of Christ.

In Mark 2:1-12 a paralytic man is brought to Jesus, and Jesus says to him, "Your sins are forgiven." The religious leaders in the crowd respond by saying, "Why does this man speak that way? He is blaspheming; who can forgive sins but God alone?" (v. 7). They recognized that Jesus was not just saying, "I forgive you" like we might say to someone who sinned against us. Jesus was proclaiming that He had the authority to forgive anyone's sins, whatever those sins might be and whoever they might be against—an authority that belongs only God. The religious leaders were outraged and accused Jesus of blasphemy.

Then Jesus proved the veracity of His claim to deity with a visible sign. He asked them, "Which is easier, to say to the paralytic, 'Your sins are forgiven'; or to say, 'Get up, and pick up your pallet and walk'?" His point was that both statements could be accomplished only by divine authority, but the second statement was harder because its accomplishment would have to produce visible results that could be verified by the onlookers. Jesus then healed the paralytic man after saying specifically that He was doing it so that "you may know that the Son of Man has authority on earth to forgive sins." He verified his claim to deity with a miracle proving that He possessed divine authority.

In Mark 14:55-65, Jesus is on trial before the Jewish religious leaders. They cannot find adequate witness against Him to justify execution, so the High Priest eventually asks Him directly, *"Are You the Christ, the Son of the Blessed One?" Jesus responds by saying "I am; and you shall see THE SON OF MAN SITTING AT THE RIGHT HAND OF POWER, and COMING WITH THE CLOUDS OF HEAVEN" (v. 61).*

When Jesus said this, the high priest tore his robe and said to the others, "You have the blasphemy." The high priest was prohibited from tearing his robe except when he was in the position of judge and he felt that blasphemy was spoken in his presence. Then, by tradition he was required to tear his robe as a response to the blasphemy. He recognized that Jesus was declaring Himself to be the Christ and the Son of God. This was equivalent to declaring Himself to be God and was considered blasphemous. Jesus was condemned by the court, not for anything He had done, but for who He claimed to be.

Two other phrases in Jesus' response are also significant: "You will see the Son of Man sitting at the right hand of power, and coming in the clouds of heaven." Here Jesus was claiming that He was the fulfillment of messianic prophecies found in Daniel 7:13 and Psalm 110:1. The high priest and the court understood His meaning and responded by sentencing Him to death for blaspheming.

2. Joel 2:32 (Quoted in Romans and in Acts)

And it will come about that whoever calls on the name of the LORD Will be delivered; For on Mount Zion and in Jerusalem There will be those who escape, As the LORD has said, Even among the survivors whom the LORD calls. (Joel 2:32)

This prophetic proclamation is quoted in two different New Testament passages referring to Jesus Christ. Thus we can see that the New Testament is clearly saying that calling upon the Name of the Lord (YHWH, Jehovah, or Yahweh) is equivalent to calling upon the Name of Jesus Christ, for He is the Lord. In other words, Jesus is God.

If you confess with your mouth Jesus as Lord, and believe in your heart that God raised Him from the dead, you will be saved; (10) for with the heart a person believes, resulting in righteousness, and with the mouth he confesses, resulting in salvation. (11) For the Scripture says, "Whoever believes in Him will not be disappointed." (12) For there is no distinction between Jew and Greek; for the same Lord is Lord of all, abounding in riches for all who call on Him; (13) for "WHOEVER WILL CALL ON THE NAME OF THE LORD WILL BE SAVED." (Romans 10:9-13)

In this passage, Paul equates confessing Jesus as Lord with calling upon the Name of the Lord. In verse 13 he quotes Joel 2:32, and the context shows that he is clearly speaking of calling upon Jesus Christ. Here we have a New Testament passage that is declaring Jesus Christ to be Lord, or Jehovah.

This takes place also in Acts 2 on the day of Pentecost as Peter is preaching in Jerusalem. He quotes Joel 2:28-32 to explain what is occurring as the Spirit of God is being poured out that day upon followers of Jesus Christ. Verse 21 is a quote of Joel 2:32. The verses that follow make it clear that in quoting this verse he is speaking to them about Jesus Christ.

> *"AND IT SHALL BE IN THE LAST DAYS," God says, "THAT I WILL POUR FORTH OF MY SPIRIT ON ALL MANKIND; AND YOUR SONS AND YOUR DAUGHTERS SHALL PROPHESY, AND YOUR YOUNG MEN SHALL SEE VISIONS, AND YOUR OLD MEN SHALL DREAM DREAMS; (18) EVEN ON MY BOND SLAVES, BOTH MEN AND WOMEN, I WILL IN THOSE DAYS POUR FORTH OF MY SPIRIT And they shall prophesy. (19) AND I WILL GRANT WONDERS IN THE SKY ABOVE AND SIGNS ON THE EARTH BELOW, BLOOD, AND FIRE, AND VAPOR OF SMOKE. (20) THE SUN WILL BE TURNED INTO DARKNESS AND THE MOON INTO BLOOD, BEFORE THE GREAT AND GLORIOUS DAY OF THE LORD SHALL COME. (21) AND IT SHALL BE THAT EVERYONE WHO CALLS ON THE NAME OF THE LORD WILL BE SAVED." (Acts 2:17-21)*
> (Note - Capitalized words in Bible verses indicates this part of the verse is quoted from an Old Testament passage.)

As Peter continues his message, he makes this statement about Jesus in verse 36.

> *Therefore let all the house of Israel know for certain that God has made Him both Lord and Christ—this Jesus whom you crucified. (Acts 2:36)*

The Greek word for Lord (Kurios) is used in both verse 21 and 36 where Peter boldly states that God has made Jesus both Lord and Christ (Messiah). So again Jesus is said to be the fulfillment of Joel 2:32, which states that everyone who calls upon the name of the Lord (Jehovah) will be saved. Jesus is proclaimed to be God.

3. Zechariah 14
In Zechariah 14:3-5 there is a reference to the Lord returning to the Mount of Olives as King.

> ***Then the LORD will go forth and fight against those nations, as when He fights on a day of battle. (4) In that day His feet will stand on the Mount of Olives, which is in front of Jerusalem on the east; and the Mount of Olives will be split in its middle from east to west by a very large valley, so that half of the mountain will move toward the north and the other half toward the south. (5) You will flee by the valley of My mountains, for the valley of the mountains will reach to Azel; yes, you will flee just as you fled before the earthquake in the days of Uzziah king of Judah. Then the LORD, my God, will come, and all the holy ones with Him! (Zechariah 14:3-5)***

This prophetic word about the return of the Lord appears to have its fulfillment in Revelation 19:6-19 where we see Jesus returning to earth as a great conquering king.

4. Hebrews 1
Hebrews 1 contains numerous references to the deity of Christ and much discussion of Him as God's Son and the messenger of the salvation message. Among them are the statements in verses 2 and 3 that declare Jesus to be the Creator of everything and that He is the radiance of God the Father's glory and the exact representation of His nature. Even more direct are the references that indicate the deity of Christ in verses 6-8.

And when He again brings the firstborn into the world, He says, "AND LET ALL THE ANGELS OF GOD WORSHIP HIM." (7) And of the angels He says, "WHO MAKES HIS ANGELS WINDS AND HIS MINISTERS A FLAME OF FIRE." (8) But of the Son He says, "YOUR THRONE, O GOD, IS FOREVER AND EVER, AND THE RIGHTEOUS SCEPTER IS THE SCEPTER OF HIS KINGDOM." (Hebrews 1:6-8)

Here the angels are told to worship Jesus. According to the Bible, only God is to be worshipped. Angels would not accept worship. The fact that the angels are told to worship Jesus is an indication that He is God. Verse 8 indicates that the Father says of His Son Jesus, "Your throne, O God, is forever and ever..." Here, God the Father refers to Jesus His Son as God.

5. Matthew 1:22-23

In Matthew 1:19-25, Joseph is told that the baby Mary is carrying is divine and that when He is born, he is to name Him "Jesus" (which means "salvation") because He will save His people from their sins. Then in verse 22-23 says that this was in fulfillment of the words of the prophet which said, ***"'BEHOLD THE VIRGIN SHALL BE WITH CHILD AND SHALL BEAR A SON, AND THEY SHALL CALL HIS NAME IMMANUEL,' which translated means, 'GOD WITH US.'"*** This is a quote from Isaiah 7:14. It is important to notice that Jesus is given the name "Immanuel," which means "God with us." Jesus is proclaimed to be "God with us" at the time of His birth.

6. Philippians 2:5-11

Have this attitude in yourselves which was also in Christ Jesus, (6) who, although He existed in the form of God, did not regard equality with God a thing to be grasped, (7) but emptied Himself, taking the form of a bond-servant, and being made in the likeness of men. (8) Being found in appearance as a man, He humbled Himself by becoming obedient to the point of death, even death on a cross. (9) For this reason also, God highly exalted Him, and bestowed on Him the name which is above every name, (10) so that at the name of Jesus EVERY KNEE WILL BOW, of those who are in heaven and on earth and under the earth, (11) and that every tongue will confess that Jesus Christ is Lord, to the glory of God the Father. (Philippians 2:5-11)

Jesus is said to have been "in the form of God" in verse 6. We are told that He was willing to empty Himself, or as the Amplified translation puts it, "But stripped Himself [of all privileges and rightful dignity]." Jesus did not stop being God when He became a man, but He laid aside all of His ability to function with divine power for that time. He ministered and performed all His miracles by the power of the Holy Spirit. Verse 6 gives us a clear statement that before Jesus became a man, "He existed in the form of God." He is now exalted and will be proclaimed by every being in heaven and on earth as Lord!

7. Colossians 2:9

For in Him all the fullness of Deity dwells in bodily form. (Colossians 2:9)

This verse refers to Jesus Christ and pointedly states that all the fullness of deity dwelled in Jesus Christ in bodily form. In other words, Jesus is God.

8. Titus 2:13

In this verse, Paul tells us that we are to be...

...looking for the blessed hope and the appearing of the glory of our great God and Savior, Christ Jesus, (Titus 2:13)

9. Matthew 7:24-29

When Jesus had finished these words, the crowds were amazed at His teaching; (29) for He was teaching them as one having authority, and not as their scribes. (Matthew 7:28-29)

As this verse shows, Jesus taught with divine authority. The teachers of the law in Jesus' day had no authority of their own. Their authority came from their use of earlier authorities. Even Moses and the other Old Testament prophets and authors did not speak in their own authority, but would say, "This is what the Lord says." Jesus, on the other hand, interprets the law by saying, "You have heard that it was said... But I say to you" (see Matthew 5:22, 28, 32, 34, 39, 44 and Matthew 7:24-29). His divine authority is shown with staggering clarity when He speaks of Himself as the Lord who will judge the whole earth and will say to the wicked, "I never knew you; depart from me, you workers of lawlessness" (Matthew 7:23). No wonder the crowd was amazed at the authority with which Jesus spoke!

Jesus recognized that His words carried divine weight. He acknowledged the permanent authority of the law and put his words on an equal plane with it: "For truly, I say to you, until heaven and earth pass away, not an iota, not a dot, will pass from the Law until all is accomplished" (Matthew 5:18); "Heaven and earth will pass away, but my words will not pass away" (Matthew 24:35).

Lunatic, Liar or Lord

The claim has often been made that Jesus was a great moral teacher but nothing more than that. In the mid-twentieth century, the apologist C.S. Lewis penned the now-famous "Lewis Trilemma" to counter this claim by showing the sheer illogic of it. The argument had its origins about a hundred years earlier from the Scottish Christian preacher "Rabbi" John Duncan, who declared that Christ either deceived mankind by conscious fraud, or He was Himself deluded and self-deceived, or He was divine. Here is the Lewis Trilemma in its entirety.

I am trying here to prevent anyone saying the really foolish thing that people often say about Him: I'm ready to accept Jesus as a great moral teacher, but I don't accept his claim to be God. That is the one thing we must not say. A man who was merely a man and said the sort of things Jesus said would not be a great moral teacher. He would either be a lunatic—on the level with the man who says he is a poached egg—or else he would be the Devil of Hell. You must make your choice. Either this man was, and is, the Son of God, or else a madman or something worse. You can shut him up for a fool, you can spit at him and kill him as a demon or you can fall at his feet and call him Lord and God, but let us not come with any patronizing nonsense about his being a great human teacher. He has not left that open to us. He did not intend to. . . . Now it seems to me obvious that He was neither a lunatic nor a fiend: and consequently, however strange or terrifying or unlikely it may seem, I have to accept the view that He was and is God. [1]

Our Great High Priest

The book of Hebrews is dedicated to presenting Jesus Christ as our great high priest, the One who both offered the sacrifice for our sin and who is that sacrifice. He is also the One who ever lives to make intercession for us. As our eternal high priest, Jesus is able to save us completely. He is the priest of the new covenant that is superior to the old covenant which was officiated by the Old Testament Levitical priests.

Throughout the book of Hebrews, Jesus is revealed to be superior. He is shown to be superior to angels in chapter 1, superior to Moses in chapter 3, and superior to the Old Testament priests in chapters 5–7. The new covenant that He has established between God and us is revealed as superior to old covenant. The sacrifice of the new covenant is shown to be superior to the sacrifices of the old covenant.

---

[1] C.S. Lewis, *Mere Christianity*, First published as a unit in 1952, p.55-56

The following verses are a sampling of many from the book of Hebrews that reveal the significance of Jesus being our great high priest. Others that will help you understand the concept are: Hebrews 2:14-18; 8:1-2; 9:14-15; and 9:24-26.

> *Therefore, since we have a great high priest who has passed through the heavens, Jesus the Son of God, let us hold fast our confession. (15) For we do not have a high priest who cannot sympathize with our weaknesses, but One who has been tempted in all things as we are, yet without sin. (16) Therefore let us draw near with confidence to the throne of grace, so that we may receive mercy and find grace to help in time of need. (Hebrews 4:14-16)*

> *For they indeed became priests without an oath, but He with an oath through the One who said to Him, "THE LORD HAS SWORN AND WILL NOT CHANGE HIS MIND, 'YOU ARE A PRIEST FOREVER'"; (22) so much the more also Jesus has become the guarantee of a better covenant. (23) The former priests, on the one hand, existed in greater numbers because they were prevented by death from continuing, (24) but Jesus, on the other hand, because He continues forever, holds His priesthood permanently. (25) Therefore He is able also to save forever those who draw near to God through Him, since He always lives to make intercession for them. (Hebrews 7:21-25)*

The Only Way of Salvation

One of the most difficult aspects of the Christian faith for some to embrace is the teaching of Scripture that Jesus Christ is the only way of salvation. Many today choose to believe that Jesus is one way to God, but there are many other ways. This is politically correct by the standards of today, but it is not what the Bible teaches. As Christians, we must commit to the truth that Jesus is the only way.

We must share our faith with others in a kind, gentle, and loving way, but we must not compromise the truth that Jesus Christ is the way of salvation.

In John 14:6, Jesus Himself says that He is the only way of salvation. *"I am the way, and the truth, and the life; no one comes to the Father but through Me."* Acts 4:12 teaches the same thing: *"And there is salvation in no one else; for there is no other name under heaven that has been given among men by which we must be saved."*

Some suggest that when you examine what all religions teach, you will find that they are really the same. This is certainly not true! In all other religions besides Christianity, a person must achieve salvation through his own good works or his ability to tap into special secret knowledge. Christianity alone offers salvation as an undeserved gift by the grace of God to the person who believes in Jesus. Salvation is received through confessing Jesus as Lord and believing that God raised Him from the dead.

> *If you confess with your mouth Jesus as Lord, and believe in your heart that God raised Him from the dead, you will be saved; (10) for with the heart a person believes, resulting in righteousness, and with the mouth he confesses, resulting in salvation. (Romans 10:9-10)*

The message of the Bible does not make sense if there are many ways to obtain salvation and to be reconciled to God. Why would God the Father ask His Son to become a man, suffer and die a brutal death upon a cross for the sins of men if there were already many other ways that people could be saved from their sin? The fact that God the Father gave His Son, and the fact that Jesus, God's Son, was willing to become a man and die for us reveals that there is no other way. The apostle Paul proclaims that there is only one mediator between God and men, and that one mediator is Jesus Christ.

> *For there is one God, and one mediator also between God and men, the man Christ Jesus, (6) who gave Himself as a ransom for all, the testimony given at the proper time. (1 Timothy 2:5-6)*

Only God Himself could become the sinless, perfect sacrifice for sin, sufficient to pay the price for the sins of every person who has ever lived. It truly is "the greatest story ever told." What a loving and caring God! What an awesome Savior!

The apostle John reveals the true reason so many reject the idea that Jesus is the way of salvation. They love their sin and darkness and do not want to turn away from it.

> *This is the judgment, that the Light has come into the world, and men loved the darkness rather than the Light, for their deeds were evil. (20) For everyone who does evil hates the Light, and does not come to the Light for fear that his deeds will be exposed. (John 3:19-20)*

That there are many paths to God and salvation is a fatal lie that we must counter at every opportunity. People need to see the love of God in our lives, and they need to hear the truth in love; Jesus is the way unto salvation.

Jesus - God Incarnate

Jesus Christ is fully God, but He also became fully man so that He could be the sacrifice for our sin and our Great High Priest forever. As God Incarnate, He became Immanuel (also spelled "Emmanuel"), which means "God with us." While here in the flesh, He laid aside His ability to function as God. He experienced  everything that we experience in life as human beings. He was tempted in every way that we are, yet He never sinned. He depended upon the Holy Spirit to lead Him (Matthew 4:1; Luke 4:1) and to empower Him to teach and perform miracles. The Bible shows us that He did not begin to minister publicly until the Holy Spirit rested upon Him at the time of His baptism (Matthew 3:16; Luke 4:1; John 1:32).

Below I have quoted two Scriptures indicating the incarnation of Christ. Others you might want to study are Isaiah 9:6-7; Philippians 2:5-8; and Hebrews 2:14-18;

"BEHOLD, THE VIRGIN SHALL BE WITH CHILD AND SHALL BEAR A SON, AND THEY SHALL CALL HIS NAME IMMANUEL," which translated means, "GOD WITH US." (Matthew 1:23)

In the beginning was the Word, and the Word was with God, and the Word was God.... (14) And the Word became flesh, and dwelt among us, and we saw His glory, glory as of the only begotten from the Father, full of grace and truth. (John 1:1, 14)

Jesus is the Christ (Messiah)

Throughout portions of the Old Testament there are various references to a coming savior who will conquer his enemies and establish his kingdom. This figure is referred to in some passages and in the Jewish belief system as the Messiah, which means "the anointed one." He will be anointed by God to fulfill God's plan of salvation. For the most part, the Jews understood this Messiah to just be a savior for the Jewish people, the people of God. However, the promise of the coming Messiah was not just for the Jews, but for all nations. This person would be "the seed of Abraham," which Genesis 22:18 says would bring blessing to all the nations.

In the Greek language, the Hebrew word "Messiah" is translated as "Christ" (Christos). It still retains the meaning, "the anointed one."

Jesus of Nazareth is referred to as "the Christ" throughout the New Testament, revealing that He is God's anointed one and the fulfillment of Old Testament prophecy and typology. Jesus is referred to as Christ about 500 times in the New Testament. He is referred to as Christ in every book of the New Testament except 3 John, which consists of merely one, short fourteen-verse chapter. From Matthew chapter 1 through Revelation chapter 20, Jesus is proclaimed to be "the Christ."

John's purpose in writing the Gospel of John was that we might believe that Jesus is the Christ, the Son of God, and that by believing we might have life in His name. In Matthew 16 Jesus asked His disciples who they said that He was. Peter responded in verse 16 by saying, "You are the Christ, the Son of the living God." This confession of who Jesus is, a truth that was revealed to him by God the Father, changed Peter forever.

Jesus warns us three times in Matthew 24 that many false Christs and false prophets will come and deceive many in the last days. We are to understand that Jesus of Nazareth is Jesus the Christ, and He alone is the Christ. Jesus, which means salvation or savior, is His Name, and Christ is His title. He holds the office of Christ, the anointed one. Some New Age thinkers today say that Jesus came to show us the Christ-consciousness that is in each of us, but this is not what the Bible teaches. The Bible clearly teaches that Jesus of Nazareth alone is the Christ.

One of the key Old Testament passages considered messianic, or prophetic regarding the coming Messiah, is found in Daniel 7. As Daniel describes a vision that God gave him, he speaks of the coming Messiah who will have dominion and who will receive an eternal kingdom.

> *I kept looking in the night visions, And behold, with the clouds of heaven One like a Son of Man was coming, And He came up to the Ancient of Days And was presented before Him. (14) And to Him was given dominion, Glory and a kingdom, That all the peoples, nations and men of every language Might serve Him. His dominion is an everlasting dominion Which will not pass away; And His kingdom is one Which will not be destroyed. (Daniel 7:13-14)*

For centuries Jewish people, especially Jewish religious leaders, clung to this promise of the coming Messiah. To the Jews the term "Son of Man" did not refer to someone who was merely human, but rather to someone who was divine. They equated the term with the coming Messiah.

Jesus Christ is referred to as the Son of Man over eighty times in the four gospels and the book of Acts. This title was the key to Jesus being condemned by the Jewish religious leaders in Mark 14. They found Him guilty of blasphemy, for to say that Jesus is the Son of Man is to say that He is the Christ.

"Son of Man" (Found in 85 times in N.T.)	
Matthew	(Found 31 times in 29 Verses)
Mark	(Found 14 times in 13 Verses)
Luke	(Found 26 times in 26 Verses)
John	(Found 13 times in 12 Verses)
Acts	(Found 1 time in 1 Verse)

The fact that Jesus is the Christ or the Messiah spoken of throughout the Old Testament brings us to another important point about His birth, life, death, burial, and resurrection. Jesus Christ fulfilled over 300 prophetic references to the Messiah in the Old Testament, even though the Old Testament was written hundreds of years before Jesus lived.

Below are a few examples of these messianic prophecies fulfilled by Jesus Christ. Notice that many of them were fulfilled solely by the actions of others without His direct involvement.

Messianic Prophecies Fulfilled by Jesus

Born of a virgin (Isaiah 7:14; Matthew 1:18, 24, 25)
Of the Tribe of Judah (Genesis 49:10; Micah 5:2;
Matthew 1:1-16; Luke 3:23-33)
Born at Bethlehem (Micah 5:2; Matthew 2:1; Luke 2:4-7)
Herod would try to kill him as a baby (Jeremiah 31:15; Matthew 2:16)
Would be called "Immanuel" (Isaiah 7:14; Matthew 1:23)
Shall be a prophet (Deuteronomy 18:18; Matthew 21:11)
Would be a King (Psalm 2:6; Matthew 27:37)
Preceded by a messenger (Isaiah 40:3; Matthew 3:1-3)
Ministry to begin in Galilee (Isaiah 9:1; Matthew 4:12-17)
Teacher of parables (Psalms 78:2; Matthew 13:34)
He would enter Jerusalem on a donkey
(Zechariah 9:9; Luke 19:35-37)
Resurrection from the Dead (Psalms 16:10; Acts 2:31)
Betrayed by a friend (Psalms 41:9; Matthew 26:49-50)
Sold for 30 pieces of silver (Zechariah 11:12-13; Matt. 26:15; 27:3-10)
Hands and feet pierced (Psalms 22:16; Luke 23:33; John 20:25)
Crucified with thieves (Isaiah 53:12; Matthew 27:38)
Garments parted and lots casts (Psalm 22:18; John 19:23-24)
His cry of being forsaken on the cross (Psalms 22:1; Matthew 27:46)
His side would be pierced (Zechariah 12:10; John 19:34)
Buried in a rich man's tomb (Isaiah 53:9; Matthew 27:57-60)

What would you say are the chances of one man fulfilling all the Old Testament messianic prophecies? The answer would involve a number beyond our comprehension. In his book Science Speaks, Dr. Peter Stoner explains a research project he conducted with his students at Pasadena City College to estimate the probability of one person fulfilling various Old Testament messianic prophecies. The research involved over a dozen different groups of students, about 600 in all. The students carefully evaluated a number of different messianic prophecies, giving very conservative estimates on the probability of one man fulfilling each particular prophecy. Here is a list of the first eight prophecies they considered and the conservative estimated probability they agreed on.

1. Born in Bethlehem (Micah 5:2) - 1 in 2.8 x 10⁵

1. Born in Bethlehem (Micah 5:2) - 1 in 2.8×10^5
2. Messenger to Precede Him (Malachi 3:1) - 1 in 10^3
3. Riding Into Jerusalem on a Donkey (Zechariah 9:9) - 1 in 10^2
4. Betrayed by a Friend & Wounded in His Hands (Zech 13:6) - 1 in 10^3
5. Betrayed for 30 Pieces of Silver (Zech 11:12) - 1 in 10^3
(Note – I think this one shows how conservative
the students were in their estimates.)
6. 30 Pieces of Silver Cast Down & Used to Buy the Potter's Field
(Zechariah 11:13) - 1 In 10^5
7. Made No Defense Though Innocent (Isaiah 53:7) - 1 in 10^3
8. Hands and Feet Pierced in Crucifixion (Psalm 22:16) - 1 in 10^4

Dr. Stoner says they then multiplied the equations together and for sake of simplicity dropped the 2.8 estimate out entirely. When multiplied together, it was found that even using these very conservative estimates, there would be a 1 in 10^{28} chance of someone fulfilling just these eight messianic prophecies. That number looks like this when written out: 1 chance in 10,000,000,000,000,000,000,000,000,000.

Dr. Peter Stoner

Even after dividing this number by the total number of people estimated to have lived since the prophecies were made, Dr. Stoner says the chances are still 1 in 10^{17}. To illustrate how small this chance is, he says that if you covered the state of Texas in silver dollars two feet thick, you would have about 10^{17} silver dollars. Now, mark any one of the silver dollars and then mix them up all across the state. Next, blindfold a man and allow him to travel anywhere in the state he chooses and pick any one of the silver dollars. The chances of him picking the marked silver dollar are equivalent to the chances of one person fulfilling these eight prophecies.

When the research project was expanded to involve forty-eight Old Testament messianic prophecies, the probability number increased to 1 in 10^{157}. To illustrate this equation Dr. Stoner turns from silver dollars to electrons. Electrons are so small that if you lined them up side by side it would take 2.5×10^{15} of them to extend one inch. His group determined that the probability of one person fulfilling forty-eight Old Testament prophecies would be like selecting just the right electron from a ball much larger than the entire universe packed with electrons. [2]

These kinds of numbers are mind boggling, but they remind us that Jesus Christ proved beyond a shadow of a doubt that He is the Christ by fulfilling every one of the Old Testament messianic prophecies.

It is unfortunate that so many Jewish people, who are looking for the Messiah have not recognized that Jesus is He. Maybe the greatest reason for this is that they have such a skewed view of the Messiah. They have focused only on the prophecies of the Messiah's conquests over all His enemies. They have not paid sufficient attention to the prophecies clearly indicating that He will suffer greatly in order to accomplish the plans of God. Isaiah 53 gives great prophetic detail of the suffering that the Messiah would endure to save many. Oh, that the eyes of our Jewish friends would be opened to see this clear picture of the Messiah that was fulfilled in the person of Jesus Christ of Nazareth!

The Lamb of God
In the first chapter of John, John the Baptist introduces Jesus as "The Lamb of God who takes away the sins of the world." The book

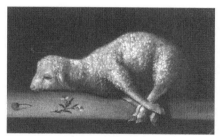

of Revelation applied the term "The Lamb" to Jesus on nine different occasions, including a reference to the "Marriage Supper of the Lamb." This title, "The Lamb of God," directs us to the fact that Jesus Christ is the sacrifice for the sins of the world. This is another example of the unity of the Bible. The Passover Lamb in the Old Testament is a type of Jesus, the Lamb of God in the New Testament. Only those who by faith applied the blood of the Passover Lamb were spared from the judgment of God that came upon Egypt immediately preceding the Hebrew's Exodus from that nation (Exodus 12). Only those who by

---

[2] Peter W. Stoner, *Science Speaks*, Chicago: Moody Press, 1963.

faith trust in the shed blood of Jesus, the Lamb of God, will be spared from the future judgment of God upon sin.

For your further study, here are three passages of Scripture that refer to Jesus as the Lamb of God: John 1:29, 36; Revelation 5:6-9; and Revelation 7:17.

The Victorious Conquering King

Jesus has defeated Satan through His death and resurrection. In contrast to His role and title as Lamb of God, the book of Revelation presents Him as a mighty conqueror who will rule forever and who has rescued mankind from sin and Satan. Hebrews 2:14 says that He destroyed him who had the power of death, that is the devil. He has conquered death by rising from the dead. He sits at the right hand of the Father awaiting final victory over all His enemies. He will return to the earth someday in great power and glory. His title of "Lion of Judah" refers also to His status as a victorious, conquering king.

One of the most powerful and dramatic Scriptures affirming the eternal kingship of Christ is Revelation 11:15:

> *Then the seventh angel sounded; and there were loud voices in heaven, saying, "The kingdom of the world has become the kingdom of our Lord and of His Christ; and He will reign forever and ever."*

For further study, other Scriptures that show Jesus as the victorious, conquering king are 1 Corinthians 15:24-27; Ephesians 1:20-22; Hebrews 1:14; and Revelation 19:16.

We Must Believe in Jesus

John 3:16 is certainly the best-known verse in all the Bible. In this one verse, God's plan of salvation is revealed quite simply and clearly. It succinctly tells us that believing in Jesus Christ allows us to be forgiven of sin, saved, and reunited with God.

For God so loved the world, that He gave His only begotten Son, that whoever believes in Him shall not perish, but have eternal life. (John 3:16)

Other verses that confirm this truth include Acts 16:31, Romans 3:21-22; 10:9-10; and Ephesians 2:8-9.

The entire Bible points to who Jesus is and what He has done, which makes our need to believe on Him obvious. As we have already noted in some detail, the importance of believing in Jesus can be seen by studying the Gospel of John, for the very purpose of John's writing his gospel is "so that you may believe that Jesus is the Christ, the Son of God; and that believing you may have life in His name" (John 20:31).

This emphasis in the Gospel of John can be easily seen in the following chart that demonstrates the multiple occurrences of the word "believe" and its variant forms in the Gospel of John, as compared to the use of these words in the other three Gospels.

Words Used	"Believe"	"Believes"	"Believed"	"Believing"	Total
John's Gospel	55	14	24	5	98
Matthew	9	0	1	1	11
Mark	10	2	3	0	15
Luke	9	0	1	0	10

In each of the ninety-eight times that the Gospel of John uses one of the four forms of "believe" the context is in reference to believing in Jesus Christ. Clearly, the Gospel of John is written to emphasize our need to believe in the revelation of who Jesus Christ and what He has done for us.

New Age teachers and followers reject the idea that belief in Jesus Christ is the key to salvation. We see an example of this in a quote from Oprah Winfrey during a discussion with New Age teacher Eckhart Tolle. She said, "God, in the essence of all consciousness, isn't something to believe.... God is a feeling experience, not a believing experience." [3]

The Bible is clear that believing in Jesus is essential. Believing in Jesus is the only way that we can be saved. He is not merely the one who shows us the way; He is "the Way"!

Jesus Is a Historical Person

Many skeptics and unbelievers question whether Jesus truly lived. They suggest that He is just a legend made up by a group of people who desired to start a new religion. In a Washington Post online article entitled "Did Historical Jesus Ever Exist? The Evidence Just Doesn't Add Up," author Raphael Lataster says,

> *Did a man called Jesus of Nazareth walk the earth? Discussions over whether the figure known as the "Historical Jesus" actually existed primarily reflect disagreements among atheists. Believers, who uphold the implausible and more easily-dismissed "Christ of Faith" (the divine Jesus who walked on water), ought not to get involved....*
>
> *The first problem we encounter when trying to discover more about the Historical Jesus is the lack of early sources. The earliest sources only reference the clearly fictional Christ of Faith.* [4]

As you can imagine, Lataster totally dismisses the gospels as having any credibility. This is an example of the types of accusations that many Christian young people face in higher education environments today. It is important to know that the Jesus seen in the Bible was a real person who actually lived is confirmed in many ways. The evidence is overpowering, though unbelievers determined not to believe are quick to dismiss it.

Here we will look at a number of evidences confirming that

---

[3] Richard Abanes, *Religions of the Stars*, Baker Books, 2009

[4]

https://www.washingtonpost.com/posteverything/wp/2014/12/18/did-historical-jesus-exist-the-traditional-evidence-doesnt-hold-up/?utm_term=.c4fcd18f6a61.

Jesus Christ lived 2,000 years ago here on the Earth. First, there are numerous secular writers from that period who refer to Jesus and His followers. Here are examples:

- **The Historical Account of Cornelius Tacitus, the Roman Historian**
  (The context of this quote is Nero's response to the fire of Rome)

> Consequently, to get rid of the report, Nero fastened the guilt and inflicted the most exquisite tortures on a class hated for their abominations, called Christians by the populace. Christus, from whom the name had its origin, suffered the extreme penalty during the reign of Tiberius at the hands of one of our procurators, Pontius Pilatus, and a most mischievous superstition, thus checked for the moment, again broke out not only in Judaea, the first source of the evil, but even in Rome, where all things hideous and
>
>
>
> Tacitus
>
> shameful from every part of the world find their centre and become popular. Accordingly, an arrest was first made of all who pleaded guilty; then, upon their information, an immense multitude was convicted, not so much of the crime of firing the city, as of hatred against mankind. Mockery of every sort was added to their deaths. Covered with the skins of beasts, they were torn by dogs and perished, or were nailed to crosses, or were doomed to the flames and burnt, to serve as a nightly illumination, when daylight had expired. Nero offered his gardens for the spectacle, and was exhibiting a show in the circus, while he mingled with the people in the dress of a charioteer or stood aloft on a car. Hence, even for criminals who deserved extreme and exemplary punishment, there arose a feeling of compassion; for it was not, as it seemed, for the public good, but to glut one man's cruelty, that they were being destroyed. (Annals 15.44)

• Josephus, the Jewish Historian Writes Concerning Jesus

But the younger Ananus who, as we said, received the high priesthood, was of a bold disposition and

exceptionally daring; he followed the party of the Sadducees, who are severe in judgment above all the Jews, as we have already shown. As therefore Ananus was of such a disposition, he thought he had now a good opportunity, as Festus was now dead, and Albinus was still on the road; so he assembled a council of judges, and brought before it

Flavius Josephus

the brother of Jesus the so-called Christ, whose name was James, together with some others, and having accused them as lawbreakers, he delivered them over to be stoned. (Antiquities 20.9.1)

Now there was about this time Jesus, a wise man, if it be lawful to call him a man, for he was a doer of wonderful works, a teacher of such men as receive the truth with pleasure. He drew over to him both many of the Jews, and many of the Gentiles. He was the Christ, and when Pilate, at the suggestion of the principal men among us, had condemned him to the cross, those that loved him at the first did not forsake him; for he appeared to them alive again the third day; as the divine prophets had foretold these and ten thousand other wonderful things concerning him. And the tribe of Christians so named from him are not extinct at this day. (Antiquities 18.3.3)

- **Pliny the Younger (a Lawyer, Author, and Magistrate of First-century Rome)   (Speaks of Jesus and His Followers)**

Pliny the Younger, in Letters 10:96, recorded early Christian worship practices including the fact that Christians worshiped Jesus as God and were very ethical. He includes a reference to the love feast and Lord's Supper

Pliny the Younger

- **Writings of the Sanhedrin Speak of Jesus' Crucifixion**

The Babylonian Talmud (Sanhedrin 43a) confirms Jesus' crucifixion on the eve of Passover and the accusations against Christ of practicing sorcery and encouraging Jewish apostasy.

- **Lucian of Samosata was a Second-century Greek Writer Who Speaks of Jesus**

Lucian, in his work, The Death of Peregrinus (or The Passing of Peregrinus) admits that Jesus was worshiped by Christians, introduced new teachings, and was crucified for them. He said that Jesus' teachings included the brotherhood of believers, the importance of conversion, and the importance of denying other gods.

Lucian of Samosata   Christians lived according to Jesus' laws, believed themselves to be immortal, and were characterized by contempt for death, voluntary self-devotion, and renunciation of material goods.

In addition to these sources, there are other evidences that point to the fact that Jesus Christ lived on the Earth and that He did the things the Bible says He did. Here are examples of these additional evidences.

• Our Calendar Speaks of the Reality of Jesus Christ (BC and AD, or as Secularists Prefer, BCE and CE)

Our calendars are dated based the estimated year that Jesus Christ was born. He so impacted the world that history is divided at the time he came to earth.

• The Rise of Christianity Amidst Much Difficulty Speaks of the Reality of Jesus Christ

The early followers of Jesus certainly did not gain a lot of earthly benefit from their proclamation of their newfound faith in Jesus. Eleven of the twelve apostles died martyrs deaths because they proclaimed the gospel of Jesus. First-century Christians were often burned to death, fed to wild animals for entertainment in coliseums, or stoned to death for their faith. To say that they endured these persecutions in order to make up a new religion and follow a person who never existed does not make sense. The rise of Christianity amidst much difficulty speaks clearly to the fact that Jesus Christ lived on Earth, performed great miracles, died on the cross, and rose from the dead.

• The Effect of Jesus Christ on Nations, Tribes and Individuals Speaks of His Reality

The movie The End of the Spear tells the true story of missionaries who went to Ecuador in the mid-twentieth century and gave their lives to reach a hostile tribe with the good news of Jesus Christ. After the tribe had killed these five missionary men, some of their wives and children came to Ecuador and led them into a relationship with Jesus Christ, transforming their lives. The love shown by the missionary families and the amazing transformation of these tribal people points to the reality of who Jesus is.

This is just one example of millions of transformed lives and people groups who have found new life through faith in Jesus

Christ. The Assemblies of God, of which I am a part, is an example of this truth. In 1914 about 300 people gathered in Hot Springs, Arkansas, to begin a new fellowship dedicated to taking the good news of Jesus Christ to every part of the world. Today, just over 100 years later, the Assemblies of God has over 68 million members. In the process of reaching this point, many missionaries have given their lives. This is just one part of the body of Christ around the world, but it shows the power, even today, that Jesus has in people's lives. This story is repeated in numerous denominations and mission organizations.

The transformation of nations when the message of Jesus has come to them is well documented. Women's rights have followed where the Christian message has been preached and accepted. Mercy and justice in legal systems have emerged in nations where Christianity has been accepted. Modern science emerged primarily through pioneers who believed in God and in God the Son, Jesus Christ.

To claim that Jesus never lived is to deny the reality of the impact He has made upon the world and the sacrifices His followers have made to proclaim His Name throughout the centuries.

• Even Other Religions and Cult Groups Proclaim the Reality that Jesus Lived

Though other religions and cult groups alter the biblical revelation of Jesus Christ, they do acknowledge Him as a historical person. Their views of Jesus vary, but nevertheless they acknowledge Him. Here are some of the things they believe and don't believe about Jesus.

(1) Judaism (Monotheistic) •Jesus was a man •Falsely claimed to be the Jewish Messiah •Resurrection – No

(2) Islam (Monotheistic) •Jesus was a man •He was a true prophet sent by God but was superseded by Muhammad •Purpose – to reveal God's will in a progressive revelation that ended with Muhammad •Resurrection – No

(3) Hinduism (Polytheistic – 330,000 gods) •Varying views of who Jesus is •An incarnation of God akin to Krishna or a wise man •Purpose – not addressed •Resurrection – not addressed

(4) Buddhism (Polytheistic – 18 gods) •Jesus was a man •A wise and enlightened teacher who taught things similar to the Buddha •Purpose – to teach people wisdom and the way to enlightenment •Resurrection – not addressed

(5) Gnosticism (Polytheistic) •Jesus was God •Divine Being sent from the Supreme God •Purpose – to rescue humanity from the material world by revealing true knowledge •Resurrection – most Gnostics reject that Jesus died at all – the human Jesus was ordinary and did not resurrect

(6) Secular Humanism (Atheistic/Agnostic) •Question whether or not Jesus Christ lived – If he did live, he was certainly just a man •May have been an interesting teacher •Resurrection – no

(7) Jehovah Witnesses •Jesus was an archangel •Son of God, Word of God, God's first Creation, the Archangel Michael •Purpose – to teach about God, to provide a model for right living, to die sacrificially for human sin •Resurrection – yes •Salvation is through faith in Christ and obeying Jehovah's laws

(8) Mormonism •Son of God, Savior, originally one of the spirit beings that all humans used to be •Has a physical body •Brother of Lucifer •Purpose - to teach about God, provide a model for living, die sacrificially for sin •Resurrection – yes •Salvation by faith in Christ, good works, ordinances, and evangelism.

A Recent Archaeological Find

In recent years, an amazing archaeological find confirms the existence of Jesus Christ in the first century AD. Note the following section of an article by Dr. John D. Morris Ph.D., about this discovery.

> *The new artifact is an ossuary, a medium-sized box in which human bones were placed for permanent burial after the flesh had all decayed away. This practice was employed for only a brief period of time from about 20 BC to AD 70. The box is made of a soft, chalky, limestone, common to the area. The contents*

have long since vanished.

Most remarkably, an inscription has been etched into the side which reads, "James, son of Joseph, brother of Jesus" in the Aramaic script of the time. Careful studies, including scrutiny under a scanning electron microscope, show the inscription to be genuine. The patina, or oxidized surface equally covers both box and the interior of the etched letters. The recognized expert on such matters, Dr. Andre Lemaire, concludes: "I am pleased to report that in my judgment it is genuinely ancient and not a fake."

All three names used were common in that era, but seldom was the deceased's brother mentioned, unless that brother was noteworthy. To have all three listed, in correct Biblical relationship certainly supports the possibility of this being the ossuary of the Biblical James.

Many other archaeological finds have confirmed various people, places, and events recorded in the gospels about the life and times of Jesus.

Jesus Christ truly lived on this Earth 2,000 years ago. Historical sources confirm this. Archaeological finds and the impact of Jesus upon nations and individuals for centuries confirm this. The rise of the Christian church in the midst of great hardship also confirms this. The world has been impacted forever because Jesus Christ came.

Confirmed Resurrection (Jesus Rose From the Dead!)

The bodily (or physical) resurrection from the dead by Jesus Christ is the central element of the Christian faith. The Old Testament prophesied that Jesus would rise from the dead. Jesus spoke numerous times to His disciples of His coming death and resurrection from the dead. His resurrection is what brings defeat to all His (and our) enemies. His resurrection is what makes it possible for us to be resurrected from the dead to eternal life. The hope of the Christian faith is found in the resurrection of Jesus. The overcoming victory within the Christian faith is found in the resurrection of Jesus.

It is not surprising that unbelievers who attack the Christian faith would target the resurrection. In most cases, those who deny the resurrection begin with the idea that it is just not possible. They deny the reality of the supernatural. They fail to look at the evidences that support the biblical account of Christ's resurrection or dismiss them because resurrection from the dead involves miraculous, supernatural power, which they deny exists.

There are many alternative theories attempting to explain away both the death of Jesus on the cross and His resurrection from the dead. They are asserted with confidence and exhibit disdain for Christian beliefs, but when examined they do not match the historical evidence.

It is comforting for believers to know the evidences that confirm the fact that Jesus Christ rose from the dead. Josh McDowell deals much more extensively with this subject in his book More Than a Carpenter, as does Gary Habermas in his book The Case for the Resurrection of Jesus. Let's look briefly at some of the primary evidences that confirm the resurrection of Jesus.

1. The Empty Tomb

The body of Jesus was placed in a tomb near Jerusalem. The religious leaders were concerned that His disciples might steal the body and claim that Jesus had risen. To prevent such a trick, they convinced the Roman authorities to place a large stone weighing 1½ to 2 tons over the entrance to the tomb. A Roman seal was placed upon the stone, and a Roman guard (probably about sixteen soldiers) was assigned protect the tomb from attempted theft of the body.

Days later, when the tomb was found empty, the Jewish leaders conspired to make up a story that the guards had fallen asleep and the disciples stole the body. The story was doggedly repeated by Jews for decades after the resurrection of Jesus.

What is striking about this story is that it shows beyond doubt that everyone knew that Jesus' tomb was empty. Had it not been empty, the disciples could not have proclaimed His resurrection right there in Jerusalem where it happened and in surrounding areas just weeks later. Jewish religious leaders could have simply pointed to the body in the tomb or produced the body to squash the resurrection message. Christianity would have been stopped cold before it ever germinated. The message of Jesus Christ's resurrection was proclaimed successfully in Jerusalem because the tomb there was empty. As Paul Althaus writes, the resurrection proclamation "could not have been maintained in Jerusalem for a single day, for a single hour, if the emptiness of the tomb had not been established as a fact for all concerned."

It is amazing that the story of the sleeping Roman guards could possibly have been seen as credible for three reasons: First, the Roman army was the most formidable and best-trained military force in the world, and for Roman guards to sleep on duty was punishable by death. It is unthinkable that they would have fallen asleep, especially all of them at once. Second, the story is illogical on its surface. How can sleeping people know what is going on around them? Sleeping guards would not have known whether the disciples stole the body. Third, there is no way that Jesus' disciples could have slipped past the guards, rolled the boulder away from the tomb, broken the Roman seal, taken the time to unwrap the dead body inside, and take it away without awakening the guards. The story of the sleeping guards is outlandishly incredible.

2. Eyewitnesses of Christ's Bodily Resurrection

The book of 1 Corinthians is believed to be the earliest written book of the New Testament. The summarized account of the gospel message found in 1 Corinthians 15:1-8 is believed to have been a creed that was very important to the early Christian church. Within these verses are proclamations about many having been eyewitnesses of the bodily resurrection of Jesus Christ.

Now I make known to you, brethren, the gospel which I preached to you, which also you received, in which also you stand, (2) by which also you are saved, if you hold fast the word which I preached to you, unless you believed in vain. (3) For I delivered to you as of first importance what I also received, that Christ died for our sins according to the Scriptures, (4) and that He was buried, and that He was raised on the third day according to the Scriptures, (5) and that He appeared to Cephas, then to the twelve. (6) After that He appeared to more than five hundred brethren at one time, most of whom remain until now, but some have fallen asleep; (7) then He appeared to James, then to all the apostles; (8) and last of all, as to one untimely born, He appeared to me also. (1 Corinthians 15:1-8)

Paul speaks of Jesus appearing to Peter, to the twelve apostles, to James, to all the disciples, and to Paul himself. He also includes another very important piece of information. He says that Jesus appeared to more than 500 brethren at one time, and that most of those eyewitnesses were still living at the time he wrote this letter to the church at Corinth. This is important because when Paul wrote this account, there were many people in the area who were alive at the time the events had unfolded. If he was not writing the truth, there would have been many who would have stood up against his claim of the resurrection.

Some attempt to explain away the resurrection of Jesus by saying those who saw Him alive afterward were hallucinating. But the fact that more than 500 people saw the risen Jesus alive at one time makes the hallucination theory utterly implausible.

Numerous eyewitnesses of the risen Christ who lived during the time that the resurrection began to be proclaimed is wonderful evidence that Jesus did rise from the dead, just as the Bible says.

3. Women Witnesses of the Empty Tomb

At the time of the writing of the New Testament, the Jewish people lived in a patriarchal society. The men were clearly dominant, and women's roles were diminished. At that time women were not even allowed to be witnesses in court cases.

This is significant, because the biblical accounts of the resurrection show that it was the women who first discovered the empty tomb and the resurrected Christ. All four of the gospel writers make reference to the fact that it was Mary Magdalene and other women who were the first to discover that Jesus has risen and reported this to the disciples (see Matthew 28:1-10, Mark 16:1-11, Luke 24:1-11; John 20:1, 11-18). Note especially Mark's description of that resurrection morning.

When the Sabbath was over, Mary Magdalene, and Mary the mother of James, and Salome, bought spices, so that they might come and anoint Him. (2) Very early on the first day of the week, they came to the tomb when the sun had risen. (3) They were saying to one another, "Who will roll away the stone for us from the entrance of the tomb?" (4) Looking up, they saw that the stone had been rolled away, although it was extremely large. (5) Entering the tomb, they saw a young man sitting at the right, wearing a white robe; and they were amazed. (6) And he said to them, "Do not be amazed; you are looking for Jesus the Nazarene, who has been crucified. He has risen; He is not here; behold, here is the place where they laid Him. (7) "But go, tell His disciples and Peter, 'He is going ahead of you to Galilee; there you will see Him, just as He told you.'" (8) They went out and fled from the tomb, for trembling and astonishment had gripped them; and they said nothing to anyone, for they were afraid. (9) Now after He had risen early on the first day of the week, He first appeared to Mary Magdalene, from whom He had cast out seven demons. (10) She went and reported to those who had been with Him, while they were mourning and weeping. (11) When they heard that He was alive and had been seen by her, they refused to believe it. (Mark 16:1-11)

Not only is Mary Magdalene credited with the other women for finding the empty tomb, she is singled out for her other activities on that morning. She spoke to the angel; it was she to whom Jesus first appeared; and it was she who reported His resurrection to the disciples. And they, at first, refused to believe it.

If you were making up a story to start a new religion, this would be all wrong. Women would not be chosen as the first witnesses. Mary Magdalene, who had a sinful past and had been demon possessed, would not be the star witness and reporter. The disciples of Jesus would not be hiding, seemingly afraid of the Jewish and Roman authorities while women went boldly to the tomb. A fabricated story meant to convince would use men as witnesses and would make the apostles look like heroes. These "truth is stranger than fiction" details found in Scripture show that it was not a made-up story, but rather a real account of events that actually happened.

4. The Changed Lives of the Twelve Apostles Who Died for Their Belief in Christ's Resurrection

I believe the greatest evidence for the resurrection of Jesus Christ is the changed lives of the disciples after His resurrection and the establishing of the Christian church amidst great persecution and hardship.

No one can deny that the Christian church exists. Millions of believers in Christ live in nations all around the world. If the Christian church exists, it had to have a beginning. If we do not accept the biblical account of its beginning, we would have to explain it in some other way.

The first preachers in the Christian church were not wealthy, bringing in great offerings and living in luxury. On the contrary, they were persecuted severely, made great sacrifices for their faith, and eventually died as martyrs for it. Why? What would have motivated these simple men who had fled when Jesus was arrested and hid after He was buried to become bold, effective preachers who would change the world and establish a faith that has impacted the world for 2,000 years?

The answer is obvious. They saw and spoke with the resurrected Jesus Christ. This interaction had such an impact on them that they were willing to be persecuted, imprisoned, exiled, and martyred for their faith in Christ.

To believe that nothing miraculous took place and yet these simple men conspired successfully to fake out the world, even though it would cost them their lives, involves a biased faith that is not based on evidence but a denial of evidence.

Jesus did die on the cross, and He did rise from the dead on the third day.

The Name of Jesus

The Bible proclaims that "there is no other name under heaven that has been given among men by which we must be saved" (Acts 4:12). Philippians 2:9-11 says that because Jesus was obedient in humbly becoming a man, He has been given a Name that is above every name. It goes on to say that every knee will bow to Him and every tongue will confess that He is Lord. Acts 3:6 indicates that in the Name of Jesus, the lame can walk. It is no wonder that the Name of Jesus, Who He is and what He did, is attacked continually. It is no wonder that the Name of Jesus is used by people to curse and express their anger. The devil hates the Name of Jesus, for he knows that at that name his demons flee and he is defeated.

Jesus is the centerpiece of the Bible and of all of history. He is the way, the truth and life. He is the only way to God the Father. Jesus is the author and perfecter of faith. Jesus is Lord of Lords and the King of Kings. Jesus is the Messiah, and He is God the Son!

Confirming Evidence - Jesus is the Son of God
Jesus is truly a Historical Person - He is Who the Bible Says He Is!

JESUS IS THE AUTHOR & FINISHER OF THE GOSPEL MESSAGE
WHO YOU BELIEVE JESUS TO BE IS THE MOST IMPORTANT ISSUE IN ALL OF LIFE!
THE UNIQUENESS OF CHRISTIANITY IS THAT IT IS BASED UPON THE PERSON OF JESUS CHRIST!
JESUS CHRIST IS REVEALED IN SCRIPTURE BY NUMEROUS TITLES & IN NUMEROUS ROLES
JESUS CHRIST IS REVEALED AS THE DIVINE SON OF GOD IN THE OLD & NEW TESTAMENTS!
THE GOSPEL OF JOHN IS DEDICATED TO REVEALING JESUS AS THE SON OF GOD & AS THE CHRIST!
JESUS OF NAZARETH FULFILLED OVER 300 OLD TESTAMENT PROPHECIES CONCERNING THE MESSIAH (CHRIST)!
BASED ON JESUS' CLAIMS HE MUST HAVE BEEN EITHER A LIAR, A LUNATIC OR LORD OF ALL!
MANY HISTORICAL EVIDENCES CONFIRM THAT JESUS CHRIST IS A REAL HISTORICAL PERSON!
THE RESURRECTION OF JESUS CHRIST FROM THE DEAD IS A CONFIRMED FACT OF HISTORY!
EVEN OTHER RELIGIONS & CULTS ACKNOWLEDGE THE HISTORICAL REALITY OF JESUS CHRIST!
JESUS CHRIST IS THE CENTRAL FIGURE IN ALL OF HUMAN HISTORY!

The Person of Jesus Christ

The Cornerstone!

Jesus Christ is said to be the Cornerstone that the church is built upon in numerous passages. Along with this, He is said to be the Stone that the builders rejected & the Stone of Stumbling!

Psalm 118:22-23, 1 Peter 2:6-8

Acts 4:10-12, Luke 20:17-18

(1)

The Person of Jesus Christ

His Deity (Pt.1)

Jesus Christ is presented in the Gospel of John as God! His deity is expressed in the 1st verse, "In the beginning was the Word, & the Word was with God, & the Word was God!" His deity is also seen through the 23 "I Am" Statements in John's Gospel.

John 1:1,   John 20:31

John 8:24, John 8:58

(2)

The Person of Jesus Christ

His Deity (Pt.2)

Jesus Christ is presented as Lord & God throughout the N.T. Note - Rom. 10 refers to Jesus as the fulfillment of Joel's prophecy about "The LORD". Other N.T. passages show Jesus as having deity & receiving worship!

Phil. 2:5-8, Titus 2:13, Heb. 1:6-8

Joel 2:32 & Rom. 10:9-10, Col. 2:9

(3)

The Person of Jesus Christ

Our Great High Priest

In the book of Hebrews Jesus Christ is presented as our Great Eternal High Priest! He is seen as both the blood sacrifice and the High Priest Who offers His blood for us in heaven. He is author of our faith & of the New Covenant between God & His people!

The Book of Hebrews

(4)

The Person of Jesus Christ

Only Way of Salvation

Jesus Christ is clearly seen in the Bible as the only way of Salvation! Numerous passages speak of this. Also, Jesus Christ is the focus of all the Bible; in the O.T. by types, shadows & prophesies, and in the N.T. by direct statements.

John 14:6, 1 Timothy 2:5-6

Acts 4:12, Romans 10:9-10

(5)

The Person of Jesus Christ

God Incarnate!

Jesus Christ is fully God but He also became fully man so He might be the sacrifice for our sin and our Great High Priest forever. As God Incarnate He became "Immanuel" which is "God with us". While here in the flesh He laid aside His deity.

Matt. 1:23,   Phil 2:5-8

Heb. 2:14-18, Is. 9:6-7

(6)

The Person of Jesus Christ

The Christ (Messiah)
Jesus fulfilled all of the O.T. messianic prophesies (over 300 of them) showing that He is "Messiah" (Hebrew) or "Christ" (Greek). This means that He is the "Anointed One" Who would bring salvation & victory!
Is. 53, Is. 9:6-7, Ps. 22, Is. 7:14
John 20:31, Matt. 16:13-17
(7)

The Person of Jesus Christ

The Lamb of God
Jesus is introduced by John the Baptist in John 1 as "The Lamb of God Who takes away the sins of the world". The book of Revelation applied the term "The Lamb" to Jesus 9xs including a reference to the "Marriage Supper of the Lamb".
John 1:29 & 36, Rev. 5:6 & 6:9
Rev. 7:17 & 19:9 & 21:23
(8)

The Person of Jesus Christ

Conquering (Victorious King)
Jesus has defeated Satan through His death & resurrection. Hebrews says "He destroyed him who has the power of death." He has conquered death. He sits at the right hand of the Father awaiting final victory over all of His enemies.
Heb. 2:14, Col. 2:13-15, Rev. 19:11-21
1 Cor. 15:23-28, Eph. 1:20-22
(9)

The Person of Jesus Christ

Life = Believing in Jesus
The purpose of John's gospel is pronounced in John 20:31, "... that you may believe that Jesus is the Christ, the Son of God, and that believing you may have life in His Name". Believing upon Jesus for salvation is seen in other scriptures also.
John 20:31, Romans 10:9-10
Acts 16:31, John 3:16
(10)

The Person of Jesus Christ

Historical Person
Some question if Jesus really lived on earth as the Bible declares. The life of Jesus is confirmed by Roman historians and the Jewish historian Josephus. The impact of Jesus upon people & nations is undeniable. Even our calendars date back to His birth! The gospels tell of His earthly life.
Luke 1:1-4, Acts 1:1-2
(11)

The Person of Jesus Christ

Confirmed Resurrection
Some question Jesus' bodily resurrection. There are many evidences of Jesus' resurrection. The bold witness of His disciples who had previously been fearful confirms the resurrection. They were willing now to die for their faith. The empty tomb, plus the rise of Christianity also confirm that He rose from the dead!
1 Corinthians 15:3-8
(12)

(Above) These 12 memorization cards deal with the Person of Jesus Christ, showing who the Bible says He is and showing external evidence for His existence, and bodily resurrection. You are encouraged to use them to help you retain the critical information within this chapter.

Memorization Cards Available for Free Download at
localchurchapologetics.org

"Sharing The Gospel of Christ"

Sharing the Gospel of Jesus Christ

The purpose of this book is to train believers to defend and share their faith in the midst of a skeptical and often hostile culture. Most of our attention has been given to learning the various evidences confirming the major tenets of the Christian faith.

In this chapter, we will turn our attention to sharing our faith, rather than defending it. Scripture is very clear that Christians are called to be witnesses for Jesus Christ, which includes verbally sharing the gospel message with others. Many Christians have never learned how to share the gospel in a simple, concise way. Here we will address how to communicate the gospel by using the five points that are listed on the memorization cards included with the chapter. You are encouraged to read and memorize these points so that you will be better prepared to share your faith with others.

In addition to memorizing this simple plan of salvation, you are encouraged to write out your own testimony and familiarize yourself with it so you can include it when appropriate as you speak to others about Jesus. To help you in writing your testimony, consider these three simple points of emphasis:

> (1) What my life was like before I came to know Jesus
> (2) How I came to know Jesus
> (3) How my life is different since I came to know Jesus

Pray before writing your testimony and ask the Holy Spirit to lead you. He is faithful and will guide you as you write.

The Gospel Message

This simple presentation of the plan of salvation is our starting point. It is easy to remember and share. After memorizing this presentation, you can add more Scriptures, thoughts, and illustrations as you continue to learn and become more comfortable sharing with others. As you are learning, you may want to practice sharing the gospel with another believer, just to get used to communicating comfortably. You might find it helpful to use the cards as you share.

(1) Created in God's Image (Genesis 1:27)

Each of us is created in the image and likeness of God. This truth helps us to understand that God loves us and has a purpose for each of us. We are not accidents, and we are known to God. From the beginning, He created us to have a personal relationship with Him. Psalm 139:13-17 is an excellent passage to add when sharing this first point.

(2) Separation by Sin (Romans 3:23)

God warned Adam that if he sinned he would die. The death God spoke of is spiritual death, which involves separation from God. Not only did Adam sin, but Romans 3:23 says clearly that "all have sinned and fall short of the glory of God." Our problem is our sin. It separates us from the God who created us and loves us. Every one of us is in this situation. We have all sinned. We see the results of our

sinfulness everywhere we look today. As long as we are separated from the God who created us, we can never experience true peace, joy, and life. Note how the card illustrates this truth with a bottomless chasm that separates us from God. (Also see Galatians 3:22 and 1 John 1:8-10.)

(3) Spiritual Death (Romans 6:23)

Separation from God because of sin also means that we are spiritually dead. Our body is alive, but our spirit is dead because it is separated from God, the source of life. Romans 6:23 declares that "the wages of sin is death." Since we have all sinned, we all are spiritually dead apart from Christ. If we die in this condition, we will experience  eternal judgment for our sin. Because we are sinful and spiritually dead, there is nothing we can do ourselves to fix our problem and get rid of our sin. We need a Savior! Fortunately, Romans 6:23 goes on to promise us that "the free gift of God is eternal life in Christ Jesus our Lord." (Also see Romans 5:12 and Ephesians 2:1-3.)

(4) Christ Is The Way (1 Peter 3:18)

Knowing that we cannot save ourselves, God came to us in the form of Jesus Christ, God's Son, to provide a way of salvation. Jesus laid aside His glory and became a human being so that He could take the sin of the entire world upon Himself. He became the Lamb of God. The Bible makes it clear that Jesus' death on the cross and His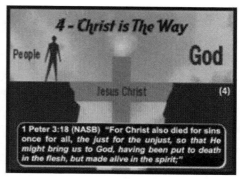

resurrection provides both payment for our sin and victory over death for all who will put their faith and trust in Him. In 1 Peter 3:18 we read that "Christ also died for sins once for all, the just for the unjust, so that He might bring us to God." Jesus cleared the way for us to come back into a restored personal relationship with God. With our sin problem taken care of, we can again be united with God and have eternal life. Note how this card illustrates this truth by showing the cross as a bridge over the impassable chasm created by our sin. (Also see John 1:29; Romans 5:8; 1 Timothy 1:15; Hebrews 2:17; 1 John 4:10.)

(5) Salvation Through Christ (John 1:12)

God has provided a way of forgiveness and salvation through the death and resurrection of His Son Jesus Christ. This is truly good news! To receive the forgiveness and salvation to eternal life that Jesus Christ offers, we must repent of our sin (turn away from sin and turn to Christ) and put our faith in Him. This step is

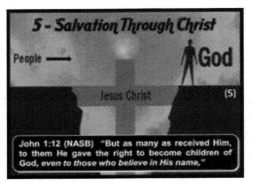

often called "receiving Jesus into our life," which is what we find indicated in John 1:12: "but as many as received Him, to them He gave the right to become children of God, even to those who believe in His Name."

Receiving Jesus Christ as our Savior and Lord is the only way that we can be forgiven of our sin and brought back into a personal relationship with the God who created us, loves us, and wants us to spend eternity with Him as His sons and daughters. In John 14:6, Jesus declares that He is "the way, the truth and the life" and that "no one comes unto the Father except by Him." Some feel that declaring Jesus Christ as the only way to salvation is harsh, haughty, or mean-spirited. If we think about it, we will realize this is not the case. If there were many ways to salvation or if we could save ourselves, God would never have sent His Son Jesus to die a terrible, brutal death on the cross on our behalf. Jesus came and died for us because there was and is no other way. Note how the illustration on the card shows the person has crossed the chasm on the cross of Christ and is now reconciled to God. (Also see John 3:16; Acts 16:31; Romans 3:26; Galatians 3:24; Ephesians 2:8-9.)

A Simple Prayer to Receive Jesus Christ Into Your Life

It is important for you to be prepared to lead a person in prayer to accept Christ when you share the gospel with him or her. You never know when God will allow you the opportunity to speak to someone at the right moment when his heart becomes open to Christ and he is ready to put his faith and trust in Him. The prayer does not have to use a particular formula or certain words as long as it expresses the point that the person is now confessing his sin and putting his trust in Jesus for forgiveness and salvation.

Here is a sample prayer you can learn or modify as needed.

"Dear Jesus, I confess to You that I have sinned.
I ask You to forgive me of my sin.
I believe that You died on the cross for my sin.
I believe that You rose from the dead to bring me victory over death.
I turn from my sin and turn in faith to You.
I invite You into my life.
Please be my Savior and my Lord.
I confess that You are Lord.
I give You all of my heart and life.
Please give me the gift of eternal life.
Thank You so much for this gift by Your grace.
I love You! Amen.

Speaking the Gospel Boldly

In the remainder of this chapter we will look at some key points in Scripture that concern our call to share the gospel with others. We will see the broad extent of the promises and provisions God gives to us when we share the gospel.

We Are Called (Commanded) to Share the Gospel

The Bible is clear that God has chosen to bring His loving message to people through those who know Him and have experienced His love and salvation.

> *And He said to them, "Go into all the world and preach the gospel to all creation." (Mark 16:15)*

> *And Jesus came up and spoke to them, saying, "All authority has been given to Me in heaven and on earth. (19) Go therefore and make disciples of all the nations, baptizing them in the name of the Father and the Son and the Holy Spirit, (20) teaching them to observe all that I commanded you; and lo, I am with you always, even to the end of the age." (Matthew 28:18-20)*

> *You will receive power when the Holy Spirit has come upon you; and you shall be My witnesses both in Jerusalem, and in all Judea and Samaria, and even to the remotest part of the earth. (Acts 1:8)*

> *Now all these things are from God, who reconciled us to Himself through Christ and gave us the ministry of reconciliation, (19) namely, that God was in Christ reconciling the world to Himself, not counting their trespasses against them, and He has committed to us the word of reconciliation. (20) Therefore, we are ambassadors for Christ, as though God were making an appeal through us; we beg you on behalf of Christ, be reconciled to God. (2 Corinthians 5:18-20)*

Bold Proclamations of the Gospel Must Be Bathed in Prayer

The apostle Paul requested the prayers of the church at Ephesus that he might proclaim the mystery of the gospel boldly. His prayer sets an excellent example for us today.

Pray on my behalf, that utterance may be given to me in the opening of my mouth, to make known with boldness the mystery of the gospel, (20) for which I am an ambassador in chains; that in proclaiming it I may speak boldly, as I ought to speak. (Ephesians 6:19-20)

Bold Proclamation of the Gospel Often Includes Reasoning with People

Paul recognized that more is involved in personal evangelism than just a rote presentation of pre-memorized points. People will have questions, and some will be resistant, which means reasoning and persuasion will be involved.

And he entered the synagogue and continued speaking out boldly for three months, reasoning and persuading them about the kingdom of God. (9) But when some were becoming hardened and disobedient, speaking evil of the Way before the people, he withdrew from them and took away the disciples, reasoning daily in the school of Tyrannus. (10) This took place for two years, so that all who lived in Asia heard the word of the Lord, both Jews and Greeks. (11) God was performing extraordinary miracles by the hands of Paul. (Acts 19:8-11)

Notice the phrase, "God was performing extraordinary miracles by the hands of Paul." This introduces a pattern that we will see in many passages of New Testament Scripture. Miracles and signs and wonders often accompany those who boldly share the gospel of Jesus in difficult or hostile situations.

Bold Proclamation is Based on Reliance Upon the Lord

And when I came to you, brethren, I did not come with superiority of speech or of wisdom, proclaiming to you the testimony of God. (2) For I determined to know nothing among you except Jesus Christ, and

Him crucified. (3) I was with you in weakness and in fear and in much trembling, (4) and my message and my preaching were not in persuasive words of wisdom, but in demonstration of the Spirit and of power, (5) so that your faith would not rest on the wisdom of men, but on the power of God. (1 Corinthians 2:1-5)

In Iconium they entered the synagogue of the Jews together, and spoke in such a manner that a large number of people believed, both of Jews and of Greeks. (2) But the Jews who disbelieved stirred up the minds of the Gentiles and embittered them against the brethren. (3) Therefore they spent a long time there speaking boldly with reliance upon the Lord, who was testifying to the word of His grace, granting that signs and wonders be done by their hands. (Acts 14:1-3)

Note Paul's emphasis on relying upon the Lord. We cannot proclaim truth boldly apart from reliance upon the Lord (His Holy Spirit).

This passage shows that God granted Paul and Barnabas the ability to perform signs and wonders as they spoke the Word of God boldly. This is another example of God granting signs and wonders to confirm the bold proclamation of the gospel of Christ.

Signs, Wonders, Miracles, and Healings Accompany the Bold Proclamation of the Gospel

Often believers ask why we do not see signs and wonders, miracles, and healings today as they did in the Bible. Many believers attest to having seen some of these things, but most have not.

One common explanation is that we do not have enough faith. Yet Jesus said that if we just have faith the size of a mustard seed, we will experience miracles. So, if our failure to experience miracles is not due to a lack of faith, there must be another reason, and I believe the Bible gives it to us.

The New Testament explains the purpose of signs and wonders, and the book of Acts shows a pattern of their occurrences in the lives of the apostles. In the following Scriptures, we will see a connection between signs and wonders and the bold proclaiming of the gospel in difficult and sometimes hostile circumstances.

> *For this reason we must pay much closer attention to what we have heard, so that we do not drift away from it. (2) For if the word spoken through angels proved unalterable, and every transgression and disobedience received a just penalty, (3) how will we escape if we neglect so great a salvation? After it was at the first spoken through the Lord, it was confirmed to us by those who heard, (4) God also testifying with them, both by signs and wonders and by various miracles and by gifts of the Holy Spirit according to His own will. (Hebrews 2:1-4)*

> *I have written very boldly to you on some points so as to remind you again, because of the grace that was given me from God, ... (19) in the power of signs and wonders, in the power of the Spirit; so that from Jerusalem and round about as far as Illyricum I have fully preached the gospel of Christ.*
>
> *(Romans 15:15, 19)*

These passages tell us that God's message of salvation was first spoken through the Lord. It was confirmed by those who heard and by the testimony of God by signs, wonders, miracles, and gifts of the Holy Spirit. These were supernatural affirmations from God testifying that the truth was being proclaimed.

> *"And now, Lord, take note of their threats, and grant that Your bond-servants may speak Your word with all confidence, (boldness) (30) while You extend Your hand to heal, and signs and wonders take place through the name of Your holy servant Jesus." (31)*

And when they had prayed, the place where they had gathered together was shaken, and they were all filled with the Holy Spirit and began to speak the word of God with boldness. (Acts 4:29-31)

Again we see a connection between bold proclamations of truth and confirming signs and wonders. Here the believers are praying after being threatened with harm if they continue preaching. Their prayer inspires us, for it was not a plea for protection, but that they would speak the Word of God with boldness. As a result of this boldness, they fully expected to see miracles, healings, signs, and wonders as they ignored the threats and continued to proclaim the gospel boldly.

If we do not proclaim God's Word boldly, we may never see God's signs and wonders displayed. We often ask for signs and wonders as we pray inside our churches, yet we are not often out in the world proclaiming the gospel in difficult circumstances.

The word of God kept on spreading; and the number of the disciples continued to increase greatly in Jerusalem, and a great many of the priests were becoming obedient to the faith. (8) And Stephen, full of grace and power, was performing great wonders and signs among the people. (9) But some men from what was called the Synagogue of the Freedmen, including both Cyrenians and Alexandrians, and some from Cilicia and Asia, rose up and argued with Stephen. (10) But they were unable to cope with the wisdom and the Spirit with which he was speaking. (Acts 6:7-10)

Stephen was obviously active in preaching the gospel of Jesus Christ boldly. Here we see the pattern again. Because he was speaking the word boldly, God granted Stephen the ability to perform great wonders and signs among the people as a testimony to the truth he was proclaiming. In Acts 7 we find that Stephen never backed away from boldly proclaiming God's truth, even though it cost him his earthly life.

When Jesus issued to His disciples the Great Commission in Mark 16:15-20, Mark ends the passage with these words: "And they went out and preached everywhere, while the Lord worked with them, and confirmed the word by the signs that followed" (v. 20). This verse tells us two things: First, the New Testament church obeyed Jesus' command to go into all the world and preach the gospel to all creation. Second, here we see the original promise that signs would follow and confirm the word they preached.

There are many other Scriptures that illustrate the point I'm making here, but I think the ones I have quoted are sufficient to make it clear that if we do not see miraculous signs today, it may be because we are not boldly proclaiming the gospel to our culture.

But before we step out to correct that deficiency, there is one more thing we must consider, and that the source of our power to accomplish what we are commanded to do. After Jesus' resurrection and prior to his ascension, He told His disciples to "stay in the city until you are clothed with power from on high" (Luke 24:49). Then in the first chapter of Acts, His message is repeated in a more complete and specific form:

> **You will receive power when the Holy Spirit has come upon you; and you shall be My witnesses both in Jerusalem, and in all Judea and Samaria, and even to the remotest part of the earth." (Acts 1:8)**

The reason that Jesus had His disciples wait for the power of the Holy Spirit was that they could not be His witnesses without the power of God working in and through them. They witnessed of Jesus by allowing the power of God to work in their lives. Both the command of Jesus and the power of the Holy Spirit led them into the world to boldly proclaim the gospel. As long as we stay inside our church buildings and do little to spread the gospel, we may see little of the manifestation of the power of the Holy Spirit of God.

We have often convinced ourselves that the truth of God cannot be boldly communicated today because of the hostile culture around us. This excuse does not wash. The early church boldly proclaimed the gospel in a very hostile culture. They were persecuted and mistreated. Some were martyred. Yet these early

Christians were very effective in getting the message out, and the gospel spread like wildfire. Even today the gospel is proclaimed effectively by brave believers in hostile places like China, Africa, Iran, and many other Middle Eastern and Asian nations. Who should determine whether we boldly communicate God's truth? The culture? Government? Us? Or God?

If we want to see miraculous signs and wonders as did the New Testament church, we need to recognize that these signs and wonders are given by God to confirm the Word of God that is proclaimed openly by His people. More proclaiming, more signs!

For further study on how the gospel is confirmed by signs and wonders, see the following Scriptures: John 20:30-31; Acts 2:19; Acts 2:22; Acts 2:43, 42-47; Acts 4:29-31; Acts 5:12-14; Acts 6:7-10; Acts 7; Acts 14:3; Acts 15:12; Romans 15:18-19; 2 Corinthians 12:12; Hebrews 2:1-4.

Reason, the Love of Jesus and the Power of the Holy Spirit

As we speak about sharing the gospel of Jesus Christ with others, let me remind you of something we covered in an earlier chapter. Though much of this book deals with preparing ourselves to reason with people about the evidence that confirms the truth of the Christian faith, there is a danger in relying too heavily on our ability to reason. No matter how informed and intelligent we may be, we will not be able to reason a person out of skepticism and into faith. To impact others for Christ, we must remember these three critical needs:

1. Reason,
2. The Love of Jesus Christ
3. The Power of the Holy Spirit

Whether we are defending our faith or sharing it, we must remember these things. Being prepared and reasoning with others is biblical and powerful, but no one will be reached for Christ apart from the love of Jesus Christ, which should be apparent in our lives. And no one will be reached without the power of the Holy Spirit, who alone can convict, convince, and change one's heart.

What about you?

Here we have given you a simple way to present the gospel of Jesus Christ to others. Will you take the time to prepare yourself so that God can use you more efficiently to share His love and truth? We are all called to be His witnesses. Who knows, you might just end up experiencing some signs and wonders along the way, and even the greatest miracle of all—a person being transferred out of death into life, through faith in Jesus Christ.

Just as Peter trusted Jesus enough to get out of the boat and walk on the water, trust the Lord enough to speak to others about your faith in Jesus Christ. If you stumble along the way, Jesus will be there to catch you, just as He caught Peter when he stumbled. Some emphasize the fact that Peter faltered. The truth is, he was the only one of the disciples that experienced walking on water with Jesus.

When I was about twenty years old, I went alone to downtown Rockford, Illinois, to tell people about Jesus Christ. I shared the gospel with a sixteen-year-old boy and then asked if he would like to accept Jesus Christ as his personal Savior. To my surprise, he said yes! We prayed together on the street that day, and later I had the privilege of leading him through some discipleship lessons. He started attending church with his grandma and soon began playing drums in the praise band each Sunday. That incident is still one of the highlights of my life. What about you? Will you share your faith with others and see what God does?

(Above) These memorization cards are designed to assist you in memorizing a short and simple presentation of the plan of salvation.

**Memorization Cards Available for Free Download at
localchurchapologetics.org**

SECTION 3: CHAPTER 13

"Dealing With the Questions
and Criticisms of Skeptics"

Dealing with Questions and Criticisms of Skeptics
This may very well be the most difficult chapter of the book for me to write, because attacks on the Bible and the Christian faith come from so many sources and take so many forms. Entire books have been dedicated to these issues. In keeping with the purpose and title of this book, Faith and Reason Made Simple, I will attempt to give some basic answers to questions and statements of skeptics without going into great detail. In some cases, I will refer to additional resources that can be consulted for further information. Up front I will recommend one website readers can consult for general information: searchcreation.org. This is a search engine for several top apologetic  websites. It gives you access to many articles dealing with the issues addressed in this chapter.

You are encouraged to use the memorization cards to memorize simple, basic answers to these questions. (There are no cards for questions #14 & #15.) To find more information, you can always go back and search out more details as needed, either from this book or from other resources.

1. If God is a loving God, why is there so much suffering in the world?
The Bible teaches that when God created the heavens and the Earth, and all that is within them, He declared in Genesis 1:31 that "it

was very good." The Bible also indicates that when God first created living things, including man, there was no death, no suffering, no hardship, etc. Man dwelt in harmony with himself, his wife, all the animals, and even with God, the Creator. Genesis 3:8 indicates that God walked in the Garden of Eden at times and conversed with man. Suffering was not a part of the world that God created. The sin of man brought suffering into the world. God told Adam that if he disobeyed God's command, the result be death.

> *But from the tree of the knowledge of good and evil you shall not eat, for in the day that you eat from it you will surely die. (Genesis 2:17)*

Adam's disobedience brought spiritual death immediately (separation of man's spirit from God's Spirit) and eventual physical death. Along with death came pain, suffering, aging, and all other parts of the Earth's present death cycle. Genesis 3:16-19 elaborates on the results of man's sin.

> *To the woman He said, "I will greatly multiply your pain in childbirth, In pain you will bring forth children; Yet your desire will be for your husband, And he will rule over you." (17) Then to Adam He said, "Because you have listened to the voice of your wife, and have eaten from the tree about which I commanded you, saying, 'You shall not eat from it'; Cursed is the ground because of you; In toil you will eat of it All the days of your life. (18) Both thorns and thistles it shall grow for you; And you will eat the plants of the field; (19) By the sweat of your face you will eat bread, Till you return to the ground, Because from it you were taken; For you are dust, And to dust you shall return." (Genesis 3:16-19)*

Here we see that suffering in the world is a result of mankind's sin, not a result of God creating a world of suffering. Romans 8:19-22 indicates that the whole world (or creation) has been subjected to futility because of man's sin. This occurred because man had been given authority over the rest of God's creation, and when man was corrupted, his authority was compromised.

Romans 8:21 gives us a picture of the hope that we have for the future because of Jesus Christ. It says that "the creation itself also will be set free from its slavery to corruption into the freedom of the glory of the children of God." Revelation 21-22 shows us that a time is coming when there will be no pain, no tears, and no suffering. Acts 3:21 says that heaven has received Jesus the Christ until "the period of the restoration of all things." Though suffering is a reality because of man's sin, Jesus Christ came not only to save us from our sin, but also to deliver us and the whole of creation from suffering, pain, and hardship.

One problem with the view that God created everything in millions of years, not in six literal days, is that it requires a process of death, disease, and suffering that occurred for millions of years before mankind sinned. This conflicts with the biblical account of why there is suffering in the world today. The Bible clearly indicates that death and suffering came about as a result of man's sin.

2. How can you say there is only one way to God?

This question is usually combined with an accusation that declaring Jesus to be the only way of salvation is arrogant and unfeeling toward others. The culture is deeply entrenched in a worldview that declares there is no absolute truth, and one person's opinion is as valid as another's.

The Bible's message is clear. Jesus Christ is the central figure of all the Bible, and its message is one of hope. Jesus Christ, God's Son, came to save us from our sin and give us the gift of eternal life. The Old Testament looks forward to Jesus Christ through many types, shadows, and prophecies. The New Testament tells us of His coming, His life, His teachings, His death and resurrection, His ascension, and His future second coming to bring to us the full measure of salvation under His benevolent rule.

John 14:6 is the most direct Scripture showing that Jesus Christ is the only way to God. Here Jesus said of Himself, "I am the way, and the truth, and the life; no one comes to the Father but through Me." Jesus not only clearly declares that He is the way to God the Father; He declares that He is the only way. The message of the rest of the Bible confirms the truth of this powerful Scripture.

Sheer logic supports the claim that Jesus is the only way. It doesn't make sense that God the Father would give His Son to suffer and die for us if there were other ways to achieve our salvation. Can you imagine God the Father saying to Jesus, His Son, "There are many ways for people to come back into a loving, intimate relationship with Us for eternity, but why don't You lay aside Your glory, go down there and live among them, let them reject You, let them spit on You, let them lie about You, let them humiliate You, let them rip Your back apart till the muscle tissue is hanging in shreds, let them drive a crown of thorns into Your head, and let them drive nails into Your hands and feet as they crucify You like a terrible criminal, so that they can have an extra way to make it to heaven." It just doesn't make sense does it?

Either the Bible's declared way of salvation is the only way, or it is not a way at all. If our works could save us, which in essence is what all other religions present as the hope of salvation, we would certainly not need Jesus Christ to do all that He did to save us. He did what He did to save us because there was, and is, nothing we can do to save ourselves.

We should not be surprised that many find it offensive that we declare Jesus Christ to be the only way of salvation. The Bible tells us that the preaching of the cross will be offensive to many (1 Corinthians 1:18; Galatians 5:11). Jesus is the stone that the builders rejected. Many have given their lives over the centuries for proclaiming this message of hope, and we must not compromise it one iota today.

Consider the warnings of the following passages of Scripture.

But I am afraid that, as the serpent deceived Eve by his craftiness, your minds will be led astray from the simplicity and purity of devotion to Christ. (4) For if one comes and preaches another Jesus whom we have not preached, or you receive a different spirit which you have not received, or a different gospel which you have not accepted, you bear this beautifully. (2 Corinthians 11:3-4)

See to it that no one takes you captive through philosophy and empty deception, according to the tradition of men, according to the elementary principles of the world, rather than according to Christ. (9) For in Him all the fullness of Deity dwells in bodily form, (10) and in Him you have been made complete, and He is the head over all rule and authority. (Colossians 2:8-10)

Jesus is the way, the truth, and the life. No one comes to God the Father except through Him. This is the message of the Bible. It is a message of great hope and great love. Because it is offensive to many does not mean that it is not true or that it should not be proclaimed.

3. How do you know that Jesus is God?

This question is addressed in greater detail in an earlier chapter of this section, but here we will give a short answer listing several Scriptures that declare Jesus to be God.

John 1:1-3: "In the beginning was the Word, and Word was with God, and the Word was God." John 1:14 makes it clear that the Word is Jesus Christ. John also tells us that He is the Creator of all things.

John 20:31 declares that the Gospel of John was written, "so that you may believe that Jesus is the Christ, the Son of God."

Philippians 2:5-8 declares that Jesus was equal with God the Father, but He voluntarily laid aside His ability to function as God for a time while He came to Earth and lived as a man.

Matthew 1:23 declares that Jesus is "Emmanuel," which means "God with us."

Isaiah 9:6 prophecies of Jesus' coming and declares that unto us "a Son is given."

Jesus is referred to as Lord in many Scriptures. A few examples are found in Philippians 3:20; Colossians 2:6; 2 Thessalonians 3:18.

Titus 2:13 refers to Jesus as "our great God and Savior, Christ Jesus."

In the following Scriptures, Jesus is said to be the Creator of everything: John 1:3; Hebrews 1:3; Colossians 1:15-17.

You might also find it helpful to review the twenty-three "I Am" statements in the Gospel of John that we discussed in an earlier chapter of this section. These statements are strong attestations to the deity of Christ.

These are samplings of the Scriptures asserting that Jesus Christ is God. If Jesus were not God, He would not have been able to take our sin upon Himself. He is God, and He is the Messiah who came to save us.

4. Aren't there many contradictions within the Bible?

To deal with this question, we need to understand two important terms related to the Bible: "inspiration" and "inerrancy."

We believe that the Bible is the inspired, inerrant, infallible Word of God. Skeptics speak of contradictions in the Bible in an attempt to attack this claim. Their own claim is that the Bible is just a fallible book written by men. We believe the Bible is inspired or "God breathed" because this claim is made within the Bible.

All Scripture is inspired by God and profitable for teaching, for reproof, for correction, for training in righteousness. (2 Timothy 3:16)

I remember from Bible College the more specific term evangelical Christians use when they speak of the Bible being "inspired." That term is "verbal plenary inspiration." This simply means that God directed the very words that the writers wrote, but He used their own personality, vocabulary, and writing style in the process. This also indicates that He often used their personal eyewitness accounts of events they reported. The gospel writers often give us more than one eyewitness account of the same event. This means we should expect to find different details recorded by different writers, different writing styles used, and in some cases, different timelines based on the experiences of the writer. In all of this, we believe by faith that God has communicated His perfect message through imperfect men. Our faith is not a blind faith, however. As we have already seen, there are many evidences that confirm our faith that the Bible is the Word of God.

We believe that the original writings of the books of the Bible were "inerrant," that is, without error. We also believe that the Bible has been very well preserved over the centuries. This does not mean, however, that we claim the translations of the Bible we have today are perfect in every way. There may have been minor scribal errors or mistranslations. In question number 9 of this chapter, we deal with the wonderful evidence that gives us great comfort in knowing we can trust our Bible to be an accurate reflection of the original message He gave to us 3500 to 2000 years ago.

All of the so-called contradictions within the Bible involve minor details that do not change its meaning or message. Most of these seeming contradictions involve the observations of two writers describing the same event. It is not uncommon for one observer to give details that another observer omits. For example, in the description of the events surrounding Jesus' resurrection, the writers of the gospels differ in the details they report. Actually, these minor differences point to the reality of the event they are describing. They all broadly report the same events and come to the exact same conclusions. The fact that they differ on minor details within the storyline confirms that they did not conspire together to make up a story. Such a conspiracy would have ironed out the differences in details. Different eyewitness accounts of the same event will always vary some in the details that are remembered and considered important by the various witnesses.

In some cases, the style of writing accounts for the apparent contradiction. (e.g. a summary account vs. a chronological detailed account) In Matthew 21:10-22 and Mark 11:10-24, we are given accounts of two events: Jesus cleansing the Temple in Jerusalem, and Jesus cursing the fig tree between Jerusalem and Bethany. In Mark's account, these two events take place within three days. Jesus observes what's going on in the temple, goes in the evening to Bethany, curses the fig tree the next morning on His way back to Jerusalem, reenters the temple and cleanses it, goes back to Bethany again that night, and walks by the now-withered fig tree the next morning as his disciples notice the tree and comment on it. In Matthew's account, the two events—the cleansing of the temple and the cursing of the fig tree—appear to take place in two days. Jesus enters the temple in Jerusalem and cleanses it; He goes to Bethany for the night, and on His way back to Jerusalem the next morning He curses the fig tree, which, to the disciples' amazement, withers at once.

Critics and skeptics point to the fact that Matthew says the fig tree withers at once while Mark says it was withered when the disciples saw it the next morning. The key to understanding this is to notice that Matthew is not writing the details of these events in chronological order. He is summarizing the events to bring forth their meaning. Mark, on the other hand, is relating the events in chronological order. This means Mark records Jesus first going to the temple, then returning to Bethany and speaking the curse upon the fig tree the next morning before He returns to the temple to cleanse it. Matthew chooses to group the details of each event together and record them separately instead of going back and forth between them. He deals first with the cleansing of the Temple in Jerusalem and completes that account, then he addresses the cursing of the fig tree and completes that account.

My study leads me to believe that what actually happened was this: The fig tree did wither at once from the roots up just as Matthew recorded. But the disciples actually saw the completed process of the withering the next morning. Matthew is summarizing each event and did not consider the exact timeline to be a priority. He did the same thing with his account of the event in the temple. His account may allow one to assume Jesus went to the temple only once and cleansed it on that single visit. But Mark gives us more chronological details, saying that Jesus went into the Temple the day before He cursed the fig tree, and then went back and cleansed the Temple later in the same day that He cursed the fig tree.

It should be noted that Mark never says that the fig tree did not wither until the next day; he simply says that it was the next morning when the disciples proclaimed that it had withered.

I like to illustrate this by imagining two sportswriters reporting on the results of a basketball tournament. One writer may choose to report it in chronological order, saying "In game 1, team A defeated team B; in game 2, team C defeated team D; in game 3, team A defeated team C; and in game 4, team B defeated team D." The other writer may choose to report in a summary fashion, saying "Team A defeated team B and team C, while Team D was defeated by team C and team B." We would not say that one of the writers was wrong because he didn't report the games in chronological order. We would not say he lied or that his report was erroneous. He simply had a different way of reporting the results, not feeling that the chronological sequence of the games was important to what he was trying to communicate.

Another example of a supposed Bible contradiction involves the three accounts of Paul's "Road to Damascus" experience. The difficulty is in the description of what happened to those who were traveling with Paul. Acts 9:7 says that they "stood speechless, hearing the voice, but seeing no one." In Acts 22:9 Paul says that they "saw the light for sure, but did not understand the voice that was speaking to me." In Acts 26:13-14 he says that the light from heaven was "shining all around me and those who were journeying with me," and that they "had all fallen to the ground."

Obviously, each of these accounts describes the details

differently, but they do not contradict one another. The companions of Paul saw the light but did not see the person of Christ within the light. They saw just the light. They heard the voice that was speaking to Paul, but they did not understand the voice. The word for "stood" in "stood speechless" can also be translated "fixed." They were so frightened that they were not able to speak. They may have fallen to the ground for a time, but they were still speechless when they again stood up.

Obviously, none of these so-called contradictions changes the essential message of what happened to Paul on the road to Damascus. Each time Paul tells the story, he references what happens to his companions a bit differently, but not in a contradictory way. In none of the situations where Paul describes this event is the exact account of what happened to the companions an essential part of what is being communicated. Even so, the bottom line is that the three accounts together give us a fuller understanding of what happened to Paul's companions.

Another example of a seeming contradiction is a comparison of 2 Kings 24:8, which says that Jehoiachin ruled over Jerusalem for three months, and 2 Chronicles 36:9, which says that he ruled for three months and ten days. The difference is probably a simple matter of the writer of Kings rounding off the number, not feeling that the ten extra days were important to communicate.

There is, however, another issue within these two passages. In 2 Kings we read that Jehoiachin was eighteen years old when he began to reign. In 2 Chronicles we read that he was only eight years old when he began to reign. There are two possible explanations for this difference. One is that Jehoiachin's father brought him alongside of him at the age of eight to begin reigning with him, as if in training. Then he began to reign on his own at age eighteen. More commentators, however, are of the opinion that the difference is due to a rare scribal error. In ancient times, the notations of numbers was such that a very minor difference would distinguish between eight and eighteen. If the difference here between 2 Kings and 2 Chronicles is due to a scribal error, it does not contradict biblical inerrancy. It merely indicates that our copies are not perfect. We should note, however, that the scribal procedures for copying the

Bible show that without question, the Bible has been accurately preserved beyond any other writings of history, by far. We should also note that the differences in the king's age in the disputed passages have no effect whatsoever on the meaning of the text.

It would be inaccurate to say that dealing with so-called contradictions within the Bible is an easy matter in all cases. Sometimes we struggle to understand why there is a difference between two passages. Critics spend great amounts of time in finding these details and pointing them out. Most of us Christians have not spent much time finding explanations for them. This is because—as we have stressed—these seeming contradictions don't affect the meaning of Scripture and seldom rise to claim our attention until we are challenged. We should be thankful for those who have taken the time to look into these matters and record explanations.

We cannot in one chapter address all or even most of the skeptics' claims of biblical contradictions. To help you respond to any specific claim of contradiction, I refer you to the following online resources where you will find detailed answers to almost any challenge.

- **searchcreation.org (search: Contradictions in the Bible)**
- **apologeticspress.org (search: Contradictions in the Bible)**
- **answersingenesis.org (search: Contradictions in the Bible)**
- **carm.org (search: Contradictions in the Bible)**
- **comereason.org (Answering Biblical Contradictions)**
- **debate.org.uk (101 Cleared-up Contradictions in the Bible)**

5. How can God be three persons and yet just one God?

Skeptics, Muslims, and sometimes Christians of particular persuasions often question the doctrine of the Trinity, the belief that God is one God eternally in the form of three persons. They sometimes accuse us of believing in three Gods.

The Bible states clearly that there is One God!

Hear, O Israel! The LORD is our God, the LORD is one! (Deuteronomy 6:4)

I am the LORD, and there is no other; Besides Me there is no God. (Isaiah 45:5a)

For You are great and do wondrous deeds; You alone are God. (Psalms 86:10)

The Bible also clearly reveals that God forever exists in the form of three Persons: God the Father, God the Son, Jesus Christ, and God the Holy Spirit. It is true that the word "trinity" is never used in the Bible. The doctrine of the Trinity is based on the consistent statements that refer to the Father, the Son, and the Holy Spirit.

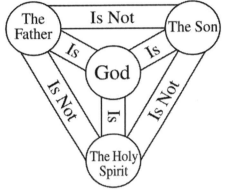

We covered the deity of Jesus Christ in detail in an earlier chapter of this section. The deity of the Holy Spirit is also well established in the Bible. The Holy Spirit is also referred to as "the Spirit of God" and referenced by God as "My Spirit." For example, Acts 2 quotes a passage in Joel where God says, "In the last days I will pour out My Spirit upon all flesh."

The Biblical acknowledgment that these three are separate persons is seen in many places. Note the following examples: (I have individually identified the three persons of God referenced in the passages)

When the Helper comes [God the Holy Spirit], whom I [God the Son] will send to you from the Father [God the Father], that is the Spirit of truth [God the Holy Spirit] who proceeds from the Father [God the Father], He [God the Holy Spirit] will testify about Me [God the Son]. (John 15:26)

But now I [God the Son] am going to Him [God the Father] who sent Me [God the Son]; and none of you asks Me [God the Son], "Where are You [God the Son] going?" (6) But because I [God the Son] have said these things to you, sorrow has filled your heart. (7) But I [God the Son] tell you the truth, it is to your advantage that I [God the Son] go away; for if I [God the Son] do not go away, the Helper [God the Holy Spirit] will not come to you; but if I [God the Son] go, I [God the Son] will send Him [God the Holy Spirit] to you. (John 16:5-7)

According to the foreknowledge of God the Father [God the Father], by the sanctifying work of the Spirit [God the Holy Spirit], to obey Jesus Christ [God the Son] and be sprinkled with His blood: May grace and peace be yours in the fullest measure. (1 Peter 1:2)

God [God the Father], after He [God the Father] spoke long ago to the fathers in the prophets in many portions and in many ways, (2) in these last days has spoken to us in His Son [God the Son], whom He appointed heir of all things, through whom [God the Son] also He [God the Father] made the world. (3) And He [God the Son] is the radiance of His [God the Father] glory and the exact representation of His [God the Father] nature, and upholds all things by the word of His [God the Son] power. When He [God the Son] had made purification of sins, He [God the Son] sat down at the right hand of the Majesty [God the Father] on high. (Hebrews 1:1-3)

Note in the following Scripture how the Genesis account of the creation of man refers to the Trinity. God is having a discussion within the Triune Godhead as He says, "Let Us make... in Our image, according to Our likeness..."

325

Then God said, "Let Us make man in Our image, according to Our likeness; and let them rule over the fish of the sea and over the birds of the sky and over the cattle and over all the earth, and over every creeping thing that creeps on the earth." (Genesis 1:26)

The Trinity is also seen during the baptism of Jesus – God the Father says "This is My Son", speaking of Jesus – God the Holy Spirit comes upon Jesus in the form of a dove. All three persons of the Trinity are seen together in this recorded event.

Jesus said in one place that He and the Father are one. He also said in John 13 that if you have seen Me, you have seen the Father. Yet, He also said things like, "I do not come to do My own will, but the will of Him who sent Me," and "Not My will be done, but Thine." We see both His oneness with the Father and the fact that He is a separate person from the Father.

These three personalities—God the Father, God the Son, and God the Holy Spirit—eternally exist together at the same time and together are the totality of the one God who created all things and has revealed Himself in the Bible.

Despite our best attempts to comprehend God, there is much about Him and the unseen spiritual world that we will never understand. This is to be expected, as God told us through the prophet Isaiah.

"For My thoughts are not your thoughts, Nor are your ways My ways," declares the LORD. (9) "For as the heavens are higher than the earth, So are My ways higher than your ways And My thoughts than your thoughts. (Isaiah 55:8-9)

Though the reality of the Trinity is hard for us to grasp, an illustration that helps a bit can be found in the egg. As I pick up an egg to fry for my breakfast, I have only one egg in my hand, but that egg has three distinct parts: the shell, the egg white, and the yoke. The three parts make up one egg. Similarly, the three

sides of a triangle are individually distinct lines, but together they form one triangle. No illustration explains the Trinity perfectly, but ultimately we accept by faith what the Bible reveals while realizing that some mysteries will remain opaque to us until we become citizens of eternity.

6. Evidence of the existence of God is not credible because it does not have a naturalistic explanation verifiable by science.

Humanists and evolutionists insist that the science classroom is no place for the discussion of God. Their reasoning is based on the prevailing philosophy of naturalism, which claims that nothing exists outside the realm of nature. In other words, there is no such thing as a supernatural realm, which means that God, who is inevitably supernatural, cannot exist. Only what science can identify, quantify, and analyze can be included in what the naturalists call reality.

In the naturalistic view, everything that science discovers must have a naturalistic explanation, no matter how much it appears to point to the existence of a wise and powerful being. Many famous evolutionary scientists have warned their colleagues that they must always remember that no matter how much what they are studying looks designed, it isn't. They are blinded to the obvious evidence by their presupposed assumptions and biases.

It is true that we cannot scientifically examine the supernatural or unseen spiritual realm for the simple reason that this realm is indeed outside of nature. But being outside of nature is not the same as being non-existent. It is not even scientific to make such a claim. What we cannot know should not automatically be closed off as a possibility. When scientific discovery brings forth evidence that an unseen intelligent designer is behind what we observe, invoking a religious explanation should not be out of bounds.

It's true that empirical evidence that proves the existence of the God who created everything cannot be found. But we do have scientific evidence that is consistent with what we would expect to find if a God who created everything exists.

Romans 1:19-20 gives us reason to expect that scientific examination of the known world will reveal evidence that points us to God.

That which is known about God is evident within them; for God made it evident to them. (20) For since the creation of the world His invisible attributes, His eternal power and divine nature, have been clearly seen, being understood through what has been made, so that they are without excuse. (Romans 1:19-20)

Actually, scientific work can be done only because we live in an orderly universe which allows us to trust the results we find through examination. If the universe came about through totally random processes as humanistic scientists claim, there would be no laws of physics and no consistent findings that could be trusted. Randomness does not produce order, which means that a universe that came about through random processes will remain chaotic and random.

The early pioneers of science were almost all Christians, or at least deists, who believed it was worth their time to study the universe. They expected to find designed things and reliable information because they believed that God had designed the universe, and it would make sense when studied.

Sir Isaac Newton

Nicolaus Copernicus, Sir Francis Bacon, Galileo, Johann Kepler, Blaise Pascal, Robert Boyle, and Sir Isaac Newton are among the early pioneers of science who all believed in a Creator. The idea that science and belief in God are incompatible is almost laughable. For a more complete list of early scientists who believed in a Creator, go to Creation Ministries International's website and search for "Scientists of the past who believed in a creator."

7. Who made God?

God's existence is assumed and proclaimed in the Bible. We see God existing and working in the very first verse, where it declares,

"In the beginning God created..." No attempt is made to explain where He came from or how long He existed before He created the heavens and the Earth.

Reason demands that something must be self-existent to account for the fact that things exist. The Bible merely identifies that self-existent being as the God who created all things. No explanation of self-existence that our finite minds could understand is possible. This is why the Bible merely declares the self-existence of God rather than trying futilely to explain it. In Exodus 3:14-15 God merely identifies Himself to Moses as "I AM," a proclamation of self-existence in the grammatical present tense that covers his existence in the eternal past, present, and future. No explanation is possible. God simply is.

Some find it hard to accept that God can exist eternally with no beginning. Perhaps it is helpful to think of the alternative. How could God have a beginning? If He had a beginning, we would still face the question, What caused Him to begin? Once we start down that road, there is no end. The question keeps repeating itself. We simply need to accept the revelation of God that is given to us in the Bible. He is revealed as the eternal self-existent One.

Logic presents us with only four possible options as to how things came into existence. Those options are shown in the chart below. Not one of these options fits into the natural universe. Each is inevitably outside the realm of nature and thus scientifically inexplicable, yet one of them must be true. That means, no matter which option you choose, you must believe it on faith, for scientific proof is impossible. The answer that the Bible gives us makes the most sense and fits best with all that God has revealed to us through His creation. God is eternal and self-existent. God created all things.

Only 4 Possibilities for the Origin of All Things	
1	**Matter & Energy are eternal and had no beginning.** Though Matter & Energy have changed over vast amounts of time there was no original source of them.
2	**Matter & Energy are not eternal but had a beginning.** Though not created, designed or purposed, Matter & Energy somehow came into existence out of _nothing_ with no creator.
3	**God is Eternal, Self Existent and Creator of all things!** (According to the Bible this Eternal God created everything & Revealed Himself through that which He made.)
4	**God is the Creator of all things but He is not Eternal.** In this proposal the origin of God is a mystery with no answer. Any answer would only lead to a greater question.

8. Is the story of Jesus just a retelling of the accounts of pagan mythical gods like Mithras?

In recent years, entertainer Bill Maher and many other skeptics have claimed that the story of Jesus is nothing more than a retelling of prior stories of mythical gods such as Horus, Mithras, or Osiris. Those who make such claims typically describe a number of shared characteristics between Jesus and prior mythological figures. They assert that the biblical account of Jesus is made up, taken from other stories that existed long before the time of Christ. This form of attack upon the Christian faith appears to have had its beginnings in the writings of Gerald Massey in the latter part of the nineteenth century. In 1887 Massey wrote a book entitled, The Historical Jesus and The Mythical Christ.

Perhaps the most persuasive example of these arguments is found in claims related to Mithras, the ancient mythological deity worshipped in Persia 400 years prior to Jesus and by Romans during the 1st through the 4th Centuries AD (or CE). The list of asserted similarities between Jesus and Mithras is quite extensive. Here is a sampling:

"Mithras" Myth

1. Born of a virgin, in a cave on December 25th
2. His birth attended by shepherds
3. Considered a great traveling teacher and master
4. Had twelve companions (or disciples)
5. Promised his followers immortality
6. Performed miracles
7. Sacrificed himself for world peace
8. Was buried in a tomb and rose from the dead after three days
9. His followers celebrated his resurrection each year;
the date later became Easter
10. Called the "Good Shepherd"
11. Identified with both the lamb and the lion
12. Was considered to be "the Way, the Truth, and the Life"
13. Also referred to as the "Logos," the "Redeemer,"
the "Savior," and the "Messiah"
14. His followers celebrated Sunday as his sacred day,
known as the "Lord's Day"
15. His followers celebrated a Eucharist or Lord's Supper

Obviously, if all these similarities were true, it would appear that the writers of the Bible borrowed them from the myths related to Mithras. Although those hostile to the Christian faith present these similarities as factual, most of them are simply false. Study the myth of Mithras as presented in Persian mythology, and here is what you will find:

1. Mithras was supposedly born out of a rock, not a from a virgin.

2. Shepherds are part of Mithraism, helping Mithras emerge from a rock.

3. There is nothing in Mithraic tradition that indicates Mithras was a teacher of any kind.

4. There is no evidence that Mithras was supposed to have twelve companion or disciples. The closest things to this are murals that depict Mithras surrounded by the twelve signs of the zodiac.

5. There is no evidence of Mithras dying for world peace. He was supposed to have killed a threatening bull.

6. There is nothing in Mithraic tradition that says Mithras even died, much less was raised from the dead. After the time of Christ, there is a reference by Tertullian indicating that Mithras believers did reenact resurrection scenes, but this was well after New Testament times. The reality is that the writers of the Bible did not take elements from Mithras beliefs, but Mithras followers after the time of Christ may have taken elements from the biblical accounts of Christ and added them to their beliefs and practices.

7. There is no evidence that Mithras was ever referred to as "Good Shepherd," "the Way, the Truth and the Life," "Redeemer," "Savior," or "Messiah."

8. Mithras followers celebrating on Sunday is only seen well after the time of Christ, again showing that later followers of Mithras may have borrowed practices from followers of Christ.

9. Mithras followers did not celebrate a Eucharist.

Much of what is presumed about Mithras comes from ancient captionless pictures and murals, so the vast majority of scholarly work on Mithras is pure speculation. Also, as mentioned above, some of what we know about Mithras was learned after the time of Christ. Skeptics have attempted to attribute beliefs and practices of followers of Mithras that began after the time of Christ, to Mithras myths originating hundreds of years before Christ. All in all, the claim that the biblical accounts of Jesus were taken from mythological accounts of Mithras are simply false.

For more information on this topic you can look up "Jesus and Mithras" in the "searchcreation.org" search engine. J. Warner

Wallace has a good article on this subject. (I derived much of my information in this section from Wallace's article.)

We find the same results when we look at other mythological stories that are purported to be the source of the biblical account of Jesus. There is a short, entertaining video clip on YouTube that addresses this entitled "Horus Ruins Christmas."

9. How do you know that the Bible you read today is an accurate translation of the original manuscripts?

Earlier in this chapter we discussed the fact that biblical "inerrancy" does not mean that the copies of the Bible that we have today are a perfect reflection of the original writings. But we do know that the Bible we have today is very reliable. Though it may contain minor copying or translation errors, it is clear that the Bible has been preserved better by far than any other ancient writing.

This claim has been amply affirmed by what is called "bibliographical evidence." This term speaks of the information known about the ancient manuscripts and manuscript fragments of the Bible. The shorter the time span between an ancient writing and its earliest copies, the more reliable those copies are considered to be. The greater the quantity of ancient manuscript copies, the more reliable they are considered to be.

Author	Written	Earliest Copies	Time Span	# of copies
Caesar	100-44 B.C.	A.D. 900	1,000 yrs.	10
Plato (Tetralogies)	427-347 B.C.	A.D. 900	1,200 yrs.	7
Thucydides	460-400 B.C.	A.D. 900	1,300 yrs.	8
Sophocles	496-406 B.C.	A.D. 1,000	1,400 yrs.	100
Catullus	54 B.C.	A.D. 1,550	1,600 yrs.	3
Euripides	480-406 B.C.	A.D. 1,100	1,500 yrs.	9
Aristotle	384-322 B.C.	A.D. 1,100	1,400 yrs.	5
THE SECOND RUNNER UP.....				
Homer (Iliad)	750-700 B.C.	200 B.C.	500 yrs.	643
AND THE WINNER IS......				
God (The N.T.)	A.D. 40-100	A.D. 125	25 yrs.	24,000+

When comparing the number of ancient manuscripts and manuscript fragments of the Bible to the number of ancient manuscripts and fragments of other ancient writings, it is clear that the Bible we have today is much more reliable than the modern copies of any other ancient writing.

Also, the oldest manuscript copies of the Bible are much closer in date to the original writings than the oldest manuscript copies of any other ancient writing. Consider the chart shown here. Clearly the Bible is well-preserved and trustworthy.

The 1947 discovery of the Dead Sea Scrolls included a copy of the book of Isaiah that was believed to be 1,000 years older than the oldest known extant copy. When the two copies were compared, only a few minor differences were found, none of which affected the meaning of the text in any way. This confirmed in a  powerful way that the Bible has been accurately preserved over the centuries.

In a presentation by Josh McDowell entitled "Touch the Evidence," he allows audiences to view up close a 700-year-old Torah Scroll ("The Torah" is what the Jews called the first five books of the Bible.) As he shows the scroll, he speaks of the meticulous process that scribes used to copy the Bible. They had to abide by about 4,000 rules when copying the Bible. These rules were strenuous and meticulous, designed to ensure that every copy was completely accurate. No other book in history has been preserved with such care. We can trust that the Bible we read today accurately presents the message of God given to us centuries ago.

10. Can you prove that Jesus really existed?

This question is covered extensively in the earlier chapter on the person of Jesus Christ, so I will simply reiterate here a few key points that address the question.

First, virtually no historians—even unbelieving historians—question the reality of the life of Jesus. Josephus, Tacitus, Pliny the Younger, and other ancient historians speak of Jesus in their writings.

Other religions acknowledge the fact that Jesus lived, though they do not believe that He is God and the Savior of the world.

The world has been radically changed by the life of Jesus. Our calendars date back to the estimated year of His birth. Nations have been changed wherever the message of Jesus Christ has been embraced. Hospitals have been built around the world in His Name. Missionaries have given their lives to take His message around the world, and hundreds of millions have experienced life-change by putting their faith in Christ.

It should be noted that the question can easily be turned around. We can ask the skeptic, "Can you prove that Jesus did not live?"

11. Aren't all religions essentially the same?

Many today say that all religions are basically the same. I find that statement amazingly ignorant of what religions really teach. When we examine the teachings of the various religions, we find that they exhibit major differences. (In a later chapter we will look at many of these teachings.) Their views of God, morality, eternity, sin, and salvation are often radically different.

Others complain about Christianity's claim of exclusiveness. As we noted above, they are offended that Jesus said that no one can come to God except through Him. In truth, other religions are exclusive as well. Certainly, today you can find teachers of all religions, including Christianity, who embrace universalism—the teaching that there are many paths to God. Still, an examination of the actual teachings of various religions shows that the major religions of the world do not even claim to lead to the same destination. There is a way that is right, which means there are also ways that are not right.

Holding firmly to the truth that Christianity is true and other religions are not true does give Christians the right to adopt an attitude of superiority, disdain, or hate. Jesus clearly taught us to love others, even those who are our enemies.

The key difference between Christianity and other religions is seen through an understanding of the word "grace." All other religions call for man to attempt to reach God or a heavenly dwelling by his own works, effort, or knowledge. Christianity speaks of God reaching out to man and offering him a restored relationship with

God and eternal life through grace. Grace is defined as undeserved or unmerited favor. God offers us salvation as a gift through grace—His undeserved favor which He freely bestows upon us. This is the key difference between Christianity and all other religions.

We see the real uniqueness of Christianity in the fact that it is the only religion in which salvation is found in a person—the Lord Jesus Christ. Other religions have key teachers or prophets who are there to help people in their journey to salvation, but Christianity alone shows that salvation is found in a person who is both God and man, who died for the sins of the world, and rose from the dead.

Note the differences in the world's major religions in the chart shown on this page.

	HINDUISM	BUDDHISM	ISLAM	CHRISTIANITY
ULTIMATE REALITY	Impersonal essence; Or many gods	No God; or impersonal "Buddha essence"	A Creator Who is unknowable	A Creator Who is personal & Who has made Himself known
THE NATURE OF HUMANITY	Divine in our essence	No personal essence	Created by God, but nothing about him is at all like God	Created by God in His image and likeness
HUMANITY'S PROBLEM	Trapped in rein-carnations in an illusory world, due to ignorance and karma	Trapped in rein-carnations in a world of suffering, due to desire and karma	Under the judg-ment of Allah, due to failure to keep the Law	Under God's judgment due to sinful rebellion
SALVATION	Deliverance from the world through knowledge, works, or devotion	Deliverance from the world of suffer-ing through the cessation of desire (by own works, or "divine" help)	Deliverance from judgment through obedience to the Law	Deliverance from judgment by faith in God's gracious provision of salvation through Jesus Christ
FINAL STATE	Merging with ultimate reality, or heavenly bliss in the presence of the gods	Extinction of suffering, desire, and individuality (Nirvana)	Paradise or Hell	Heaven or Hell

12. Why is so much evil done in the Name of God?

If Jesus taught that His followers were to love others as themselves and speak blessing upon others, why does history record times when people did horrible things in the name of Christianity? Those who ask this question often point to the Crusades, which occurred about 800 years ago, when Christians brutally killed many Muslims.

Others point to the Spanish Inquisition or the fighting between Catholics and Protestants in Ireland. Some even claim that Hitler had religious leanings that influenced his instigation of the Holocaust.

To answer the question, we must briefly examine what it means to be a Christian. The word "Christian" means "a follower of Christ." Many claim an affinity with Christianity but do not follow the teachings of Jesus. If a person is not a follower of Christ and His teachings, he is not truly a Christian, even if  he claims to be. Today 80 percent of Americans claim to be Christian, even though it is obvious that the majority are not followers of Christ and His teachings. Even in our churches we often see people who are not following Christ.

The fact that so many wear the name Christian without following Christ explains why much evil has been done in the Name of God. Individuals, organizations, or governments that have done evil in the name of Christianity were not following the teachings of Christ.

It is true that even genuine Christians still have a wicked, fleshly nature that often prods them to sin (see Luke 9:23; Romans 7:14-24; 8:13; Galatians 6:7-8; 1 John 2:15-16). The Bible indicates that the Christian must put this wicked, fleshly nature to death each day, or in other words, not allow it to dictate the daily decisions and directions of life. This means that even true Christians may be guilty of evil acts when they respond to the pull of their fleshly nature instead of being led by the Spirit of God. When this happens, the true believer must quickly confess his sin and be motivated by godly sorrow to repent of it.

It should also be pointed out that though there have been evil things done by people claiming to be Christian over the centuries, there have been many, many more good things done in the name of Christianity. The world, nations, communities, families and individuals have been affected in many wonderful ways by those who choose to follow the ways of Christianity! As an example, until recent years most hospitals in America and other nations were established by Christians and Christian organizations.

13. If God is good and all-powerful, how can the existence of evil be explained?

This question differs from question 1 in that it does not merely address human suffering, but the very existence of evil. The question involves these factors: If God is all good, He would want to prevent evil. If God is all-powerful, He would be able to prevent evil. Since evil exists, God must not want to prevent evil or He must not be able to prevent evil. Therefore, the existence of evil shows that either God does not exist or that He is not good or that He is not all-powerful.

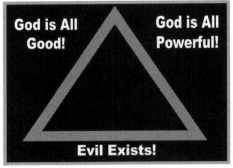

The answer to this question (or accusation) involves an understanding of human free will, which God gave to man along with ruling authority over all the Earth (Genesis 1:27-28). God created the world in a perfect state and intended that it should remain that way. But in giving man free will and rule over the earth, He allowed man to choose either to submit to God and keep the world in its perfect state or to reject God and lose the power to rule the world and prevent the intrusion of evil.

Satan tempted man to sin, and when man sinned, he rejected God's rule and evil entered the world. The essence of evil is simply the absence of God. At that point, all creation was afflicted with evil because man was no longer joined to God.

The goodness of God is vindicated not only by His giving man the power of free will, but also by His promise of redemption, which will include the restoration of the complete goodness of the Earth as it existed in God's original creation (Romans 8:18-25).

14. How can a loving God send people to hell to suffer eternal conscious suffering?

When it comes to hell and eternal judgment, we must admit that there are things that we cannot clearly understand. Though the Bible makes it clear that there is a place of judgment called hell, there are some verses, such as Hebrews 10:26-31, that could lead us to believe that those who face the judgment of hell will be consumed by the fire of hell and cease to exist. Other verses seem to indicate that those in hell will experience eternal, conscious suffering.

We must allow the revealed nature and character of God to trump our lack of understanding about eternal matters that we do not comprehend. This includes hell and eternal judgment. We do not have a good understanding of eternal things beyond the grave, but we do have a good understanding of God's character. Because we know that He is loving, holy, full of grace, merciful, just, and unchanging, we can trust that His judgments on people are just and consistent with His revealed nature. When we encounter questions beyond our understanding, we must let our understanding of God's revealed character uphold our faith in Him.

God's nature and character are clearly revealed in the following verses of the Bible:

- **God is Love:** 1 John 1:8; Romans 5:8
- **God is Holy:** (perfect, whole, lacking nothing): Isaiah 6:3; 1 Peter 1:15-16; Revelation 4:8
- **God is a Giver of Grace:** Ephesians 2:8-9; Romans 3:23-24; John 1:16-17
- **God is Merciful:** Psalm 86:15; Psalm 119:156; Titus 3:5
- **God is Just:** Psalm 89:14; Psalm 119:137; Romans 3:26
- **God does not Change:** Malachi 3:6; Hebrews 6:17-18; James 1:17

To accuse God by saying "If God were a loving God, He would never send someone to hell", is to abandon the clear revelation of Scripture concerning God's nature and character. I may struggle to understand and comprehend some things about eternity and the unseen world but my understanding of who God is should trump my lack of understanding. I may not totally understand hell or eternal judgment but I know that God is love and God is just and God is holy, so whatever His judgments are they will be right and just.

15. Why are there so many denominations?

Because there is human involvement within the church, imperfections within the church of Jesus Christ are inevitable. We don't always handle disagreements as we should and we don't always treat one another as we should. Some of the factors that brought about many various denominations over the centuries have been disagreements in governmental policies, structural policies and methodologies. Christians have often been guilty of allowing minor differences to become points of division. The humanness involved in the church of Jesus Christ has often created schisms that have remained for decades and even centuries.

On the major doctrines of the Christian faith most denominations, in their statements of faith, agree. Still, minor differences in doctrine have certainly been the root cause of divisions within the body of Christ on many occasions. As individuals we often find ourselves feeling more comfortable with one interpretation of Scripture over another interpretation. It is important to remember that in almost all cases these differences in interpretation do not change the major doctrines of the Christian faith. There are some groups that vary in major doctrines, such as the deity of Jesus Christ, which are not considered a part of the Christian church though they may claim to be a part of mainstream Christianity. They are considered "cults" because they hold to doctrines that have not been held by the Christian church since its beginning.

It should be noted that though there are many denominations most true Christians get along well, following Jesus' command to love one another. I have found throughout my life that many of my best friends within the body of Christ were a part of a different denomination than I am. Those who know Jesus Christ as their personal Savior are brothers and sisters in Christ though they may attend churches that are part of different denominations.

For further answers to questions asked by seekers or skeptics, I recommend the following website:
http://carm.org/evidence-and-answers
(Christian Apologetics & Research Ministry)

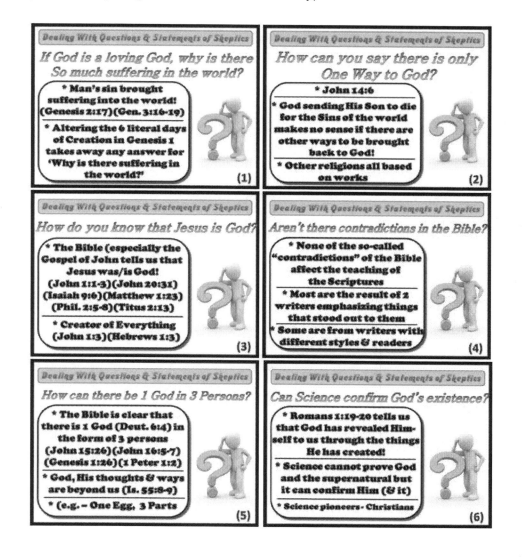

Dealing With Questions & Statements of Skeptics

Who made God?

* **The Bible assumes the existence of God! (Gen. 1:1)**
* **God is revealed in the Bible As the self-existent One – "I Am" – Exodus 3:15**
* **Only 4 explanations of how Everything came into being** (Eternal M & E) (M & E from Nothing) (Eternal God) (Created God)

(7)

Dealing With Questions & Statements of Skeptics

Is the story of Jesus a retelling of accounts of mythical god's like Mithras?

* **These accusations involve faulty information**
* **The accurate details of pre-existing myths do not line up with the details of the Biblical Jesus. Some of the myths came after Jesus.**

(8)

Dealing With Questions & Statements of Skeptics

How do you know your Bible is an Accurate translation of the original?

* **Bibliographical Evidence provides more assurance than with any other ancient writings**
* **Dead Sea Scrolls provide confirmation of accuracy**

(9)

Dealing With Questions & Statements of Skeptics

Can you prove that Jesus really lived?

* **Historians, including Josephus refer to details of the life of Jesus.**
* **The world has been greatly impacted by Jesus. (Nations, Hospitals, Calendar, Etc.)**
* **Turn the question around!**

(10)

Dealing With Questions & Statements of Skeptics

Aren't all Religions basically the same?

* **Religions are very different in their views on (Nature of God) (Nature of Man) (Eternity) (Salvation) (Incarnation) (Etc.)**
* **Only Christianity focuses on God's work of salvation (All others – Man's Works)**
* **"Grace" sets Christianity apart**

(11)

Dealing With Questions & Statements of Skeptics

Why so much evil done in God's Name?

* **No one, following the teachings of Christ could resort to evil methods**
* **Many who call themselves "Christian" are not followers of Christ. Those who do evil at the supposed direction of "the church" or "Christianity" are not following Christ. True Christians have often the victims of violence**

(12)

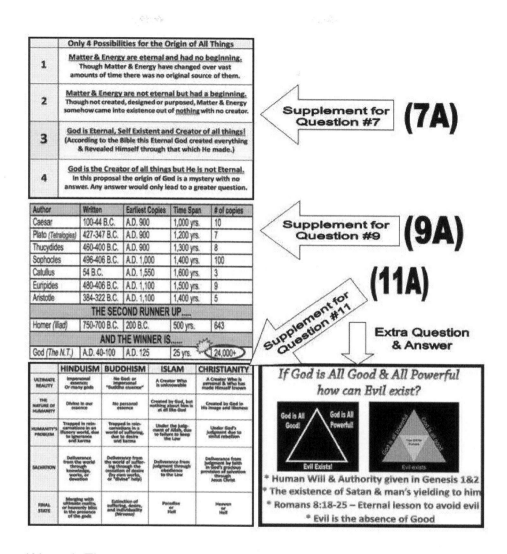

(Above) These memorization cards are designed to assist you in remembering key points in answering the questions that people may ask you about your Christian faith whether they are a sincere seeker or a skeptic attempting to attack your faith.

Memorization Cards Available for Free Download at
localchurchapologetics.org

"Dealing With Homosexuality and Other Social Issues"

Dealing with Homosexuality and Other Social Issues

In America today we experience increasing pressure to view homosexuality as an acceptable and godly lifestyle. In 2015, President Obama proclaimed June to be LGBT Pride month across the nation. He repeated the proclamation for June of 2016. Gay and lesbian lifestyles are not only accepted in America today, they are often celebrated. In reality, the phrase "celebrate diversity" actually means "celebrate homosexuality."  Those who dare say that homosexuality is a sin are accused of hate, homophobia, or bigotry.

On June 26, 2015, the Supreme Court ruled that the Constitution guarantees homosexuals the right to marry each other,  making same-sex marriage legal in America. That night, many buildings across America, including the White House, were bathed in rainbow-colored lights in celebration of the decision. Even Niagara Falls was lit up with rainbow colors.

In 2015, the Justice Department threatened to withhold federal funding for states that required school children to use the restrooms designated for the gender recorded on their birth certificates. The government demanded that students be allowed to use restrooms that corresponded to their self-chosen gender identity. As of the fall of 2016, thirteen states had filed lawsuits in response to the directive.

These examples show how rapidly the acceptance of homosexual and transgender lifestyles is increasing in America. The speed and suddenness of these changes make it difficult for churches and Christians to know how to respond. Christian young people tell me that this is the number one issue that they are facing with their peers. For this reason, I felt it essential to include in this book a chapter dealing with the issue.

Speaking the Truth in Love

The apostle Paul gives us a simple, straightforward directive that can guide us in dealing with today's social issues.

> *Speaking the truth in love, we are to grow up in all aspects into Him who is the head, even Christ. (Ephesians 4:15)*

Notice the two parts of this directive. The first is "speaking the truth." We are to hold to the truth of God's Word and speak it no matter what the culture around us believes. The second part of the directive is "in love." Our words, attitudes, and actions should express the love of Jesus to everyone around us, including those involved in immoral lifestyles. Name-calling, bullying, crude jokes, or mistreatment of any kind must not be a part of a Christian's response to those engaged in immorality.

I am convinced that name-calling and mistreatment of homosexuals normally comes from non-Christians. It is unfortunate, however, that the actions and words of a few misguided Christians or so-called Christians have at times created a distorted image of Christianity.

I am also convinced that the problem with most Christians' response to homosexuality is not the "in love" part, but rather the "speaking the truth" part. The fear of rejection or accusations of bigotry have caused many Christians to remain silent on these issues. A lack of understanding of what the Bible says also contributes to that silence.

Another passage that gives us direction in this matter is 1 Peter 3:15. You may remember that this is the key verse related to apologetics. Notice the last part of the verse.

> **Sanctify Christ as Lord in your hearts, always being ready to make a defense to everyone who asks you to give an account for the hope that is in you, yet with gentleness and reverence. (1 Peter 3:15)**

Whenever we are defending our faith or communicating specific aspects of it, we should maintain the right attitude. "With gentleness and reverence" is closely related to "in love." Having a Christ-like attitude is essential. Speaking the truth may still bring on accusations of hatred or bigotry, but being falsely accused is nothing new for Christians. Speaking truth has come at a cost throughout the centuries. We are not exempt today. We are called to faithfully proclaim the truth in love, even if the truth offends others and persecution comes to us as a result.

Knowing when to speak and when not to speak is also important. We know that the Holy Spirit lives inside us and that we are to be led by Him. Romans 8:14 tells us that all who are children of God are led by the Spirit of God. We should pray and ask the Holy Spirit to direct us as to when to speak truth and when to not speak. That applies not only to the issue of homosexuality, but also to all other issues in life. Trust the Holy Spirit to lead you to know what to say and when to say it. Remember that the only way for people to be set free is by the truth (John 8:32). Christians must not abandon the truth just because it is unpopular in the current culture. We are called to be the light of the world and the salt of the earth (Matthew 5:13-16). Salt is a preservative and light gives direction. Truth sets people free. Actually, "speaking the truth" and "in love" go together perfectly, because to speak truth to others is the loving thing to do, even if one must pay a price for speaking it.

If love, kindness, compassion, grace, mercy, gentleness, reverence, and concern for others is not in our heart, our words will most likely not produce good fruit. Our response to these cultural issues  should be directed by the same principles that have directed believers for centuries. Love God and other people with all your heart, and hold to God's truth and speak it as you are directed by the Holy Spirit. When you are asked, be ready to speak the truth with a right attitude (1 Peter 3:15).

What Does the Bible Say About Homosexuality?

Here we will look at numerous passages of Scripture that deal with homosexuality, either directly or indirectly.

Today several church denominations and segments of denominations are attempting to reinterpret the Bible to condone homosexuality. Linda Seiler has a superb presentation on this issue entitled, "Homotextuality: How Pro-Gay Advocates Revise the Bible." You can read this article on her website, lindaseiler.com.

The Bible has much to say about sexual immorality in general. It does not single out homosexuality for special condemnation; it clearly calls all sexual immorality sin. Our words and responses should make this point clear. We should never treat someone who is practicing the sin of homosexuality differently than those practicing other sins. Adultery and fornication are sinful and immoral acts. In the same way, homosexual acts are sinful and immoral. Homosexuality does take things a step beyond by violating God's creative order of sexual intercourse being between a man and a woman. Also, Romans 1 specifically says that when homosexuality becomes prevalent within a culture, it is a certain sign of that culture refusing to honor God as creator. Still, these things do not equate to homosexuality being a separate type of sin that should be treated differently than other sin. For all sin the answer is the same. When we sin we need forgiveness, mercy and grace which all come through faith in Jesus Christ, the Savior of the world.

Christians are often accused of attacking homosexuality as though it is a greater sin than others. But I find that it is usually not Christians who single out homosexuality for special treatment, but its defenders. They attempt to take homosexuality out of the category of sin altogether and declare it to be acceptable to God. People do not normally claim that other acts condemned in the Bible are not sinful—acts such as theft, lying, adultery, and murder (except in the case of abortion). Yet many claim that homosexuality is not sinful. Because Christians counter this claim with biblical injunctions against homosexuality, they are often falsely accused of singling out homosexuality for special condemnation.

With that thought in mind, let's look at what the Bible says about homosexuality and those who practice it.

New Testament Passages That Specifically Show that Homosexuality is a Sin

> *Or do you not know that the unrighteous will not inherit the kingdom of God? Do not be deceived; neither fornicators, nor idolaters, nor adulterers, nor effeminate, nor homosexuals, (10) nor thieves, nor the covetous, nor drunkards, nor revilers, nor swindlers, will inherit the kingdom of God. (11) Such were some of you; but you were washed, but you were sanctified, but you were justified in the name of the Lord Jesus Christ and in the Spirit of our God. (1 Corinthians 6:9-11)*

Notice that the Bible here does not single out homosexuality as worse than other sins but it does identify it as sin. It clearly places homosexuality with other sinful acts that prevent those who practice them from inheriting the kingdom of God.

> *Law is not made for a righteous person, but for those who are lawless and rebellious, for the*

ungodly and sinners, for the unholy and profane, for those who kill their fathers or mothers, for murderers (10) and immoral men and homosexuals and kidnappers and liars and perjurers, and whatever else is contrary to sound teaching. (1 Timothy 1:9-10)

The New Testament teaches that the purpose of the law is to show us our sin and our need for Christ. This passage relates the purpose of the law specifically to revealing the error of sinful practices. It specifically identifies murder, homosexuality, kidnapping and lying as sin.

Old Testament Passages that Specifically Show Homosexuality to be a Sin

If there is a man who commits adultery with another man's wife, one who commits adultery with his friend's wife, the adulterer and the adulteress shall surely be put to death. (11) If there is a man who lies with his father's wife, he has uncovered his father's nakedness; both of them shall surely be put to death, their bloodguiltiness is upon them. (12) If there is a man who lies with his daughter-in-law, both of them shall surely be put to death; they have committed incest, their bloodguiltiness is upon them. (13) If there is a man who lies with a male as those who lie with a woman, both of them have committed a detestable act; they shall surely be put to death. Their bloodguiltiness is upon them. (14) If there is a man who marries a woman and her mother, it is immorality; both he and they shall be burned with fire, so that there will be no immorality in your midst. (15) If there is a man who lies with an animal, he shall surely be put to death; you shall also kill the animal. (16) If there is a woman who approaches any animal to mate with it, you shall kill the woman and the animal; they shall surely be put to death. Their bloodguiltiness is upon them. (Leviticus 20:10-16)

Note that homosexuality (v.13) is included within the Old Testament law as among the immoral acts that were to bring very strict punishment to those who committed them. The harshness of the punishment is difficult for us to comprehend in today's culture, which views most of these practices as either acceptable or not preferable or maybe even disgusting—but not sinful or detestable. We need not be distracted from our point by the severity of Old Testament punishments. Our focus here is on the fact that the Bible condemns all forms of immorality as sinful violations of God's moral law.

> *You shall not have intercourse with your neighbor's wife, to be defiled with her. (21) You shall not give any of your offspring to offer them to Molech, nor shall you profane the name of your God; I am the LORD. (22) You shall not lie with a male as one lies with a female; it is an abomination. (23) Also you shall not have intercourse with any animal to be defiled with it, nor shall any woman stand before an animal to mate with it; it is a perversion. (Leviticus 18:20-23)*

This passage shows that God considers homosexuality and other forms of sexual immorality to be abominations.

Passages Dealing with God's Judgment upon Sodom and Gomorrah

> *And the LORD said, "The outcry of Sodom and Gomorrah is indeed great, and their sin is exceedingly grave. (21) I will go down now, and see if they have done entirely according to its outcry, which has come to Me; and if not, I will know." (Genesis 18:20-21)*

> *Now the two angels came to Sodom in the evening as Lot was sitting in the gate of Sodom. When Lot*

saw them, he rose to meet them and bowed down with his face to the ground. (2) And he said, "Now behold, my lords, please turn aside into your servant's house, and spend the night, and wash your feet; then you may rise early and go on your way." They said however, "No, but we shall spend the night in the square." (3) Yet he urged them strongly, so they turned aside to him and entered his house; and he prepared a feast for them, and baked unleavened bread, and they ate. (4) Before they lay down, the men of the city, the men of Sodom, surrounded the house, both young and old, all the people from every quarter; (5) and they called to Lot and said to him, "Where are the men who came to you tonight? Bring them out to us that we may have relations with them." (6) But Lot went out to them at the doorway, and shut the door behind him, (7) and said, "Please, my brothers, do not act wickedly. ... (12) Then the two men said to Lot, "Whom else have you here? A son-in-law, and your sons, and your daughters, and whomever you have in the city, bring them out of the place; (13) for we are about to destroy this place, because their outcry has become so great before the LORD that the LORD has sent us to destroy it." (Genesis 19:1-7, 12-13)

The story of Sodom and Gomorrah found in Genesis 18–19 reveals the judgment of God upon a people and place where homosexuality had become commonplace. The Merriam-Webster online dictionary says this concerning the origin of the word "sodomy": "Middle English, from Anglo-French sodomie, from Late Latin Sodoma Sodom; from the homosexual proclivities of the men of the city in Genesis 19:1–11." Though some say that the sin of the men of Sodom was a lack of hospitality, there is nothing in Scripture to support this. Scripture does support the premise that sexual immorality—particularly homosexuality in this passage—is an abomination to God and worthy of judgment.

If He condemned the cities of Sodom and Gomorrah to destruction by reducing them to ashes, having made them an example to those who would live ungodly lives thereafter; (7) and if He rescued righteous Lot, oppressed by the sensual conduct of unprincipled men (8) (for by what he saw and heard that righteous man, while living among them, felt his righteous soul tormented day after day by their lawless deeds). (2 Peter 2:6-8)

...just as Sodom and Gomorrah and the cities around them, since they in the same way as these indulged in gross immorality and went after strange flesh, are exhibited as an example in undergoing the punishment of eternal fire. (Jude 1:7)

These two New Testament passages refer to God's judgment upon Sodom and Gomorrah and confirm that judgment came to them as a result of gross sexual immorality. The context of the passages indicates that they are recorded in the New Testament as examples for us to learn from.

New Testament Passages Dealing with Sexual Immorality in General

Flee immorality. Every other sin that a man commits is outside the body, but the immoral man sins against his own body. (19) Or do you not know that your body is a temple of the Holy Spirit who is in you, whom you have from God, and that you are not your own? (20) For you have been bought with a price: therefore glorify God in your body. (1 Corinthians 6:18-20)

Now the deeds of the flesh are evident, which are: immorality, impurity, sensuality, (20) idolatry, sorcery, enmities, strife, jealousy, outbursts of anger, disputes, dissensions, factions, (21) envying, drunkenness, carousing, and things like these, of which I forewarn you, just as I have forewarned you, that those who practice such things will not inherit the kingdom of God. (Galatians 5:19-21)

But immorality or any impurity or greed must not even be named among you, as is proper among saints; (4) and there must be no filthiness and silly talk, or coarse jesting, which are not fitting, but rather giving of thanks. (5) For this you know with certainty, that no immoral or impure person or covetous man, who is an idolater, has an inheritance in the kingdom of Christ and God. (6) Let no one deceive you with empty words, for because of these things the wrath of God comes upon the sons of disobedience. (Ephesians 5:3-6)

For this is the will of God, your sanctification; that is, that you abstain from sexual immorality. (1 Thessalonians 4:3)

Each of these passages clearly indicate that sexual immorality is sinful and if practiced will prevent a person from experiencing eternal life with God.

Romans 1 – Homosexuality within a Culture that Denies God

For the wrath of God is revealed from heaven against all ungodliness and unrighteousness of men who suppress the truth in unrighteousness, (19) because that which is known about God is evident within them; for God made it evident to them. (20) For since the creation of the world His invisible attributes, His eternal power and divine nature, have been clearly seen, being understood through what has been made, so that they are without excuse. (21) For even though they knew God, they did not honor Him as God or give thanks, but they became futile in their speculations, and their foolish heart was darkened. (22) Professing to be wise, they became fools, (23) and exchanged the glory of the incorruptible God for an image in the form of corruptible man and of birds and four-footed animals and crawling creatures. (24) Therefore God gave them over in the lusts of their hearts to impurity, so that their bodies would be dishonored among them. (25) For they exchanged the truth of God for a lie, and worshiped and served the creature rather than the Creator, who is blessed forever. Amen. (26) For this reason God gave them over to degrading passions; for their women exchanged the natural function for that which is unnatural, (27) and in the same way also the men abandoned the natural function of the woman and burned in their desire toward one another, men with men committing indecent acts and receiving in their own persons the due penalty of their error. (28) And just as they did not see fit to acknowledge God any longer, God gave them over to a depraved mind, to do those things which are not proper. (Romans 1:18-28)

This passage describes the pattern that occurs when a culture, nation, or people group first begins to deny God. When they suppress the truth that is revealed to them about who God is and what He has done, God gives them over "in the lusts of their hearts to impurity" (v.24) and "to degrading passions" (v.26). Verses 24 through 27 make it clear that the sin described here is homosexuality.

Verses 28-32 describe the next moral step downward after a culture endorses homosexuality as normal. That culture is given over to "a depraved mind, to do those things which are not proper." In verse 32, which follows the passage quoted above, Paul tells us that in a depraved culture even those who do not practice these abominations "give hearty approval to those who practice them." Wow! What an accurate description of America today!

In the mid twentieth century, American public schools began to teach our children that God did not create us, but rather we have evolved from nothing. According to these teachings we have no God, no purpose in life, no eternity, no special place within creation. By the 1960s, we took Bible reading and prayer out of our public schools. We pushed God out of our culture and in many ways "did not honor Him as God." According to Romans 1, this exclusion of God that began fifty years ago meant that we could have begun at that time to expect homosexuality to become prevalent within American culture. It has! Romans 1 can be seen clearly in America today.

It should be noted that individuals who struggle with homosexuality are not more responsible for what has happened within the culture than those who do not struggle with it. What the Bible is saying is that when a nation or people deny God, the entire culture will be given over to, or become more susceptible to, these unnatural passions, so that they become much more prevalent. Just as people are more likely to become alcoholics or thieves in some cultures than in others, a culture that suppresses the truth about God and does not honor Him as God is more likely to struggle with homosexuality. Everyone is tempted to sin in some way, but God has warned us that denying Him as Creator can increase tendencies toward homosexuality and other sexual sins, which have consequences.

A Summary of Chapter 6

I believe the Christian's appropriate response to the issues surrounding homosexuality can be summarized quite simply. Love people! Be kind to them, care for them, and show compassion to them. Jesus was known as a friend of sinners. We should show ourselves friendly to others, whether or not they are practicing conspicuous sins.

Speak the truth in love. We should never compromise God's Word. It is the truth that will set people free. With a loving heart, a gentle spirit, and an attitude of kindness, we should speak the truth found in the Bible as we are led by the Holy Spirit of God who lives within us.

We would not hesitate to share the truth with a neighbor who is bound in alcohol or drugs or going through a divorce or tired of the stress of life. We should treat the homosexual in the same way. Tell him or her that God loves them and that forgiveness and freedom are available to them in Christ.

> *For God so loved the world, that He gave His only begotten Son, that whoever believes in Him shall not perish, but have eternal life. (John 3:16)*

> *If we confess our sins, He is faithful and righteous to forgive us our sins and to cleanse us from all unrighteousness. (1 John 1:9)*

> *In Him we have redemption through His blood, the forgiveness of our trespasses, according to the riches of His grace. (Ephesians 1:7)*

> *So if the Son makes you free, you will be free indeed. (John 8:36)*

"Christianity and Other World Religions"

Christianity and Other World Religions

Today Christians face the growing influence of a type of universalism which teaches that all religions contain a path to God. Most who hold to this type of universalism believe that religious truth is found within all religions, each contributing its own aspect of truth to the whole. This belief is rapidly gaining prominence in America today.

This universalism brings with it a new definition of tolerance. To a growing number of people, tolerance now means that you acknowledge other religions to be just as right and valid as your own. To assert that you are right and another person is wrong is now considered intolerant. The concept lurking behind this new universalism is that all truth is relative, which means one person's truth or religion is just as right and valid as another's.

This definition of tolerance is a gross distortion of the word's true meaning. Showing tolerance to others does not mean accepting their religion or opinions as valid truth. It means choosing to co-exist with them in a peaceful way, even while believing their religion or opinions are wrong. It means respecting their right to hold their beliefs even though I do not endorse them. It is biblical to be tolerant of others, but not to accept all religions and opinions as true.

In this chapter we will look briefly at the differences between the major religions in the world and show why it is impossible to claim that all offer a valid path to God or heaven. We will look at what makes Christianity unique among all other religions. This chapter will merely provide an overview of these subjects, but I will provide suggested resources where the reader can go to dig more deeply.

Comparing World Religions

We will structure our comparison of world religions on what each teaches in five critical areas as follows:

> (1) What Religions Teach about God
> (2) What Religions Teach about Man
> (3) What Religions Teach about the Afterlife
> (4) What Religions Teach about Salvation
> (5) What Religions Teach about Jesus Christ

1. What Religions Teach About God

The beliefs of world religions about God fall into five categories: monotheistic, polytheistic, pantheistic, atheistic, and animistic. We will examine the primary beliefs that define each category and identify the religions that fall into it.

Monotheistic Religions

The word "monotheism" is derived from the Greek roots monos, meaning "one" and theos, meaning "God." Monotheistic religions believe that there is one God. In most cases, they believe that this one God should be worshipped and He alone should be worshipped.

Major Monotheistic Religions: Christianity, Judaism, and Islam

(Deism could also be considered monotheistic. Deists believe in a God who created everything but is not involved with his creation and cannot be known to man.

Polytheistic Religions

The word "polytheism" is derived from the Greek roots poly, meaning "many" and theos, meaning "God." Polytheistic religions believe that there are many gods. In most cases, they worship those many gods.

Major Polytheistic Religions: Hinduism, Ancient Greek and Roman Religions, Confucianism, Taoism, Shintoism, some forms of Buddhism

Pantheistic Religions

The word "pantheism" is derived from the Greek roots pan, meaning "all" and theos, meaning "God." Pantheistic religions believe that the entire universe is God. They believe that God is in everything and that the combined substances, forces, and natural laws which we see around us are manifestations of God.

Major Polytheistic Religions: Paganism, Neo-Paganism, New Age, some forms of Buddhism)

Atheistic Religions

The word "atheism" is derived from the Greek roots a, meaning "against" and theos, meaning "God." Atheistic religions are against God or against the belief that there is a God or gods.

Major Atheistic Religion: Secular Humanism (See the Humanist Manifestos)

Agnosticism is often related to atheism. Agnosticism is not a total denial that God exists, but agnostics doubt that He exists because they do not find the evidence convincing.

Animistic Religions

The word "animism" is derived from the Latin animas, meaning "breath, spirit, or life." Animism is the belief that entities in nature—such as animals, plants, and often even inanimate objects—possess a spiritual essence. Animism is closely related to pantheism.

Major Animistic Religions: Paganism, Neo-Paganism, Wicca

Already we can see that all religions are not the same. Some teach that there are many gods, some teach that everything is a part of god, and some teach that there is no god. Only the monotheistic religions teach that there is one God who created all things and who is involved with His Creation. Within the three major monotheistic religions, only Christianity and Judaism believe that there is one God who can be known personally by human beings. Islam believes that God (Allah) is the creator and is involved with His creation, but they do not believe that humans can enter into a personal relationship with him. Even Judaism does not teach that we can enter into a personal relationship with God to the degree that Christianity does.

Even when we just look at what various religions believe about God we can see that Christianity is unique. It is unique in that it represents God as existing in three persons—the Father, the Son, and the Holy Spirit. The Christian God is unique in that He alone came into this world, became a man to pay the price for man's sin, and now offers us a restoration of intimate relationship with Him for eternity through faith in Christ. Only in Christianity can the believer experience God the Holy Spirit coming to live within the believer's heart and life. People who claim that all religions are the same are very much mistaken. The personal, loving God of the Old and New Testaments who made mankind to be His own sons and daughters and who humbled Himself by becoming a man to redeem fallen mankind is nowhere close to being the impersonal, distant gods claimed by all other religions.

2. What Religions Teach About Man

Christianity – Man is created in the image and likeness of God. Man consists of body, soul and spirit. He was created to rule over creation. Man sinned and has been separated from God by his sin. Since Adam's sin, mankind has inherited a sinful nature and all have sinned against God, thus being separated from God. All creation has been affected by man's sin. Man is an eternal being. Christ came to save man from death and give to us the gift of eternal life. Redeemed mankind is restored to a personal relationship with God, will dwell with God for eternity, will receive an eternal inheritance, and will rule with God. Man's moral values and understanding of what is right and wrong are determined by God and His Word the Bible.

Judaism – Man is created in the image and likeness of God. He was created to rule over creation. Man must keep God's law in order to be declared righteous, to be blessed by God, and to dwell in heaven after death. The concept of original sin is rejected by Judaism. In Judaism it is believed that man has the ability to choose good or evil and that man can be declared righteous by keeping God's law. Man's moral values and understanding of what is right and wrong are determined by God and the Old Testament Torah (Law).

Islam – Man is created by God (Allah). Man is born in a natural state of submission to God. Man can find salvation by repentance and submitting to God and His will. Man is created to rule over creation as God's servant and agent. Human beings are not believed to be inherently sinful, but are equally capable of both good and evil. Humans are capable of achieving life beyond the grave through submission and obedience to God's will. Man is required to be in submission to Allah's will as revealed through Mohammed in Islam's holy writings, the Quran and the Hadith, which is of lesser importance than the Quran. "Hadith" means "narrative" or "report" and collects the sayings and deeds of Muhammad and his followers.

Buddhism – In Buddhism the self, along with all other creatures, is believed to be an illusion. Man's aim is to avoid suffering and to gain enlightenment and release from the cycle of rebirth (reincarnation), or at least to attain a better rebirth by gaining merit. The state of "nirvana" is the ultimate goal of the individual in Buddhism. Nirvana is described in Buddhism as the cessation of all afflictions, actions, and individual consciousness, as well as the cessation of rebirths and suffering that are a consequence of afflictions and actions. It is a state of liberation described as coming to the place of "non-self." In Buddhism, liberation is achieved by severing ones attachments to the transient things of this world. During the cycles of reincarnation before reaching nirvana, it is believed that a person obtains good or bad "karma" based on his or her actions in the current life. Karma is believed to determine the fate of the person in future existences.

Hinduism – In Hinduism, humans are in bondage to ignorance and the illusion of life and reality. Man's purpose is to escape bondage to the illusion of reality and gain release from rebirth, or at least to achieve a better rebirth. Humans are not created individually by a personal God. Humans are responsible to the gods for how they live their lives. In Hinduism, personhood (the sense of personal identity—the "I") is the main source of suffering. The ultimate goal is to escape suffering through total abandonment of self, called Moksha, to Nirvana, which is the knowledge of true Self (Atman) and the acceptance of its universality and unity with metaphysical Brahman. During ongoing reincarnation cycles before reaching nirvana, a person obtains good or bad "karma." Karma is believed to be determined by the sum of a person's actions in this life and previous lives. Karma is believed to determine the fate of the person in future existences. According to Hinduism, all present suffering is exactly deserved, being the paying back of one's karma,

New Age – Man is in an evolutionary process, which includes spiritual evolution. Man will eventually evolve into a higher form of creature and be god-like. Since New Age teachings are often a blend of Western and Eastern religions, man's relationship to God, to gods, or to spiritually enlightened guides varies within the experiences of different individuals. In New Age teachings, there are many different paths that can lead to the same end result of advancement to a higher evolved state.

Secular Humanism (Atheism) – Man is an evolved creature with no distinct purpose or destiny. Man has evolved, just as all other living things have evolved, and has no more value than any other living or non-living part of the universe. Man has no life beyond death. In secular humanistic thinking, moral values are derived from what the majority of people deem to be right and good at a given time. No source or basis for absolute moral values can be found within a secular humanistic system.

3. What Religions Teach About the Afterlife and Eternity

Christianity – Christianity teaches that God is eternal and that He created man as an eternal being. God's purpose for man is for him to dwell with God as His son or daughter for eternity in a heavenly place, best presented in Revelation 21 and 22. Christ will come again to set things right in this fallen world, and at that time there will be a bodily resurrection of all who have died, some to eternal life, and some to eternal death. Those who are raised to eternal life will be "heirs of God, and co-heirs with Christ" (Romans 8:17), reigning with Him and sharing His glory (2 Timothy 2:12; Revelation 22:5; Romans 8:17-18; Colossians 1:27; Hebrews 2:10). They will be given a glorious resurrected body like His glorious body (Philippians 3:20-21). Eternal life is the gift that God offers to all through Jesus Christ (John 3:16). God does not want anyone to perish but rather to have eternal life. Those who leave this life still in their sin, having rejected Jesus Christ's sacrifice and offer of forgiveness, will be eternally separated from God and will perish in the lake of fire known as hell (Hebrews 12:26-31; Revelation 20:12-15).

Judaism - Jewish sacred texts do not place great emphasis on the afterlife. The Torah and Talmud both focus primarily on the purpose of earthly life, which is to fulfill one's duties to God and to fellow man. Succeeding in this brings reward; failing at it brings punishment. The Old Testament does give indications of existence beyond the grave. Many death accounts in the Torah speak of the deceased as being "gathered to his people." In numerous passages in Psalms and elsewhere in the Old Testament, a biblical image of the afterlife is presented as a shadowy place called Sheol. Daniel 12:2 speaks of a time of resurrection from the dead, some to everlasting life and some to disgrace and everlasting contempt. Within Jewish tradition there is a belief in life beyond the grave in heaven or in hell, yet no one view has ever been officially agreed upon. Some may recall that even in the book of Acts there is recorded a dispute among Jewish religious leaders where the Pharisees believed in the resurrection of the dead and the spirit world while the Sadducees did not believe in either (Acts 23).

Islam – Islam teaches that there will be a judgment on the last day when Allah will physically resurrect humans. Each person will be judged by the balance of his good deeds and his bad deeds. Those whose good deeds outweigh their bad deeds will be granted admission into paradise, where they will experience spiritual and physical pleasures forever. Those whose bad deeds outweigh their good deeds will be condemned to hell, where they will experience spiritual and physical torment for eternity. Islam describes the day of judgment as passing over hell on a narrow bridge in order to inherit paradise. Those who fall because they are weighted down by their bad deeds will spend eternity in hell. Islam states two exceptions to this judgment process: Warriors who die fighting for the cause of Islam will be ushered immediately into Allah's presence while enemies of Islam will go straight to hell at the time of their death.

Buddhism – Buddhism teaches that beyond this life there is either reincarnation or nirvana. Reincarnation involves the continual cycle of life and death, with each life being different from the previous life yet affected by the previous life. The ultimate end of these life-and-death cycles is nirvana. Buddhism teaches that mankind suffers because of desires. Nirvana is described as the state in which a person has ceased from having desires and is thereby freed from suffering and, according to most sources, from individual consciousness. Buddhism does not clarify whether on reaching nirvana one ceases to exist or whether he experiences some kind of heavenly existence.

Hinduism – Hindu beliefs center on reincarnation. In Hinduism death is not seen as permanent. Rather, life-and-death cycles are temporary. Hinduism teaches that souls are immortal and imperishable. A soul goes through repeated cycles of life and death in order to be liberated from the impurities of attachment, delusion, and laws of karma. Death is therefore not a calamity, but a natural process, a resting period during which the person recuperates, reassembles his resources, adjusts his course, and returns again to earth to continue his journey. Hinduism does teach that the period of time between reincarnated earthly lives can be either more heavenly or hellish, based on the deeds of the person's past life or on what he was thinking at the time of death. According to Hinduism, the goal to be achieved at death is not heaven but liberation. Liberation is attained through acts of self-denial, discipline, devotion, self-surrender, and the help of a guru, or god. The ultimate state in Hinduism is that of merging with the ultimate reality or bliss in the presence of the gods.

New Age - The New Age movement views death and the afterlife in many ways, but all forms of New Age religion believe in the continuation of the individual after death. New Age practitioners usually possess a generally positive view of death as merely a doorway to the next life. New Age teachings postulate that the soul reincarnates through a succession of lives as it evolves from a lower state of spiritual awareness toward a higher one. New Agers tend to view incarnation as a human being on earth as just one option among many for a reincarnating soul. Most believe that reincarnated souls can take on life in various forms on a variety of planets and planes of existence.

Secular Humanism (Atheism) – Secular Humanists and atheists believe that this life is all there is and that death is the end of existence for humans and all other living things.

4. What Religions Teach About Salvation

Christianity – Christianity's teachings about salvation differ radically from those of every other religion. Judaism and Islam teach that salvation comes through a person's good works. Buddhism and Hinduism teach that salvation is the process of separating from self and desire to blend with the universe and the gods in a state of bliss. New Age teachings speak of man evolving to a higher state rather than being saved from sin. Secular Humanism teaches that man is a temporal being, with nothing to be saved from. Only Christianity teaches that man is created with a high purpose and calling, but has fallen away from God into sin. Sin results in spiritual death that cannot be remedied by good works. Only Christianity teaches that the God who created man has lovingly paid the price for man's sin so that man can be forgiven, cleansed, and restored to a loving, intimate relationship with God, his Creator. A summary of Christianity's doctrine of salvation is as follows:

- Man is created in the image and likeness of God but is also born into sin because of Adam's original sin, the results of which are passed down to every person.
- Mankind is separated from God and spiritually dead because all have sinned.
- All creation is under the curse of sin as a result of man's sin because man was given dominion over all creation by God.
- Man is incapable of atoning for his sin by his own effort, works, or goodness.
- God sent His Son, Jesus Christ, who is Divine, but who became a human being to take upon Himself the sin of all other human beings. Jesus Christ also became our great high priest. He is both the sacrifice for sin and the high priest who offers the sacrifice on

our behalf.
- Jesus' death on the cross is the propitiation (substitutionary sacrifice) for man's sin.
- Salvation (forgiveness of sin) is available to all through repentance (turning away from sin) and faith in Christ's sacrifice. (This involves receiving Jesus Christ as Savior and Lord.)
- Salvation involves "reconciliation," which means a restored personal relationship with God.
- Salvation involves being "born again" which means being born spiritually. A person is born again when the Holy Spirit of God comes to live in his life, uniting with his spirit.
- Jesus Christ will return to Earth again to bring with Him the full measure of salvation, which involves inheritance and redemption of the body for the saved believer, as well as the setting free of all of creation which has been held in bondage because of sin.

No other religion offers anything close to this plan of salvation presented in the Christian faith.

Judaism – The views of Judaism regarding salvation are consistent with its lack of focus on the afterlife. Judaism does not teach the doctrine of original sin and places no emphasis on individual salvation. Salvation is viewed as God's promise to the nation of Israel and will be achieved at the coming of the Messiah, who will bring a lasting victory and deliverance to the nation. Jewish belief does hold to a basic accountability for one's works, good or bad, but does not define a specific state of alienation from God or a plan of salvation for individuals. Jews place a high priority on individual morality as defined by the Old Testament Torah.

Islam – The Quran teaches that both faith in Allah and good works are necessary for salvation. Islam teaches that each person has two "watcher" angels, one on his right shoulder and one on his left. The angel on the right records the person's good deeds and the angel on the left records his bad deeds. Salvation and entrance into paradise require that a person's good deeds outweigh or outnumber his bad deeds. The five pillars of Islam are key aspects of a Muslim's required works for salvation. The five pillars are as follows:

> 1. Proclamation ("Shahada") of Allah as God and Muhammad as His Prophet
> 2. Prayer - Five times a day facing Mecca
> 3. Fasting - During the month of Ramadan
> 4. Alms Giving - Benevolent donations to help the poor
> 5. Pilgrimage to Mecca ("Hajj") - At least once during a person's lifetime

Buddhism – The primary belief of Buddhism is that salvation is ultimately the escaping of suffering by the burning out of karma and an annihilation of the illusion of an existing self. This state is referred to as nirvana. There are different versions of Buddhism, so the end goal varies somewhat from one sect to another. In Mahayana Buddhism, instead of seeking nirvana just for oneself, the disciple of Mahayana Buddhism aims to become a "bodhisattva", a celestial being that postpones his own entrance into parinirvana (final extinction) in order to help other humans attain it. He swears not to enter nirvana until he fulfills this noble mission.

Hinduism – In Hinduism, salvation involves the escape from continual cycles of reincarnation, the annihilation of desire and the illusion of self, and the entry into a state of oneness with the Brahman (which is all the gods put together). This liberation is called Moksha. This kind of liberation is actually an impersonal fusion of atman (eternal self—the real self beyond ego, and false self—the soul) with Brahman, resembling the fusion of a raindrop with the ocean, thus becoming one with the gods. This liberation from the illusion of self can only be attained through intuitive or metaphysical knowledge. Since this liberation from self is not an attainable option for most Hindus, most adopt a devotion to the gods as an attempt to transcend the world of suffering.

New Age – Since New Age teachings do not view man as sinful or lost, New Agers tend not to discuss the concept of salvation, which they reject as a Christian or Jewish-Christian concept. Instead, they stress self-development and spiritual advancement. New Age practitioners accept a form of salvation predicated on the progressive evolution of the individual soul in the current and future lives. Though this evolution may take many lifetimes, New Agers look to it as the ultimate goal of human existence.

Secular Humanism (Atheism) – Secular Humanism does not teach that mankind is created, in a lost condition, or capable of life beyond the grave. Therefore, there is no concept of salvation in Secular Humanism, other than possibly the salvation from harmful, superstitious thought processes in this life.

5. What Religions Teach About Jesus Christ

Christianity – Jesus Christ is the central figure of the Christian faith. Christianity teaches that Jesus Christ is God the Son (the second Person of the Triune Godhead), God incarnate, the world's Messiah (or Christ) ("anointed one") who became a man and died to save mankind from eternal death, and the King who will return to Earth and establish His eternal kingdom of glory and perfection. He is seen in the Old Testament through types, shadows, and prophecies. He is seen in detail in the New Testament. Without Jesus Christ, there would be no Christianity.

Judaism – In Judaism, Jesus is not believed to be God or a mediator for man to God. Judaism also denies that Jesus is the Messiah. In Reformed Judaism, anyone who accepts Jesus Christ as his Savior is considered apostate and is no longer recognized as a Jew. Judaism does acknowledge the historical existence of Jesus but believes Him to be a false messiah.

Islam – In Islamic belief, Jesus was a prophet, but was inferior to Mohammed. Muslims refer to Jesus as "Isa." In Islamic teachings, Jesus was born of the virgin Mary and performed miracles, but He is not believed to be God or the Son of God. The idea of the Trinity or of God having a Son is unacceptable in Islam. Muslims do not believe that Jesus died on the cross for sin or that He rose from the dead. Islam does teach that Jesus will come again to defeat the Antichrist and to declare that He never claimed divinity, directing people's allegiance to Allah.

Buddhism – In Buddhism Jesus is considered to have been an enlightened being much as Buddha was. Popular and prolific Buddhist author Thich Nhat Hanh reports in his book, Living Buddha, Living Christ, that his personal shrine contains images of both Buddha and Jesus, whom he deems spiritual brothers, both worthy of veneration.[1] In 2001 the Dalai Lama stated that "Jesus Christ also lived previous lives," and added, "So, you see, he reached a high state, either as a Bodhisattva, or an enlightened person, through Buddhist practice or something like that" [2] Buddhism does not accept Jesus as creator or his death on the cross as redemptive. The Christian concept of grace is contrary to Buddhism, which teaches that a deity cannot interfere with the karma of an individual.

Hinduism – Some Hindus believe that Jesus was raised in India and trained by a guru there. They believe that he then went to Israel, where He taught and healed people by methods He learned from the guru. Hindus believe that Jesus was one of many holy men. Some Hindus believe that He was an "avatar" which is an incarnation of one of the millions of gods recognized by Hinduism that are all part of the impersonal, supreme being that Hindus believe fills the universe.

New Age – In New Age teaching, Jesus is considered to have been an enlightened teacher. Some within the New Age movement

---

[1] Internet article - Jesus and Buddha: Two Masters or One? (Article ID: DJ660) by: Douglas R. Groothuis - http://www.equip.org/article/jesus-and-buddha/
[2] Wikipedia article entitled "Buddhism and Christianity"

believe that He was a spiritual master who ushered humanity into the "age of Pisces." New Agers believe that the age of Pisces is now ending (or has just ended), and greater spiritual masters are leading humanity into another new age, which is the "age of Aquarius."

Secular Humanism (Atheism) – Some within secular humanism believe that Jesus lived but was not divine and did not rise from the dead. Others believe that Jesus never existed, but that the story of His life, death and resurrection was invented to establish the Christian religion.

A Summary of This Chapter

The purpose of this chapter is to help the reader see that all religions are not the same or anything close to it. Christianity is unique among all religions. This fact is amply revealed by what the various religions teach about salvation. It is interesting to note that all religions acknowledge Jesus in some form. Though this acknowledgment helps to confirm the fact that Jesus was a historic person, it is important to note that Christianity presents Him in a way that does not fit with any other religion. It presents Him as God and the only way of salvation. This is the clear message of Christianity, and Christianity alone.

The Christian faith cannot be blended with other religions. If Christianity is true, then all other religions are false. If any other religion is true, then Christianity is false.

It is true that many religions teach various things about loving others and doing good things. On these points we can agree but that is a long way from saying that all religions are essentially the same. Christians can and should get along with people of other religions. We are commanded to love the people around us, even if we are convinced that their beliefs are wrong. Loving others does not mean that Christians are to declare all belief systems equal and valid. Christians are to proclaim the gospel of Jesus Christ as God's wonderful and only plan of salvation. They are to do this with a kind and loving heart.

For additional information about the varied beliefs and practices of different religions, I recommend the following books:

- World Religions Made Easy by Mark Water
(available at Christian Book Distributors)
- Christianity and World Religions: Wrestling with Questions People Ask –
Participant's book by Adam Hamilton
(available at Christian Book Distributors)
- Christianity, Cults and Religions – by Rose Publishing (available at CBD)
- So What's the Difference? Updated and Expanded Edition by
Fritz Ridenour (available at Christian Book Distributors)

	HINDUISM	BUDDHISM	ISLAM	CHRISTIANITY
ULTIMATE REALITY	Impersonal essence; Or many gods	No God: or impersonal "Buddha essence"	A Creator Who is unknowable	A Creator Who is personal & Who has made Himself known
THE NATURE OF HUMANITY	Divine in our essence	No personal essence	Created by God, but nothing about him is at all like God	Created by God in His image and likeness
HUMANITY'S PROBLEM	Trapped in rein-carnations in an illusory world, due to ignorance and karma	Trapped in rein-carnations in a world of suffering, due to desire and karma	Under the judg-ment of Allah, due to failure to keep the Law	Under God's judgment due to sinful rebellion
SALVATION	Deliverance from the world through knowledge, works, or devotion	Deliverance from the world of suffer-ing through the cessation of desire (by own works, or "divine" help)	Deliverance from judgment through obedience to the Law	Deliverance from judgment by faith in God's gracious provision of salvation through Jesus Christ
FINAL STATE	Merging with ultimate reality, or heavenly bliss in the presence of the gods	Extinction of suffering, desire, and individuality (Nirvana)	Paradise or Hell	Heaven or Hell

"Christianity and Islam"

Christianity and Islam

The growing prevalence of Islam in America poses another challenge to Christian believers in living and sharing their faith. What are the differences between Islam and Christianity? What do Muslims believe about Jesus Christ? How can I relate to Muslims? How can I  reach out to Muslims with the good news of Jesus Christ? These are among the questions that Christians must answer as they encounter Muslims in everyday life.

The Differences Between Christianity & Islam

The differences between Christianity and Islam were summarized in the previous chapter, but in order to make this chapter complete and cogent, it is worthwhile to expand on those differences here.

The Doctrine of God

Both Christianity and Islam portray God as creator, lawgiver, and judge. Christianity shows God to be self-existent, eternal, and a unity of three distinct persons, the Father, the Son, and the Holy Spirit. In

Christianity, the second person of the Trinity, the Son, became incarnate and lived among men in the form of Jesus, who is truly God and truly man. The God of the Bible is both approachable and personal. He is unchanging, consistent, good, loving, just, and all-powerful.

In contrast, Islam denies the Trinity and says that God has no Son. The God of Islam is called Allah. He is not approachable, nor does he desire a personal relationship with humans. The God of Islam also is recognized to be unpredictable, causing even the devout Muslim to be unsure about their coming judgment.

The Doctrine of Jesus

Both Christianity and Islam declare that Jesus was born of the virgin Mary. In both religions, Jesus performed miracles and was a prophet and a teacher. Christianity declares that Jesus is divine, the second person of the Trinity, the Son of God. Islam denies that Jesus is God.

The central truth of all of Christianity is that Jesus Christ died on the cross for the sins of the world and bodily rose from the dead three days later. Islam denies that Jesus died on the cross and denies that He rose from the dead. Christianity  declares that Jesus is the Savior of the world and the Lord of all creation. Islam denies both claims. Christianity says that Jesus Christ is the only way of salvation while in Islam Jesus has nothing to do with salvation. Christianity teaches that Jesus Christ will come again to establish His eternal kingdom, defeat all His enemies, and bring to His people the full measure of the salvation He purchased by His death and resurrection. Islam teaches that Jesus will come again to defeat the antichrist, to clarify that He is not God, and to point people to Islam.

The Doctrine of Salvation

Both Christianity and Islam show man as having been created by God and as having capability of life beyond the grave. Christianity teaches that Adam sinned, which separated him from God and resulted in spiritual death. This condition of sin and spiritual death was passed on to all humans ever born except Christ. Islam denies the doctrine of original sin and Christianity's teaching that man has a sinful nature. Islam teaches that man is equally capable of good and evil. Christianity teaches that man is incapable of saving himself and that Jesus Christ came into the world to save us. Christ's death on the cross is said to be the propitiation, or substitutionary sacrifice for our sin. Christianity proclaims that God offers forgiveness of sin and complete cleansing for all who will repent of sin and put their faith in Jesus Christ and the sacrifice for sin He made on the cross. God offers salvation and eternal life as a free gift through His grace. Christianity teaches that salvation involves eternal life, an eternal inheritance as a child of God, and sharing in God's glory for eternity. Christianity also teaches that those who accept Jesus Christ as their Lord and Savior have assurance of salvation and eternal life.

In contrast, Islam teaches that man is saved by a combination of Allah's mercy and man's good works. All of a person's works, good and bad, are recorded, and at the end of life salvation can be obtained if the good outweighs the bad. The angel recording the bad deeds does not write them down if the Muslim feels remorse for the sin and repents of it within six hours. Part of the good works required for the Muslim's salvation involves being faithful to the Five Pillars of Islam (see below). Even devout Muslims do not have assurance of salvation but hope that their good works will outweigh their bad and that Allah will have mercy upon them. In Islam, there are two exceptions to the normal judgment process. First, those who die as a warrior fighting for Islam will go immediately to paradise after death. Second, those who die as enemies of Islam will go immediately to hell.

As these comparisons clearly show, Christianity and Islam are radically different. Even Islam's Allah is not the same God as the God of Christianity.

Understanding Key Aspects of Islam

Muhammad and Islam's Beginnings

Muhammad was born in AD 570 in Mecca. He married around the age of twenty-five or thirty to a wealthy woman named Khadijah, who was about fifteen years older than he. Muhammad was a man who was seeking something. As a camel caravan driver, he had numerous contacts with many Christians. When Muhammad began to have visions in a cave, he questioned whether he was going mad. His wife suggested that he wasn't mad but was rather a chosen prophet. He continued to have visions and to receive revelations from what he believed to be the angel Gabriel. The revelations were written down and became the Quran.

Muhammad was not accepted at first in Mecca, so he moved to Medina. There he quickly began to accumulate numerous followers. As his following grew and he gained power, Muhammad and his followers began to use violence and force to influence people toward Islam. Muhammad died in AD 632. Within 100 years of his death, Islam became a great empire. Though Muhammad is considered to be Allah's prophet and the one through whom the Quran was delivered, he is not considered divine or perfect in Islam.

The Quran

The Quran is revered as the Word of Allah in Islam and is considered to be perfect. Muslims believe there exists a perfect Quran before Allah in heaven that was perfectly transmitted to Earth through Gabriel to Muhammad. Islam teaches that the Quran brought correction and completeness to all previous divine revelations.

378

Half of the Quran was written in Mecca, and the other half was written in Medina after Muhammad became a powerful leader. The second half (chronologically) is quite different from the first. It is much more stern and violent and is where jihad is encouraged. Some of the revelations in the second half contradict revelations in the first half, such as instructions about how to relate to Christians and Jews.

Islam teaches that there is truth in the Torah (the Law) of the Bible and in the Gospels. Muslims believe in all the prophets of the Bible, but they believe that Jews and Christians have changed and corrupted the original text to the point that biblical revelations can no longer be trusted. They believe that any teaching of the Bible that contradicts the Quran has been corrupted. In contrast, they believe the Quran is perfect and uncorrupted and corrects the errors contained in the Bible.

The Islamic Faith

To the Muslim, Islam is perfected Judaism and perfected Christianity. They believe Islam to be the authentic religion of Adam, of Abraham, and of all humanity. They believe that the Old and New Testaments

of the Bible revealed Islamic revelations and teachings before they were corrupted by Jews and Christians. They believe that Moses, David, and Jesus were all prophets. Though Muhammad did not receive the revelations that brought about the Quran until the sixth and seventh centuries AD, Islam claims to preclude all other religions of the world. Islam says the Quran always existed with Allah and had previously been given to the Jews and Christians who corrupted it in their Bible. Muslims believe the principles of Islam were finally received and recorded in perfect form by Muhammad.

Understanding their deep belief that the Bible has been corrupted is key to understanding what Muslims believe about Islam's origins and beginnings. Islam sees itself as overcoming the limitations of Judaism's incomplete justice and Christianity's idealistic love. Muslims see Islam as the way of reality within the world today.

The Hadith
Though the Quran is the Holy Book of Islam, the Hadith contains the sayings of Mohammed and the records of his life. A hadith is a saying of Muhammad or a report of something he did. The Hadith is a guide to Muslims in understanding how to live their life and follow the teachings of Islam.

Submission
The word "Islam" means "submission," and "Muslim" means "one who submits." Islam emphasizes the need to submit to Allah and his will. Ultimately, Islam teaches that Allah's will is for the entire Earth to be filled with Islam, which will then bring peace on Earth. The Muslim is to submit to this ultimate goal and purpose in life. There are some obvious similarities to this goal and the Christian's call to take the gospel of Jesus Christ to every part of the world.

Jihad
In order to bring Islam to the entire world, Muslims are to engage in "jihad." To many Muslims, this does not mean what we might think it means. The word jihad literally means "struggle or striving." In Islamic teachings, there is more than one type of jihad.

"The greater jihad" is what most Muslims feel called to. This is "the inner struggle to live in and obey the will of Allah." Secondary to this inner struggle is "a community's struggle to influence its community for the cause of Islam and to bring more people into the Islamic faith through their life and appeal."

"The lesser jihad" involves "holy war to spread Islam by violence and force." Though many Muslims neither believe in nor participate in this type of jihad, there are obviously large numbers of Muslims who do. To deny this, would be to deny the realities of the world we live in today. We need to understand, however, that the majority of Muslims reject this type of jihad and have disdain for those who promote and participate in it. It's a mistake to assume that all Muslims are terrorists or terrorist sympathizers. Many of them feel the same antipathy toward terrorism as do non-Muslims.

Ummah

The "ummah" is the Muslim community, and community is very important to Muslims. The Quran speaks of the ummah as the preeminent community given by Allah to man. When Muslims move into an area, they develop a Muslim community built upon three things:

1. Consensus of worldview
2. Consensus of heart (values)
3. Consensus of arms
(the living out of their values in their society)

The Five Pillars of Islam

In Islam, Muslims are called to fulfill the Five Pillars of Islam as their duty to Allah. Devoted Muslims are very diligent in their commitment to live out these pillars and they believe that this diligence is critical to their salvation. The 5 Pillars of Islam are as follows:

The Five Pillars

1. "Shahada" - The Confession: "There is no God by Allah, and Muhammad is His prophet."
2. "Salat" - Prayer (5 times a day facing Mecca)
3. "Zakat" - Giving alms to help the poor
4. "Sawm" - Fasting the month of Ramadan
5. "Hajj" - Pilgrimage to Mecca at least once in a lifetime if capable

---

Sharia Law

Sharia law is the religious law governing the members of the Islamic faith. It is derived from the religious precepts of Islam, particularly the Quran and the Hadith. The term "sharia" comes from the Arabic sharīʿah, which means a body of moral and religious law derived from religious prophecy, as opposed to human legislation.

Sharia deals with many topics, including crime, politics, marriage contracts, trade regulations, religious prescriptions, and economics, as well as personal matters such as sexual intercourse, hygiene, diet, prayer, everyday etiquette, and fasting. Adherence to sharia has served as one of the distinguishing characteristics of the Muslim faith historically. In its strictest definition, sharia is considered in Islam as the infallible law of God. [1]

Relating to Muslims and Sharing the Gospel with Them

There are over 7 million Muslims in America today, compared to just 100,000 in 1965. The annual population growth rate of Muslims in America is 6 percent, whereas the annual population growth rate overall in America is only 0.9 percent. Our first reactions to these figures may be concern and fear. Most of us have seen enough terrorist violence in the news and accounts of strong-handed sharia law in other nations to give us great concern about an increase of Muslims in America. As Christians, we must keep in mind that ultimately our calling and purpose in life is to share the love of Jesus Christ with everyone God brings into our path. Remembering this can change our view of Muslims who become a part of our communities, schools, workplaces, and lives.

Dr. Mark Hausfeld, president of the Assembly of God Theological Seminary, served as a missionary for over twenty years in Muslim countries. He points out that as Christians, we should approach Muslims with the love and truth of Jesus Christ. He points to Acts 17:26-27 as an indication that God brings people to specific places in His time in order that they may come to understand His loving plan for their lives.

> *He made from one man every nation of mankind to live on all the face of the earth, having determined their appointed times and the boundaries of their habitation, (27) that they would seek God, if perhaps they might grope for Him and find Him, though He is not far from each one of us. (Acts 17:26-27)*

---

[1] Wikipedia (Article on Sharia) - https://en.wikipedia.org/wiki/Sharia

We should ask, "What is God doing in this world?" and "What does God want to do?"

The first step in relating to Muslims is to pray for them and look for opportunities to befriend them and show the love of Jesus to them. If we view Muslims as enemies or undesirable neighbors, we will obviously never be successful in helping them know the love of Jesus.

Over 86 percent of Muslims, Hindus, and Buddhists do not even know a Christian. This percentage is certainly less for Muslims living in America, yet the reality is that most Muslims who live in America relate primarily to their Muslim community. Some live in America for years without ever experiencing the friendship of a Christian. The Bible teaches that it is not the responsibility of the non-Christian to befriend the Christian, but rather the opposite: The Christian is to befriend the non-Christian.

If we do not reach out in love to Muslims in America, it will not change the fact that they are here and will continue to come. If we do reach out in friendship, kindness, and love, we may find that God will use us in marvelous ways to reach them for Christ.

Adult Muslims in America are on average younger and better educated than non-Muslims. They tend to work in technical and well-paying occupations. Here is a list of the top seven occupations that Muslims in America are involved in.

1. Student
2. Engineer
3. Physician or Dentist
4. Homemaker
5. Computer Programmer
6. Corporate Manager
7. Teacher

Muslims have been incorporated into the fabric of American life. Many Christians can now interact with and befriend Muslims without leaving their own city. Could this be an opportunity that has come from God because of His love for Muslim people and His desire to see them come to know the saving love and grace of Jesus Christ?

In the Middle East, unprecedented numbers of Muslims are turning to Christ. Many have experienced supernatural dreams in which Jesus has revealed Himself to them. Many others have developed doubts about Islam because of the violence perpetrated by Islamic terrorists. Some reports from Iran have estimated that there are now over 1 million Christians in Iran. [2] Ninety percent of the Christians in Iran are former Muslims.

David Garrison, author of A Wind in the House of Islam: How God is Drawing Muslims Around the World to Faith in Jesus Christ, wrote an excellent Internet article for Premier Christianity entitled "Muslims turning to Christ—a global phenomenon." In this article, Garrison tells how he began investigating increasing reports of significant movements of Muslims to Christ in 2011. He defined a movement of Muslims coming to Christ to be "at least 100 new churches started or 1000 baptized believers, all of whom have come to Christ over the past two decades." He states that history shows only five such movements prior to the twentieth century. Yet in the first twelve years of the twenty-first century we can document sixty-nine movements of Muslims to faith and baptism in Christ and that several of these contemporary movements number in the tens of thousands. [3]

If Muslims are coming to know Christ in unprecedented numbers around the world, it should not be difficult for us to believe that God could use us as Christians in America to show the love of Jesus to Muslims who move to this country and settle in our communities.

The methods of engaging Muslim people are the same as those used to reach out to any people group. We must pray, and we must show the love of God to people in word and in deed. Our lives must display the love of Christ whether we are reaching out to a

---

[2] "Record number of Muslims coming to Christ in Iran" Sunday, March 6, 2016 I Michael F. Haverluck – OneNewsNow.com -
https://www.onenewsnow.com/missions/2016/03/06/record-number-of-muslims-coming-to-christ-in-iran
[3] "Muslims turning to Christ – a global phenomenon" by David Garrison Ph.d -
https://www.premierchristianity.com/Past-Issues/2016/June-2016/Muslims-turning-to-Christ-a-global-phenomenon

Muslim, Hindu, secularist, or just a "good ole boy."

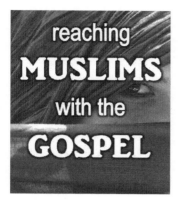

Much of the information in this chapter comes from Dr. Mark Hausfeld who has served as the director of the Center for Islamic Studies within the Assemblies of God and a professor of Urban and Islamic Studies. The following lists of suggestions on how to engage Muslim people are adapted from Dr. Hausfeld's seminars and presentations.

• Show kindness
(Mother Teresa: "The first step to love is kindness")
• Live out the love of Jesus
• Treat them with respect and dignity
• Be intentional and friendly
• Build relationships with people
• Look at immigrant and refugee communities as opportunities to reach out to people
• Begin an Internet outreach
• Begin a prayer initiative for Muslims in your church
• Involve yourself in a local Muslim outreach ministry
• Dialogues with Mosques
• Classes for immigrant parents
• Cooking exchange for women
• Hosting international students
• Be hospitable – Invite others into your home

Consider these suggestions concerning special things to avoid when attempting to engage Muslims.

• Don't cross the gender line
(Minister only to those of your own gender)
• Avoid pork and alcohol
• Muslims don't like dogs in the house
(Hunting dogs outside are acceptable)

- Attire – Dress with modesty
- Gestures – Never touch Muslims with the left hand. Use your right hand
- Religious items – Keep your Bible in a place of honor
- Don't get into arguments (Dialogue is good until it becomes argumentative and hurtful)

Dr. Hausfeld shares the result of a survey of 700 Muslims who came to know Christ as their Savior. They were asked to give the number one reason that they were drawn to the Christian faith. Here are the top answers:

> **1. Observing the Lives of Christians**
> **2. Given a Bible**
> *(Suggestion – Give them a Bible translated into their first language)*
> *(Suggestion – Wrap it in green paper and don't write in it)*
> **3. Signs, Wonders, and Miracles**
> *(Suggestion - Pray for them in the Name of Jesus)*
> **4. Understanding that God is Love**
> **5. Disillusionment with Islam**

For a superb website that gives instructions and suggestions on how to reach out to Muslims, I recommend, sayhelloinfo.com.

In summary, it is important to know differences between Christianity and Islam so we can answer questions related to the differing beliefs of the two religions. It is also important to know some of the history and beliefs of the Islamic faith so that we can better understand Muslim people. Finally, it is important to pray for and lovingly reach out to Muslim people that the Lord brings into our lives. Our goal is to lead them to experience the saving grace of Jesus Christ.

Faith and Reason Made Simple

(SECTION 4)

Bringing Apologetics Into the 21st Century Church

"Reason, Love and Holy Spirit Power"

Reason, Love and Holy Spirit Power

Unbelievers commonly accuse Christians of holding to their beliefs on the basis of blind faith rather than relying on concrete evidence. We know that we have ample evidences for our faith, and those evidences are rational and highly defensible. Yet when Christians fail to learn and defend these evidences, we can hardly blame unbelievers for their accusations. Understanding the underpinnings of our faith requires study and thought. I fear that in too many cases we have been guilty of not doing the difficult work of thinking.

In the following quotes, Ravi Zacharias emphasizes the importance of believers using their ability to think:

> The Bible places supreme value in the thought life. "As a man thinketh in his heart, so is he," Solomon wrote. Jesus asserted that sin's gravity lay in the idea itself, not just the act. Paul admonished the church at Philippi to have the mind of Christ, and to the same people he wrote, "Whatever is true ... pure ... if there be any virtue ... think on these things." Thus, the follower of Christ must demonstrate to the world what it is not just to think, but to think justly. [1]

---

[1] http://www.azquotes.com/quote/1275722

Every worldview has to bring together reason and faith. [2]

Reason is very important to evangelism, especially in our highly secularized, postmodern culture. As Ravi Zacharias has pointed out, *"what I believe in my heart must make sense in my mind."* [3] I need to understand why I believe the Christian faith, and I need to speak with others in a way that helps them to see that believing in the Christian faith is rational and intellectually defensible.

The words "reasoned" and "reasoning" are used six times in Acts 17–19, all referring to Paul's ministry. He reasoned with his hearers from the scriptures. Then we have Peter's oft-quoted admonition to "always be ready to give a defense to everyone who asks you a reason for the hope that is in you, with meekness and fear" (1 Peter 3:15). Faith and reason are not opposites; They walk hand-in-hand as partners in the discovery of truth. Faith must be based on reason, and reason leads to faith. Faith is not an absence of reason or a belief held in spite of reason. Reason leads the way for faith to follow and launches faith into realms where evidence points.

While apologetics deeply involves reason, evidence, and rational thinking, I want to caution readers that communicating these activities of the mind alone is not enough to bring people to belief. There are two other biblical essentials needed for evangelism and touching the lives of others. These are the power of love and the power of the Holy Spirit.

During the time since I have realized that the Lord was calling me to a ministry devoted to apologetics and reason I have had some powerful moments while reading God's Word when He reminded me very clearly of the need to combine the love of Jesus Christ and a dependency upon the Holy Spirit to apologetic reasoning. These three things together are very powerful and effective. Apologetic reasoning alone, apart from the love of Jesus Christ and the power of the Holy Spirit will not win people to Jesus.

---

[2] https://www.goodreads.com/author/quotes/3577.Ravi_Zacharias?page=2
[3] ibid.

The Power of Love

The Bible makes it clear that apart from love we are nothing and that we cannot effectively minister to others without the love of Jesus flowing through us. Consider these scriptures from the New Testament:

If I speak with the tongues of men and of angels, but do not have love, I have become a noisy gong or a clanging cymbal. If I have the gift of prophecy, and know all mysteries and all knowledge; and if I have all faith, so as to remove mountains, but do not have love, I am nothing. And if I give all my possessions to feed the poor, and if I surrender my body to be burned, but do not have love, it profits me nothing.
(1 Corinthians 13:1-3)

But now faith, hope, love, abide these three; but the greatest of these is love.   (1 Corinthians 13:13)

And He said to him, "YOU SHALL LOVE THE LORD YOUR GOD WITH ALL YOUR HEART, AND WITH ALL YOUR SOUL, AND WITH ALL YOUR MIND." This is the great and foremost commandment. The second is like it, "YOU SHALL LOVE YOUR NEIGHBOR AS YOURSELF."   (Matthew 22:37-39)

You have heard that it was said, "YOU SHALL LOVE YOUR NEIGHBOR and hate your enemy." But I say to you, love your enemies and pray for those who persecute you.   (Matthew 5:43-44)

Now concerning things sacrificed to idols, we know that we all have knowledge. Knowledge makes arrogant, but love edifies.   (1 Corinthians 8:1)

For the love of Christ controls us, having concluded this, that one died for all, therefore all died. (2 Corinthians 5:14)

Speaking the truth in love, we are to grow up in all aspects into Him who is the head, even Christ. (Ephesians 4:15)

We know love by this, that He laid down His life for us; and we ought to lay down our lives for the brethren. But whoever has the world's goods, and sees his brother in need and closes his heart against him, how does the love of God abide in him? Little children, let us not love with word or with tongue, but in deed and truth. We will know by this that we are of the truth, and will assure our heart before Him. (1 John 3:16-19)

Neither you or I will ever win anyone to Jesus by argument. Yes, we reason with others, but our proofs and evidences must be served on a platter of love. People don't care how much you know until they know how much you care. The love of God is central to the gospel message. It is the love of God that warms the coldest heart and brings life to the one who is dead in sin and hopelessly lost.

Ravi Zacharias has said, *"If truth is not undergirded by love, it makes the possessor of that truth obnoxious and the truth repulsive."* [4] One of things that I admire about Ravi Zacharias is that though he is extremely intellectual, he is gentle in spirit and very loving when he speaks with people, even those who attempt to contradict him. I've noticed the same about John Lennox, who is another leading Christian thinker and debater of our time.

When you pursue reason, remember to do so in love. Reason will help to reach people's mind, and love will reach their heart.

---

[4] https://www.goodreads.com/author/quotes/3577.Ravi_Zacharias?page=2

The Power of the Holy Spirit

The Apostle Paul recognized the need for the power of the Holy Spirit to reach and minister to people when he wrote...

> *My message and my preaching were not in persuasive words of wisdom, but in demonstration of the Spirit and of power, so that your faith would not rest on the wisdom of men, but on the power of God. (1 Corinthians 2:4-5)*

The apostle Paul—this man who used reason on a regular basis—also recognized that if his words were merely expressions of human understanding, they would fall short of impacting anyone for the kingdom of God. He depended upon the power of the Holy Spirit whenever he ministered to people. He did not want to give people words and ideas based on "the wisdom of men," and neither should we. None of our own reasoning will transform lives apart from the Spirit of God who causes a person to be born of the Spirit and transformed when they believe. The Holy Spirit lives in those who are believers, and we should always be depending upon Him whenever we minister to anyone, in any way. We are called to be led by the Spirit (Romans 8:14) and to walk by the Spirit (Galatians 5:16, 25).

Jesus told His disciples that they would receive power when the Holy Spirit came upon them, and then they would be witnesses of Jesus throughout the world (Acts 1:8). If we are to be effective witnesses, we need to rely upon the Holy Spirit and His power just as those disciples did.

The Bible tells us that the Holy Spirit searches the deep things of God and reveals them to us.

> *For to us God revealed them through the Spirit; for the Spirit searches all things, even the depths of God. For who among men knows the thoughts of a man except the spirit of the man which is in him?*

Even so the thoughts of God no one knows except the Spirit of God. Now we have received, not the spirit of the world, but the Spirit who is from God, so that we may know the things freely given to us by God. (1 Corinthians 2:10-12)

Jesus said that the Holy Spirit would reveal truth to us and bring to our remembrance the things that He said.

But when He, the Spirit of truth, comes, He will guide you into all the truth; for He will not speak on His own initiative, but whatever He hears, He will speak; and He will disclose to you what is to come. He will glorify Me, for He will take of Mine and will disclose it to you. (John 16:13-14)

Jesus also said that it would be the Holy Spirit who would convict people of sin, righteousness, and judgment. Without conviction no one will come to repentance and salvation.

But I tell you the truth, it is to your advantage that I go away; for if I do not go away, the Helper will not come to you; but if I go, I will send Him to you. And He, when He comes, will convict the world concerning sin and righteousness and judgment; concerning sin, because they do not believe in Me; and concerning righteousness, because I go to the Father and you no longer see Me; and concerning judgment, because the ruler of this world has been judged. (John 16:7-11)

As we can see, it is the Holy Spirit who leads us into all truth. It is the Holy Spirit who brings conviction to the hearts of people we speak to. It is the Holy Spirit's power that Paul ministered in as he proclaimed the gospel to so many people.

The Bible also teaches that the Holy Spirit brings gifts to

believers that He indwells. Among those gifts are "words of wisdom" and "words of knowledge." (1 Corinthians 12:8) Often when we speak to people about Jesus and salvation, we are unaware of situations in their life or thoughts in their hearts that are hindering them from opening their heart and mind to the gospel. The gifts of wisdom and knowledge, both given when needed by the Holy Spirit who lives within believers, are often His means of helping people break through those hindrances.

Jesus exemplified the use of specially granted knowledge for us when He ministered to the woman at the well in John 4. This woman was not very open to anything Jesus was saying until he told her to go and get her husband. She responded that she didn't have a husband. Jesus told her that she was absolutely correct in saying that she didn't have a husband. In fact, he told her that she had already had five husbands and that the man she was now with was not her husband. This was a word of knowledge—information that Jesus did not glean from research, but which was revealed directly to Him. This word of knowledge completely changed the woman's attitude about Jesus and the entire trajectory of their conversation. The results included not only her salvation, but also the salvation of many people who lived in the area.

I experienced the wonder of the Holy Spirit's wisdom a number of years ago during a marriage counseling session. I was attempting to help a couple in the church I pastored who were struggling in their marriage. During the session the couple began to argue more and more. As their argument heightened I could tell that at any moment one of them who get up and leave. It was out of control and it seemed hopeless. I stopped attempting to say the right thing and just sat there and prayed that the Holy Spirit would guide me. Within a few minutes I felt the Holy Spirit directing me and giving me wisdom. To my amazement within 5 minutes the husband and wife were holding hands and crying together. Their hearts became soft and their marriage began to be healed. I can tell you that they are still married and they are now pastoring a church. The Holy Spirit's wisdom and power is truly amazing!

Submit yourself to the Holy Spirit, and the ways He works in your life may surprise you.

In the past, believers often attempted to reach people for Christ by the power of emotion with very little reason applied. In today's skeptical climate, reason is critical to our attempts to bring people to faith in Jesus Christ. But as we have emphasized in this chapter, reason alone is never enough. To be effective we need to combine reason with the love of Jesus Christ and the power of the Holy Spirit!

Reason, Love and Holy Spirit Power!

"Equipping The Church and Family"

Equipping the Church and the Family

It is clear from scripture and from experience that God's chosen institutions for making disciples are the family and the local church. It is easy to see, therefore, that any effective movement to train believers in defending and sharing their faith must focus on equipping the local church and equipping Christian parents to minister in their home. In this chapter, we will touch on a few basic things that should be remembered if effective ministry involving apologetics is going to occur in the local church and in Christian homes.

Children's Ministries

Often we think that apologetics involves information that is over the heads of most adults in the local church, and even higher over the heads of teens and children. It is true that the challenges to the Christian faith involve some arguments that are a bit complicated, yet if we can back away for a moment from the intensity of the battle and look at the overall picture, it becomes clear that children and teens must be  equipped and informed, since they are either at or nearing a time in life when their faith will be confronted, challenged, or even attacked.

To leave apologetics for the adults is to miss the point of what is happening in our culture. It is our youth who are leaving the church in great numbers. To wait until they are adults to introduce them to information that will help them defend their faith is often too late. In many cases they are already gone.

Given the occasional complexity and general fear of apologetics, it often seems that getting believers to spend time learning this information is like trying to get kids to eat their vegetables. Everyone knows it is a good thing, but most have an appetite for other things that are easier and more enjoyable.

So what can be done?

To help people develop interest in apologetics, the more complex issues must be broken down into simple, bite-size pieces. Also, the information needs to be communicated at an age level which grabs the attention of children and teens. Various ministries have already developed many resources that accomplish these goals. A resource list is included at the end of this book.

We should not shy away from these issues merely because they may at times be a little complex. Children and teens need to be challenged. They are challenged at school. They are challenged in sports and in other activities such as drama, music, or art. Too often churches become so focused on making things fun that children and teens come to feel that church is unimportant and non-essential as it relates to real life. Ultimately, people like to be challenged. They want to feel that they are accomplishing something valuable.

I have actually had very positive experiences speaking to children and teens about apologetics. I have found them to be very interested, engaged and receptive. I believe that the perception that many church leaders have of how children and teens will receive apologetic teaching is often skewed. Apologetic teachings must obviously be presented at a child or teen level to be effective but kids and teens are surprisingly receptive.

Local churches need to come up with a game plan concerning how they are going to equip their children and teens to defend and share their faith. One technique is for Children's ministries to use curriculum that includes apologetics. Another is to acquire supplementary apologetics material and incorporate that into their general teaching schedule. For instance, a ministry could decide to incorporate a five-minute "truth window" every week in their time with their children. This time would be dedicated to answering questions children will likely be asked about their faith. This window may include verbal communication only or print material. It could also include short video clips or hands-on experiments. Below is a list of potential questions that could be covered. (These are merely examples and are not meant to be exhaustive.)

- Doesn't evolution explain how we got here without the need of a creator?
- What evidence of God's creative work do we observe in the finely tuned universe?
- Does the Bible we read today say the same thing the original scriptures did?
- Is there historical evidence that Jesus Christ lived here on earth?
- How does archeology confirm that the Bible is God's Word?
- Does the function of your cells show evidence that God created you?
- What does the Bible say about homosexuality and other sexual sin?
- Is Christianity the same as Islam?
- Is evolution really proven by science?
- How do monarch butterflies show God's wisdom and power?
- What special traits of a giraffe show that God is our creator?
- If God is a loving God, why do people go to hell?

By using the "truth window" technique, over a period of time the children can become prepared with answers when they are confronted with difficult questions concerning their faith. Finding materials or curriculum that will work for a particular local church children's ministry is a small challenge that can be easily met through the widespread availability of published material. The larger challenge is to bring the church leaders to a point of commitment to teaching their children how to defend and share their faith. We will certainly not succeed if we never try.

Another way that a children's ministry can teach apologetics is through VBS. The Answers in Genesis organization produces VBS curriculum that incorporates apologetics. This is another great way to bring attention to key issues. I strongly suggest that a local church not use VBS as their only method of incorporating apologetics. It needs to become a part of the regular fabric of children's ministry. One week out the year is not sufficient.

Another supplemental possibility is to plan a camping trip that combines fun activities with pre-planned curricula using nature to teach the amazing design features that God has placed within all of life on the earth. The teaching would include examples of insects, birds, animals, seeds, plants, water, the water cycle, the balance of oxygen and carbon dioxide in the atmosphere, etc.

Every local church leadership team should prayerfully consider what their plans will be to bring apologetics to their children and teens in age-appropriate ways. Without a determined plan, it probably will not happen.

Youth Ministries

Approaches to youth ministry within a local church can be very similar to those of the children's ministry. The obvious difference is to use materials and curriculum that are age appropriate.

Once the church leadership makes a commitment, youth ministries can incorporate plans to prepare and equip their young people to defend and share their faith. Teaching modes can include a weekly window of time, regular teaching series, small group discussions, video materials, print materials, college prep  classes, high school prep classes, junior high prep classes, special speakers, camping trips or retreats with a focus on learning along

with fun, and other modes as unlimited as your imagination. A list of resources can be found in the back of this book.

At school, teens learn about anthropology, paleontology, geology, biology, astronomy, physics, history, archaeology, etc. These subjects are aspects of the real world, or reality. If our teens cannot connect what they learn at church with reality, opponents to the faith are often able to convince them that what they learn at church is based on myth and superstition. Church teachers must show how everything we experience in the real world relates to the God who created it and to the Word He has given us. We may have to study a bit harder to learn the basics of these subject ourselves, but the end results are worth it. We will have a group of young people who know what they believe, why they believe it, and who will be able to defend it against all challenges.

There is a difference between "teaching" and "training." To truly impact the lives of teens, it is important to incorporate training that goes beyond mere teaching. This involves putting young people into situations where they are challenged to use the knowledge they learn at church. For instance, a youth pastor might take a group of high school students to a local college to speak with a group of atheist or agnostic college students. In a follow-up session afterward, he could help them devise responses to the things they heard from the college students. Learning becomes exciting when seen as needed and useful. Also, it is much better for young people to encounter challenges while in a protective, nurturing environment than waiting till they are on their own with no support system. Parents could be brought into this kind of training to learn together with their kids.

Another approach could be to take a group of young people into a public park, a local fair, or shopping area to talk to people about faith issues. As they encounter pushback and skepticism, they will be challenged to learn how to defend and share their faith using evidence. Follow up times for teaching and training will be essential for this approach to be effective.

No approach to equipping young people in the church to defend their faith will be perfect, but any planned approach will be more effective than no approach.

Local Church Lending Libraries

Another effective way that a local church can help its people grow in their ability to defend and share their faith is to establish a lending library within the church. This library should include video and print materials that can be borrowed and used by those who attend the church. A section dedicated to children can be established with teaching materials and wholesome entertainment.

In the church that I recently pastored, we established a lending library that included about 2500 books and about 2500 DVDs. We funded the library by taking a regular offering during our Wednesday night Bible study classes. Our DVD section started with

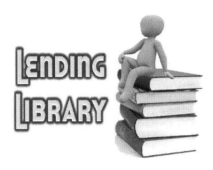

about 50 DVDs but eventually grew to over 2500. The DVDs include not only teaching and preaching, but also Christian movies and entertaining programs to give families access to wholesome entertainment in their home. We found that DVDs were utilized much more than books, so we continued to increase the number of DVDs we offered. We placed a great emphasis on obtaining quality apologetics materials for the Lending Library in both video and print formats.

Once the lending library is established, there are many creative ways to use it to promote learning in the home. There is a supplement in the back of this book offering additional details on how to establish a local church lending library.

Preaching with Apologetics

In an earlier chapter, we examined the difference between Peter's message in Acts 2 and Paul's message in Acts 17. Both preached the gospel of Jesus Christ, but Paul's starting point was different because he was speaking to a different culture.

The gospel of Jesus Christ is the same today as it was 50 years ago or 200 years ago. The bottom line of the message has not changed. Jesus Christ is the way, the truth and the life, and no one comes to the Father apart from Him.

What has changed is the starting point for those who proclaim the gospel. Decades ago we could assume that most people believed that they were created by God. Most by far believed that the Bible was a holy book and a book that could be trusted. This is no longer the case. Many today have been taught that the Bible is not dependable and is not God's Word. Many believe that science has proven that we are not created beings, but rather the result of millions of years of undirected processes. So the starting point for our message must be different from what it was in a more believing era.

To be effective in proclaiming the gospel today, we must learn how to incorporate apologetics into our preaching and teaching. That doesn't mean that every sermon or lesson must be an apologetics presentation. Sometimes, it will simply mean that we incorporate a few items of evidence along with our proclamation.

Let me give you an example. Let's say that within your gospel message is the phrase, "You, my friend, were created in the image of God, and He loves you dearly." You could add this extra bit of information: "You, my friend, were created in the image of God and He loves you dearly. The vast amount of usable information found in the DNA within every cell of your body—information that directs all the designed functions of your body—confirms the wonder of God's creative work in you. Usable information always points to a source of intelligence, and your DNA points to your wise and loving creator."

This added information might add thirty seconds to your message, but it reminds the hearer that there is evidence that confirms the faith statements we make. If people hear these kinds of evidential statements often, they will come to understand that we are not promoting a blind faith, but rather a faith that is confirmed by much evidence. From a scriptural point of view, we are applying the truth found in Romans 1:18-22. God has revealed His invisible attributes, His eternal power, and His divine nature to us through the things He has made. Because of this, no one has an excuse not to believe in God and His Word. When we proclaim evidence from our observations of what God has made, we are not diminishing faith; we are magnifying faith.

I have learned to incorporate apologetics statements even during funeral messages. Apologetics certainly does not become the main theme of the message, but it is very appropriate to include evidence statements along the way. As I speak of the meaning of life at a funeral, I often reflect that life has meaning now and beyond the grave because we are created by God. I like to include a quick evidence statement to reinforce this point, knowing that a number of people present may have dismissed faith because they believe science has shown that creation didn't happen. I may include a statement like, "though propaganda promoting secular humanism may deny that we are created, true science confirms over and over again that we are created beings designed by a wise, powerful, and loving God."

None of these examples involve enough information to adequately address the issues related to creation or the inspiration of the Bible, but short evidence statements are enough to let people know that we are aware of the cultural attacks on the Christian faith, and we are equally aware of the evidence that supports the faith. Over time, I believe this low-key insertion of evidence on appropriate occasions can be important ways to hold the line and show that we do not give ground to the cultural attacks on Christianity.

Training Believers in the Local Church

While these low-key snippets of evidence have meaning, within the local church we must devise more in-depth programs and methods of teaching apologetics if we are to be effective in equipping our people. I strongly recommend the use of sermon series and regular teaching series in classes. We need to preach and teach on the scientific evidence that confirms Biblical creation, the historical, archeological, and bibliographical evidence that confirms the Bible as God's Word. And we need to preach and teach how those same evidences confirm Jesus Christ as a real figure of history and God the Son and who died on a cross and rose from the dead. It is not enough just to proclaim that "God created us," "The Bible is the Word of God," or that "Jesus Christ rose from the dead." We need to expose people to the evidence that confirms these statements as fact, and not just unverified religious belief.

In addition to integrating the teaching of apologetics into all aspects of church ministry, I strongly recommend special training specifically designed to teach believers how to defend and share their faith. I encourage local churches to offer classes utilizing the training portions of this book or any of the many other good apologetics materials now available.

If the teachers in your local church lack expertise in this area, that should not be an obstacle. Excellent resources are available in all media, for all age groups, and in all kinds of teaching settings. You can get printed material, videos, movies, CDs, and Powerpoint presentations. You can buy material that works in classroom settings, in small groups, in informal discussions, or as presentations to large audiences as in seminars or assemblies.

One of the easiest methods for a teacher untrained in apologetics is to show a video that takes up much of the class time, and then offer discussion in the remaining time. Most videos include printed discussion guides specifically for this purpose. So there is little excuse for failing to take up this teaching challenge I'm issuing to the local church.

Using books like More Than a Carpenter for teaching series can be very helpful. Using some of the great video resources available today that deal with issues like creation vs. evolution, the dependability of the Bible, etc., can also be very effective. For a list of useful resources, see the appendix in the back of this book. Section 3 of this book is the foundation of an apologetics training for believers by the same title, "Faith and Reason Made Simple." You can go to localchurchapologetics.org to learn about DVD teachings, Powerpoint slides, memorization cards, etc. that are available to help you present this material within a group setting.

I want to challenge every pastor and church leader to begin adjusting the starting point that you use as you proclaim the gospel of Jesus Christ. The bottom line of the message has not changed, but the culture certainly has. Our new starting point must be evidence that what we preach is true. As we have noted above, we can no longer rely on the old assumptions of a general knowledge of our faith. Proclaiming the confirming evidence along with our faith will show how wonderfully Christianity explains the real world we live in.

Training Parents to Teach Their Children – Ministry in the Home

While the church can help teach the faith to children, the primary responsibility for this has always been vested in the parents. As Moses told the people of Israel, "And these words which I command you today shall be in your heart. You shall teach them diligently to your children, and shall talk of them when you sit in your house, when you walk by the way, when you lie down, and when you rise up" (Deuteronomy 6:6-7). Paul noted that Timothy's faith was strong because he had been taught by his grandmother Lois and his mother Eunice (2 Timothy 1:5).

The teaching children receive from parents is much more effective, first because it is based on relationship, and second because what is taught can be modeled in the lives of the parents. I  have seen a tendency for many busy parents to neglect teaching their children because "they are getting it at church." But I urge you parents to take responsibility for your own children's Christian education and to be intentional in teaching them not only the facts of Christianity, but also the underlying reason we know those facts to be true.

The local church must be ready to help parents who feel overwhelmed by the task of teaching and training their children. Tools and materials can be provided in the church lending library or through the church office. (See the list of available resources in the appendix of this book.) Classes can be offered to expose parents to available materials and to train them in how to communicate truth to their children. The equipping of parents for this task should be a priority in every local church.

If you are a parent who has children still at home, I challenge you to begin spending time teaching and training your children to defend and share their Christian faith. If you are already doing so, I applaud you and commend you. One great resource for parents is a 365 day family devotional entitled "Have You Considered: Evidence Beyond a Reasonable Doubt". This amazing book includes a scripture verse and an apologetic devotional for each day. The entire book is full color with beautiful illustrations. It is available at localchurchapologetics.org or at searchforthetruth.net.

If you are a local church leader, I challenge you to be intentional in issuing the challenge, training, and resources enabling parents to teach and train their children at home.

Avoid Confusing Pictures and Language

We expect art for children to be simple, cute, colorful, and often whimsical or cartoony. Much of the art in our children's Bible story books and illustrations on walls of church classrooms is rendered in these styles. But this kind of art, while visually appealing, can be a problem when illustrating historical events. Children are inundated with cartoons and fantasy stories in books, videos, and on TV using whimsical or cartoony art. And when Bible stories are made to look no different from cartoons and fantasies, the idea that "this is not true; it's just a story" is subtly planted into their minds.

A classic example of this kind of art is the use of cute pictures of Noah's Ark that decorate the nursery or children's area of many churches. The illustration on this page is typical. It fosters the idea that the whole story of Noah's Ark is just an unbelievable fairy tale. Can you see how this picture unintentionally communicates the idea that "there is no way that Noah got all of those animals on that boat"? At some point in his or her future, every child in your church will probably be confronted with skeptical claims that Noah's flood could not have happened. If their experience in their church classes has been merely the telling of Bible stories illustrated with cute fairy-tale style pictures in their books or on the walls, they may easily succumb to the skeptic's words.

The second illustration of the Noah's Ark on this page shows a much better rendition of the structure. It's true that it's not a

children's illustration, but it is clear and precisely rendered so that a child can understand it. Instead of a fun, entertaining picture, it is an accurate educational picture. When it comes to communicating biblical truth, accuracy and education must trump fun and entertainment. We need to be careful to communicate truth in reasonable terms that confirm the truth of scripture.

The teacher using this illustration could say, "Some claim that Noah could never have gotten all of the earth's animals on the ark, which proves that the story is not really true. Actually, Noah did not have to carry two of every species of animal on the ark, but just two of every kind of animal. For example, he didn't have to take two poodles, two German shepherds, two beagles, etc. He just had to take two of the dog kind. From those two dogs, all of the species of dogs we have today could develop. Since the ark had three levels, it had over 100,000 square feet of floor space. That is about as much as three football fields. Modern researchers have found that there would have been plenty of room for all the kinds of animals, plus room for food and supplies. Even baby dinosaurs could have fit on the ark. Also, modern research has shown that the shape and dimensions of the ark would have been very effective in keeping it afloat. So you can see that the story of Noah's ark in the Bible is not just a fairy tale; it is true history."

If a fun animated picture of Noah's Ark is on the wall clarification can be made showing the difference between a fun reminder and a historically accurate picture representation.

It is important to examine how we are communicating to our children, teens, and adults in the church. Do our words, illustrations, and décor help people believe the reality of the message of scripture, or is it possible that we are inadvertently contributing to the misrepresentations of the skeptical world around us?

"A Challenge to Churches"

Bringing Apologetics into the Twenty-first-century Church

This closing chapter is written particularly for pastors and church leaders. Some of the material in this chapter is a repeat of the previous chapter but I want to close by speaking to the heart of church leaders as one that has spent the majority of my life as a local church pastor.

God has given great opportunity and responsibility to pastors and church leaders as the gatekeepers of the congregations they lead. To a great degree they determine what is allowed in or out, what is emphasized, and what is taught.

Please hear my heart as you consider what place apologetics will have in the life of the congregation you help to lead.

The local church and the family are the two institutions that God has established to accomplish the task of training up the next  generations. In this culture, at this critical hour, it is essential that both local church leaders and parents recognize the need to prepare children and teens for the attacks that will come against their Christian faith. Today, training up children in the way that they should go should include apologetics. We must help kids know what they believe and why they believe it.

What is your church doing to equip children and teens in the area of apologetics? Are you preparing them for the day they will be taught evolution in a middle school classroom? Do you offer a college prep class to help them before they go off to college? Is there an environment in your church that encourages kids and teens to vocalize their questions and doubts so they can find answers in a loving, supportive setting?

If you are a pastor or church leader. I challenge you to evaluate these questions and take appropriate action. If you are a layman, I encourage you to talk about them to your pastor and church leaders in a respectful way. Offer to be a part of the solution. Be willing to involve yourself in the work of helping your church address these issues.

I hope that by the time you read this, one aspect of our ministry vision will be at least partially in place. We intend to build a website at localchurchapologetics.org to provide church friendly and age appropriate apologetics materials. I encourage you to check to see if this website can enhance your ministry in the area of apologetics. The appendix at the end of this book is designed to guide church leaders and concerned believers to wonderful apologetic materials that are available from various creation and apologetic ministries. A more complete aid in locating great materials can be downloaded from our website listed above.

Equipping Parents to Fulfill Their Responsibilities
Much of the training of children to survive and thrive as Christians in this culture needs to happen within the home. Loving parents that instruct and train their children within the home are the most effective messengers in communicating God's Word to the next generation. The local church and parachurch ministries can supplement and assist, but no external ministry will be more effective than mom and dad. If you are a  parent or grandparent, I challenge you to evaluate what you are doing to equip your children.

As mentioned in the previous chapter, every local church should take steps to help equip, challenge, and inspire the parents within their church to teach and train their children at home.

410

Churches can provide valuable training and find valuable resources to assist parents in their home teaching. Lending libraries and information on resources that can be purchased online and in Christian bookstores are very helpful to parents. Identifying and informing church families of good websites and phone apps is a key to addressing this critical need. The appendix of this book includes information on many resources that will not only be helpful to churches but to families as well.

I challenge pastors and church leaders to evaluate what you are doing to assist the parents in your church to better equip their children at home. That should be a priority in every local church.

An Apologetics Slant in Evangelism

As we saw in section 1, chapter 2 to effectively communicate the gospel of Jesus Christ, we need to understand the culture we live in. Missionaries do this as a matter of course. In Acts 17 we see Paul adjusting his evangelistic starting point to fit his audience. In America today that adjustment will often include incorporating apologetics to meet the challenges of an increasingly skeptical culture. The good news is that communicating evidence about creation, the Bible, and the person of Jesus Christ is not only faith-building, but exhilarating as well.

I am convinced that many believers today are not sharing their faith with others because they are afraid of being asked questions to which they have no answers. We must remember that there is nothing wrong with saying, "I don't know the answer to that question but I'll be glad to look into it." Studying apologetics will take you a long way toward overcoming this fear. I hope that after reading this book, you will feel much more comfortable sharing your faith with others and helping many come to know Jesus Christ as their Savior.

Evangelistic sermons and gospel musical and drama presentations can easily be adjusted to include an apologetics slant. This approach will reach many who otherwise might not respond to the presentation. Apologetics doesn't have to be dry and boring, it can be exciting and inspiring!

Teaching a Christian Worldview

It is important that we not only believe in Jesus Christ for our salvation, but that we also have a biblical worldview. We should view all of life and the world around us through the truths taught in the Bible. That means, for example, that we view people as having been created in the image of God, human life as having great value, morality as being determined by God's Word, family life as being directed by God's Word, and marriage as a sacred institution defined in the Bible.

Apologetics is important in developing a biblical worldview because it provides a key to the confidence we need to trust the Bible and its revelation of God and His will. Pastors and church leaders need to teach their congregations not only how to know Jesus as Savior, but also to view every aspect of life through the lens of Scripture.

Experiencing Greater Worship Times

Can teaching apologetics impact the worship of a local church. The answer is yes! Worship within the local church is based on our understanding of, and relationship to the God we are worshipping. As a local church engages in learning more about the awesome things God has done in creation and seeing how amazing the Bible is, the ability of the people to worship God will be enhanced. The more we see how great God is the more we can worship Him with all our heart!

Pastoral Leadership

As I close this book, I want to encourage and challenge every pastor that may read it. In responding to God's call, you have been given a sacred opportunity and responsibility. You are the key to so much of what happens in your local church. People look to you as a shepherd and as someone they trust to provide leadership in spiritual direction. In most churches, the pastor's vision is key in establishing the priorities of ministry the church pursues.

With this in mind, I challenge you, pastor, to lead the way in making apologetics a priority in your church. The need within this culture, in this hour, is obvious. You may have to reevaluate priorities, sermon topics, and budgets to address the need, but many eternal lives are dependent upon the ministries your church will provide. Obviously, the starting point is prayer. Pray that God gives you greater understanding, directs you, and empowers you to address this pressing need.

You don't have to know everything about apologetics in order to make a difference. The Lord never calls us to a task without equipping us to fulfill it. Just as He has equipped and empowered you to do all that you have already done, He will equip and empower you to address this need. As you start down the path of learning and leading others in this area with a humble and teachable spirit, the Lord will pour into you the knowledge and ability to meet the need.

If I can help you in any way in these matters, please contact me. I have dedicated the rest of my life to assisting pastors and believers with these issues.

Being Led by the Holy Spirit

In closing, I encourage you to remember that "greater is He who is in you than he who is in the world" (1 John 4:4). John also tells us that "this is the victory that has overcome the world—our faith" (1 John 5:4).

The Bible tells us that as children of God we are to be led by the Holy Spirit (Romans 8:14). We also are to trust Him to instruct us and show us what to say when we face challenging situations (Matthew 10:16-20). As you study apologetics, always remember to depend on the Holy Spirit to teach you (John 16:13-15), direct you, and empower the words that you speak to others so that they will be impacted (1 Corinthians 2:4-5). Remember that Jesus is the vine and we are but branches. We can do nothing apart from Him. Defending and sharing our faith must be done through the power of the Holy Spirit.

Christians should be equipped with reason, logic, knowledge, and evidence. Yet we must always keep in mind that we will never argue another person into faith. We should always remember that no one will come to know Jesus unless we approach them with the love of God and the power of the Holy Spirit. Pray that God helps you to show the love of Jesus to everyone you encounter and that the Holy Spirit empowers you to be an effective ambassador of Jesus Christ, who has entrusted the message of reconciliation to you.

God bless you!
Rick McGough

SECTION 4: CHAPTER 4

Appendix

This appendix has been included in an attempt to assist you in bringing materials into your local church, and/or family that will help to equip you and others in knowing how to defend the Christian faith in the midst of the skeptical, unbelieving culture we live in today. I have attempted to show here curriculum and materials that could be used within the local church for adult ministries, teen ministries and children's ministries. As you will notice, there are many more materials available for adults and teens than there are for children. I have listed materials for adults and teens together with a sub category of items designed specifically for teens. I have given brief descriptions of materials in most cases and in some cases information on how to purchase the materials.

Please note that you can obtain a free download of a much more developed version of this appendix, including color photos on our website localchurchapologetics.org. I encourage you to download the full appendix for use in your church or family.

At the end of the suggestion sheet I have listed a number of websites that you will find helpful for many additional resources, as well as many articles valuable for research and general learning.

Please note that the suggestions here are by no means a complete list of apologetics materials that you and others would find helpful. There are lots of books, teaching DVDs, audio teachings, magazines, etc. that are available and helpful. I have, for the most part limited the items listed here to items that could easily be translated into local church ministries for small groups, mid-week service series, training seminars, etc.

If I can be of help to you in your ministry in any way please feel free to contact me at rick@lcapologetics.org or at 309-738-4863. With the Lord's help our website entitled "localchurchapologetics.org" will be stocked with curriculum and materials designed to assist the local church and local church leaders in the future. **I am also available to speak & do training at local churches upon invitation.** God bless you!

Rick McGough (Local Church Apologetics)

Curriculum and Material For Adults and Teens

Great Materials From ICR
(Institute for Creation Research)

Unlocking the Mysteries of Genesis	Made In His Image	Uncovering the Truth About Dinosaurs

These 4 to 12 week video sessions are some of the best apologetics materials I have seen. They have a contemporary feel and they are very well done. The information is great! These materials would be great for a small group Bible study group, a family, or an individual. Unlocking the Mysteries of Genesis deals with the basic issues of Creation and the book of Genesis (12 weeks). Made In His Image deals with aspects of the human body (4 weeks). Uncovering the Truth About Dinosaurs shows how Dinosaurs fit within a Biblical worldview (4 weeks). These video series can be purchased from the Institute for Creation Research or at amazon.com.

Great Video Series

The Truth Project	**Lee Strobel Series**	**God's Not Dead 1 & 2**

These video series are all well done and would be great for Bible study groups or for use in the home. The Truth Project, with Dr. Del Tacket is produced by Focus on the Family and can be purchased at thetruthproject.org. The Lee Strobel series includes The Case for Creation, The Case for Christ, and The Case for Faith. These can be purchased at Christian Book Distributors. God's Not Dead study series 1 and 2 go along with the movies and can also be purchased at Christian Book Distributors.

"Beginnings" Exploring Biblical Creation

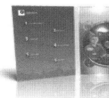  

Beginnings is a great DVD small group curriculum that covers foundational topics of science and evolution. Each of the 6 sessions by Eric Hovind lasts between 29-39 minutes. The included guide features a "something to think about" introduction & "what to watch out for" section which explains the lesson with further detail. Discussion questions and application allow participants to think and talk about what they've learned. Available at Creation Today or at CBD.

Ray Comfort Video Series

In this series of 4 video presentations Ray Comfort uses His God given gift of street interviewing to deal powerfully with 4 major issues of our time. ("Creation vs. God" – 38 min.) ("Audacity" {Homosexuality} – 55 min. - Includes a short movie with interviews woven into the movie) ("180" {Abortion} – 33 min.) ("The Atheist Delusion" – 62 min.) These videos are very effective & can be used individually or as a series. Each can be purchased for apx. $5 at Living Waters (.com) or Creation Today (.org). Bulk rates are available including 10 DVDs for $20.

"Foundations" By Ken Ham

"Foundations" is a set of 6 DVDs that includes 12 – 30 minute teachings that can be used for small groups or mid-week study series. This series includes topics dealing with the alarming state of Christianity in America today. What are the root problems and what can be done to address the crisis? Available for at answersingenesis.com. Leader's guides and participants workbooks are also available.

"Body of Evidence" Dr. David Menton

"Body of Evidence" is an 8 DVD series dealing with the Human Body. Each video lesson reveals the marvels of God's creation seen within various aspects of the human body. Dr. David Menton is the teacher within each of these lessons. Each DVD contains 2 teachings that are 30-40 minutes each. A study questions guide is also available. The series can be purchased for at answersingenesis.com.

Intelligent Design Videos (Illustra Media, Plus)

These video documentary presentations by Illustra Media are very well done. "Unlocking the Mystery of Life" presents clear evidence of Intelligent Design, broken into 6 chapters that would work well for a 3 week mid-week or small group session. "Icons of Evolution" is a great companion video showing the false assumptions that the theory of evolution are built upon. "Metamorphosis" wonderfully deals with the wonder of butterflies. "Flight" deals with design in birds. "The Privileged Planet" shows great design in the planet Earth. "DNA by Design" reveals the wondrous design in DNA. Each available at CBD for apx. $12 as well as at other apologetic web site stores.

Evidence for the Bible Videos

These videos deal with the evidence that confirms that the Bible is the Word of God and giving answers to the so-called contradictions within the Bible. Four of these are teaching videos by Charlie Campbell available at "Always Be Ready" from $11.95 - $14.95. "The Bible On Trial" & "The Bible: Fable, Fraud or Fact?" are documentary videos dealing with the reliability of the Bible. Both of these DVDs are available at CBD for $11.99 & $9.99. Excellent for church presentations. Also consider Josh McDowell's book "Evidence That Demands a Verdict" as a resource.

Videos on The Person of Jesus

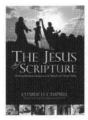   

Various Videos Showing Evidence for Jesus Christ
Teaching video by Charlie Campbell "The Jesus of Scripture" is available at Always Be Ready. "The Uniqueness of Christ" is a teaching by Ravi Zacharias available at CBD. "All About Jesus" is a documentary considering the case for Christ from history, archaeology, and ancient texts. It also shows the impact of Jesus on history. (Also available at CBD) "The Case for Christ" by Lee Strobel is also a documentary video (6 Session Study) showing evidence confirming Jesus' historicity, deity and resurrection. (Also available at CBD)

"Risen" Video Series

"Risen: Without a Doubt" by Tim Chaffey & Eric Hovind deals with the evidence that confirms the historical event that all of Christianity is built upon, the resurrection of Jesus Christ. The set includes: Six one-hour DVDs, each divided into two sessions for a total of twelve 30-minute sessions and Small Group Curriculum Discussion Guide. Set also includes bonus videos "Shrouded In Mystery" and "In Defense of Easter: Answering Critical Challenges to the Resurrection of Jesus". Available at creationtoday.org

Understanding Islam (Videos)

In the video study "Seeking Allah, Finding Jesus", Nabeel Qureshi presents valuable information about Islam and how to reach out to Muslims, along with his personal testimony. The study includes eight 30 minute sessions. Leaders and student guides are available. Available at CBD for $108.99. "More Than Dreams" is a dramatized video presentation showing the testimonies of four different Muslims who became Christians through supernatural encounters with Jesus. Apx. 2 ½ hours total length. Available at CBD for $7.99.

Short Apologetics Videos

Short Videos – Great For Church Uses

"Check This Out" includes 6 fast moving clips, 3-4 minutes each. Available at Answers in Genesis. "That's a Fact" is a series of 60 fast moving, 1-3 minute video clips by Institute for Creation Research (ICR) available at ICR web site or on You Tube. "The One Minute Apologist" (Bobby Conway) features over 900 categorized short videos (1-3 minutes) covering a variety of apologetics subjects. (Includes interviews of numerous experts) Excellent Resource – Go to oneminuteapologist.com

"Creation Today" (T.V. Shows)

CREATION TODAY

"Creation Today" is a 30 minute television program with Eric Hovind that deals with various apologetics subjects, especially topics related to creation. Five seasons of programs are available on Creation Today's web site (over 100 programs) These programs are very well done and could be used in small group settings, for mid week services or in Youth Services. Some of the programs are available on DVDs at Creation Today. Others are available on YouTube.

30 DVDs on a USB Drive

Charlie Campbell Apologetics Videos

ABR Always Be Ready.com
The Always Be Ready Apologetics Ministry

Teachings by Always Be Ready Ministry

Charlie Campbell may be the most versatile apologetics speaker in the nation. His teaching deal with Creation, The Bible, The Person of Jesus, Eschatology, Other Religions, Cults, Current Social Issues, Etc. Charlie's video teaching can be used by churches for mid week services/series or in small group settings. Available as a package or separately at Always Be Ready.

"The Stones Cry Out" Series

Produced by
Search for the Truth Ministries
These 6 sessions by Bruce Malone bring a visual, interactive, and relevant series on the evidence to creation to your church, fellowship, or youth group! Filmed at locations across America with video illustrations and animations, these lessons are not a boring technical lecture. Each session is 45 minutes long. A leaders discussion guide is available with the series. Available for $39.95 at Search For The Truth web site.

"Awareness of the Need" Videos

Produced by Answers in Genesis
In these 3 video presentations Ken Ham presents timely information that reveals the desperate situation that the Christian church in America is facing today. Young people have little confidence in the Bible and are leaving the Christian faith in alarming numbers. These videos include research statistics and data. These videos would be very effective in communicating to church leadership teams, parents and grandparents. Available at Answers in Genesis.

Apologetic Videos & Books

COLD-CASE
CHRISTIANITY
WITH J. WARNER WALLACE

Short Videos on Various
Apologetics Issues
J. Warner Wallace has made over 100 short video teachings available on his Cold Case Christianity web site. These teachings (sometimes interviews) could be very helpful supplements for local church use in various settings to quickly give confirming evidence helping believers understand and defend their faith. Jim's books are also available on the site.

Christian Response to Homosexuality

Compassion without **Compromise:**
A Christian Response to Homosexuality

6 Session video teaching series by Linda Seiler based on her master's thesis (Assemblies of God Theological Seminary, 2014) addresses the following: God's Purpose for Sexuality, What the Bible Says About Homosexuality, Is There a Gay Gene? What Does Science Say?, How Same Sex Attractions Develop, How Transformation Happens, Spiritual Warfare & the Stronghod of Homosexuality, Practical Tips to Reach Loved Ones Who Embrace a Gay Identity. Available at lindaseiler.com. or at Amazon. (Rental) Thesis PDF is also available at Linda's site.

Resources Specifically For Teens
(Note that many of the above resources are also good for Teens)

Debunking Evolution (Teen Videos)

The main characters in the videos are teens. The 12 video clips are both educational and entertaining. Companion book and student guides are available. The videos can be viewed and used through the web site and YouTube or purchased on DVD at numerous creation web stores. PDF copies of the book and student guides can also be downloaded. (A free copy of the DVD & Book is available for teens on the web site. Great tool for youth ministry!!!! For more information go to **genesisapologetics.com**. Books also available on "Debunking Human Evolution Taught in Public Schools.

Unshakable (Apologetics Training)

"Unshakable" is a 2 year, 4-course, online curriculum designed for teens. It features many top-apologetics speakers including Ken Ham, Carl Kerby, Ray Comfort, Kevin Conover, Eric Hovind and more. The 4 semester courses include (1) "NATURE: Created or Evolved?", (2) "RELIGION: Who's Right?", (3) THE BIBLE: Myth or Fact?", and (4) CULTURE: The Bible Applied". The courses will be available for local church use as well in the near future. For more information go **to creationtoday.org. or unshakablefaith.com**

Video Series (Does God Exist?) (Is The Bible Reliable?)(Who Is Jesus?)

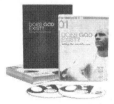

Focus on the Family's "TrueU" video curriculum offers an introduction to apologetics (a defense of belief in God). Featuring Christian worldview experts like Dr. Del Tackett, Dr. Stephen Meyer, Lee Strobel, Dr. Gary Habermas, and more. Set 1 deals with evidence for a Creator. Set 2 deals with evidence confirming the Bible is God's Word and set 3 deals with evidence that confirms Jesus is Who the Bible says He is. Each of the 3 sets involve 2 DVDs with 5 (30min. sessions) each. Available at CBD. Discussion guide available and sold separately for $6.29.

Resources Specifically for Children

Answers Bible Curriculum

Answers Bible Curriculum, from Answers in Genesis addresses the real-life issues that confront Christians every day. Students get a thorough understanding of the authority and primary teachings of Scripture. All ages will be equipped to defend the Bible, becoming conformed to the image of Christ, as they apply God's Word in their everyday lives. For use in Sunday School or other children's classes. Includes apologetics for kids. Available at answersingenesis.org

Buddy Davis Kids Videos

In these videos kids can join adventurer Buddy Davis on four exciting adventures: a trek through beautiful Alaska, an amazing world beneath the earth, a dinosaur dig in the Badlands of Montana, and a journey through the everglades. This real-life dinosaur researcher inspires kids with his solid creation teaching and infectious passion for the gospel. Available at Answers in Genesis together or separately.

What's In The Bible? (Series)

By Phil Vischer
The Bible Made Easy for Kids! Buck Denver and his friends take your children through the whole entire Bible. Each of the videos take on a different part of the Bible beginning in Genesis and ending in Revelation. Kids will be able to visualize the Bible in a different way than they had before. Phil Vischer was the creator of Veggie Tales. He has now used his God given talent to teach kids an overview of the entire Bible. The videos are very educational and very entertaining. These could be used in Kid's Ministry as well as at home. Available at CBD.

Clive & Ian's Wonder-Blimp

Produced by Phil Vischer
The "Clive & Ian: Wonderblimp of Knowledge" videos are supplements to the What's In the Bible series. In these 2 video presentations Phil Vischer helps kids answer 13 questions about God in a very entertaining way. Incorporates some apologetics for young children. These videos are available at CBD for just $5.00 each.

"Digger Doug" Kids Apologetics Series

Produced by Apologetics Press

Digger Doug's Underground is a children's program based on the characters Digger Doug, Iguana Don, Sing-a-Long Sycamore, Professor Whitecoat, and the rest of the gang. In each of the 20 episodes they explore basic Bible teachings about God, His Word, and His amazing creation. Each episode is 30 minutes long and would work well for teaching children apologetics at home or at church. This is a great resource!!! Available at apologeticspress.org for $12.00 or for $6.00 each if you buy 6 or more of the 10 DVDs available.

"Awesome Science" Video Series

Produced by Answers in Genesis

The Awesome Science DVD series takes kids, teens and adults on a field trip around the world to explore geologic and historical evidence which supports the Biblical record. Each 30-minute program is hosted by teenager, Noah Justice. There are 12 DVDs involved in the series. They can be purchased individually or as a complete set at Answers in Genesis. The entire set can also be purchased as a video download.

Apologetics (Parents/Kids)

Produced by Natasha Crain

Natasha Crain is a mother of 3 who has been studying apologetics for some time and has focused on how to communicate apologetics to her children. Her book, "Keeping Your Kids On God's Side" gives 40 conversations to help them build a lasting faith. She has also written a papers on "14 Ways I Teach Apologetics to My 5-Year Olds" and "65 Apologetic Questions Every Parent Needs to Learn to Answer". Available at keepingyourkidsongodsside.com. or at christianmomthoughts.com

Additional Resources

Search Creation Web Site (Search Engine)

 Search creation

Produced by Creation Today (Eric Hovind)
Search Creation is a search engine that searches the top creation and apologetics web sites for articles and products and will help you in finding answers to questions that come up about various creation and apologetics issues. **This is an extremely valuable tool and it is totally free!!!** Search Creation is a part of the Creation Network which also includes sites for Creation Speakers, Creation Events & Visit Creation (Museums, etc.) **(Go to searchcreation.org)**

APOLOGETICS WEBSITES

(The websites listed below may be helpful to you in finding online answers to apologetics questions, as well as in finding good apologetics books, videos and other resources.)

Local Church Apologetics - localchurchapologetics.org
College Prep America - collegeprepamerica.org
Creation Today Ministries – creationtoday.org
Josh McDowell Ministries – josh.org
Faith Search International - faithsearch.org
Living Waters Ministries – livingwaters.com
Answers in Genesis – answersingenesis.com
Willie Herath Books - readysetquestion.com
Search Creation – searchcreation.org
Institute for Creation Research – icr.org
Creation Ministries International – creation.com
Search for the Truth – searchforthetruth.net
Ravi Zacharias Ministries – rzim.org
Always Be Ready Ministries – alwaysbeready.com

Apologetics 315 – apologetics315.org
Apologetics Press Ministries – apologeticspress.org
Dave's Creation Resources – davescreationresources.com
C.A.R.M Ministries – carm.org
Faith Search International – faithsearch.org
Cold Case Christianity – coldcasechristianity.com
Lee Strobel Ministries – leestrobel.com
Genesis Apologetics Ministries – genesisapologetics.com
God's Not Dead Ministries – ricebroocks.com
What's In the Bible – whatsinthebible.com
Keys For Kids Ministries – keysforkids.org
Creation Moments Ministries – creationmoments.com

Family Devotional Materials

Keys For Kids Ministries – keysforkids.org
That's A Fact Short Videos – thatsafacttv.com
Creation Moments Ministries – creationmoments.com
Genesis Apologetics Ministries – genesisapologetics.com
College Prep America – collegeprepamerica.org
Answers in Genesis – answersingenesis.com
Jelly Telly T.V. – jellytelly.com
Life Church Kid's Videos – life.church/kids/
Short Apologetics Videos – creationminute.com
EquipU Videos - equipu.kids4truth.com/
The Dig (Devotional for Kids) - thedigforkids.com

Apologetics Devotional (Full Color) (Amazing)
"Have You Considered:
Evidence Beyond a Reasonable Doubt"
365 Devotional Pages – A Per Day
Search For The Truth Ministries
searchforthetruth.net

For additional information go to localchurchapologetics.org